FIGURING THINGS OUT

A TRAINER'S GUIDE TO NEEDS AND TASK ANALYSIS

FIGURING THINGS OUT

A TRAINER'S GUIDE TO NEEDS AND TASK ANALYSIS

Ron Zemke
President,
Performance Research Associates

Thomas Kramlinger
Senior Project Manager,
Wilson Learning Corporation

Addison-Wesley Publishing Company
Reading, Massachusetts • Menlo Park, California
London • Amsterdam • Don Mills, Ontario • Sydney

Library of Congress Cataloging in Publication Data

Zemke, Ron.
 Figuring things out.

 Bibliography: p.
 Includes index.
  1. Organizational effectiveness. 2. Employees, Train-
ing of. I. Kramlinger, Thomas, 1937-   II. Title.
HD58.9.Z45   658.3'12404   81-12805
ISBN 0-201-09098-8   AACR2

ISBN 0-201-09098-8
ABCDEFGHIJ-AL-8987654321

CONTENTS

ACKNOWLEDGMENTS xi

SECTION 1 INTRODUCTION 1

CHAPTER 1 WHY THIS BOOK? 3

A Word About Words 4
How This Book Works 5

CHAPTER 2 THE STRATEGY OF, AND TACTICS FOR, CONDUCTING AN FTO STUDY 7

Tactics of Figuring Things Out 8
Tactic One 8
Tactic Two 8
Tactic Three 11
Tactic Four 12
Tactic Five 13
Tactic Six 14
Summary 15

CHAPTER 3 FINDING A PLACE TO START—OR, WHY YOU HAVE TO HAVE A MODEL 17

Where Our Model of Human Performance Comes from—More or Less 18

SECTION **II** WATCHING PEOPLE WORK: OBSERVATIONAL
APPROACHES TO FIGURING THINGS OUT   27

CHAPTER **4** SIMPLE OBSERVATIONS, TIME STUDIES,
AND TASK LISTINGS   29

Task Listings: Second Generation of Task Analysis   33

CHAPTER **5** DEVELOPING AND USING S-R TABLES: THE DETERLINE
APPROACH TO TASK ANALYSIS   39

Conclusion   46

CHAPTER **6** BEHAVIORAL ALGORITHMS: AN INFORMATION-
PROCESSING APPROACH TO TASK ANALYSIS   47

On to the How-To's   50
More About Algorithms   50
Guidelines for Doing Algorithm Task Analysis   61

CHAPTER **7** USING BEHAVIORAL FREQUENCY COUNTS   69

Some Guidelines   79

SECTION **III** TALKING TO PEOPLE ABOUT WORK   83

CHAPTER **8** TALKING TO PEOPLE IN GROUPS: THE FOCUS GROUP
DISCUSSION   85

A Focused Group Is a Group Focused   86
Phases of the Focus Group Study   86
Some Focus Group Tips and Tricks   94
Some Pros and Cons to Focus Groups   96
A Final Note on the ROI of Focus Groups   97

CHAPTER **9** DOING IT FACE-TO-FACE: MAKING THE MOST OF
ONE-ON-ONE INTERVIEWS   99

The Structured Interview   100
The Informal or Conversational Interview   100

Anatomy of the Structured Interview   101
Limits and Things   114

CHAPTER **10** LET YOUR FINGERS DO THE WALKING: GATHERING INFORMATION OVER THE TELEPHONE   117

The Questions Are the Thing   119
Analysis of Results   123
Avoid these Mistakes when Using the Telephone   124
Keeping Your Balance   126
Satisfaction Almost Guaranteed   126

SECTION **IV** PLAYING TWENTY QUESTIONS   127

CHAPTER **11** TELL ME A STORY: THE CRITICAL INCIDENT TECHNIQUE   129

The How-To's   130
Using the Critical Incident Technique   134
Detailed How-To's   134
Summary   138

CHAPTER **12** MAKING ORDER FROM CHAOS: USING CONSENSUS GROUPS   141

Few Tasks, Low Disagreement   142
Many Tasks, Low to Moderate Disagreement   147
Complex and Unclear Tasks, Probability of Disagreement High   149
Conducting the Priority Grid and Consensus Survey Group Meetings   151
A Quick Review   154

CHAPTER **13** USING SURVEYS AND QUESTIONNAIRES   155

So Why Bother?   156
Effective Survey Research Begins with Leg Work, Not Pencil Work   158
Follow the KISS Principle (Keep it Simple, Stupid)   159
Pilot Testing a Survey to Avoid Pitfalls   163
The Case of XYZ Manufacturing, Inc.   163

Survey Dos   165
Survey Don'ts   168
Cross-Tabs   176
Bottom Line: Observation, Imagination, and a Pocket Calculator   178

SECTION V ODDS AND ENDS   181

CHAPTER 14 LOOKING AT PERFORMANCE INFORMATION: READING THE OTHER PERSON'S WATCH   183

Needs Analysis   184
Assessing the Value of an Intervention   186
Identifying High and Low Performers   188
Making Hypotheses About What the Performance Problem Is   189
Determining the Most Opportune Locus for an Intervention   190

CHAPTER 15 FAULT TREE ANALYSIS: MAKING PROGRESS WORKING BACKWARDS   193

To Be Continued . . .   200

CHAPTER 16 PYRAMID POWER: USING LEARNING HIERARCHIES IN TASK ANALYSIS   201

Gagne's Hierarchy   202
Stimulus Recognizing   203
Response Generating   203
Chaining (Procedure Following)   204
Terminology Using   205
Discrimination Making   206
Concept Forming   207
Rule Applying   207
Problem Solving   209
First Application—Teaching Strategies   210
Second Application—Task Analysis Strategies   211
Summary   213

SECTION **VI** MATCHING TECHNIQUES AND PROBLEMS   215

CHAPTER **17** DECIDING WHEN TO USE WHAT:
ORGANIZATIONAL CRITERIA   217

Does or Doesn't an Important Performance Problem Exist?   222

CHAPTER **18** DECIDING WHEN TO USE WHAT: TECHNICAL
CRITERIA   227

Matching Technique to Task   228
The Problem of Prioritizing Tasks   234
Summing Up   236

CHAPTER **19** A FLOW CHART APPROACH TO SELECTING
THE RIGHT TECHNIQUE   237

Job-Description Techniques   238

SECTION **VII** IN SUMMARY   243

CHAPTER **20** REPORTING RESULTS TO MANAGEMENT   245

CHAPTER **21** BEYOND FIGURING THINGS OUT: SOLUTIONS STILL
PAY THE RENT   255

For Instance . . .   256

APPENDIX **A** GAGNE DEFINES TASK ANALYSIS   263

Some Representative Military Tasks   264
Learning   266
Principles   267
Using these Assumptions and Principles in Training Design   267
What is Applicable to the Design of Training?   271
Summary   274
References   275

APPENDIX B THE CRITICAL INCIDENT TECHNIQUE   277

Background and Early Developments   278
Developmental Studies at the American Institute for Research   280
Studies Carried Out at the University of Pittsburgh   282
The Procedure in Its Present Form   286
Uses of the Critical Incident Technique   302
Summary and Conclusions   311
Notes   313

APPENDIX C EMERGENCY KIT STATISTICS   319

Not Nearly Everything You Need to Know About Statistics   319

BIBLIOGRAPHY   337
INDEX   341

ACKNOWLEDGMENTS

Accumulating the contents of this book took fifteen years and a very large, sturdy cardboard box. Figuring out a way to fit it all together took three years, plenty of trial and error, patient clients, and a bit of luck. Also involved were numerous individuals who contributed to our efforts to develop a cohesive set of tools for identifying and separating problems of knowledge and skill from problems of motivation, unclear goals, inappropriate incentive structures, unsupportive environment, and the like.

First, there were the inspirers: Dr. E. A. "Gene" Rocklyn, who insisted that task, needs, and organizational performance problems could be studied, researched, and measured—given the time and the right tools. Of course, to Gene, *all* things human must be considered measurable, explainable, understandable, and improvable—given time and effort and patience.

Then there were Dr. Norm Williard, Dr. Howie Mase, and Larry Wilson. Each in his own way gave us room to run and encouraged us to "Try it! Risk it! Do it, do it, do it!" And we did and we succeeded and we failed and we learned and we have finally gotten it together.

Then there were the inventors, the people who had the ideas, defined the processes, and invented the techniques we've put in this text. It's a very personal pantheon: Dr. Robert B. Miller, Dr. Robert M. Gagne, Dr. Robert Mager, Dr. William A. Deterline, Dr. John C. Flanagan, Dr. Ogden Lindsley, Dr. Thomas Gilbert, Dr. Lev Landa, Dr. Ivor K. Davies.

Next come the translators, those individuals who labored hard to translate the big ideas and exotic approaches into usable, workable tools and techniques. Another very personal list: In it belong Dr. Wells Hiveley III, Dr. Geary Rummler, David Markel, Dr. Marvin Dunnette, Paul Friesen, Joe Harless, Dr. Ann Dell Duncan, Dr. Russell Burris, Dr. John Campbell, Dr. Paul Johnson, Dr. Tom Ainsworth, Dr. T. Kirshnamurdy, Dr. Ed Greene, Dr. Robert Jones, Ivan S. Horbin, Dr. Susan Markel, and Dr. Gary Latham.

Then come the practitioners, those individuals who, by example and hard work, showed us how to get the most out of the tools and techniques. Some have worked directly with us, some have never heard of us. Among them are Molly Post, Tom Touhey, Nancy Ball, Chris Yates, Judy Ragland-Armstrong, Jeanne Kausch, Dr. Ruth Peters, Carl Gambello, Dave Walonick, Dr. Jack Anderson, Doug Berdie, Al Anderson, and Eldon Arden.

There is a group of patient but uncompromising critics to be noted as well, people who kicked us about when we were hard-headed, who gave us important corrective feedback, and who generally told us when we were making sense and when we were barking up a blind alley (mixed metaphor intended and appropriate). This group of grinches includes Dr. John Gunkler, Dr. Dave Larson, Dr. Tom Connellan, Dr. Bill Lorimer, and Ray Sandborgh.

Last, but by no means least, is a small fraternity that encouraged, aided, and abetted our pen-on-paper efforts and occasionally just nourished our spirits. They are Phil and Susan Jones, Frances Meritt Stern, Charlie Peers, Susan Murray-Zemke, and Maureen Kramlinger.

A final set of thank you's, a tip of the hat, and a deep bow are also owed Linda Standke, who put us in front of so many audiences, and Audrey Kupers, whose ability to read neurotic sanscrit put readable words before our editors.

SECTION **I** INTRODUCTION

The three chapters of this first section focus on our approach to training needs and task analysis studies in organizations. They explain the way we have learned to approach performance problem analysis and give you a look at the underlying philosophy that has led us to choose and use the tactics and techniques presented in this book. This section is not just a way of making the book longer.

We believe you need to know what business we think we are in, and exactly how we look at the world of work, if you are to make the best use of our ideas and approaches. Asking you to accept our approach to organizational needs and task studies on faith is not one of the businesses we are in.

An analogy: In 1973, THE WHO recorded a rock opera titled *Tommy*. The plot line is instructive. Tommy is a young English boy beset by hysterical blindness. He is, in fact, deaf, dumb, and blind. Despite these handicaps, Tommy becomes the "pinball wizard"; champion pinball player in the Empire. One day, while demonstrating his skills, Tommy is cured of his afflictions. He becomes a spiritual super-star, gets an agent, and goes on the speaking circuit to proclaim the wonder of his miracle cure. Eventually, Tommy forms a training company and opens a center—Tommy's Holiday Camp. At the camp, Tommy and his facilitators help others to find miracle cures and personal growth by—what else?—playing pinball while wearing blindfolds, gags, and earplugs. After an initial flurry, enrollments plummet and Tommy, Inc., goes broke. The point is, the training and development field is chocked full of Tommys and miracle cures. We want to avoid being a part of the salvation shuffle. Hopefully, the three chapters of Section I will show you exactly what pinball machine we've been playing. Adding up the score, and deciding whether we've brought in the winner we hope we have, is up to you.

CHAPTER 1 WHY THIS BOOK?

This book is about the techniques and tactics we apply to the problem of figuring out what successful people do when they do something successfully. That's the positive side. On the negative side, this book *also* describes the techniques and tactics we employ when someone in an organization asks some version of Dr. Robert Mager's famous question, "They really oughta wanna do better. Why don't they?" Or its more common and more strident version, "These people can't do anything right. We need some training around here!" The *techniques* for looking at both these situations, positive and negative, are the same, but the tactics of applying them are different.

In essence, this book offers a systematically organized description of the way we approach the analysis of human performance problems. For years, the performance-problem-analysis business has survived through a combination of seat-of-the-pants intuitions, the blind application of past success formulas to new problems, and the ability to skate quickly across the thin ice of what we didn't know about gathering and analyzing information on human performance problems. Thanks to Mager, Pipe,[1] and Harless[2]—when a client hollered, "I've got a training problem." or "My people need some motivation!"—we knew that (a) the *real* problem wasn't being mentioned and (b) the solution to the problem might be something entirely different once the problem had been properly analyzed. Managers and others who are responsible for getting things done through people usually have a highly developed clinical sensitivity to "things not being right around here," but they don't always have the training, knowledge, objectivity or time to adequately pinpoint the cause or causes of the problems they perceive.

---

[1]Robert Mager and Peter Pipe, *Analyzing Performance Problems or 'You Really Oughta Wanna'* (Belmont, Calif.: Fearon Publishers, 1970).

[2]Joe Harless, *An Ounce of Analysis Is Worth a Pound of Objectives* (Falls Church, Va.: Harless Educational Technologies, 1970).

Helping pinpoint causes is one of the jobs the professional Human Resource Development (HRD) person is paid to tackle tactfully. We both quickly learned that when our rejoinder to the client's "They need some training!" was a smug "How do you *know* it's a training problem?" we were in for a bit of turbulence. Specifically, we learned that we'd better turn down the smug-control knob and have a pretty good set of procedures at hand for confirming or modifying that management intuition if we were going to succeed at playing the "What you have is a performance problem and we'll tell you whether the solution is training or not" gambit. Or, as a friend of ours says, "Don't try to play hard ball if you haven't got a glove." This book represents the "glove" we've stitched together for playing human-factors specialist in the Organizational Performance Problem League. It also represents our effort to share with you the investigative techniques and tactics we have found useful in our performance-problem analysis work, the specific things we've learned to do when we reach the decision box in one of those ubiquitous "Systems Approach to Training" flowcharts.

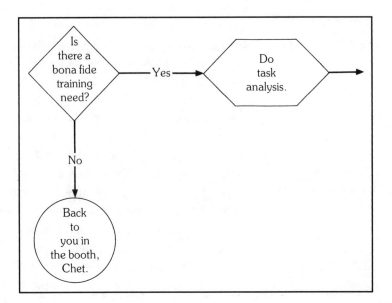

A WORD ABOUT WORDS

Over the past years, we have conducted workshops and seminars based on our approach to doing a "Figuring Things Out" study. Originally, we simply called what we were trying to communicate "Advanced Task Analysis Techniques." Little did we appreciate the Humpty Dumpty nature of words in the wonderful world of training and development! About an hour into our second workshop, a participant with a brand new doctorate in instructional technology rose to his feet and hotly announced that we obviously didn't know anything about task analysis. The gentleman was clearly agitated, and it took more than a mite of courage to call us down in public like that. As every trainer has learned, you never win by fighting with a member of the audience. So in response to our crafty "Could you tell us more about that?" he said, "Task analysis is a concept invented by R. B. Miller* and refined by my graduate advisor, professor Joseph, and refers to a specific set of procedures for describing the behavioral and procedural elements of a job task."

In the ensuing minutes, additional members of the audience made their views known about who invented what and before long, at least one thing was perfectly clear to us: We had stepped into the middle of a jargon jungle where words mean neither more nor less than the person using them wants them to mean. The same nasty problem exists for such terms as needs analysis, organizational analysis, performance analysis, and behavior analysis.

Since neither of us has the patience or capacity for sorting and sifting the sands of such a word game, we compromised. We decided to call what we do an FTO (Figuring Things Out) study and subtitled this book, "A Trainer's Guide to Needs and Task Analysis." As you will soon see, many of the techniques that can be used to help us sort out organizational obstacles can also be used to sort and order a list of job tasks. It has been our experience that the people we work for, the managers and other non trainers we call clients, could care less what we name the toys and tools of our trade. What they do care about is how quickly and how well we are able to pinpoint the cause or causes of the human performance problem at hand and how we solve it.

Call what we do task analysis, needs analysis, or Fred, if you like. When pressed, we simply say that our job is to identify the human factors or "people parts" of important organizational problems and determine the cause or causes of those human performance problems. We look at problems, try to find causes, and suggest solutions. In a nutshell, we Figure Things Out.

HOW THIS BOOK WORKS

There are seven sections to this book. In Section I, Getting Started Figuring Things Out, we try to convey both the strategic and tactical approach we take to the task of analysing human performance problems and some sense of the important human and organizational factors that influence performance and achievement in an organization.

---

*This, of course, conflicts with the story we heard—specifically, that the term task analysis was coined by Dr. Edgar L. Shriver, who was a colleague of Miller's at the American Institute of Research (AIR) from 1951 through 1953.

In Sections II through V, we explain in detail the techniques and procedures we use to figure out performance problems. Each section deals with related techniques and procedures. Since at one time or another we have used every one of these techniques in our own work, we're able to illustrate quite vividly the application of each technique.

Section VI consists of three short chapters on choosing the right technique or combination of techniques to apply to the study of a given performance problem. We wrote three chapters because we wanted to separate the political from the technical considerations.

Section VII deals with the importance of properly reporting the results of an FTO study to management. We think the value of a good reasonable presentation can't be overstated; that's why we devoted a full chapter to it.

Between the lines of this book is a subliminal message or two. The first is that it *is* possible for people like us, professional trainers and human resource development specialists, to look for and find the *real* causes of human performance problems. And the second message is that the "figuring things out" business is a fascinating, stimulating, and organizationally significant one to be in.

CHAPTER 2 THE STRATEGY OF, AND TACTICS FOR, CONDUCTING AN FTO STUDY

In some contexts, words like *strategy* and *tactic* seem argumentative and adversarial. They shouldn't. Used here, at least, they simply mean *what* we are trying to accomplish and *how* we are going to do it. Ben Tregoe and John Zimmerman of Kepner-Tregoe offer a lucid definition of strategy in their book, *Top Management Strategy*. In the organizational context, they define strategy this way:[1]

> Strategy is a vision directed at *what* the organization should be, and not *how* the organization will get there. We define strategy as *the framework which guides those choices that determine the nature and direction of an organization.*

In our context, that of doing a successful performance-problem analysis or FTO study, strategy refers to our overall goal, namely:

> Finding the significant human-factors components of important organizational performance problems and determining the primary cause or causes of those human performance problems.

So much for strategy—the *what* in "What should I do when the phone rings and somebody hollers, 'Help! I need a training problem.'?" That statement of strategy isn't especially new. For some time now, all of us in the wonderful world of training and development have been telling one another that analyzing human performance problems is the driving force of our business. But beyond the blarney, we have been a lot better at talking "what to's" than "how to's." Until now, the tool kit of "how to's," the tactics and procedures for analyzing performance problems, has been next to nonexistent.

In a way, we've been behaving like a group of Johnny-One-Notes. Historically, Professor Shemp invents technique Beta and declares it as the only idea you'll ever need; Consultant Curly comes up wth cute idea Zeta and calls it the best thing since sliced white bread; and Practitioner Moe solves all problem-solving problems with Trusty Rusty Survey Seven, a thing *his* mentor invented

---

[1]Ben Tregoe and John Zimmerman, *Top Management Strategy* (New York: Simon & Schuster, Inc., 1980), p. 17.

that has gained acceptance in the organization. There are, of course, times when Beta is a great technique, when Zeta is the perfect tool, and when Survey Seven hits the spot, but there are also times when each is inappropriate for analyzing the problem at hand.

To deny reality and continue to believe in the "one technique fits all problems" myth is as silly as believing the only tool an electrician needs is a screwdriver. If we really want the rest of the world to recognize our business as being concerned with human-factors problem solving, we must develop a tool kit of ways to approach and solve human performance problems. This book is our attempt to move the rock along in that direction.

TACTICS OF FIGURING THINGS OUT

We follow six overriding "how-to" rules when designing and conducting an FTO study. We "learned" them through trial and error—mostly error. Our 20/20 hindsight tells us that, whenever we botched one, it wasn't because the tools in our kit didn't work or were lacking. Rather, we made some sort of tactical mistake up front.

TACTIC ONE
ALWAYS WORK FROM A MODEL OF HUMAN PERFORMANCE

Chapter 3 deals exclusively with the issue of why we need a workable model of human performance if we're in the performance problem-solving business. At this point, we'll just say that working with an *organizationally relevent* model of human performance in mind facilitates and greatly enhances the processes of choosing the right factors to study and picking an appropriate method of studying them. Perhaps most importantly, it gives us a framework for analyzing and reporting results to management.

TACTIC TWO
START THE STUDY AS HIGH IN THE ORGANIZATION AS POSSIBLE AND WORK YOUR WAY DOWN

This is another of those concepts we've talked into the ground, but rarely seem to apply. When you start and end your problem analysis at the performer level, you never know exactly how the problem is perceived organizationally. Nor do you find out who is and who isn't concerned. And you never know what the problem is costing the organization, or why someone really cares enough to solve it, or if, in fact, you are playing the goat for someone in the organization who doesn't want the *real* problem solved.

One approach to the "start at the top and work down" tactic is practiced and reported on by Dr. Ann Deden-Parker of San Francisco State University. She calls her straightforward approach the Three-Phase Needs Analysis Model.

Figure 2-1 is adapted from an article in the Fall 1980 issue of the *Journal of Instructional Development* wherein Deden-Parker explains the three-phase model using, as an example, the analysis of the branch loan officer job at the Wells Fargo bank. The analysis began when senior management decided there was a problem; namely, branch loans were below dollar goals, and some questions of compliance with federal regulations were being raised. Phase one, Organizational Analysis, captured the concerns of senior managers and quantified the differences between desired and actual loan performance. Then loan officers at all levels in the bank were inteviewed to get a variety of impressions regarding lending responsibility at various credit-generating levels and to gather perceptions concerning the possible contingencies affecting performance, information needs of the job, extent of current training, and feelings about adequacy of current training.

Phase two, Operations Analysis, was characterized by interviews with subject-matter experts to capture in-depth behavioral and operational descriptions of the job tasks. These descriptions were, in turn, used to survey incumbents to determine the importance of the various tasks.

Fig. 2-1 Three-Phase Needs Analysis.

Phase of Analysis	Function/Purpose	Example from Loan Officer Needs Analysis
1. Organization Analysis	Identify and prioritize discrepancies between corporate performance and goals.	Bank divisional management identifies a problem as "number and quality of loans are below goals."
2. Operational Analysis	Perform in-depth job/task analysis to capture discrete behaviors.	Sample analysis entry: "Loan officer can identify parts of credit analysis to which Regulation B applies." Sample questionnaire to field items: How often do you perform this task? "Identify portions of credit analysis to which Reg. B applies." *Never Rarely Occasionally Frequently* 0 1 2 1
3. Individual Analysis	Assess each employee's performance on identified tasks.	Sample test question: "Which of the following (a–d) most accurately reflects the scope of Reg. B?" a. _____ c. _____ _____ _____ b. _____ d. _____ _____ _____

Adapted from Ann Deden-Parker, *Journal of Instructional Development* (Fall 1980).

Phase three, Individual Analysis, consisted of administering a paper-and-pencil test to incumbents, interviewing incumbents, and reviewing individual performance records.

Our approach to actualizing Tactic Two, "start at the top and work down," is similar to Deden-Parker's three-phase needs analysis, but there are enough differences to merit detailed description. At the Organizational Analysis level, we also engage in management discussions and ask those "Where does it hurt?" and "How much does it hurt?" questions that help us learn how current performance compares to organizational goals, the relative *impact and importance* of the difference between actual and desired performance, and management's initial impression of problem causes. But we also follow the lead of McGill University's Henry Mintzberg; Robert Doktar, University of Hawaii; and a number of strategic-planning people who see upper management's most critical function to be holistic, strategic thinking.

Toward the end of honoring that concept, we spend some of the precious time we wrangle out of senior managers trying to capture the image these managers have in their minds of a well-functioning branch, department, or division. We try to capture that ideal so we can use the same criteria effectiveness. Management rewards, punishes, and adjusts what's happening in the organization on the basis of a "mental model" of what the organization must look like if it is to actualize the mission. We need to know the key elements of that picture if we are to point out inappropriate behavior and help engineer appropriate behavior.

As Zemke and Larson have shown, this "mental model" or "idealized mission statement" of the organizational entity under consideration is the "comparator" senior management uses to judge performance, correct plans, and reward and punish subordinates. In a sense, this model of the management way sees the organization ideally operating in its mind's *eye* is as important to understanding the "organizational problem" that precipitated the request for help as it is to understanding the numerical and behavioral indicators of the specific problem at hand. In our view, the mission of an organization, any organization, is a vision or hunch held by a single entrepreneur or a policy group of the business in which the organization can be successful. For example, if Sam Smith believes the world is pining for 7¢ buggy whips, that's a business proposition. Sam won't know if his proposition is good or bad until he actually makes and tries to peddle buggy whips for 7¢ apiece (12 for 79¢). If the organization cannot turn out 7¢ buggy whips, Sam's proposition will remain untested. If the organization *is* able to produce 7¢ buggy whips, but eventually goes under, then we can say some nasty things about Sam's silly ideal.

The point is *all* organizations stand or fall on the marketplace testing of their prime mission, their idea, or their driving force. The investing in, and policing of, that mission is essentially what senior managers do for a living. The rest of us spend our time trying to actualize that mission or at least trying to keep the organization healthy and vital and aimed in the right direction. We, all of us staff folk, get paid not on the ultimate success or failure of the mission but on the basis of how well we help maximize the factors that help the mission get a fair trial in the marketplace. To do that, we have to know what that mission and model are.

Our step two under Tactic Two is to investigate the performance environment. Since our performance model places great stock in the effects of reward and punishment, feedback, objectives, and support systems on individual and small group performance, we spend considerable time asking, "Who does what to whom?" "Who gets punished around here?" and "How do you know how you're doing?" By asking, we mean applying the appropriate FTO technique(s) for getting the data that "answer" these questions. In this phase, the individual performer and the performer's supervisors and coworkers often play the role of informants. In addition, we spend time observing the environment in action—watching people interact, management manage, salespeople sell, machine operators operate, and customers do their thing.

Step three of Tactic Two is to focus on the individual performer. Here we observe the behaviors and results of performers in action, and again we use the individual as an informant. This time, however, we are seeking information on how the performer thinks *about* the job and *on* the job, as well as information about what the individual can and can't do and does and doesn't know. The details of how Tactic Two operates will become clearer as we look at the other tactics.

TACTIC THREE
ALWAYS KNOW WHOM YOU ARE STUDYING

From time to time, we all get so carried away in our quest to capture the skills, knowledge, and behaviors of a job that we forget to look at and consider the relative effectiveness of the people we are observing and tapping for program content information. Purposely reversing this situation is an invaluable tactic. Specifically, we have found that by separating job incumbents into high and low (or high, low, and medium) performing groups, and looking carefully for the skills, knowledges, behaviors, and attitudes that discriminate between the two groups, we can gather very telling information for the solution-building process. For instance, many a traditional task-analysis study of the sales management job includes dozens of pages describing the paperwork, form-filling-out responsibilities of the sales manager. Yet we have never heard of a sales manager being fired for sloppy paper work. But based on the content outlines of the sales management courses that result from the traditional "capture everything" task analysis process, precise paper shuffling would seem critical to job success.

In a sense, this tactic helps us—forces us, really—to apply the Pareto principle or 80/20 rule to the figuring things out process. When we shift the focus from capturing all relevant job-performance factors to capturing only the knowledges, skills, behaviors, and attitudes that distinguish or discriminate between high and low performers, we're more likely to end up with only critically important information about performance. We realize, of course, that occasionally we must have a complete, detailed behavioral description of the job under study. But it has been our experience that, even in those situations, we get more bang for the buck by also pinpointing the few critical behaviors and performance factors that separate high- and low-performing individuals or performance units. This "critical difference" information gives us a basis for making emphasis decisions for the training of new employees and for choosing the content for refresher and advanced training programs.

We have successfully applied this good guy/bad guy structure to such diverse situations as selling, banking, and manufacturing. Using such disparate good guy/bad guy performance criteria as sales figures, loan applications, pieces assembled, customer complaints, service recall orders, grievances, and turnover, we have applied this tactic to the study of high- and low-performing sales reps, bank loan officers, flight crews, blackjack dealers, assembly lines, drug stores, business machine branch sales offices, and automobile service departments. In sum, we have found the "know whom you are studying" tactic to be invaluable in sorting the wheat from the chaff of on-job behaviors and performance environments.[2]

TACTIC FOUR
NEVER USE JUST ONE INFORMATION-GATHERING TECHNIQUE

Every data gathering technique and data analysis procedure known can and does distort the reality it is designed to study. There is no such thing as a foolproof process or technique. If we always study the performers and performance in question in at least two independent ways, we more than double our chances of being on target. For instance, a needs survey may tell us that a majority of sales reps at LMQ Corporation feel they need to improve their time-management skills, cold-calling approach, and skill at asking for the order. But one-to-one interviews, focus groups, and check-rides with sales reps confirm only that

---

[2]If this tactic still seems dubious to you, perhaps you can be persuaded by Dr. David McClelland, Harvard's "need to achieve" researcher who has been looking at the issue of competency lately. His view is in "Testing for Competence Rather than for Intelligence," *The American Psychologist* 28 (1973): 1-14.

cold calling and asking for the order are problematic; they give virtually no evidence that poor *time management* is impinging on performance. In that case, we'd advise skipping the time-management indicator and concentrating on the cold-calling and "asking for the order" problems, which are quadruply indicated. The time management indication may be what statisticians call a false positive. In fact, we know that time management is often a false positive outcome of the ever popular "pick your biggest problem" type of needs survey. Repeated surveying we and others have been involved in shows that 30 to 40 percent of all sales people will, when asked, name time management as one of their top improvement needs.

This "try two techniques" tactic is technically known as the use of non-repetitive redundant measures. Translated this simply means that if you wear a belt *and* suspenders, your pants are pretty sure to stay up.

TACTIC FIVE
LET LINE MANAGERS MAKE THE CRITICAL DECISIONS

Peter Drucker has said that managers make far too many decisions. We say that trainers too often get roped into making management's decisions about human-factors issues and performance problems. In the heat of problem solving, we frequently forget who is line, who is support staff, and who is responsible for what. Example: You ask Manager Tom of the shipping department which inventory check-in system is the best for his operation: the one the night shift uses or the one the day shift uses. You need to know for program content. Tom shrugs his shoulders and says, "I don't know. What do you think? Which one should we be using?" Dilemma. As a nurturing training type and as a person with a deadline, you want to get the decision made and Tom off the hot seat. But the decision is Tom's to make, not yours. If you jump in and decide, then it's *your* decision, not Tom's; therefore, Tom has no need to be committed to it or to support it later. The same thing can happen when you need management to specify the criteria for picking the good guys and bad guys to study, when you need that clear statement of mission or strategy, or when you need someone to determine the importance of the problem and the price the organization is willing to pay to solve it.

Once upon a time, in a world far away, we were making a presentation to the personnel vice president of Big City Bond Company. We began on an unfortunate note: "Turnover in the operations division is at 7 percent and our study shows that part of that can be attributed to poor selection practices on the part of line supervisors." That's when the roof caved in. "Do you consider a 7 percent turnover rate to be a serious problem?" Asked the personnel v.p., an individual with a black belt in bad mouth and an advanced degree in "gottcha" logic. "Well, yes, I think so," we said, walking fly-like into his verbal parlor. "From now on keep your thoughts on such matters to yourself. I make the personnel decisions around here, not you," he snapped. "If I say 7 percent is high, it's high. If I say it's low, it's low. That's what I get paid for."

Though the experience was unpleasant, it highlights the point: Line managers—and personnel VPs, as well—get paid to exercise judgement and make certain decisions for the organization. Let them do their jobs. Playing line manager and making other people's decisions is fun and ego boosting when you call the right shots. But you can also end up carrying your head tucked underneath your arm or at least nursing severely chaffed knuckles when you call the wrong ones.

TACTIC SIX
REMEMBER THE KISS PRINCIPLE

As Paul Friesen used to say, "when it comes to doing studies of the problem, Keep It Short and Sweet." Doing a big-deal study for the sake of doing a big-deal study sets big-deal expectations and can lead to big letdowns.

Over the years, we have learned to underpromise and overproduce. We prefer to stun a client with how much we've learned of his or her organization and its problems rather than disappoint the client with lacklustre results. And the very same problem investigation and results findings can have either reception depending solely on how they are positioned up front and subsequently conducted.

We frankly get very nervous when a client decides to "show 'em in the field that we are working on the problem." When he or she mandates that we survey the entire work force instead of a small sample and that we interview every line manager instead of our preferred, carefully chosen set of a few high and low performers, we get nervous on two accounts. First, the spotlight treatment leads key people to have high expectations of our work; since time is money, the size of the bill we must run up for this sort of "good PR" reinforces the unrealistic expectations. Secondly, the spotlight treatment puts people on notice. It's better the branch manager in Kankakee forgets you're coming rather than spend two days drilling the staff on what to say when "the hotshot from home office" starts asking questions.

Rule of thumb: In twenty to forty working days you can conduct 99 percent of all the performance-problem studies you are ever called upon to perform. In this era of future shock and rapid technological change, by the time you finish one of those big-deal "call a task force and take a year" studies, half the jobs involved with the performance problem may no longer exist. Run too many pointless, big deal studies and your job may become extinct.

SUMMARY

If there is a single theme underlying the strategy and tactics of figuring things out, it's this: Training and HRD people get hired to prevent and/or solve human-performance problems within an organization; the core of our craft is the art/science of *finding* the right problems and *understanding* them fully. That requires careful thought, a touch of subtlety and ingenuity, and the appropriate tool kit. When we have followed our own advice, we have consistently found that well-analyzed problems suggest their own solutions. And often these natural solutions have a simple *elegance* and grace that, in themselves, make the "figuring things out" process extremely rewarding.

CHAPTER **3** FINDING A PLACE TO START— OR, WHY YOU HAVE TO HAVE A MODEL

Tactic One states, "Always work from a model of human performance." That was a hard-won truth. We used to believe if you had the right tools, you didn't have to adhere to any particular theory of human performance. Experience has taught us however that in order to be effective, those tools must be applied to the job of looking for the presence or absence of *something.* And that something is what a good, usable theory of human performance names as factors that significantly affect human performance. When it became obvious to us that a person with a behaviorist view of performance and one with a cognitive or decision-making belief system can look at the same performance and see different "key influencing factors," it also became obvious that we had to be keenly aware of our own theory of human performance to succeed in analyzing performance problems. And it is equally essential that we work from a practicable base or theory that is consistent with the culture of the organization.

Actually, we're not as interested in theory in the strict sense as we are in a plausible, consistent, and at least scientifically defendable[1] set of general principles that can be used to explain observed facts. Perhaps for our purposes *model* is more descriptive, and slightly more accurate, than *theory.* Whatever you choose to call it, each of us has to have a fairly concise, integrated concept of the key factors that influence the behavior and performance of people who work in our organization.

It's not imperative that you accept *our* model of human performance in order to use the tactics and techniques we employ to sort out a work environment and look for the presence or absence, strength or weakness of those forces

---

[1]By defendable we simply mean there must be a logical relationship between the elements of your model and research findings of some decent quality. Most of the elements in our model draw on social learning (behavior modeling) research and cognitive behavior modification. But the bloodline is far from pure and there is even a hint of Freud and Gestalt in some of the factors.

or factors that affect performance in an organization. But a quick look at our model probably will help you understand the vignettes and examples we use throughout this book and will clarify what we mean by a model of human performance.

WHERE OUR MODEL OF HUMAN PERFORMANCE COMES FROM — MORE OR LESS

Our current working model is pretty much a mix of performance models borrowed from others. For example, in *Analyzing Performance Problems,* Mager and Pipe use a human performance model that they explain by means of a flow chart (Fig. 3-1).

This model leads you, the performance analyst, to ask and attempt to answer twelve key questions and a series of subquestions.[2]

1. What is the performance discrepancy?
   ► What is the difference between what is being done and what is expected?
   ► What is my evidence?
   ► How reliable is my evidence?

2. Is the discrepancy important?
   ► Why?
   ► What happens if we do nothing?
   ► Is it worth making better?

3. Is it a lack of skill?
   ► Could the performers do it if their lives depended on doing the job correctly?
   ► Are present skills at least adequate?

4. Were they able to perform successfully in the past?
   ► Have they forgotten?
   ► Do they know it's still expected of them?

---

[2]Adapted from the Quick-Reference Checklist by Robert Mager and Peter Pipe, by permission of Pitman Learning, Inc., Belmont, Calif. If you haven't a theory of performance you use already, you absolutely *must* read Mager and Pipe's book *Analyzing Performance Problems* (Belmont, Calif.: Fearon Publishers, 1970). No overview can really do their ideas justice.

Fig. 3–1   The Flow-Chart Version of Mager and Pipe's Human Performance "Model."

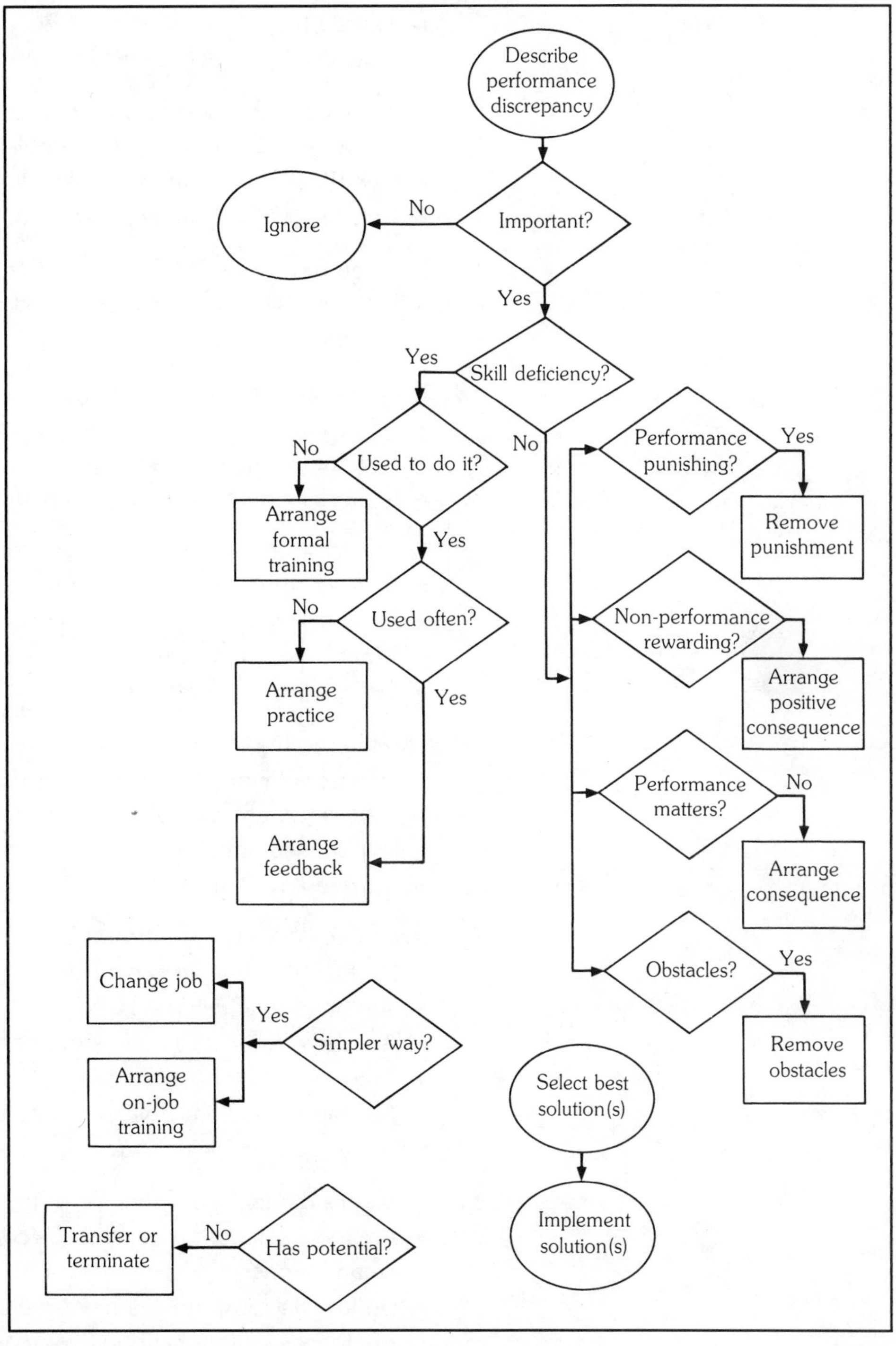

From Robert Mager and Peter Pipe, *Analyzing Performance Problems or 'You Really Oughta Wanna'* (Belmont, Calif.: Fearon Publishers, 1970).

5. Is the needed skill used frequently?
   - ► Do they get regular feedback on how well they are/are not doing?
   - ► Exactly how do they find out how they are doing?
   - ► How do they view the way they are told?

6. Is there a simpler way to do the job?
   - ► Would job aids clear up the problem?
   - ► Can they learn/relearn by watching others?
   - ► Can the job be changed some way?

7. Do they have what it takes to do the job?
   - ► Is the physical and/or mental potential there?
   - ► Are they overqualified?

8. Is the desired performance inadvertently being punished?
   - ► What's in it for the performer to do it right?
   - ► Is doing it somehow self-punishing?
   - ► Is there some pressure not to perform?

9. Is not doing the job rewarding in some way?
   - ► Is there some reward for doing it wrong?
   - ► Does doing it wrong draw attention?
   - ► What rewards the wrong performance now?
   - ► Do performers worry less or get less tired if they do less work?

10. Does doing the job right really matter?
    - ► Is there a favorable outcome for doing?
    - ► Is there an unfavorable outcome for not doing?
    - ► Is there self-pride in doing? Not doing?
    - ► Is there any status or lack of it connected with the job?

11. Are there obstacles to performing?
    - ► Do they know *what* is expected?
    - ► Do they know *when* it is expected?
    - ► Are there too many competing demands?
    - ► Are time and tools available?
    - ► Are there tradition, policy, or ego barriers?
    - ► Is the job physically a mess?

12. What are the limits on possible solutions?
    - ► Are there solutions that would be considered unacceptable to the organizations?
    - ► Do key decision makers have preferred solutions?
    - ► Are there solutions beyond the organization's time and money resources?

When we began collecting the information-gathering techniques that comprise this book, we were simply looking for ways of addressing the questions that flow out of Mager and Pipe's human-performance problem model. Since then, we've learned more and more ways to figure things out, and our interpretation of the model has taken on many strange barnacles. But it owes its birth impetus to the Mager and Pipe model—credit where credit is due we say.

THERE ARE MODELS AND THEN THERE ARE MODELS

There is, of course, a variety of models for one to cling to as "truth until further notice." Your model can be behavior-modification based, social-learning based (behavioral modeling), problem-solving based, transactional-analysis based, or purely cognitive. It can even be an amalgam of all these plus a cup of orange peels. The important thing is that *your* model helps *you* to analyze and understand performance problems in your organization and then to select appropriate solutions to apply to those problems. When the model stops working for you, it's time to discard it and pick a new, more appropriate touchstone.

By the way, the model you use for your training and development work doesn't necessarily have to be totally consistent with the one you pick for your organizational development work or the one you use for doing price negotiations with your neighborhood audiovisual dealer.

We already took a quick look at the Mager and Pipe model, which we are quick to admit is very close to the one we use. But there are plenty of other models we like and have also borrowed pieces from. The social-learning model of Albert Bandura has stood many a trainer in good stead in recent years, and one trainer/researcher mentioned earlier, Dr. Fred Luthans of the University of Nebraska, has done a fine job applying Bandura's social-learning model to the study of management. Another yeoman bit of work has been done by Dr. Geary Rummler; Rummler has spent most of a lifetime defining the strategy and tactics of trainer as performance engineer and developing a vocabulary—and performance model—to match the concept. Rummler's colleague and mentor, Dr. Thomas Gilbert, has captured much of this same performance model in his book, *Human Competence: Engineering Worthy Performance* (McGraw-Hill, 1978).

Lest this sound like a litany of Skinner student spin-offs, there are a number of useful performance models that owe their shape and being to von Bertalanffy and general systems theory, psychocybernetics, transactional analysis, Blake and Mouton and their multitude of grid applications, and Malcolm Knowles and his concepts of adult learning. The model or models you use can have any number of philosophical and theoretical parents and grandparents. The key remains pragmatism. A performance model that helps you analyze and solve human-performance problems in the immediate culture/environment/organization is a "good one," and one that gives you no help is a "bad one."

Not incidentally, the instruments and techniques of a performance model reflect the nature of the model. So, as you will notice later, the techniques we have in our preferred tool kit tend to reflect our model. And conversely, as we have learned of and tried new figuring-things-out tactics and techniques, we have modified our little model to accommodate these new approaches to gathering and analyzing information about human-performance problems. No doubt you will experience the same gratifying maturation process.

OUR MODEL   Our model is fairly simple. It has to be to accommodate the large number of techniques we embrace and to work in the wide variety of organizations where we have done FTO studies. You will recognize in it the ideas and influence of Mager and Pipe, as well as those of Rummler and Gilbert. But it also shows the creative influence of Dr. John Gunkler, Dr. Thomas Connellan, Larry Wilson, Joe Haubenhoffer, Dr. David Larson, and Dr. Olaf Isachsen. And if some of the wording seems familiar to some readers, you may be recognizing the magical wordsmithing of Tom Kramlinger's colleagues at Wilson Learning. Listen, we know a well-turned phrase when we borrow it. In short, our model is really quite an eclectic stew.

The model is composed of six factors or *categories of variables* that seem to us to capture the major variables that researchers have found to affect performance in organizations. Figure 3-2 is a graphic representation of these factors and their relationship to an organization.

Basically, we look at organizations as semi-open systems, influenced in their choices of mission, goals, strategy, tactics, and plans by the men, women,

Fig. 3-2   The Zemke-Kramlinger Model of the Major Human and Organizational Factors that Affect People Performance in an Organization.

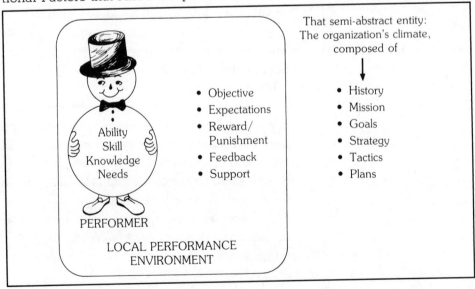

laws, and societies around them. But, at the same time, organizations have identifiable, consistent, and constant climates and cultures of their own. Of course, the climate and culture of an organization are products of missions and goals, people and place, time and size, but it is equally true that organizations have a fairly persistent summative Gestalt or nature. This "feel of the work-place," as Steele and Jenks call it, has been prodded and poked, studied and measured, as if it really were an independent life force. The names Lewin, Likert, Litwin, Katz, and Kahn spring to mind as representative of the leading practitioners of the art.

In our model, there are two direct links between the organization as an entity and people who work in the organization. The first is the body of *objectives and expectations* individuals and small groups of individuals must meet. The second link is the system of *reinforcement and performance feedback* that tells the employee or group how he, she, or they are doing at meeting the formal or informal performance demands of the organization, the same system that rewards and punishes "good" and "not so good" performance. A secondary, but occasionally very powerful influence is *support,* or the availability of help, counsel, and general personal psychosocial sustenance the individual is allowed to experience both as a person and as a performer or achiever within the organization. The final factor, a very important one, is the combination of *ability, skill, knowledge, and need* within the individual that comes to the organization and job.

When we conduct an FTO study, we look for the roots of the given performance problem by:

A. Capturing the climate and culture of the organization and interpreting the effect that culture has on individuals who are involved some way with the performance problem of the organization. We tend not to look at climate and culture in an organizational-development sense with an eye for hanging it. We tend to look at the *match* or *mismatch* of people and the weather of the work place. These sorts of mismatches can result from changes in mission and goals, limitations on available personnel, and simple organizational drift. When a significant mismatch occurs—for instance, if an organization switches from the mechanical device business to the electronic device business, there could be a sudden bear market in mechanical engineering degrees and a bull market in electrical engineering degrees—something has to give. Sometimes it's the organization, sometimes the people.

B. Understanding the mission and goals of the organization and trying to figure out how well the mission is understood at functional/operational levels in the organization and how well the mission is being translated into actions. In addition, we try to get a sense of how well today's mission fits with old ways of doing things in the organization. As Henry Mintzberg and others have found out, yesterday's ideologies and ways of thinking and doing things live on, ghost-like, long after the helm has been turned toward fresher breezes.

C. Finding out how people who work in the organization perceive the organizations incentive system. In essence, we try to get people to tell us, in a variety of ways, what the organization pays off for, what it punishes for, and how people find out how they are meeting the objectives and expectations they believe they are working toward.

D. Capturing the critical skill requirements of the job or jobs involved in the performance problem and determining how various "good" and "not so good" performers differ in performing those tasks and why that difference seems to exist. Sometimes they haven't the abilities, sometimes they don't know how, and sometimes there are organizational obstacles that make doing the job as expected virtually impossible.

E. Determining how much support exists in the work place and how critical or incidental support is in the specific organization.

Before you panic, please note that we have almost never, ever had to search for all these factors in a single study. Once or twice, we have done a full audit on a small company, and two or three times we have done the "big study" number on a division or a department. But even then, we've had a specific performance problem in mind and have only done quick checks on some of the less suspect factors. There are six key questions a typical employee might ask when he or she starts a job. When we go hunting for human-performance-problem causes, we too seek answers to those questions. These six key queries are:

1. "Will this be a comfortable place for me to work? Will I fit? Will I like them and they like me?" We all have similar climate/culture/environment questions when we take on a new job, even when the new job is in a different part of the same organization.

2. "What's expected of me here, on paper and otherwise?" That of course is the objectives and expectations question. It acknowledges that we all are aware that job-performance requirements are only a *part* of the criteria we are judged on in an organization.

3. "How do I do what's expected of me?" This is the skill/knowledge/ability question boiled to the bones. How it's answered has to do with hire-versus-develop and replace-versus-update strategies and the cost effectiveness of each for an organization at given points in time. Also included is the acquirable skill-versus-hirable skill sort of question that drives line managers, personnel directors, and industrial psychologists up the wall.

4. "How am I doing?" That's the formal feedback question. It illustrates the need for a view of the performance from an external source, human and otherwise, and it tells the employee whether to maintain or change his or her behavior to meet goals and expectations.

5. "What's in it for me?" Money, recognition, praise, sanction, incentive, and all other aspects of the reinforcement and punishment picture are components that answer this deceptively simple-sounding query.

6. "How do I get help when I'm in trouble?" Research tells us that some high-stress jobs can only be borne when there is a strong support system for the incumbent. In some jobs, camaraderie and group belonging are more "nice" than "necessary." In others, the reverse is true.

When we do an FTO study, we generally are called upon to answer one or more of these questions as they pertain to a specific job with a specific associated performance malady. As you already know, we think there is no big trick to answering these questions well and in a satisfactory time frame when they are asked of the *right* people in the right way. And that, of course, is the subject of the remainder of this book.

A final reminder: We are not trying to "sell" you our specific model of how people behave in organizations. But it is important that you have a workable, comfortable performance theory or model with which to work. As you are already seeing, our performance model greatly influences the way we do our work. It will eventually be the same for you if you pick a truly meaningful, useful model.

SECTION **II** WATCHING PEOPLE WORK: OBSERVATIONAL APPROACHES TO FIGURING THINGS OUT

The "Figuring Things Out" techniques explained and illustrated in this section share a common focus: each involves direct observation of the performer at work. Sure, chatting with the performer and asking questions about the job he or she is doing are also parts of these methods, but actually *watching* the individual perform is the critical feature of all these approaches.

The techniques in the first three chapters of this section—simple observation, time-and-motion studies, task listings, S-R Tables and algorithms—are the classics of task analysis. Their primary value lies in capturing the specific details of the tasks of a job. In the figuring-things-out context, these techniques come into play when:

1. The performance-problem analysis has shown that many performers don't know how to do the job, and training is indeed an appropriate solution.

2. There is an agreed-upon master performer, a "good guy" who does the job tasks the way consensus has decided everyone should do them.

The final chapter in this section explains and amply demonstrates the behavioral-frequency-count approach. It is especially valuable for observing high and low performers in their natural setting and ferreting out the differences between them. It is especially useful in answering questions of how much, as in "Do highly successful salespeople really ask for the order more frequently than less successful salespeople?" and "What behaviors differentiate between liked and disliked supervisors, and is there a *frequency* factor involved?"

CHAPTER **4** SIMPLE OBSERVATIONS, TIME STUDIES, AND TASK LISTINGS

The most commonly practiced task analysis technique is simple observation. Observational task analysis is part common sense—if you have to teach someone something, watch the good ones do it and document what you *see*—and part time-and-motion study. Though early industrial engineers are often characterized today as Frankensteins who invented assembly lines and made work mindless,[1] their tools—such as time-and-motion, work place layout, tool design, and human factors studies—still help us figure out what people need to learn to perform a job successfully.

Time-and-motion and methods studies have become fairly sophisticated over the years and can expedite our task analysis efforts. The industrial engineer sits or stands next to a performer, a qualified incumbent, whose job is to perform some highly observable task, such as counting out money and strapping it into bundles or assembling automobile door handles. The engineer/analyst records the performer's movements and operations, usually using a combination of standard symbols and simple prose descriptions. To get more specific about the "how-to's" the industrial engineer uses, we would have to wrestle with a number of definitional tigers. For instance, under the rubric of methods analysis fall operations studies, man-machine studies, and micromotion studies. The same holds for another group of industrial engineering tools work measurement or time studies.

In general, *methods analysis* is concerned with analyzing work activities in order to increase the efficiency of the job. The methods analyst often works with standardized operations charts and standardized symbols. In the old days, methods analysts spent hours looking over people's shoulders and charting what they

---

[1]We'd like to go on record in favor of a more reasoned and balanced view of the pioneering work of such early industrial engineers as Frederick W. Taylor and Frank and Lillian Gilbreth. Yes, they invented scientific management, piecework, and the assembly line. But it can also be argued that their work kicked off the second industrial revolution and moved all of us a big step away from work as dray animals toward work as creative, thinking beings.

observed. That's how they developed a reputation as company snoops. Today, jobs are often videotaped or filmed so the analyst can study the job under consideration at a more leisurely pace and without the pressure of "getting off the worker's back" in a timely fashion.

Here's one set of symbols that is popular in operations studies and, generally, in work efficiency/work improvement studies.

Symbol	Name	Activities Represented
○	Operation	Modification of object at one workplace. Object may be changed in any of its physical or chemical characteristics, assembled or disassembled, or arranged for another operation, transportation, inspection, or storage.
▷	Transportation	Change in location of object from one place to another.
□	Inspection	Examination of object to check on quality or quantity characteristics.
D	Delay	Retention of object in a location awaiting next activity. No authorization is required to perform the next activity.
▽	Storage	Retention of object in location in which it is protected against unauthorized removal.

Figure 4-1, an operation-chart analysis of the task of assembling a ball-point pen, shows these symbols in use.

A *time and motion* study is usually conducted for one of five reasons:

1. To measure productivity

2. To develop performance incentive systems

3. To determine product/manufacturing costs

4. To estimate costs and procedures for projected new products

5. To develop work-load and crew-assignment schedules

Figure 4-2 shows a "pure" time-study chart; it is concerned only with determining the actual time of an operation, in this case the operation of drilling three holes in a piece of metal destined to become a brake shoe. Its ample detail can be helpful to both engineer and trainer.

Fig. 4–1 An Operation Chart of the Task of Assemblying a Ballpoint Pen.

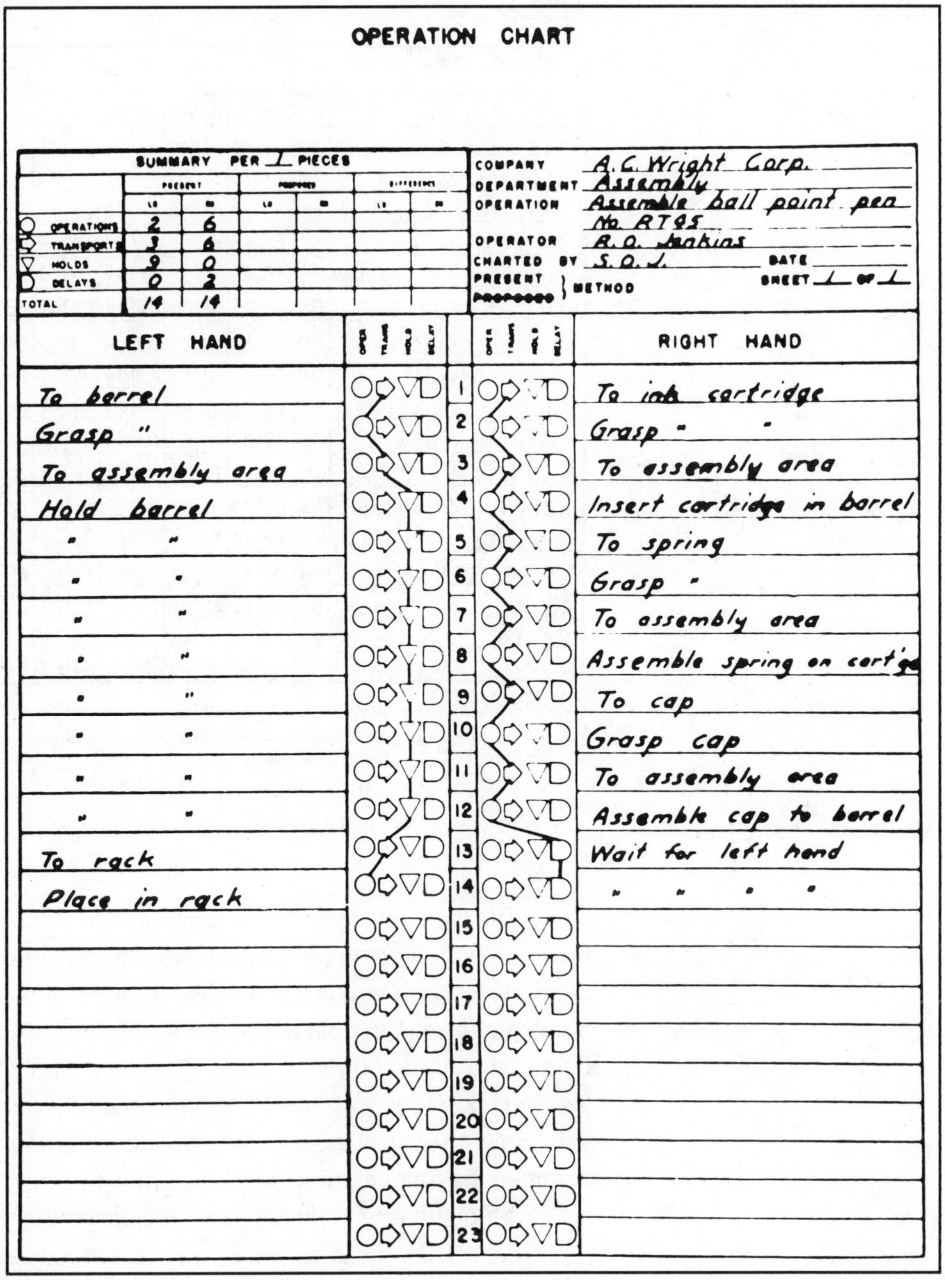
OPERATION CHART

SUMMARY PER 1 PIECES	PRESENT LH	PRESENT RH	PROPOSED LH	PROPOSED RH	DIFFERENCE LH	DIFFERENCE RH
OPERATIONS	2	6				
TRANSPORTS	3	6				
HOLDS	9	0				
DELAYS	0	2				
TOTAL	14	14				

COMPANY A. C. Wright Corp.
DEPARTMENT Assembly
OPERATION Assemble ball point pen No. RT95
OPERATOR R. O. Jenkins
CHARTED BY S. O. J. DATE
PRESENT / PROPOSED METHOD SHEET 1 OF 1

LEFT HAND	No.	RIGHT HAND
To barrel	1	To ink cartridge
Grasp "	2	Grasp " "
To assembly area	3	To assembly area
Hold barrel	4	Insert cartridge in barrel
" "	5	To spring
" "	6	Grasp "
" "	7	To assembly area
" "	8	Assemble spring on cart'ge
" "	9	To cap
" "	10	Grasp cap
" "	11	To assembly area
" "	12	Assemble cap to barrel
To rack	13	Wait for left hand
Place in rack	14	" " " "
	15	
	16	
	17	
	18	
	19	
	20	
	21	
	22	
	23	

Notice that left- and right-hand movements are recorded separately. Now that's about as microscopic as a task analysis can get!

From Amrine, Ritchey, and Hulley, *Manufacturing Organization and Management,* 3rd ed., © 1975, pp. 120–123. Reprinted by permission of Prentice-Hall, Inc., Englewood Cliffs, New Jersey.

Fig. 4–2 Time Study of the Operation of Drilling Three Holes in a Brake Shoe Blank.

											RATING 100%		SELECTED NORMAL		
Pick up Piece	05	04	05	06	05	05	06	05	05	04				
Place in Jig	07	06	07	08	07	07	07	08	06	06				
Tighten 2 Screws	10	11	10	10	12	10	11	10	10	11				
Locate Under Spindle	05	06	05	01	06	05	06	06	05	06				
Lower Spindle	05	05	04	04	05	04	05	05	05	05		.05		
Drill 1 Hole 1"dia. 1"deep	39	38	39	31	39	38	31	39	39	38			.38	
Raise Spindle	04	03	04	04	03	03	04	03	03	03				.03
Shift To Next Hole	10	09	10	10	09	09	08	10	10	09				
Lower Spindle	04	04	04	05	04	05	04	04	04	04		.04		
Drill 1 Hole 1"dia. 1"deep	42	41	42	40	42	40	40	39	39	40			.40	
Raise Spindle	05	05	04	03	04	04	05	05	05	05				.05
Shift To Next Hole	10	10	9	12	9	12	10	9	10	10				
Lower Spindle	03	03	03	02	03	03	03	04	03	03		.03		
Drill 1 Hole 1"dia. 1"deep	45	42	43	44	42	41	43	42	45	43			.43	
Raise Spindle	04	04	03	04	04	03	04	04	04	03				.04
Loosen 2 Screws	07	05	07	07	06	08	07	07	08	06				
Remove Piece	05	04	06	06	04	07	06	06	05	05				
Piece Aside	04	03	04	03	04	04	04	04	05	04				

The time-study analyst broke the process into 18 steps (far left column), observed and timed an operator through 10 repetitions (center column), estimated that the operator was working at 100 percent efficiency, and selected a set of normal or average times for 9 of the 18 operations or steps.

We won't belabor the conduct of time-and-motion and methods studies. If however, you work in an industry or company that uses these industrial engineering tools and you aren't availing yourself of the results, you're overlooking a training information gold mine at least as a first step in your training task analysis. If time-and-motion or methods studies exist for a job you're going to prepare training for, you can short cut the time needed to do your task analysis, develop valid training objectives, and extrapolate the core motor skills and perceptual discriminations trainees must learn in order to master the job tasks.

Step one is to verify the study by observing the job as it is currently being performed. If the job is still being done essentially as it was time studied, you're in business. If the job to be learned is a relatively simple one, you may need only to do some videotaping and simple simulation building for the training. A more complex set of tasks may require additional analysis and organization. Many seemingly simple manufacture and assembly tasks, such as the manufacture and assembly of many computer components, require a more detailed analysis than, say, the production of parts for a kid's swing set.

Even when your analysis must be more sophisticated than existing time studies, you can utilize existing studies of similar tasks to estimate what the training will look like, what it will cost, and how long it is likely to take.

Obviously, not all jobs can be studied successfully with stop watch, clipboard, and a vocabulary of standard movement notation. Jobs with important or complex decisional elements, and even manual work requiring a number of optional routines and procedures, are not readily amenable to time-and-motion techniques. For these jobs, the task-listing approach, which is more flexible than the time-and-motion technique, is often indicated.

TASK LISTINGS: SECOND GENERATION OF TASK ANALYSIS

What we think of as a second generation of task analysis, one step beyond time-and-motion studies, is task listing, the process of capturing, sorting, and sequencing job tasks. It definitely qualifies for what R. B. Miller called an "art form", but it does have rules, rhymes, and intrinsic reason.[2]

The task-listing approach is used extensively in military training where it has proved to be quite useful. To give it a fair shake, we should start with the military understanding, or at least definition, of *task*. A 1973 U.S. Air Force training-design handbook describes a task this way:

- ► A task is a group of related manual activities directed toward a goal.
- ► A task usually has a definite beginning and end.
- ► A task involves people's interaction with equipment, other people, and/or media.
- ► A task, when performed, results in a meaningful product. (Products are not always tangible. For example, a "correct decision" is a meaningful product.)
- ► A task may be of any size or degree of complexity. But it must be directed toward a specific purpose or separate portion of the total duty.

Another military publication, this time from the Navy, goes on to specify the steps of analyzing tasks as they are defined by the five criteria just mentioned.

---

[2]Specifically, Miller called task analysis "a branch of technology dependent on invention rather than science, which is dependent on research and discovery in the classic sense. . . . Task analysis is an art, and, as an art, is largely dependent for its excellence and ability on the expertise of the task analyst" (*Journal of Performance Improvement,* 1972).

This particular approach is best understood by starting with this definition of *job analysis*:

> The breaking down of a job into a series of levels of job tasks of increasing specificity. In Navy terms, job analysis is analyzing a billet into duty assignments, these into tasks, and these into task elements.

This approach of analyzing a job by developing a list or outline of *duties,* broken into *tasks,* which are broken into *sub-tasks,* which are broken into *task elements,* was formalized by Edward A. Rundquist. It usually yields something akin to the task listing in Fig. 4–3.

Fig. 4–3 An Example of a Job Task Broken Down by Task Levels and Sequenced According to the Rundquist Method.

LEVEL I JOB TASK

1.0   Participates in a detail operating the main steam propulsion plant

Analysis of Level I job task 1.0, "Participates in a detail operating the main steam propulsion plant," can be further subdivided into:

LEVEL II JOB TASKS

1.1	Operates and monitors steam generating system.
1.2	Monitors expansion phase equipment, and adjusts as needed.
1.3	Operates and monitors mechanical propulsion gear.
1.4	Monitors lubrication system.
1.5	Monitors condensation system.
1.6	Monitors feed system.

Analysis of Level II job task 1.1, "Operates and monitors steam generating system," can be further subdivided into:

LEVEL III JOB TASKS

1.1.1	Operates, inspects, and maintains steam generator.
1.1.2	Monitors, inspects, and maintains oil-burning equipment.
1.1.3	Monitors, inspects, and maintains air-distribution equipment.
1.1.4	Monitors, inspects, and maintains feed-water system.
1.1.5	Employs chemistry equipment.
1.1.6	Monitors and inspects automatic controls.

Analysis of Level III job task 1.1.1, "Operates, inspects, and maintains steam generator," can be further subdivided into:

LEVEL IV JOB TASKS

1.1.1.1	Lights off steam generator.
1.1.1.2	Operates steam generator.
1.1.1.3	Secures steam generator.
1.1.1.4	Applies emergency procedures (casualty control).
1.1.1.5	Inspects, maintains, and repairs steam generator.

(continued)

Analysis of Level IV job task 1.1.1.1, "Lights off steam generator in a cold plant with auxiliary steam available, by performing (11) tasks in the following sequence," can be further subdivided into:

LEVEL V JOB TASKS

1.1.1.1.1	Establishes water level in steam generator.
1.1.1.1.2	Establishes oil supply for steam generator.
1.1.1.1.3	Establishes air supply for steam generator.
1.1.1.1.4	Lines up vents, drains, and steam protection.
1.1.1.1.5	Lights off steam generator (forms steam).
1.1.1.1.6	Secures vents.
1.1.1.1.7	Realigns drains.
1.1.1.1.8	Realigns steam protection.
1.1.1.1.9	Maintains water level in steam generator.
1.1.1.1.10	Raises steam to operating pressure.
1.1.1.1.11	Opens steam stops

Analysis of Level V job task 1.1.1.1.2, "Establishes oil supply for steam generator by performing (11) subtasks in the following sequence," can be further subdivided into:

LEVEL VI JOB TASKS

1.1.1.1.2.1	Lines up fuel oil suction to pump.
1.1.1.1.2.2	Lines up fuel oil heater.
1.1.1.1.2.3	Lines up fuel oil supply to burner.
1.1.1.1.2.4	Checks operation of quick-closing valve.
1.1.1.1.2.5	Opens recirculating valve.
1.1.1.1.2.6	Starts fuel oil service pump.
1.1.1.1.2.7	Checks operation of relief valves.
1.1.1.1.2.8	Cuts in steam to fuel oil heater.
1.1.1.1.2.9	Ensures oil temperature is raised to operating temperature.
1.1.1.1.2.10	Assembles fuel oil burners of lighting-off size.
1.1.1.1.2.11	Installs fuel oil burners thus assembled.

Note how specific Level VI tasks are. The analysis stops at this point because, given instructions, any student will be able to do these simple tasks. They are like turning a knob or adjusting a dial.

In case you didn't recognize it, the job being analyzed in Fig. 4–3 is that of a Navy BT-2 or Boiler Tender, somebody who keeps the steam engines running on a ship.

According to Rundquist, there are six critical operations in the task-listing approach to the task-analysis process.

1. *Enumerating and agreeing upon job duties.* If the experts don't agree on the assignment of responsibilities and duties, you have a different level of problem to work with. (We'll cover that later in the section on Consensus Techniques.)

Fig. 4-4 A Job/Task Breakdown Modeled after Rundquist's (1970) Analysis of a Specific Naval Position.

	LEVEL I TASK
7.0	Relieves the watch.
	LEVEL II TASKS
7.1	Checks stored data prior to relieving the watch.
7.2	Determines systems status prior to relieving watch.
	LEVEL III TASKS
7.1.1	Sights, using checklist if desired, stored data required to administer the watch, assuming custody for classified material. (1)
7.1.2	Determines information, events, and procedures applicable to his watch by reviewing: pertinent operation orders and operations plans, CO's night orders, pass-down-the-line (PDL) log, and pertinent messages. (2)
7.1.3	Amplifies and interprets data derived from operation orders, night orders, PDL log, and messages by referring to doctrinal publications, fleet and ship standard operating procedures (SOP), intelligence materials, and RADFO messages. (2)
7.2.1	Inspects, interprets, and evaluates surface summary plot to determine presence, location, and degree of threat of surface contacts. (3)
7.2.2	Inspects, interprets, and evaluates air vertical plot to determine presence, location, and degree of threat of air contacts. (4)
7.2.3	Inspects, interprets, and evaluates electronic warfare status board to determine information pertinent to radar and intercept search guards, EMCON, and current or anticipated intercepts. (4)

2. *Selecting the right action verb for describing job tasks.* As with instructional objectives, job tasks are best expressed using verbs that tell exactly and unequivocally what job actions are to be taken. As you can tell from the task listing in Fig. 4-4, Rundquist prefers to err on the side of overexplicitness.

A job task such as "solders a copper wire to a lug" appears explicit, yet the verb is not really job-oriented. The writer prefers the job statement, "connects a copper wire to a lug by soldering," the verb *connects* being the job-oriented *what* and the soldering being the *how*. Both are needed in the job task statement. Frequently, the point of how (by what action) the job incumbent does these tasks is missed when identifying job tasks. (Rundquist, 1970)

3. *Managing the numbers of the job tasks.* Rundquist advises that numbering keeps the tasks in proper hierarchial perspective. The numbering system specifies the level of every detail of every task and task element. Decimals help keep the levels straight.

Level I tasks:	1.0	2.0	3.0, etc.
Level II tasks:	1.1	2.1	3.1, etc.
Level III tasks:	1.1.1	2.1.1	3.1.1, etc.
Level IV tasks:	1.1.1.1	2.1.1.1	3.1.1.1, etc.

He further suggests that, early in the analysis, Level I tasks be kept on separate cards so they can be sorted for sequencing. In nonlinear jobs, jobs with optional routines, the separate card system is helpful for keeping the optional routines separated from "mainstream" tasks.

4. *Building a hierarchy of tasks and elements.* In a completed hierarchy of tasks, each task or task element should be clearly distinguishable from the one above or below it. When done properly, the whole thing should logically and visually "add up." Adding up simply means that one cluster of Level IV tasks, taken as a whole, should be equal to the Level III task just above it. All the Level III tasks add up to the Level II tasks immediately above them, and so forth. Level I tasks are, of course, the discrete units that make up the job duty being described and that name the task being analyzed.

5. *Using subject matter experts (SMEs).* Rundquist suggests using a panel of three or more SMEs to agree upon the sequencing of Level I and II tasks. But he prefers that one SME be designated as *the* authority for the approval, development, and sequencing of Level III, IV, V, and so on, tasks and elements.

6. *Determining criteria for stopping the dissection.* The job task identification ends when all tasks that are to be trained are identified. There are four rules for recognizing when it's time to stop dissecting the duty in question into smaller and smaller pieces:
    a. Stop when the job tasks clearly and accurately express what needs to be trained.
    b. Stop when further analysis involves a complex skill that can be assumed or that must be learned outside the job-learning context.
    c. Stop when a task level is reached that the designer/analyst is confident the job instructor can further analyze into lower-level tasks on his or her own should that become necessary.
    d. Stop when a job task is reached that the course entrant is supposed to be able to do prior to training.

This system and others like it are extremely laborious and detailed and somewhat tedious to do. But they work well when the job to be done requires the trainee to make a few very simple decisions and when the job is extremely linear or has many linear parts.

Rundquist did an excellent job of describing and illustrating task listing, a classic and time-honored approach to task analysis. This approach, however, doesn't suggest or use any criteria for specifying the psychological processes that job tasks usually demand.[3] The next evolution, the S-R Table approach, is a form of task listing that corrects for this missing piece.

---

[3]Two psychologists, Glaser and Resnick, defined and made a case for task analysis as "the description of tasks in terms of the demands they place on such basic psychological processes as attention, perception, and linguistic processing." (*The Annual Review of Psychology*, 1970, p. 385).

CHAPTER 5 DEVELOPING AND USING S-R TABLES: THE DETERLINE APPROACH TO TASK ANALYSIS

Dr. William Deterline of Deterline Associates in Palo Alto, California, teaches and practices a more sophisticated form of the task-listing approach to task analysis. It's called the S-R (stimulus-response) table approach.[1] Deterline defines task analysis as the "specification of all overt and covert behavior involved in the performance of a job." Accordingly, the analyst's job is to develop a behavioral blueprint consisting of three elements:

- ► Stimulus response (S-R) table
- ► Behavioral objectives
- ► Criterion test items

Development of the S-R table begins with observation. Deterline recommends, as a first step, passively watching the job. If you close your mouth, empty or quiet your mind, and just watch—patterns and repetitive movements begin to emerge. Once you see these patterns, you can begin to experimentally anticipate actions. Say, for example, you're watching a drill press operator. She reaches for a part. You anticipate that when the part is in hand, she will move it to the bed of the drill press and secure it in the drilling jig. But she crosses you up. She moves the piece to the drill press, but instead of fastening it in place, she looks at it quizzically, turns it over in her hands, and finally tosses it in a barrel marked "Re-work."

Your first hypothesis, using Deterline's notational system, would have looked like this:

Cue or Stimulus	Action or Response
1. Need blank to drill	⟶ Reach out and obtain blank from bin
2. Blank in hand	⟶ Move to drill press bed
3. Blank at drill press bed	⟶ Secure blank in drilling jig

---

[1] There are other S-R task analysis systems, but Deterline's approach, as formalized in his "Instructional Technology Workshop," was the first we encountered and is the one we use, so we give him the credit.

But as you watched, you discovered a need to add the new task element: 'Inspect part blank for defects." Your revised S-R table would look like this:

Cue or Stimulus		Action or Response
1. Need blank to drill	⟶	Reach into bin and secure blank
2a. Blank in hand	⟶	Inspect blank
2b. Inspect blank—reject	⟶	Put in reject barrel (back to cue 1)
2c. Inspect blank—accept	⟶	Move blank to bed of drill
3. Blank at bed of drill press	⟶	Secure blank in jig

Once you have developed a rough S-R outline—first in your head, then on paper—you interview the incumbents while they work.[1] Eventually, these chats with the people who do the work will help you compile a list of "whys" and "wherefores" for their behavior, the informal rules they use for self-guidance, descriptions of what constitutes reject conditions, cues for taking procedural short-cuts, and the general rationale or cognitive structure behind the behaviors you have nailed down on the S-R table. The procedure is to ask such simple questions as: "How did you decide that one was a reject?" and "How do you know when to call the expediter?" By the way, the more naive and less threatening you are, the more information you get.

One caution on interviewing master performers. Supervisors naturally will want you to watch their best person work. Often, this department hotshot is the person the supervisor assigns to train newcomers and you qualify. Be careful not to accept at face value the "performance theories" the hotshot gives you. He or she may have just made them up to help novices remember the procedural routines. This is especially true of computer mop-up jobs. A senior reconciliation clerk once gave us an elaborate rationale why a computer made certain errors and why corrections had to be entered in a certain fashion. Turned out, in fact, that a "glitch" in the computer programming necessitated a very odd re-entry routine, but no one had ever told the reconcilers that, so they made up their own explanation.

To be safe, check your S-R tables for the job against the performance of more than one operator/performer. Tap on everyone you can for tips and tricks, short-cuts, and procedural rationale as well. If you don't maintain a broad base for information gathering, you won't find out until it's too late that you've been working with the departmental whiz kid, overachiever or eccentric and have therefore, developed an S-R table that is worthless for the average performer.

---

[1]There is a "good judgment" factor to exercise here. Interviewing skin divers, fire eaters, and demolition derby drivers while they are working is considered beyond the call, unless you're doubling as a correspondent for one of those "really incredible people" television shows.

It is also appropriate to check your analysis with departmental supervisors and "lead people," as those skilled artisans who buffer management from the actual work are sometimes called. But bear in mind that supervisors don't always know the jobs well enough to perform them at expected production levels, and lead people are often ex-overachiever superstars. That sometimes makes the input from these two groups less helpful in designing training for the average performer.

One more acid test is to do the job yourself, guided by your own S-R table. If you're like us, that is pretty good verification. Our general rule of thumb is, "If *we* can learn to do it, *anybody* can." After all, one attribute of a good trainer is being a bad trainee, isn't it?

While the Deterline System looks simple, it has a number of notational and conceptual subtleties that make it a bit tricky to use. But its advantage over simple task-listing systems is that basic conceptual and decisional task parameters can be captured and eventually utilized in the training. There are roughly six steps in the development of an S-R table.

1. *Record Observable Behavior of Incumbents.* As mentioned earlier, Deterline recommends beginning with very passive observation. The details go like this:

   a. Once you have management's positioning on why the job needs a training program and you've determined that training is indeed an appropriate intervention, have management select at least four "experts" for you to observe and learn the job from. These four people should be of distinctly different skill levels, from hotshot to barely competent.

   b. Be sure you introduce yourself or have yourself introduced and positioned in a nonthreatening manner. With incumbents, this intro has worked for us.

   I'm _____ from the training department. I'm going to be developing a training program for new operators. I asked to work with a number of people in the department. You're one of the "lucky ones" who was nominated. I guess you get me first. Would it bother you if I sat next to you and watched you for a while? Just treat me like any new hire you might be breaking in. I don't know much about the job yet, so tell me everything you think I should know to do it right. Okay?

   There will be a certain amount of threat in your presence, so some congenial banter is in order. The *worst* thing you can do is try to play "rank" games with line people. If you do, they'll burn and bury you—figuratively, of course. The usual gambit is to clam up and only give you what you ask for. That's a guaranteed, time-honored way to "help" the fancy trainer-type perform the big banana peel stunt on him- or herself. It's called malecous obedience. If you haven't learned that a little humility—make that a *lot* of humility—goes a long way in this profession, consider this a first lesson.

c. Watch for repeated movements, the individual pieces of behavior that make up the flow of performance. Look for pauses; these are often decision points. But mostly just watch. That isn't as easy as it sounds. Watching someone work, with the intent of understanding what he or she is doing, is *exhausting*. If your eyes get tired, your concentration flags, and you are mentally numb at the end of a full day of observation, you're doing the job right.
Caution: Don't start right out taking notes. This can scare your informant, and it interferes with your actual learning of the tasks. Save that till the second day or very late on the first day.

d. Once you start making scribbles, do so mostly in response to your informant's answers to your questions. You can write what you please, but be sure the operator understands that you are trying to capture the *job,* not spy on the operators.

e. The process we described earlier of trying to guess the performer's next move is a frustrating but effective exercise. Once you *think* you understand the job, try to guess what the next step will be. Try to guess what the next response to the current stimulus might be.
An operator who has doubled as an on-job trainer for the department will often enjoy cooperating with you in this effort. That also helps you identify the natural decision points.

2. *Determine the Stimuli for Each Response.* Here comes one of the tricky parts. Most job behavior is actually chains of behavior, not discrete S-R units. Technically it looks like this:

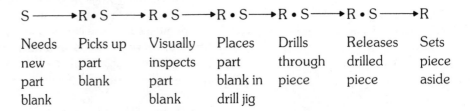

| S → R • | S → R • | S → R • | S → R • | S → R • | S → R • | S → R |

| Needs new part blank | Picks up part blank | Visually inspects part blank | Places part blank in drill jig | Drills through piece | Releases drilled piece | Sets piece aside |

In most behavior repertoires, a response is *also* a stimulus for the next response. In S-R table form, the preceding chain would look like this:

Stimulus		Response
1. Needs new part blank	⟶	Picks up part blank
2. Puts blank in hand	⟶	Visually inspects blank
3. Blank acceptable for processing	⟶	Places blank in drill jig
4. Blank seam in drill jig	⟶	Drills through piece
5. Piece drilled	⟶	Releases piece
6. Piece released	⟶	Sets aside

3. *Classify the S-R elements as:*

MP *Motor Performance*—things the performer does. Lifts cog, stacks reports, files orders, and so on are examples of MP.

VP *Verbal Performance*—things the performer does with words or numbers. Speaking, writing, working equations on paper are examples of VP.

VB *Verbal Background*—things the performer says to him- or herself to direct performance. "The fare goes in the FBZ box," "Stale dated check," and "Multiply bill by 25 percent nuisance tax" are examples of VB.

D *Discriminations*—distinctions the performer makes that tell when a performance is finished, a part is to be rejectd, or an operation is to begin. Scans list for city code, scans ticket for fare box, feels valve lock tight are examples of D.

All S-R unit learning requires the performer to make some sort of discrimination. The use of D here is, therefore, best understood as a seek-and-find operation, such as looking for a zip code in a list. In some cases, low-level but critical, decision making is a D—deciding that a part is faulty, for example.

Figure 5-1 is a simple example of a task fully analyzed, with S's and R's properly sorted and classified using the Deterline notational system.

4. *Classify Discriminations (D) As Single or Multiple.*   Tasks sometimes have different discriminating qualities. This is important to the eventual instructional strategy.

EXAMPLE: *The task "Must be able to find the correct picture when told, 'Find the triceratops' " is different from "Must be able to name all the dinosaurs in picture 7-Z."*

In the first case, we would simply teach "not triceratops" to the non-examples and "is triceratops" to the example. In the second case, we would teach "is stegosaurus," "is allosaurus," "is triceratops."

Fig. 5–1   The Task of Replacing a Ballpoint Pen Cartridge Using the S-R Table Task Analysis Approach.

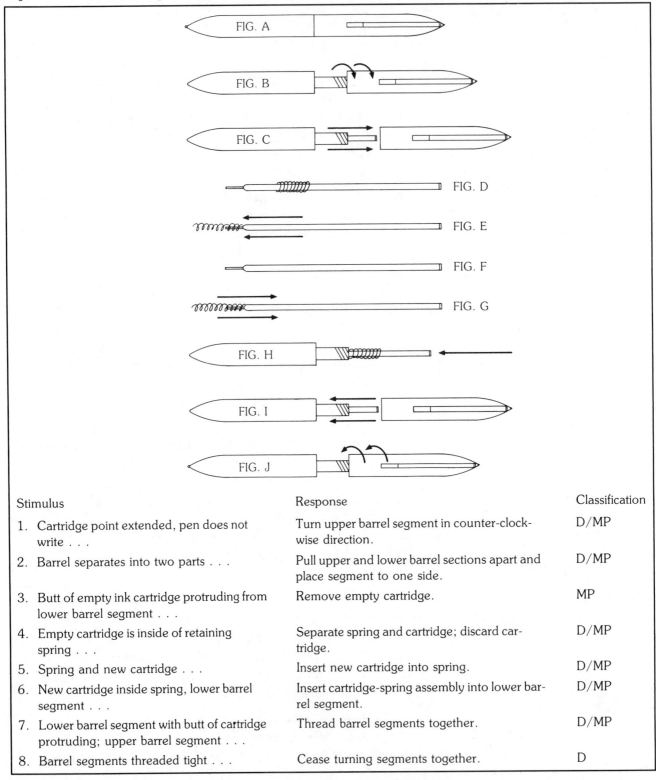

Stimulus	Response	Classification
1. Cartridge point extended, pen does not write . . .	Turn upper barrel segment in counter-clock-wise direction.	D/MP
2. Barrel separates into two parts . . .	Pull upper and lower barrel sections apart and place segment to one side.	D/MP
3. Butt of empty ink cartridge protruding from lower barrel segment . . .	Remove empty cartridge.	MP
4. Empty cartridge is inside of retaining spring . . .	Separate spring and cartridge; discard cartridge.	D/MP
5. Spring and new cartridge . . .	Insert new cartridge into spring.	D/MP
6. New cartridge inside spring, lower barrel segment . . .	Insert cartridge-spring assembly into lower barrel segment.	D/MP
7. Lower barrel segment with butt of cartridge protruding; upper barrel segment . . .	Thread barrel segments together.	D/MP
8. Barrel segments threaded tight . . .	Cease turning segments together.	D

Compare this analysis with the time-and-motion analysis of the same task from Fig. 4-2.

5. *Classify All S-R Units As One-Way or Two-Way.* S-R units have a definite direction to them. Back to the dinosaur farm:
  ► If the task is: "Say *triceratops* to this picture,"

we're talking one-way S-R unit. Given the picture (S), say the sentence (R).
  ► If the task is: "Given these three pictures, you will point to A when told to 'point to the triceratops,' "

we're still talking one-way S-R learning.

► If, however, the task is to: "Say *triceratops* when shown this picture" and to
"Find this picture in response to 'find the triceratops,' "
then we're looking at a two-way S-R learning task. Given the (S) do [name, find] (R) and given (R) find [do, name] (S).

6. *Determine Relevant Verbal Mediators.*   Some VBs are verbal mediators or close to it, but let's save this term for special cases such as:
"In fourteen hundred and ninety-two, Columbus sailed the ocean blue."
Or is that . . .
"In fourteen hundred and seventeen, Columbus sailed the ocean green"?
Or perhaps . . .
"In fourteen hundred and ninety-three, Columbus sailed the deep blue sea"?

Anyway, save the *mediator* tag for mnemonic devices and other special aids to learning and performance. ROY G. BIV is a good example. The seven letters represent the color code for the resistance hierarchy of electrical resistors. This mnemonic is a classic example of a verbal mediator.

CONCLUSION

The various observational task analysis methods we have explored are very useful for analyzing the content of jobs with a mix of simple verbal behaviors, lower-level decisional aspects, and myriad significant, non-arbitrary, procedurally dictated actions. Small motor repair, prepping scuba-diving equipment, flight ticket preparation, and the assembly of electronic modules are all examples where these techniques, especially the S-R table approach, have had successful application. Not surprisingly, a number of variations on these approaches have been developed. For example, Michael A. Companion and Warren H. Teichner (1977), under the auspices of a U.S. Air Force grant, designed a variation on the Deterline System that you might want to look over to see if it fits your working style.

CHAPTER **6** BEHAVIORAL ALGORITHMS: AN INFORMATION-PROCESSING APPROACH TO TASK ANALYSIS[1]

We know an individual who thinks an algorithm is a variation of the Latin Hustle! Actually, the word is commonplace to mathematicians, computer programmers, and systems analysts. According to training consultant Ivan Horabin, an algorithm is:

> An orderly procedure or exact prescription for solving a problem. An algorithm leads the user from a collection of input data to a desired result. Strictly speaking, *all* rules and regulations are algorithms. But in this context (training), we limit the use of the term *algorithm* to presentation of rules and regulations in specific forms. In this sense, an algorithm is usually a decision tree and always a presentation in which the physical layout shows the relationships between inputs, data and outcomes. The algorithm replaces continuous prose as an instrument for communicating complex rules and regulations.[2]

Expatriate Russian educational psychologist Dr. Lev Landa believes that the algorithm is an accurate model of the way humans actually think and function. Therefore, educational psychology should be primarily concerned with the classification and clarification of general algorithms for general classes of performance and the development of expeditious algorithmic application by the novice. Or, as Landa puts it:

> In order to teach effectively the ability to solve problems when the underlying problem-solving process is algorithmic in nature (when there are operations and conditions to follow), the teacher must know the corresponding algorithms.[3]

---

[1] Subtitle respectfully borrowed from "Task Analysis—An Information Processing Approach," a 1976 article by Paul F. Merrill, *NSPI Journal*, vol. xv, no. 2.

[2] From Horabin's *Achievement* newsletter, No. 5, September 1971, © 1971 by Ivan Horabin, Summit Point, West Virginia.

[3] Lev Landa, *Algorithmization In Learning and Instruction*, p. 27.

At least we *think* that's what he thinks. To be quite honest, his two master-ful but somewhat difficult texts on algorithms as a model of the mind explain themselves better than we can explain their essence:

- ► *Algorithmization In Learning And Instruction* Educational Tech-nology Publications, Englewood Cliff, NJ (1974)
- ► *Instructional Regulation and Control: Cybernetics, Algorithmiza-tion, and Heuristics in Education.* Educational Technology Publi-cations, Englewood Cliff, NJ (1976)

Anyway, Dr. Landa's research, parallel studies in the cognitive decision-making process by Dr. Herbert A Simon and Dr. Paul Johnson, and field work by Dr. John Rhetts and Dr. Russell Burris give us confidence that the algorithm is a major but underutilized tool in the task analysis arsenal. The algorithm is *the* analysis technique of choice in tasks that are highly decisional in nature and that have fairly simple operations and processes. Translation: When thinking and deciding are more complex than doing—as in a medical diagnosis—then the algorithm is helpful in sorting and ordering what is to be learned and performed.

Still baffled? Just think of an algorithm as a flow chart of the processes, operations, and decisions it takes to do a task. Figure 6-1 is an algorithm devel-oped by Paul Merrill for reconciling his bank statement and his checkbook.

One of us, the senior author in this case, uses a somewhat different algo-rithm to obtain agreement between his bank statement and checkbook. Figure 6-2 shows that algorithm.

The difference between the Merrill and Zemke algorithms points up an important characteristic of algorithms: They are somewhat atheoretical. Yes, using algorithms does assume that there is an orderly and maximally efficient flow between the entry and exit points of the algorithm and that cognitive pro-cesses may be more important than behavioral. But the algorithm itself doesn't dictate content or the flow of operations; it only captures performance. The Mer-rill algorithm, for example, assumes that there is some reasonable probability that the bank might make an error in Merrill's account *and* that he will be able to find it. The Zemke algorithm assumes that the bank is unlikely to err and that, even if it does, Zemke would be unlikely to find the mistake. Both approaches to solving the problem can be analyzed—and taught to others—using the algorithm technique.

An algorithm is neither right nor wrong, only a detailed exposition of con-sensus among subject matter experts (SMEs); basically, it's a reflection of the way a local culture has decided to solve a particular problem. Zemke claims that his approach to the checkbook problem has saved him about 500 hours of work and several bottles of aspirin in the five years he has been using it. He likes the assumptions and the savings. Some of us like to argue with our banks, and some of us do not.

Fig. 6-1   Information Processing Flow Chart for Reconciling a Bank Statement.

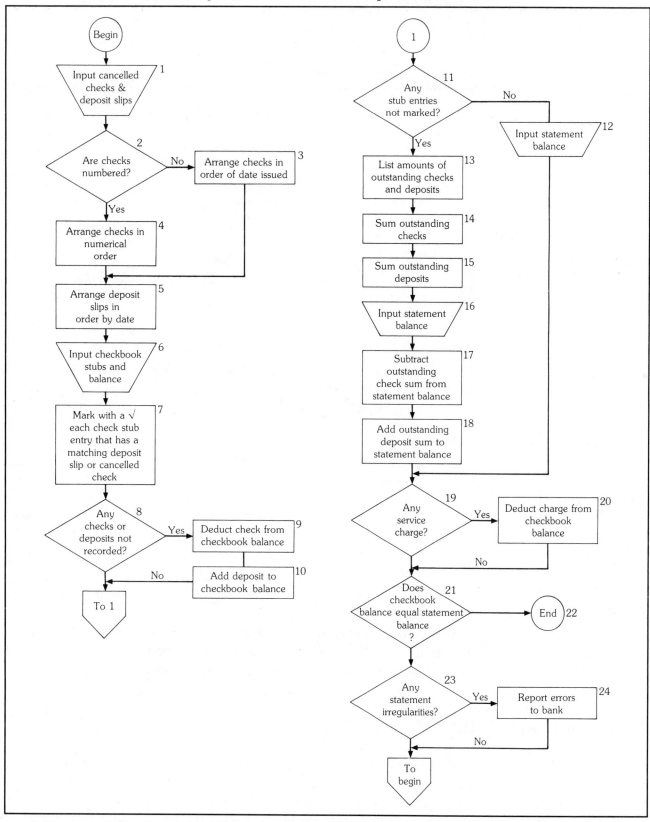

Fig. 6–2   Another Approach to the Checkbook Balancing Task.

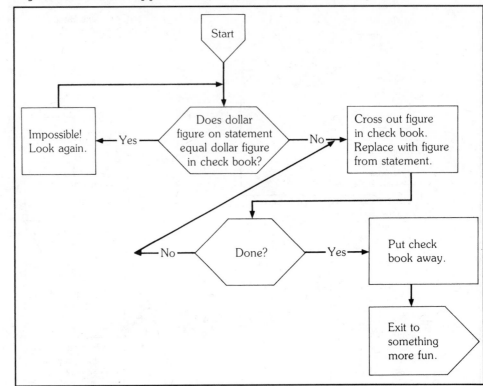

ON TO THE HOW-TO's

The algorithm has many of the characteristics of the old "branching" programmed texts of the early sixties, as well as significant commonality with computer-assisted instruction. Just for the devil of it *and* to give you a feel for the algorithm as an instructional device, we've algorithmized the remainder of this chapter on using algorithms for task-analysis purposes (Fig. 6–3).

MORE ABOUT ALGORITHMS

When programming a computer, the task is to break most decisions into questions that have simple yes/no answers followed and/or preceded by equally simple operations. As a training tool (job aid), the algorithm has been honed to perfection by Ivor K. Davies and Ivan S. Horabin, who have used a strategy similar to computer programming.

Fig. 6–3   Algorithm for Remainder of this Chapter.

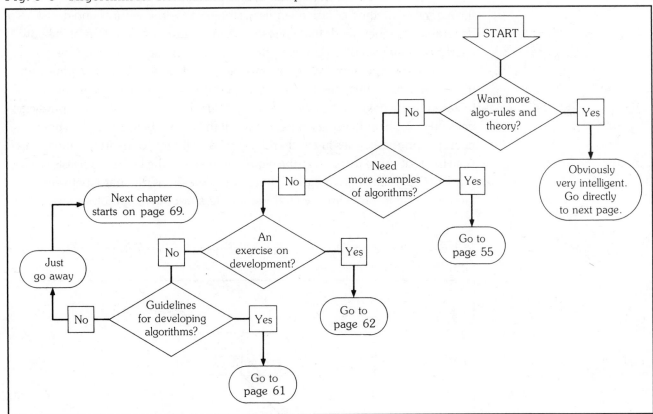

As a task-analysis technique, the exercise of forcing large, complex, and conditional repertoires into relatively simple instructions and yes/no questions can bring order to apparent chaos. Analysts armed with the algorithm mentality have attacked such seemingly complex and multiple procedure-bound jobs as medical diagnosis, computer repair, chess playing, and the filing of one's income tax.

The procedure for developing the algorithm is a fairly straightforward one sometimes referred to as *protocol development.* The analyst begins by having an SME give a running commentary on what he or she is doing and thinking while performing the task. The analyst encourages the SME's verbal explanations by asking questions such as "What did you just do?" and "Why did you decide to do that?" After the analyst has recorded a full job cycle and observed two or more performers, the observations are combined, and an acceptable compromise protocol is developed. One group we know uses the tape recorder extensively. SMEs are encouraged to chat with the analyst as one would with a student: "Here's what I'm doing. At this point, I could do A, B, or C. I'm going to do B. Here's why. . . ."

Two medical educators, Drs. John E. Rhetts and James H. Moller, used the algorithm method of task analysis to structure the procedures and decisions a general practitioner needs to diagnose pediatric heart diseases. Part of the flow chart they developed to represent the procedure is shown in Fig. 6-4.

The first operation is to look at the fingernails of the child. The physician pinches the tip of the finger and looks at the color of the nail when pressure is released. If the color of the flesh under the nail is bluish (cyonotic), the physician goes on to order and inspect chest X-rays. If the telltale blue color does *not* appear, the physician goes in another direction and listens for heart murmur. This specific "test" is the first step in the algorithm because the heart specialists working with Rhetts and Moller agreed that it was a major discriminator between families of heart problems. Therefore, all the subsequent symptom checks

Fig. 6-4   Part of an Algorithm of the Process Used for Diagnosis of Childhood Heart Disease.

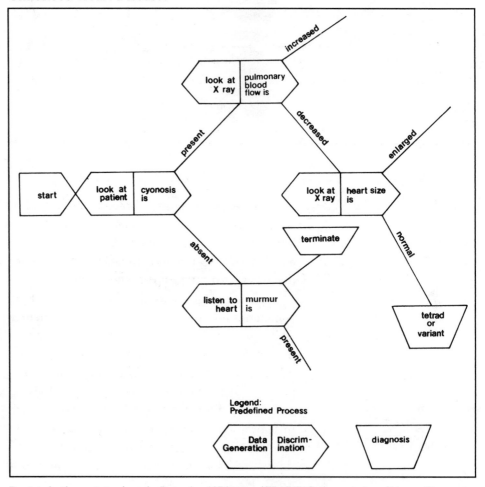

toward the top of the figure will tend to be oriented toward looking for blood-flow restrictions; those toward the bottom of the figure will be aimed at sorting for other symptom families. Notice also that this algorithm does *not* use yes/no decision points.

The goal was to break diagnosis steps and decisions into manageable pieces and a logical flow that a neophyte, in this case a general practitioner, could follow in a learning context. The final algorithm that Rhetts and Moller developed did not, in fact, represent any specific heart specialist's *personal* diagnosis procedure after the first, or cyonotic fingernail test, step. Rather, the algorithm the training analysts finally developed was a compromise struck by the panel of SMEs they had observed while gathering data for the algorithm. Later we'll discuss the consensus strategy used in this case, but for now we'll simply say that the criterion the panel used for agreeing on the final algorithm was "What would the *safest* algorithm for GP's to follow look like?"

In most cases, the algorithm we are trying to develop is merely an efficient way of capturing the decisions, discriminations, operations, processes, procedures, and knowledge pieces the learner must master. Only in a minority of cases do we want the algorithm to reflect a rigid lock step blueprint that trainees must follow forever. Working with volatile chemicals and expensive electronic gear, flying commercial airliners, and running nuclear power plants are among the minority of cases that spring to mind.

The process/decision flow chart, or algorithm approach is, of course, useful in analyzing and organizing the elements of jobs composed of decisional tasks less critical than pediatric cardiology. Take the problem illustrated in Fig. 6-5, the myriad rules, discriminations, and decisions a bank teller must master to perform the "simple" task of cashing a check. By forcing the mass of observationally gathered information through such questions as "What usually happens first?," "How do you decide what to do next?," and "Why did you do that?," an algorithm for check cashing emerges.

One trainer we know made a job aid of the process/decision flowcharts he designed for teaching trainees how to repair the 100 most common faults of calculating machines. Training time was reduced by 45 percent and repeat repairs by 30 percent. Going with the flow can be an effective way to tighten and strengthen many training programs.

Fig. 6-5   Process/Decision Flow Chart of the Check-Cashing Process.

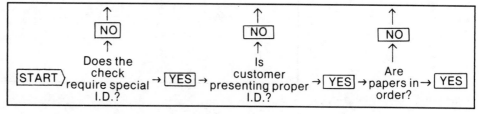

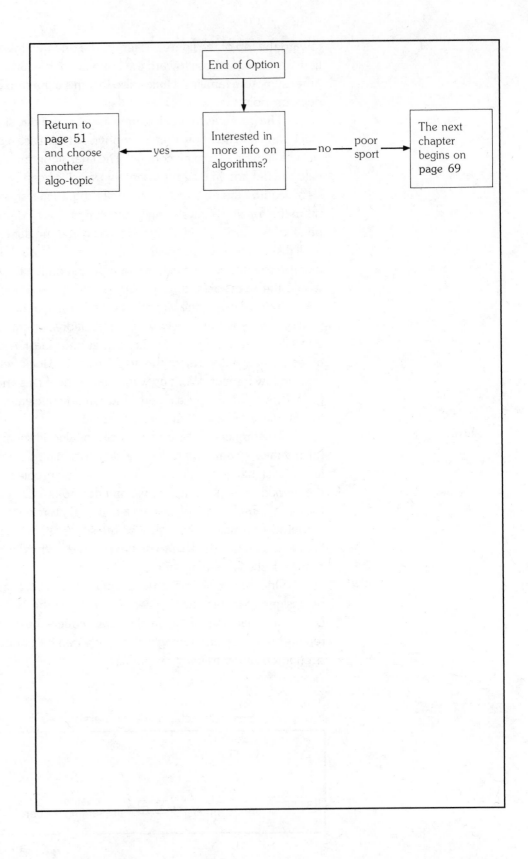

MORE EXAMPLES
OF ALGORITHMS
USED TO ANALYZE
JOBS AND TASKS

▶ There are three more examples of algorithm task analysis in this section.

▶ Remember Ivan Horbin's definition of an algorithm? "A precise set of instructions for solving a well-defined problem." Figure 6-6 shows a set of instructions and the resulting algorithm.

Fig. 6-6   Instructions and Resulting Algorithm.

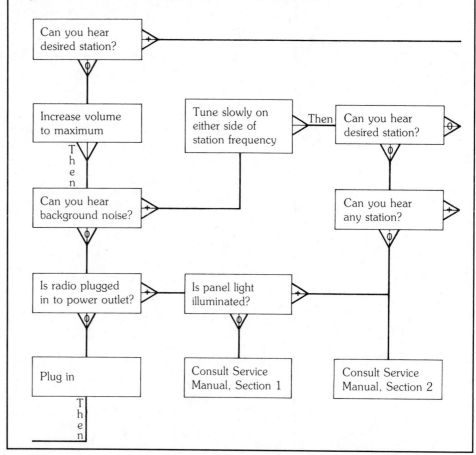

INSTRUCTIONS:

Turn the tuning control to put the pointer on the desired station frequency. If you don't hear the desired station, turn up the volume to maximum. If you don't hear a station or any background noise, first check that the set is plugged in to the power outlet, then check that the panel light is illuminated. If the panel light is not illuminated, refer to Section 1 of the Service Manual. If the panel light is illuminated, refer to Section 2 of the Service Manual.

If you can hear background noise with the volume at maximum, tune slowly on either side of the station frequency. If you still can't get the station you want but you hear other stations, consult Section 3 of the Service Manual. If you can't hear any station at all, consult Section 2 of the Service Manual.

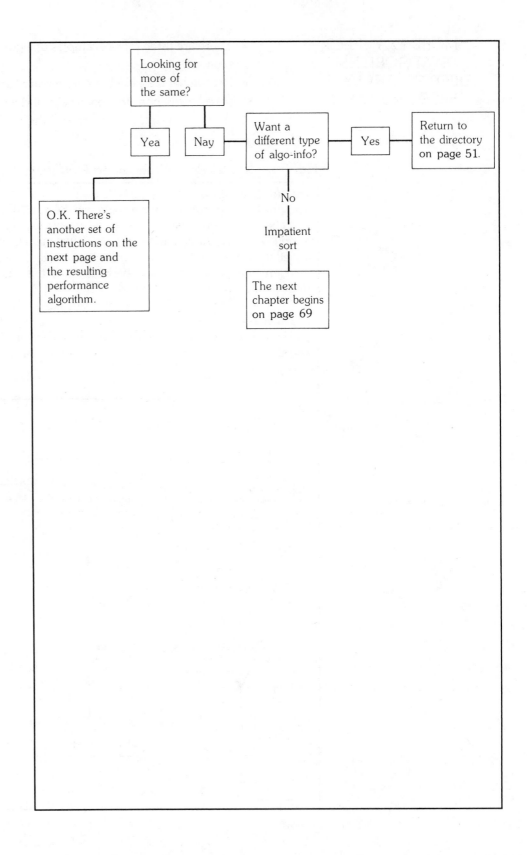

INSTRUCTIONS:

If the asset consists of stocks or shares with values quoted on a stock exchange or of unit trust units whose values are regularly quoted, the amount of tax chargeable or allowable depends upon the relative sizes of the *cost price* of the asset, its *market value* on April 6, 1964, and the *selling price* of the asset.

If the selling price is greater than the market value and if the market value is greater than the cost price, tax is charged on the selling price less the market value (less allowable expenses). If the selling price is greater than the market value and if the market value is *less* than the cost price, two possibilities arise. Either the selling price is greater than the cost price, in which case tax is charged on selling price less the cost price (less expenses). Or the selling price is less than the cost price, in which case no tax is either charged or allowed.

If the selling price is less than the market value and the market value is less than the cost price, tax is allowed on the market value less the selling price (plus allowable expenses). If the selling price is less than the market value and the market value is *greater* than the cost price, two possibilities arise. Either the selling price is less than the cost price, in which case tax is allowed on the cost price less the selling price (plus expenses). Or the selling price is greater than the cost price, in which case no tax is either allowed or charged.

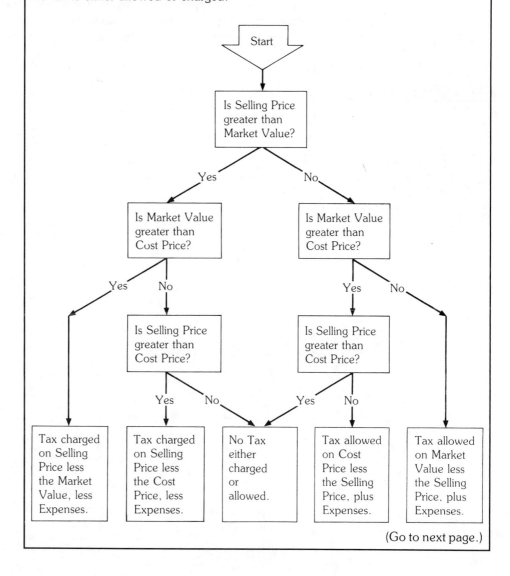

(Go to next page.)

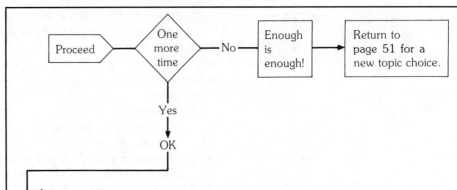

The algorithm on the facing page was developed to teach supervisors in a nonunion shop proper procedure to follow during a unionization attempt. It fulfills the requirements of both NLRB guidelines *and,* we think, good industrial relations judgment. In any case, it demonstrates that algorithms are a pretty flexible analysis tool, since they capture a complex subject matter in a fairly compact manner.

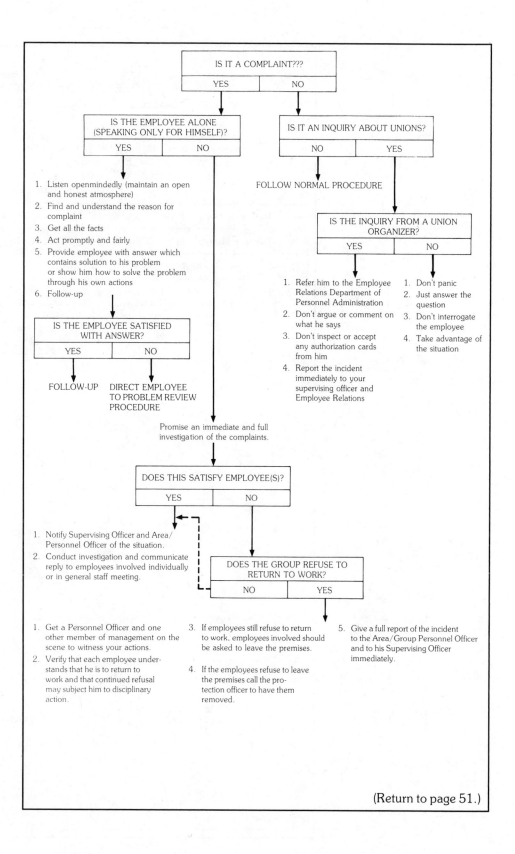

(Return to page 51.)

HEY! THERE ARE NO INSTRUCTIONS
THAT CAN GET YOU TO THIS PAGE.

This is known as the "gottcha" page. Every branching text *must* have one, whether it makes sense or not. Now that you have been "gotched," you have four choices:

Decision Matrix

A.	Return to page 51 for more algo-info.
B.	Go to page 69 and begin the chapter on the behavioral frequency approach.
C.	Turn the page and read the section on Guidelines for Doing Algorithm Task Analysis.
D.	Ignore all this wonderful advice and do whatever you please.

GUIDELINES FOR DOING ALGORITHM TASK ANALYSIS

OVERVIEW. Algorithm task analysis is a way of capturing rule-oriented, sequential data. Technically, an algorithm is a sequence of operations and decisions for solving a problem or performing a task. Theoretically, an algorithm is guaranteed to produce the "correct results" if "done correctly", that is. An algorithm task analysis gives the training designer three things:

1. An agreed-upon set of sequences the trainees must learn to perform. When done well, an algorithm task analyses provides SMEs with decided priorities of subtasks and maximally efficient routines for trainees to follow.

2. A clearly defined set of decisions and discriminations trainees need to learn.

3. A detailed accounting of the steps in all operations trainees must master.

The algorithm approach works best where there are: (a) correct answers; (b) specifiable inputs and outcomes; (c) logical rules that govern decisions and operations; and (d) a number of operations the trainee must learn that are "if . . . then" in nature or only required under certain definable conditions.

WHAT DOES A FINISHED ONE LOOK LIKE? We prefer using a notational system that mimics the computer programmers. Whether you use our notational system or not, the end product should, in a sense, be a model or simulation of the performer's behavior. An SME, or any fairly knowledgeable person for that matter, should be able to "read" your algorithm and tell you that he or she "gets the picture" of what is expected of the performer. The notational system we use involves four symbols, some arrows, and lots of Yes/No (Y/N) directional indicators.

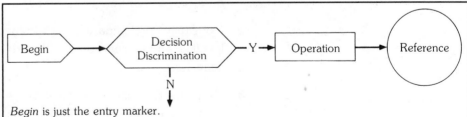

Begin is just the entry marker.
Decision is just that—decisions to be made, something the performer must say yes/no or go/no-go to.
Discriminations are a bit different. Is the indicator light red or green? Is the reading high, medium, or low? Is the check above or below your check-cashing limit? These are typical discriminations that might be made at a discrimination/decision point.
Operations are sequences, procedures, or continuous activities that are cued up by the decision or discrimination.
Reference is what computer programmers refer to as off-line operations. Looking up a piece of input from a table or going to a manual would be a reference operation. It can *also* be used to stand for movement to another algorithm.

HOW DO YOU DO IT? The following steps illustrate our general approach to developing a performance algorithm for task analysis purposes:

1. Observe the performer doing the task(s). Write down and/or tape record what you observe. The first part of the procedure we outlined for the Deterline process fits here.

2. When working on the description of tasks for a job that does *not* have a high number of primary verbal components, have the performer "think out loud" while performing the task.
   ► Ask "who, what, when, where, and why" questions of the performer.
   ► Have him or her speak into a tape recorder while performing, talking out loud and answering your queries.
   ► Encourage this kind of chatter from your SME:
   "Here's what I'm doing . . ."
   "At this point, I could do A, B, or C . . ."
   "But I'm doing B and here's why. . . ."
   If the job is highly verbal, as in sales or people management, record what you see and hear. Write out specific questions about what you see and ask them as soon as possible, while the incident you observed is still fresh in the performer's mind. Generally encourage the performer to debrief him/herself into the recorder.

3. Ask questions that probe and help define sequence (What comes before that?) and that clarify discriminations and decisions (Why? What happens if . . . ?).

4. Define and put in separate "piles" the *operations and procedures*, the *decisions and discriminations* that are made, and the *major sequence,* or "natural" flow, of activity.

5. Construct a preliminary flow chart that (a) has a least-effort or mainline flow and (b) subordinates the "sometimes" and "occasionally" activities.

6. Using one or more of the consensus techniques in Chapter 12 (and a long-handled wooden spoon), obtain verification of your algorithm from an appropriate subject-matter-expert panel.

SOME TIPS AND TRICKS.
   ► The specific format and notation you use should be appropriate for the population of SMEs you are working with. (Don't turn them off to the method.)
   ► Step size and operation complexity are somewhat arbitrary. The keys are really the *population* you are working with and the *criticality* of the decisions and operations. Isolate very critical operations or discriminations.

► It is better to make the steps too big than too small. Just as it is easier to beef up a programmed text than it is to trim it, it is easier to "fatten" an algorithm than trim one. This rule of thumb requires that you pilot test the algorithm. Pilot testing is especially helpful when you are going to use the algorithm later as a job aid or learning guide. It's a little less critical, but still a good idea, when the algorithm will be used exclusively as a design guide.

► Existing job documents, manuals, procedural guides, and the like can be helpful in forming questions to ask your SMEs *and* for finding tasks your master performers may have forgotten to show you.

The following is an algorithm for developing algorithms:

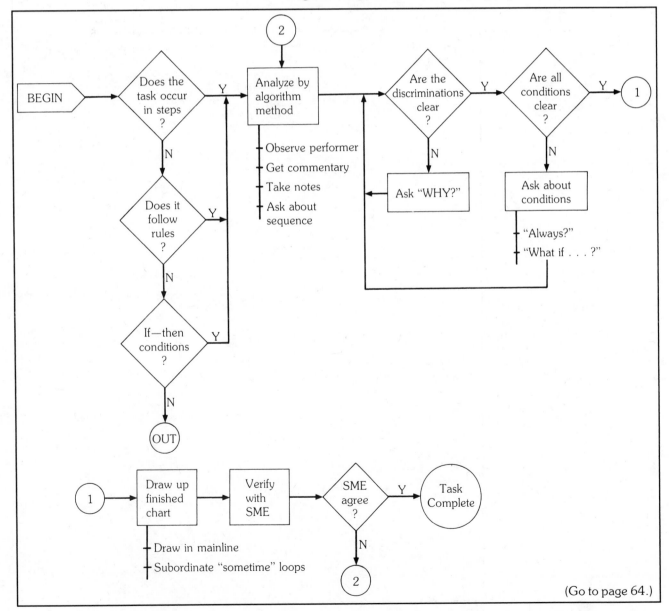

(Go to page 64.)

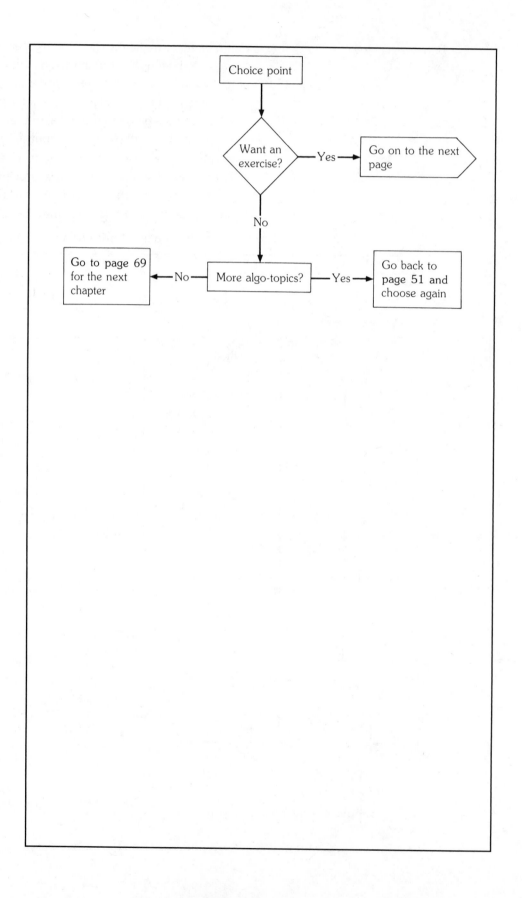

AN EXERCISE IN ALGORITHM TASK ANALYSIS.   Okay, *you* asked for it! Grab a pad of lined paper, a flowchart template, a pencil, and some cut-and-paste tools. Here is the symbol, or notational, system we use:

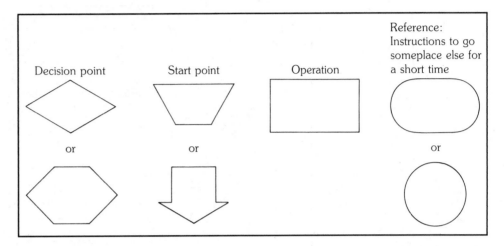

Now you're all set. We promise that the following set of procedures can be effectively put into algorithm format. Give it a go and check *your* algorithm against the one on the next page.

Declaration of Estimated Tax for Individuals

1. Purpose of declaration-vouchers.—The declaration-vouchers are provided for paying currently any income tax (including self-employment tax) due in excess of the tax withheld. Therefore, declarations are required only from individuals whose wages or other income exceed the amounts specified in Instruction 2. In general, the definitions of income, deductions, exemptions, etc., are the same as those on Form 1040.

2. Who must make a declaration.—Under the law every citizen of the United States or resident of the United States, Puerto Rico, Virgin Islands, Guam, and American Samoa shall make a declaration of his estimated tax if his total estimated tax (line 14 of worksheet) is $40 or more and he:

    (a) can reasonably expect gross income to exceed—
        (1) $10,000 for a head of household or a widow or widower entitled to the special tax rates;
        (2) $5,000 for other single individuals;
        (3) $5,000 for a married individual not entitled to file a joint declaration;
        (4) $5,000 for a married individual entitled to file a joint declaration, and the combined income of both husband and wife can reasonably be expected to exceed $10,000; OR
    (b) can reasonably expect to receive more than $200 from sources other than wages subject to withholding.

7. Changes in income, exemptions, etc.—Even though your situation on April 15 is such that you are not required to file, your circumstances may change so that you will be required to file a declaration later. In such case the time for filing is as follows: June 15, if the change occurs after April 1 and before June 2; September 15, if the change occurs after June 1 and before September 2; January 15, 1971, if the change occurs after September 1. The estimated tax may be paid in equal installments on the remaining payment dates.

(Go to next page.)

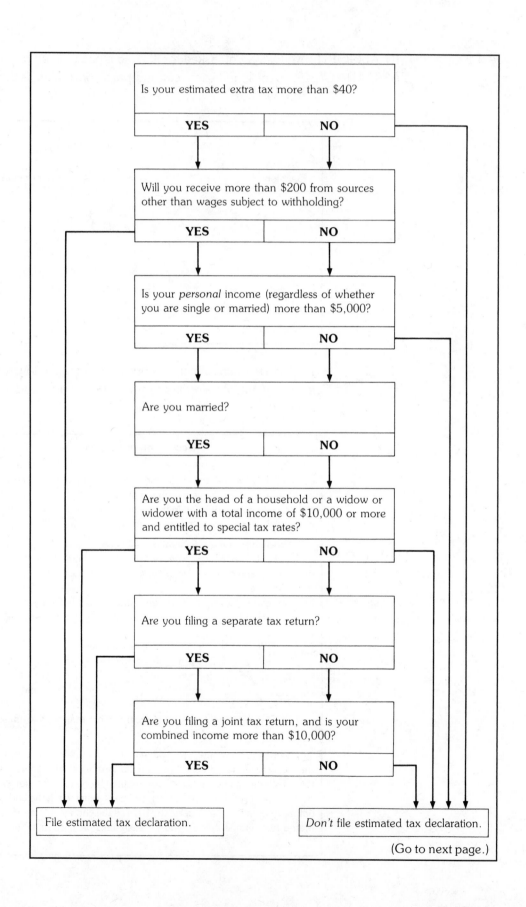

Is your estimated extra tax more than $40?

| **YES** | **NO** |

Will you receive more than $200 from sources other than wages subject to withholding?

| **YES** | **NO** |

Is your *personal* income (regardless of whether you are single or married) more than $5,000?

| **YES** | **NO** |

Are you married?

| **YES** | **NO** |

Are you the head of a household or a widow or widower with a total income of $10,000 or more and entitled to special tax rates?

| **YES** | **NO** |

Are you filing a separate tax return?

| **YES** | **NO** |

Are you filing a joint tax return, and is your combined income more than $10,000?

| **YES** | **NO** |

File estimated tax declaration.   *Don't* file estimated tax declaration.

(Go to next page.)

CHAPTER 7 USING BEHAVIORAL FREQUENCY COUNTS[1]

Bottom line, the two major contributions of the Skinnerian school of behavioral psychology are the concepts of reinforcement and behavioral frequency. Most trainers are familiar with the concept of reinforcement—a behavior followed by favorable consequences for the performer tends to increase in frequency, while a behavior followed by unfavorable consequences (or *no* consequence) for the performer tends to decrease in frequency.

Frequency, the measure of how *often* a behavior of interest occurs in a given unit of time, is often overlooked as a separate and powerful idea because it is so closely tied to the concepts of punishment, extinction, and reinforcement. Behavioral frequency is the measurement touchstone that "tells tales" or gives feedback on the effects of all behavioral interventions. Actually, the concept of behavioral frequency, the idea that the *rate of occurrence of a behavior* is critical, is with us in a number of day-to-day situations. We all use the concept of frequency to describe routine behavior, though we are only marginally aware of it. We refer to one person as "quick" and another as "slow." We describe a third party as "fast-talking" or "high energy." These are all imprecise references to frequency of speech, frequency of particular speaking habits, and frequency of certain body movement.

Frequency is important to trainers and others in the performance-problem business because we all have behaviors within our "behavioral repertoires" that are judged appropriate or inappropriate, acceptable or unacceptable, strictly on the basis of how often they occur in a given situation. For example, none of us speaks in complete sentences or uses perfect grammar 100 percent of the time. But a frequency of 80 to 90 percent grammatically correct speech can give the impression that we speak the King's English all the time. Conversely, a grammatically correct rate of, 50 to 60 percent gives the impression that we speak a

---

[1]This is the first technique we look at that has wide application potential. That is, the count-and-chart, or behavioral frequency technique can help us in task analysis, needs analysis, and organizational-effectiveness studies.

nonstandard, improper English. The difference is simply rate or frequency of correct and incorrect speech habits.

Often the traits we attribute to people are really handy word summaries based on our observations of the occurrence of certain desirable and undesirable behaviors. For example, Dr. C. Aubrey Daniels, of Daniels and Associates, and Larry Miller, of Fran Tarkenton Associates, have determined that supervisors who scold employees four times as often as they praise them are perceived by their employees as cold, hard, stern, and difficult to work for. Supervisors who reverse this ratio and praise four times more often than they scold are perceived as warm, friendly, helpful, and easy to work for. A similar relationship exists between customer-contact people and a customer's perception of their helpfulness and warmth.

This behavioral-frequency approach to studying performance is the offspring of the first nonlaboratory uses of operant psychological principles. In the late 1950s, Dr. Ogden Lindsley, utilizing the basic principles developed by his mentor, B. F. Skinner, developed behavior modification and a teaching/research technology called precision teaching and a self-management system called precise personal management. The key tools of this system, translated to a figuring-things-out context, are:

Pinpointing   Selecting for study a large, repeatable behavior that can be validated.

Counting   Enumerating the occurrence of the pinpointed behavior for a specific period of time.

Charting   Recording the behavior per standard time period of performers who produce different outcomes. Sometimes the time period is behaviors per minute, sometimes behaviors per hour or half hour.

This seemingly simple approach to studying behavior and performance is useful in the study of managerial, sales, line-manufacturing, and customer-contact skills. A study we conducted in Nevada is a good case in point. Our task was to study the effectiveness of blackjack dealers in a number of Nevada casinos. We were to determine which, if any, dealer behaviors were correlated with a high nightly "take" and which with a low one. The theory was that if we could identify dealer behaviors and behavioral frequencies consistently related to high productivity, supervisors—or "pit bosses," as they're called in that environment—could be trained to look for and positively reinforce occurrences of those dealer behaviors.

While we did not find a single set of behaviors that consistently fit that bill, we did manage to learn more about behavioral frequency observations in a unique environment. Our study method entailed observing a dealer for a fifteen-minute period, during which we made a frequency count of the *hands dealt* and the *dealer/player verbal transactions.*

During pilot testing, we found that it was possible not only to count the number of verbal transaction episodes but to rate the quality[2] of the transactions as well. We found that two moderately, experienced behavior observers, working independently, could reach 90 percent agreement on the number of dealer/player verbal transactions *and* the quality of those transactions. The actual procedure was to have two analysts observe each dealer. One analyst timed the observation period and counted the number of hands the dealer dealt. The second analyst counted and rated each player/dealer verbal transaction episode. We observed ten dealers in each of eight casinos (eighty dealers in all) and compared our frequency counts across performance-effectiveness ratings. Actually, we ended up with seventy-two dealers, (forty-three rated as high producers and twenty-nine rated as low producers). These ratings made by their managers were based on the dollars generated by the dealers and management's assessment of high or low production amounts.

Figure 7-1 is a somewhat stylized version of the kind of data we collected and analyzed using this approach and procedure.

Fig. 7-1 Stylized Results of Casino "21" Dealer Study.*

	High Producers	Low Producers
1. Number of dealers	49	23
2. Minutes observed	720	350
3. Hands dealt	528	192
4. Verbal transaction quality		
a. Value added	58 (17%)	15 (11%)
b. Polite	147 (43%)	49 (36%)
c. Indifferent	123 (36%)	59 (42%)
d. Rude	14 (6%)	15 (11%)
Total	342 (100%)	138 (100%)
5. Hands/dealer/hour	43	33
6. Percent of transactions rated as "value added" and "polite"	58%	47%
7. Percent of transactions rated as "indifferent" and "rude"	42%	53%

*High- and low-producer rating came from management. Data from frequency-count observations of approximately fifteen minutes per dealer. Conversion to hours per for standardization of comparisons.

---

[2]The quality rating of transactions we used was very simple. The observer simply rated each transaction as *rude, indifferent, polite,* or *value added.* Since then, we have found that the same rating system can be successfully applied to transactions between customers and cashiers, tellers, clerks, waiters and waitresses, and bank officers.

As you can see, there was a statistically significant difference in customer treatment, but the biggest difference was in number of hands dealt. By the way, size of tips and frequency of tipping had more to do with *winning* than with quality of dealer/player interpersonal transactions. And as we moved from the $2-minimum to the $50-minimum tables, some of the relationships we found between customer treatment and productivity became less important, and the number of hands dealt became more important. In other words, because we chose *not* to start training people on the basis that "better customer relations can't do anything but *help* us" and, instead, spent time looking for the effectiveness relationships, we decided that improving dealing skills, not customer-relations skills,[3] would stimulate more rings of the cash register.

Speaking of cash registers, the frequency-count approach has been used to document the existence and impact of specific selling behaviors. Dr. Thomas Connellan, of The Management Group, Ann Arbor, Michigan, has found an interesting phenomenon associated with the pinpoint "makes a verbal closing statement" (asks for the order). Connellan discovered that salespeople who typically make four or five closing statements can accurately report having asked for the order that number of times. The customer/prospect, however, when asked his/her impression of how often the salesperson asked for the order typically answered, "One or two times." Connellan additionally found that sales reps with higher "ask rates" (seven to nine times per interview) tended to have more sales than reps with low "ask rates" (two or three times per interview).

The behavior-counting approach also helps put the importance or impact of specific behaviors into perspective. For example, the following data were gathered by watching sales clerks ring up purchases in a fashionable teen-oriented clothing store. The purpose of the study was to determine the effectiveness of different strategies for stimulating "add-on" items to a sale. Though this data is stylized—no accounting for supervision is made—it does represent a real situation and a real study.

	Salesperson		
	A	B	C
Number of ring-ups observed	6	7	6
Small talk (bursts)	7	3	3
Clerk asks, "Anything else today?"	4	8	2
Clerk suggests specific add-on item	1	3	5
Average "add-on" $ per ring-up	$1.85	$2.10	$5.36

---

[3]In fact, a companion survey study showed that casino patrons had no problems with dealer interpersonal skills. About 80 percent of those surveyed rated dealer treatment of patrons and dealer attitude toward patrons as either "acceptable," "good," or "very good."

As you can see, the "suggest specific add-on item" strategy was more effective in generating the sale of additional items than was the "Anything else today?" query. Clerk C, who made specific purchase suggestions five times more frequently than clerk A, generated more than twice the dollar amount of "add-on" business. The trainer who had asked the original "what should we be doing?" question changed her retail-selling program to emphasize *specific* rather than *general* suggestive selling strategies.

The pinpoint-count-chart or behavioral-frequency approach has been used successfully to study telephone-contact situations, teller/customer relations, performance-review effectiveness, and group problem-solving.

One well-known sales situation where the results of a frequency study have been used to shape the selling situation involves an ingenious general life insurance agent, O. Alfred Granum of Northwestern Mutual Life, who assigns his new agents a sales-point system. Granum's new agents earn x points for making a phone call, y points for arranging a client lunch and z points for making a formal proposal. By demanding specific performance frequencies of new agents, Granum was able to see the development of a behavioral pattern which he then studied and validated for his agent.[4] Does it work? You can count on it! Granum's Chicago-area insurance agency is one of the most prosperous in the country.

The behavior-counting approach can be an invaluable tool in the trainer's bag of tricks for ferreting out the subtle differences between effective and ineffective performance and for determining whether performance differences really affect the bottom line. As we have seen, the behavioral-frequency approach can be used to study questions as narrow as "What specific behaviors and behavioral frequencies differentiate highly productive from less productive "21" dealers?" and "What behaviors differentiate between high-dollar and low-dollar sales clerks?" The behavioral-frequency method also can be helpul in understanding the performance of a department store, branch office, agency, or any other cohesive work group.

To better understand the efficacy of the behavioral-frequency approach, let's consider the results of a hypothetical study of departmental absences. The scenario is fairly typical. ABC Manufacturing is experiencing an uncomfortable absence rate; factorywide, the rate is over 6 percent. Personnel and senior management wants to institute a new, highly punitive absence-control policy. Tom and Tina Trainer are assigned to communicate the new policy to the troops and to train supervisory personnel to enforce it. But a quick look at the personnel director's data suggests to our hero and heroine that there is quite a dif-

---

[4]Alfred Granum, *The Science and Art of Building a Life Insurance Clientele,* National Life Underwriters, Cincinnati, Ohio. In this book, Granum tells about where the data came from that showed him *exactly* what the high-impact behaviors were and how he turned that data into a feedback and incentive system.

ference in absence rates among departments and that a policy change may not be the most effective solution. Tom and Tina separate departments into two groups: those with absence records higher than 6 percent form one group, and those with absence records below 6 percent form the other. Tom and Tina chart one month of daily absences for each department. Figure 7–2 shows the "pay dirt" they hit using the count-and-chart approach. It is a comparison made between two departments, one with low absenteeism and one with high absenteeism. Both departments are similar in function, structure, and number of employees, so the comparison is a fair one. Two important pattern differences are clear.

One big difference is *trend.* As trend line *A* indicates, Department I has a steady rate; that is, the trend line shows no acceleration. Department II, however, has not only a higher rate of absences but also a rate that is increasing, as trend line *B* clearly indicates.

A second important difference is that absences in Department II are cyclical in nature. The absence spikes at *A, B, C,* and *D* are all Mondays. Department I has a similar but much less severe and less predictable pattern of Monday spikes.

On the basis of this analysis, Tom and Tina decide to look closely at differences in supervisory styles and methods, as well as at differences in physical work environments of the high- and low-absence departments. They recommend that ABC management delay introducing the new policy until these hypotheses can be checked out.

THE BIG CITY   The behavioral-frequency technique can also be used to help study larger, more
BANK STUDY   nebulous questions such as "What differentiates high-profitability branches from low-profitability branches?" Actually, that is exactly the question we undertook to study for a large New York bank. And one of the most important tools in that study was the count-and-chart approach.

In one of those rare instances where a client opens the doors, the records, and the checkbook and says, "Do it," we conducted approximately sixteen

Fig. 7–2   A Comparison of Departmental Absences Using the Count And Chart Method. (Courtesy of TRAINING Magazine.)

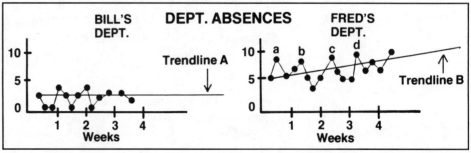

separate studies, used almost *every* technique in this book, and as a result, were able to give management an *extremely* comprehensive report on the "who what when where and whys" that were affecting performance in the organization. During that mega-study, we used the behavioral-frequency method to examine:

► Customer traffic and sales opportunities
► Platform and teller sales behaviors
► Teller/customer interpersonal transaction quality and teller transaction skills
► Teller/supervisor/manager relations

Though the details of these studies must remain confidential, a look at a stylized version of some of the results illustrates the power of this seemingly simple technique.

SQUARE ONE: SEPARATING HIGHS AND LOWS. As you would expect, one of our first steps was to inveigle the individual in charge of the branch system to rank order the branches from best to worst in terms of his perception of their effectiveness. In debriefing this exercise, we found that he had used numerous factors to make his ranking decisions. He used a number of financial indices: profitability, balances, loan portfolio, new accounts opened, and the like. But one important criterion was the division manager's perception of how well the individual branches matched his mental model of how an effective branch should look—physically, on the books, and behaviorally. As we pointed out earlier, this is an appropriate approach within the context of the performance model we use.

Once the branches were separated by high-, medium-, and low-performance levels, we were able to embark on a number of ventures. We did interviews, surveys, and focus groups. We extracted some performance algorithms. But key to the success of this project were the many observational studies we conducted. One of the observational studies was especially helpful in testing some long-held middle management beliefs about branch traffic, the number of transactions employees could perform in a given period of time, the "sell potential" of certain job classes in certain geographic locations, and the need for a proposed sales training program.

BIG BANK STUDY A: "THE BUSINESS IS WEST OF HERE" Managers of Big Bank's lower-performing branches tended to explain away low numbers of new account openings and poor cross-sell numbers by saying, "This neighborhood is saturated. The new business is all west of here." We decided to test the twin resultant hypotheses of this belief that:

a. Low-sales-volume branches are low in sales because the customer base (traffic) is low, and

b. Most of the traffic that does exist involves bus change and check cashing, not qualified sales-prospect traffic.

To start, we observed, timed, and counted customers coming to the sales platform and asking for assistance. In addition, we counted the number of "buying signals" we heard these customers and prospective customers make. Our approach was to first observe and code by type of transaction all platform personnel/customer transactions that began with a customer walking up to a branch service counter. Observations were conducted in thirty-minute units, during which all transactions were recorded by type—using a simple, predesigned record form. The same procedure was followed in high-, medium-, and low-performing branches.

The following two tables, and our interpretation of the data, indicate how useful the simple observe-and-record procedure was in testing the belief that low-sales branches were low because sales potential in those branches was low.

The results shown in Table 7-1 represent many hours of observation, but for comparison purposes they are reported in terms of average number of transactions per half hour. How was this conglomeration of percents, hours, and transactions per half hour used to answer the two original hypotheses? Watch.

Question 1:   Do high, medium, and low branches differ in the actual amount of sales-counter traffic?

Answer: A little bit, but not as predicted. In fact, the high-performing branches encounter less sales-counter traffic than either low- or medium-performing branches.

Reasoning: a. Low-performing branches were observed for 10.5 hours. During that time the low-performing branches had 58 sales-counter contacts or 2.76 customer contacts per half-hour.

b. Medium-performing branches were observed for 11.5 hours. During that time the medium branches had 20 sales contacts or 3.04 customer contacts per half-hour.

c. High-performing branches were observed for 8.5 hours. During that time, there were 44 sales contacts or 2.58 contacts per half-hour.

Table 7-1   Summary of Branch Observations of Type and Volume of Transactions in High-, Medium-, and Low-Performing Branches.

| Branch rating | Customers observed | Hours observed | Customer transactions per ½ hour | Type of transaction (percent) | | | |
				New account information	Check approval	Account servicing	Other
High	44	8.5	2.58	20.4	17.2	36.2	26.2
Medium	70	11.5	3.04	22.8	14.0	41.0	22.2
Low	58	10.5	2.76	22.4	16.3	35.0	26.3

Question 2: Do high-, medium-, and low-performance branches differ in the proportion of *sales opportunities* branch personnel meet at the sales/service counter?

Answer: No. Some would argue that *every* warm body is a sales opportunity. But even at Big Bank, where sales opportunities are considered *asking for new account information,* there is little difference among branches. In fact, both low- and medium-performing branches encounter a greater proportion of people asking about bank services than do high-performing branches.

In addition, there was little difference between high-, medium-, and low-performing branches in the "Other" transactions category, where we recorded the bus change and other nonbanking information requests. The same *no difference* finding holds for *check approvals,* the other category of nonsales opportunity that was supposed to separate high- and low-performing branches.

If you noted that we may have dispelled a local myth but failed to enlighten the client as to the cause or causes of different sales records, you would get the gold star for performance analysis logic. But the second half of this study addresses the problem of what *is* causing the difference in sales records.

At the same time we were recording sales/service counter traffic and types of transactions, we also were recording *attempts to sell something.* The next table, Table 7–2 shows how a little simple arithmetic, combined with simple observation, gave us and our client some very valuable information.

Question 1: Are there more *sales opportunities* in some branches than in others?

Answer: Again the answer is no. High-, medium-, and low-performance branches have a similar proportion of sales opportunities presented to sales/service counter personnel. In fact, the proportion of sales opportunities in high-performing branches is smaller than the proportion in medium- and low-performance branches (20.4 percent versus 22.8 percent and 22.4 percent).

Table 7–2

Branch rating	Number of transactions	Sales opportunities No.	Ratio	Attempts to sell No.	Ratio	Conversion of attempts No.	Ratio	Conversion of opportunities
High	44	9	20.4%	7	78%	3	43%	33%
Medium	70	16	22.8%	9	56%	4	44%	25%
Low	58	13	22.4%	6	46%	3	50%	23%

Question 2:   Are there significant behavioral differences among sales/service counter personnel in high-, medium-, and low-performance branches?

Answer: Yes. Look at the column headed *Attempts to sell.* The percentage figures in that column are a ratio of the number of *attempts to sell* divided by the number of *Sales opportunities.*

In high-performing branches, sales personnel made a sales pitch 78 percent of the time a clear sales opportunity arose. In medium- and low-performing branches, these "effort ratios" were 56 percent and 46 percent respectively.

But even if we ignore our assessment of what *is* and *is not* a sales opportunity and simply look at the relationship between *observed transactions* and *attempts to sell,* counter personnel in the high-performing branches are still ahead. Specifically, people in high-performing branches attempted to sell something 16 percent of the time, while low performers tried only 10 percent of the time.

Question 3:   Is there a sales skill problem—that is, a difference in sales skills—between high-, medium-, and low-performing branch personnel?

Answer: Some but not a lot. How did we come to *that* strange answer? Easy. Look at the column in Table 1-2 headed *Conversion of attempts.* This is the ratio of the number of *attempts to sell* divided by the number of actual sales (*conversion of attempts*). Look how close these numbers are: High, 43 percent; medium, 44 percent; low, 50 percent.

If anything, the personnel in low-performing branches are more successful than those in high-performing branches on an attempt-by-attempt basis. But, at the same time, personnel in low-performing branches *attempt to sell* 32 percent less often (78 percent − 46 percent). So when push came to shove, we couldn't recommend that Big City Bank invest more money in sales training than they had just finished doing six months earlier. Instead, we suggested they look at sales management and the perception of sales opportunities among branch personnel.

Later on, as an outcome of focus group discussions with branch sales personnel, we found that salespeople in high-sales branches believed, "If customers can sign their names, they should have a checking account." On the other hand, sales personnel in low-performing branches held the more conservative view: "A check is a lethal legal instrument, and the bank must be protected from people who might misuse such an instrument."

When probed further, performers in high-sales branches told us they had a simple formula for identifying sales prospects: "If they don't have some sort of account with us, they should have. If they come in here they have money. If they have money, we want it."

At the same time, performers in low-sales branches were more likely to explain: "You can tell by their looks. The scruffy-looking ones and the young ones aren't worth bothering with. They cause more trouble than their business is worth."

The moral of this case study is that simple observational studies, done carefully and thoroughly, can provide critical data about performance and prevent us from making costly mistakes in the prescription-of-remedy department.

SOME GUIDELINES

Behavioral observation studies are deceptively simple-looking. So much so, in fact, that they can be easily confused. There are two places you can stumble and fall—*pinpoint picking* and *observing the behavior.*

Picking the pinpoint is our shorthand for "selecting and defining the behavior or behaviors to be counted and compared." The most common pinpointing errors are *definitional rigidity* and *premature pinpointing,* and they are related. Pinpoint selection should be a fairly flexible process. We have found that regardless of how much time we spend talking to clients and subject matter experts, the choice of behaviors to observe really only solidifies through field work. We just can't sit in the office and adequately define the behaviors to be observed. Our working rule is that it takes about half a day of observing the performers in their natural setting to compile the list of behaviors to be observed and another half a day to describe them clearly enough for others to observe the same behavior. Even at that, we frequently have had to refine, redefine, and add behaviors to the observational checklist later in the study.

Remember the little scale we developed for coding blackjack dealer/customer transactions? Recently we were involved in a study of customer relations in a swank resort, and we found that our old, reliable *Value Added Polite Indifferent Rude* classification scheme could be applied to rating the quality of customer-contact behaviors. But even though we had previously used this scale in a variety of settings—including hotel and food establishments—it took a day to adapt the rating system to the specific environment in question. In fact, the form used for recording the observations went through three refinements in the three days spent observing eleven front desk employees. Why? Because we kept finding new behaviors to include in our observation—behaviors that had eluded us, behaviors we did not see until the second and third shifts, and subtle behaviors that we had at first lumped with "coarser" and more easily observable behaviors. Part of the final observation sheet is reproduced in Fig. 7-3.

Fig. 7-3 Part of Observation Sheet Used to Record Behavior of Front Desk Personnel at a Swank Resort.

	Greets guest	Asks task Q's	Makes small talk	Gives info/ inst.	Explains/ clarifies policy	'Reflects' guest statements	Wishes pleasant stay/ journey	Time	Value added	Polite	Indif- ferent	Rude
Clerk 1												
Clerk 2												
Clerk 3												

Observed Front Desk Verbals — *Length of Time Obsvd.* — *Overall Transaction Quality*

We have to allow the pinpoints, the behaviors to be observed, to recommend themselves by allowing ourselves to take the "risk" of not defining before we have had a chance to sit still, shut up, and just watch the people work. Following this period of active nondoing, it is easy to specify where a behavior begins and ends, to describe the critical topography of a behavior, and to record both the frequency of occurrence of the behavior and the events and situations that occasion or prompt the behavior to occur.

Observing the behavior can be problematic due to the psychological equivalent of the Hisenberg principle. The Hisenberg principle cautions that the act of measuring a substance changes the substance, especially in the case of thermometers and liquids. The act of observing behavior can change the behavior, especially when observers make a big deal of their presence. It has been our experience that a very low key, nonassertive demeanor is important to a successful observation study. An advantage we enjoy as consultants, of course, is that we lose no status appearing stupid. We can use our nonplayer, outsider position to put people at ease and provide a framework of anonymity for the performers we observe. Whether we are making sales calls with reps, standing behind a teller line watching customer-teller transactions, or making repair calls with service people, we can readily admit to a lack of knowledge about the jobs we are observing and position ourselves as "just trying to learn what the job is like from the inside" with the people we are observing. We have been able to limit the threat we pose as observers by adhering to these four guidelines:

1. Undercommunicate with the field.

Sure, the visit has to be announced so we get some cooperation, but the lower the profile the better. The best response we can get to our arrival in the Denver branch of LMN Sales is "Oh, yeah. I remember getting that memo a couple of weeks ago. Is that today? What was it you wanted to do again?" Better to lose some time while the manager fishes about the office looking for someone for us to ride with than to have him or her greet us with a timetable and an interview schedule. We want to see people doing their jobs in a routine, everyday fashion, not be an audience of one at a song-and-dance act written and directed for our benefit. We usually need people to be at their *average* to understand the factors that may be influencing performance.

2. Be boring, thick, and uninteresting.

The task is to observe the performer in action, not create a lasting impression on someone. Swapping lies and stories with a salesperson is a lot of fun, but that's not the task. The task is to shut up, look, and listen. Likewise, it would be a lot more exciting to put on a bellhop uniform and playact bellhop for a day to "learn about bell hopping." But, there is much more to be learned sitting in the hotel lobby with the look of a bored conventioneer, observing the whole front desk and bell stand crew interacting with one another and guests. Our rule of thumb for most studies is that when you find yourself as ignored as the worse cocktail party bore you know, you have effectively set the stage for doing observations.

In situations that require interaction with the subjects such as salespeople there is a tendency to abandon the data-gathering mode and be a real person between calls on customers. Our preference is to use that time to ask simple questions about the job and the person's approach to it and to let the person talk about what interests him or her.

By remaining quiet and really listening, we have been able to catch some fairly subtle differences in both behavior and attitude between high and low performers. For example, in one study of sales reps, we noticed that the high performers' in-car time was spent talking about customer calling—debriefing themselves aloud about the last call; describing objectives, opportunities, and strategies for the next call; and trying to solicit feedback and ideas from the ride-along observer. In sharp contrast, the low performers spent their in-car, between-call time talking sports, hobbies, the opposite sex, and the weather. While this may not seem an important difference at first glance, a number of studies by psychologists of the cognitive behavior therapy persuasion have found that the "self-talk" associated with a verbal performance such as selling is the best predictor of the outcome of the performance.

3. Bumble and mumble.

We sometimes refer to this as the Columbo principle after Peter Falk's bumbling, dumb like a fox, television detective of the 1970s. As you may recall, Falk's character dressed like a mildewed laundry bag, could never seem to find a match or pencil, and continually annoyed suspects with his seeming inability to grasp the answers to simple questions. We find that if we dress modestly, have a script of fairly simple and, perhaps, naive questions available, and don't play "can you top this" with our subjects, we learn a lot. The goal is to be a *stimulus* for job performance and job related talk, not a *shaper* of that performance and conversation.

The bumble and mumble routine also puts the people we are observing at ease. It adds credibility to our remonstrations that we are "here to learn how to do the job" and not spies, efficiency experts, or hatchet men for some ubiquitous "they" or "them."

4. Keep data collection unobtrusive.

Though we always design observational schedules, scales and forms for recording our observations ahead of time, we often begin our observations with a blank piece of paper. Whipping out The Form has a way of intimidating those we are observing.

If we are working side by side with the subject, we take notes and, in effect, rebuild the record form on the spot. There have been times when we have had a perfectly good form in the briefcase and have simply rebuilt it on a lined yellow pad, mixed in among conversation notes. If you feel that you absolutely must use a form of some sort to keep data straight, sketch it by hand instead of typing it. If your ego requires boxes and squares on white paper, transfer the data to the polished form back at the hotel. When timing a performance such as a sales call, teller transaction, or hotel front desk checkout routine, keep the timing procedure as simple and unobtrusive as possible. The "stopwatch and white coat" number intimidates most people.

It's okay to sacrifice precision in favor of performer comfort. For example, timing a sales call to the nearest minute is sufficiently accurate and can be done with a quick glance at a wristwatch when the call begins and then again as it ends. Consistency in the method you use is more important than split-second accuracy. What your need is comparable time *bases,* not factual reporting of just how long a typical sales call lasts.

The overall message of these four principles is that observing behavior is a simple but powerful analysis technique *if* the observer is willing to make like a fly on the wall. The key is to do *everything* you ethically can to obtain unsullied representative slices of real-life behavior and then to work like hell understanding their impact on critical desired outcomes.

SECTION III TALKING TO PEOPLE ABOUT WORK

This section deals with the myriad rich data we can garner simply by talking to people about the work they do. Granted, the techniques discussed in the last section do contain talking-to-people elements, but the primary information source in the watching-people-work techniques was the evidence of the analyst's eyes. Talking to people about work becomes a primary data-gathering approach when there are important elements of the work that can not be directly observed. Sure, the pediatric cardiologists we discussed in Section II did most of their work in their heads, but there also were significant, albeit subtle, operations performed on the environment. That is, they did things—significant things—that a trained watcher could observe and capture with little or no interpretation and guesswork.

Attitudes, opinions, explanations, historical happenings, thoughts, desires, and frustrations can be most easily and accurately assessed by talking to people. You can *observe* the outcome of an attitude—sort of—and the by-product of a belief—more or less. But, to really know how people feel about their work, the organization, the obstacles and opportunities it presents, and the areas where they think they need more training, you have to Ask Them.

Oddly enough, the best tools for talking to people about work come not from psychology or any of the other social sciences but, rather, from the field of market research. Market researchers and advertising people have developed numerous techniques for finding what people do in the marketplace. HRD people can use many of these techniques to obtain rich data for such tasks as specifying training outcomes, pinpointing organizational problems, and developing training content.

For example, a sales training manager in a major West Coast bank utilized the services of a market-research firm to perform part of a sales training task analysis for calling officers. The researchers studied the buying habits and styles of the clients with whom the bank's calling officers worked. In addition, the firm studied preferred sales behavior and preferred call frequency. Needless to say, this information facilitated the sales training director's search for a new program and the development of a new call strategy.

Need more encouragement? Not too many years ago, a major auto-mobile manufacturer hired a consumer-research specialist to pinpoint the differences between service operations with high and low customer-complaint histories. The outcome of the study had predictable implications for service manager selection and training, as well as some surprising ones for dealer and sales rep training.

Note, please, that we would never advise talking-to-people techniques or any other market research approach as the only method for uncovering needs. But, at the same time, we would never suggest that any one of the observational techniques is "all ye need to know." The market-research people have devised some ingenious ways to figure out what is going on in people's heads. We need that kind of input for training, just as we need observational data or survey data or psychological data.

In this section, we will be looking at three "talking to people about work" techniques that market researchers use regularly: *focus group discussions, personal or face to face interviews,* and *telephone interviews.* Market researchers also use the mail survey or anonymous questionnaire to augment these three techniques; we will save the survey for the next section, where we discuss more-structured, brain-picking techniques.

CHAPTER **8** TALKING TO PEOPLE IN GROUPS: THE FOCUS GROUP DISCUSSION

Market researchers use the focus group to find out what consumers like and dislike about a specific product or service and why they buy certain products instead of others. We see focus groups as useful for comparing the attitudes, approaches, and even skills of high- and low-performing managers; capturing the cognitive processes, experiences, and job approaches of successful salespeople; and ferreting out organizational performance obstacles. We have even used the focus group technique to find out how consumers of an organization's product or service view the skills, salesmanship, friendliness, knowledgeability, and so forth of an organization's customer-contact employees. Balanced against customer-contact employees' views of the customers, this strategy has provided some stunning organizational insights.

To be completely technically accurate, the objective of a focus group is to acquire a set of responses from a group of people familiar with the topic, service, experience, or product being discussed. It is a qualitative rather than a quantitative study. It gives you a feel for important issues but doesn't give you any numbers for judging how widespread a concern or idea might be or how strongly an opinion is held. The value lies in the richness of the data the focus group discussion generates and the leads it provides in looking for patterns of experience. For example, a set of focus group discussions among sales reps of a major airline revealed that the reps felt they were well-paid "gophers" whose main value to the organization lay in "going to the airport to pick up and chauffer VIPs and company VPs and to look for key clients' lost luggage." This sales rep sentiment led management to examine the way it was using and abusing sales reps; and that reassessment eventually prompted the airline to develop a competency description of the sales rep job that put "gopher" work off limits.

Another frequent goal of the focus group is to develop hypotheses to be tested via subsequent surveys or observational techniques. Specific turns of phrase or word pictures that focus group participants generate can often aid in the development of questionnaire items. And, of course, the greenest training rookie can see that a spin-off of the focus group is a wealth of case-study and critical-incident material for use as training content, should training be a feasible "solution" to the problem under investigation.

A FOCUS GROUP IS A GROUP FOCUSED

An actual focus group usually consists of eight to twelve people working with a moderator to express opinions and attitudes and to discuss a specific topic that all group participants are familiar with. They may qualify because they sell chocolate ice cream or drink Old Swamp Water; they are, in other words, peers who share some important criteria.

A typical focus group session runs from one to two hours. A group that meets longer has usually stopped being a focus group—a discussion of a specific topic—and has turned into either group therapy or a seance. A focus group discussion differs from the organizational development consultant's "deep sensing group" by virtue of the focus and the depth of treatment of material. A sensing group is a much more broadly aimed device that concentrates on employee attitudes toward the organization. A focus group *may* focus on job satisfaction and attitude issues, but it is just as likely to uncover differences in cold call strategy between high- and low-sales performers or find why some supervisors use less overtime or have teams that make parts with fewer defects.

PHASES OF THE FOCUS GROUP STUDY

Al Anderson, president of Anderson Research in Minneapolis, says that a focus group study has eight specific stages:

1. Initial client meeting

2. Development of the interview guide

3. Second client meeting

4. Conduct of the groups

5. Transcription of the proceedings

6. Internalization

7. Organization and writing

8. Presentation of the findings

If you don't care for all those stages, just think of these three phases:

I Planning the study

II Running the groups

III Compiling the analyzing results

PHASE I—PLANNING THE STUDY

Focus groups are highly susceptible to the "garbage in garbage out" phenomenon. A concise definition of the problem under investigation and the kinds of input needed for understanding the nature of the problem is critical. The culmination of the planning process should be:

1. A statement of the problem

2. Identification of a specific population of people who should have valuable input and insight into the problem

3. An interview outline for conducting the actual focus group discussions

STEP 1. INITIAL CLIENT MEETING.

The purpose of this meeting is to scope out the problem and the parameters. This is where you learn which people are involved with the problem, what management thinks the problem causes might be, and what the value of solving the problem is.

This is also the time to discuss high and low performers. Yes, using the high and low tactic applies to focus groups as well as to every other technique. Part of the clients' homework at this meeting is finding the highs and lows for you to talk with. They own the criteria, so they have to identify the bodies.

We once studied bank calling officers by sorting high and low performers into different piles and holding separate focus groups with a sample of people from each pile. We found that the two groups had very different approaches to selling bank services. Those with sluggish sales records turned out to be overly selective in the calls they made, while the high performers were banging on many more doors per day *and* were less selective about the doors they banged on.

STEP 2. DEVELOPMENT OF THE INTERVIEW GUIDE.

This is an outline of what you want to know and some things you want to remember to say. Among the important things to make clear to the group are the purpose of the meeting and the kinds of information you are seeking. Actually the outline, besides stating the focus you want to specify and providing a nicely worded promise of anonymity, is mostly a back-up tool. The act of thinking your way through the development of the outline is enough to focus *you* on the issues.

The outline also reassures management that you aren't going on a fishing party or aren't going to pry into forbidden closets. Furthermore, the discussion outline provides a stick-to-it framework for the moderator. Of course, he or she has to know—sense, really—when the group is more concerned about topics not on the outline. In that case, he or she must just "go with the flow." Sometimes the best moderator is the one who knows when it's time to shut up and listen.

STEP 3. SECOND CLIENT MEETING. At this client meeting, you go over the outline to verify what will be covered. This is the clients' last shot at input, so listen to them. It is especially important to find out if there are any organizational taboos. For example, in one electronics manufacturing organization, we were told to avoid the topic of compensation in our groups. Naturally, compensation came up without our asking, which doubly reinforced our report that employees were still "hot" about an earlier pay faux pas.

This is also where you cross-check that you are getting the groups you wanted. It is best to remind the client liaison person that you need groups of *peers only*—no bosses and subordinates—and that high and low performers aren't mixed in the same group. We have, unfortunately, seen both these common sense rules broken. One client thought it would be good if bosses and employees could hold an honest dialogue. But, we said we weren't interested in refereeing a cat fight. Another client thought that *we* would be able to sort out high and low performers later, since we were taping the session. The lows might learn something from the highs at the same time. Nice try, but no cigar.

This is also when you solidify the "whens," "wheres" and "how manys." We have worked with Al Anderson on about a dozen sales needs-analysis studies, using focus groups as one of the techniques. Al has convinced us that it takes a maximum of *five* focus groups to cover the turf—if, as he says, we do a "diamond." Anderson's focus group diamond is illustrated in Fig. 8-1.

Anderson feels that the five groups in Fig. 8-1 will yield all the important information a focus group can find about sales performance problems. Group 1, the immediate supervisors of the sales reps, usually have some good instincts about the differences between high and low performers, as well as some ideas about what they themselves and their brother and sister managers might be doing to impede the performance of their charges. The least you get from this group is a description of current management practices, which forms a useful counterpoint to the sales rep groups' perceptions and interpretations of how they are actually being managed. A description of what one group is trying to do to help another succeed and a complementary description of how successful or unsuccessful those efforts are can be pretty valuable.

Fig. 8–1   Anderson's Sales Needs-Analysis Focus Group Diamond.

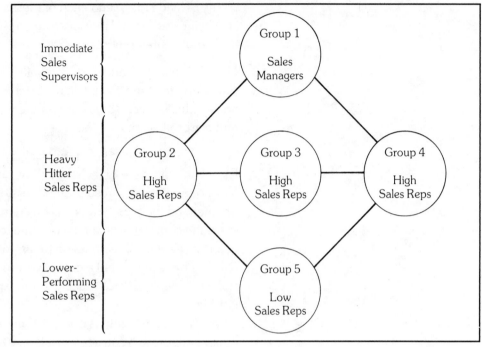

Group 5, the single low-performers group, generally generates all the low-performer opinion we need to form a significant counterpoint to the ideas, impressions, and thoughts of the high performers. Yet we seem to need three high performer groups (groups 2, 3, and 4 in the diamond) to tap completely the good ideas and tips and tricks of the high performers. High performers also seem to generate more ideas about the management support they feel they need to perform even better. Management learns more about what they are doing *right* from the high performers, so this input is doubly valuable.

PHASE II—RUNNING THE GROUPS   If well-planned, the actual group discussions can be fun.

STEP 4. CONDUCT OF THE GROUP.   The following ten suggestions should go a long way toward keeping you out of trouble.

1. Conduct the discussions on neutral turf. A conference room at a convenient company facility or even an off-site hotel/motel would be appropriate.

2. Give the chosen attendees (no fewer than five, no more than twelve) plenty of lead time. Send each of those selected for the group a letter specifying the general purpose of the meeting and its time, location, and length (preferably 2 to 2½ hours).

3. Have lots of coffee and goodies available in the meeting room. These and the time spent talking, listening, and doing general relationship building can break the ice before you turn on the recorder and start the session.

4. When you're ready to begin, have everyone sit around the table. Explain the purpose of the study, how and why the participants were chosen, and how the results of the session content will be used. Do *not* mention the high/low selection criteria. During this introduction, stress the confidentiality of the information. When all questions have been answered, ask permission to turn on your taping equipment. (No, we have never had a group ask us not to tape a session. Occasionally, there is a bit of "talking to the tape" behavior, but it doesn't last long.)

Anderson cautions not to scrimp on the quality of recording equipment used. "You'll regret it later if you do," he insists. Use a high-quality recorder, with two good microphones—one for each end of the table—and use new, high-quality tape. Put a heavy tablecloth or felt pad on the table; recorders pick up lots of table noise.

5. Begin the session by asking the group members to identify themselves and to tell where they work and how long they have been with the organization. This approach (a) loosens up the group, (b) gives you feedback on how well the participants meet the selection profile, (c) gives the participants a chance to get used to the recording equipment, and (d) gives your typist/transcriptionist a chance to become familiar with participants' voices.

6. Move from general to specific questions. "How do you approach the job of selling widgets to the Wobegone?" is a nebulous but useful starter. Later, you can ask more detailed questions, such as, "Exactly what *do* you say when you are trying to set up an appointment with someone you've never met?" In fact, the group members will usually volunteer the specifics once they have warmed up on the general questions.

7. Keep your comments nonjudgmental and your probe questions focused on information clarification. Always ask for clarification of technical terms, local jargon, and complex ideas.

8. When a group member makes a strong statement or has an interesting but novel idea, find out how others feel about it. In so doing, be sure to "protect" the original speaker.

9. Give everyone in the group an opportunity to contribute to every topic or question in your outline. This entails encouraging some people to talk and tactfully diverting attention away from those who like to talk a lot about a little.

10. When you're sure the participants have covered everything on your outline and have gotten all the "hot topics" off their chests, conclude by saying, "We seem to have covered quite a bit of territory. Is there anything I should have asked or we should have discussed but didn't?" Usually someone has been holding back or waiting for the right question before telling you something important.

One quick coda: If you are running groups from Bangor to Phoenix and back again, as is usually the case, take care to take care of yourself. Burn-out, which is a real danger for the facilitator, can destroy the energy of the group and diminish your results.

PHASE III—COMPILING AND ANALYZING RESULTS Once all the groups have been conducted, you'll tackle the difficult part of the study. At this point, you could opt for the easy way out and simply listen through the groups' tapes again, make some notes, and write up some general findings. But we recommend a more rigorous approach. Experience has proved to us and others we've talked with that enduring the tedium of the following process pays off in more precise, usable findings and a more persuasive, finely tuned report.

STEP 5. TRANSCRIPTION OF THE PROCEEDINGS. To work effectively with the data from even one group, you need a transcription of the tape. This requires an expert typist and a lot of time: one hour of focus group discussion can easily require five hours of transcribing.

As the transcripts become available, the moderator should simultaneously listen to the tapes and edit the transcription for meaning. Often the typist will mis-hear local jargon as legitimate Webster's English. Some typists get quite good at typing what they thought they heard as opposed to what was actually said. Some even editorialize from their subconscious or out of general boredom.

STEP 6. INTERNALIZING THE DATA. When you are running the groups, running for the plane, and getting just plain run down in the process, you don't really have the time and energy to understand what the people in the groups are actually telling you. Although nervous management, usually the people who authorized your work, will want instant analysis, never decide the results in the hallway. You will hear things on the tape and read things in the transcript that you won't remember hearing or saying during the group. When you are busy keeping the group moving and on focus, you can't be effectively processing and analyzing content.

This is when you should put your feet up and let yourself be puzzled. Of course, this is also a good way to get fired—putting your feet up and pondering. So we've devised a bit of semi busy-work that keeps the client and the boss happy and helps you process the information on the transcripts.

a. Read through the transcripts and make notes about possible key ideas.

b. When you think you have an exhaustive list of the key ideas contained in the transcripts, grab your scissors. Go through a photocopy of each transcript, cut out sections of dialogue and monologue that refer to entries on your initial key ideas list, and put them in labeled envelopes—one for each key idea.

c. Once you've cut the wheat from the chaff, so to speak, it's time to fine-sort and cull the kernels. Go through the contents of each envelope, looking for subtopics, usable quotes (you'll want lots of these for the final report) and substantiation of the key idea.[1]

Don't be afraid to change your mind about entries on your key ideas list. You may have thought that hiring a skywriter was a novel, worthwhile idea; but after reviewing the transcripts of four groups, you realize that only one (eccentric) participant mentioned using skywriting, and even his group considered the idea dubious. So throw out the skywriting envelope or include the quote under another heading—"Unique Marketing Ideas," perhaps.

STEP 7. ORGANIZING   This is the creative writing part, where you have to make flour of the grain
AND WRITING.   and bake some bread. You need a narrative to explain the key idea and
its subparts and to hold the supporting quotes together. And you must create this without any fictionalizing or subtle editorializing. For example, if someone in each of four groups casually mentions a disparity between union and nonunion benefits, a summary statement such as "Some nonunion employees voiced at least a little concern that they receive lower dollar-value health care benefits than bargaining unit members" would probably convey the tone of the comments more accurately than "All groups of nonunion employees expressed concern over the disparity between union and nonunion benefits and pointed to this as an example of a job dissatisfier."

---

[1] Some prefer a computer to our modest envelope routine. Ms. Janet E. Freeman, at Stop and Shop Stores, utilizes computer program for compiling focus group and interview data. If you have access to such goodies, use them. We prefer a more pure-think approach, mainly because we can't always get the necessary computer time.

No matter how you do it, bringing order from the chaos of a set of focus group transcriptions is like unraveling spaghetti. Once we have a set of envelopes that relate to specific topics, we try to cluster those envelopes into themes—a sort of loose, by-hand, factor analysis, if you will. What we end up with are piles of envelopes, each of which provides a major heading for our written outline.

A very brief description of what was done, a listing and explanation of the main factors differentiating high and low performers, and a summation of your recommendations should form a three- or four-page management overview section of the report and give you the structure of the rest of the report. Figure 8–2 gives a visual relationship between the management overview and a regular report section. An important inclusion at all levels of the report and especially in the management overview section is the direct quote. Saying "We found that three factors discriminated high- and low-performing clerks: pay, training, and nose size" isn't very dramatic. But saying

> "We found that promotional opportunities—or a lack of them—distinguished between high and low performers. As one low performer put it: 'Sure I could bust my hump. But without that golden MBA, you don't get on in this organization. That's what really counts.'"

seems to nail down both the concept and the import of the issue for a lot of senior managers. The final writing task is to condense all your findings into a one- or two-page executive summary. This helps you continue the process of distilling the information you have gathered. And it gives you a summary of the study to show to others as support for the recommendations you'll eventually

Fig. 8–2. The Relationship Between Management Overview Entries and Actual Report Units or Modules.

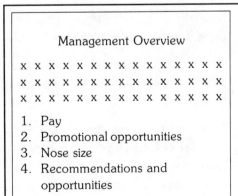

Management Overview
x x x x x x x x x x x x x x x x x x x x x x x x x x x x x x x x x x x x x x x x x x x x x
1. Pay 2. Promotional opportunities 3. Nose size 4. Recommendations and opportunities

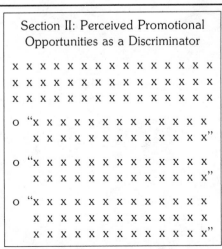

Section II: Perceived Promotional Opportunities as a Discriminator
x x x x x x x x x x x x x x x x x x x x x x x x x x x x x x x x x x x x x x x x x x x x x
o "x x x x x x x x x x x x x x x x x x x x x x x x x x x" o "x x x x x x x x x x x x x x x x x x x x x x x x x x x" o "x x x x x x x x x x x x x x x x x x x x x x x x x x x x x x x x x x x x x x x x"

make. Besides, only you, other trainers, and a few corporate masochists will ever read the entire report. The executive summary will satisfy management people who say they want to read the report but who really only want a brief idea of what you found.

STEP 8. REPORTING THE FINDINGS. The final chapter of this book is devoted to reporting findings. That's how important we feel the topic is. We won't go into it here except to say that at the last dance you find out who goes home with whom. The staging is crucially important.

STEP 9. THE OPTIONAL DOUBLE-CHECK STEP. Darrell R. Griffin, Corporate Performance Systems Inc., suggests that it is sometimes prudent to test the findings of the focus group study in one-on-one interviews. Specifically, he recommends finding and interviewing four or five additional members of the population from which the focus group members were chosen. If the individual interviews yield information similar to the focus group information, you can be quite confident in your findings. If the one-on-one interviews don't confirm the focus group findings, you should consider doing additional work, perhaps conducting a survey study based on the key ideas from the focus group study.

SOME FOCUS GROUP TIPS AND TRICKS

Over the years, those of us who have been using focus group discussions to gather information for the HRD effort have developed both a thick skin and a passel of useful guidelines. Here, in no particularly refined order, are some of our hard-won lessons:

1. Keep the group size manageable. We are most comfortable with eight to ten people; twelve is our absolute maximum.

2. Set up the groups about a week in advance. You need to give people enough warning but not so much lead time that they forget to attend.

3. Don't reveal too much of the content of the group discussion. We overfocused a group once, and eight people arrived with prepared statements to be read into the record. We ended up with something more akin to an Iranian militant's press conference than a focus group.

4. Management will sometimes offer to send along an observer to "help out" with content clarification, finding the offices to be visited, and the like. We learned to say "no thanks" after an observer from the head office decided to "defend the company" against "the awful things those people were saying about us." No shotgun riders, no one-way mirrors, no showing of tapes and names.

    It is okay to have a trainee along, someone you are training to run groups. But only one person moderates, and the trainee's role must be made perfectly clear.

5. Use normal-size chairs and a square or round table. Keep people closed in around the table—jammed in a bit if you can—both to develop an intimate atmosphere and to give your tape recorder the best possible shot at picking up voices.

6. Keep the microphones and tape machine visible. Reduce the threat by being upfront about recording and then ignoring the machine as best you can.

7. Have food and coffee in the room, but don't stage or offer any breaks. You want the group to form, function, and disband. Any interruption in the flow costs you information.

8. Keep your interview outline in plain sight and refer to it. Even though the real outline may be in your head, you want to keep the meeting focused.

9. As the meeting starts, check to see that there are no bosses and subordinates in the same group. Likewise, do anything you can to ensure homogeneity of the group.

10. The moderator has some specific functions, and there are "dos" and "don'ts" in abundance. Among the more critical are these seven.
    ▸ Don't be threatening. Better they see you as a bumbler than as the inspector general.
    ▸ The first few minutes are critical. You must start the talk flowing and stroke every contribution. "You really have some good ideas on the subject" sounds a bit corny but works. Show you appreciate what is being said, but *don't* suggest that you agree.
    ▸ Assume a passive, gentle, guiding manner. Let the participants carry the ball whenever you can.

► Orchestrate the flow so that ideas piggyback but voices don't. If you don't understand a point, don't worry about it; you can go over the tape later.

► Use questions and statements that elicit discussion and give people a chance to express divergent ideas.

► It's probably *impossible* for the moderator to shut up too much. Pauses aren't hazardous to your health.

► The interview guide isn't cast in stone. You and some other people sat down and wrote it, remember? Don't be surprised if the participants want to wander from it. If the guide isn't stimulating discussion, don't force it. Go with what the participants are hot about.

Some people worry that the focus group is too free-form and doesn't produce more than impressions. Even if that criticism were justified—which it isn't—getting out of your office and gathering some real information beats the heck out of sitting around guessing.

SOME PROS AND CONS TO FOCUS GROUPS

We tend to use focus groups to balance out the quantitative aspects of an FTO study. They add depth and some "blood and guts" to what we learn and confirm using other techniques. But there are some who don't share our enthusiasm for the technique. So, to be fair, let's look at both the pluses and minuses of using this group-centered, talking-to-people technique. First, the pluses:

► Focus groups give you easy, fairly reliable access to the ideas and attitudes of a work group. Be they salespeople, secretaries, or division managers, focus group participants tend to relax and interact well verbally.

► The group make-up can be carefully controlled and double-checked simply by having the participants introduce themselves and speak about their background for a few minutes.

► Video- and audiotaping of the sessions make the extra dimensions of nonverbal behavior and vocal information available to the analyst. Groups rarely object to recording, and transcripts of the session are invaluable for recollection analysis and comparison purposes.

► Focus groups are especially useful for gathering input that can be turned into questionnaires for a quantitative study.

The minuses are pretty obvious:

► The results of a focus-group study are *qualitative,* not *quantitative:* there's no way to tell how widespread the group's attitudes and skills are in the populations from which the participants were drawn. And, as Al Anderson cautions, "Many times a client foregoes follow-up quantitative study because of the cost and delay. That can lead to overemphasis of some relatively minor problem or idea."

► Considering the cost of getting interviewees together, focus groups are fairly expensive.

► Just gathering representatives from some populations can be a problem. One researcher, who was conducting a management-skills study with district managers of an oil company, relates that a busy manager sent his secretary halfway across the country to attend the focus group for him. Though he certainly demonstrated his delegating skills, his creative solution for being in two places at once didn't add much to the research effort.

A FINAL NOTE ON THE ROI OF FOCUS GROUPS

Focus-group research is a lot of work. A focus-group study with four group discussions, each lasting one hour, can require 120 to 150 manhours of typing, analyzing, writing, cutting and pasting, and hair-pulling to produce a first-class finished study. Is it worth the Return On Investment? It depends.

An airline, we're familiar with, did focus-group studies with airline sales reps and travel agents and discovered that company policy and paperwork were inadvertently keeping sales reps from delivering the kind of service they had been trained to deliver and wanted to do. A West Coast financial institution discovered that part of a customer-complaint problem they were experiencing resulted from undertraining their telephone reps.

For these two organizations, the return on investment and effort was a good one. Obviously, focus-group research is not a panacea. But, in the right circumstances and with the right problem, it could have a good payoff for you and your client(s).

CHAPTER **9** DOING IT FACE-TO-FACE: MAKING THE MOST OF ONE-ON-ONE INTERVIEWS

The personal interview is the most common information-gathering technique. Face-to-face interviewing is the primary information source for dozens of occupations. Reporters do it, recruiters do it, trainers do it, managers and market researchers do it. But few do it well.

Dr. Gary Latham of Washington State University contends that even though the face-to-face interview is the least reliable technique for hiring someone, it continues to be the number-one way people are hired. "Despite the data, the face-to-face interview feels right," says Latham. "When you think of it, how many people do you know who would hire someone without interviewing them? It really *wouldn't* feel right, would it?"

For two reasons, we continue to use—and advocate the use of face-to-face interviews for information-gathering purposes. First of all, they are, as Latham suggests, expected. What senior manager would accept a report from a consultant–internal or external—if the consultant hadn't interviewed him or her and demonstrated that his or her views were being duly noted and recorded? *No one* in management is going to accept an FTO report he or she hasn't contributed to. But, more importantly, certain pieces of critical information, things that shape, make and break an FTO study, can only be garnered face-to-face.

Social scientists and market researchers, well aware that the interview has much potential for error, have proposed and tested numerous "solutions" to the error problem. Extensive interviewer training has been shown to help increase both the reliability and validity of interview-gathered data, as have random selection of people to be interviewed, selective assignment or "matching" of interviewers and interviewees, and mathematical treatment of interview data.

Our tactic is to use the face-to-face interview as a primary information-gathering tool only where we must and then to control as many troublesome factors as we can. When we work in this mode, we refer to what we are doing as a structured interview. When we use the interview process as only part of the information source—for instance, when we *observe* sales behavior and *talk with* a field sales rep—we refer to what we are doing as either a conversational or informal interview. Let's take a quick look at the two.

THE STRUCTURED INTERVIEW

Four features characterize the structured interview. First, the interview is the only contact we will probably have with the informant. Second, the interviewee is in a unique position and is privy to information we can only obtain from him or her. Third, the interview is positioned as a formal, fact-finding affair; it is scheduled, planned, has rules of conduct, and a defined focus. Fourth, the results are formally analyzed in some fashion. By the way, because of the criticality of the information in many structured-interview situations, we will frequently give the respondent an opportunity to review a summary of key points from the interview.

We undertake the structured interview on two specific occasions. First we interview senior management of an organization to determine the nature and implications of the problem under consideration; we try to obtain the information we need to make a succinct statement about the difference between what exists and what management wants. In short, we use the structured interview technique when we are trying to find the preceived problem and determine why people are in an uproar over it.

We use the structured interview when investigating differences in performance units. If part of the question under study has to do with why some branches, sales offices, departments, or shifts have more or fewer errors, absences, sales, or complaints, we will use the structured interview format when we talk to the key managers of these performance units. This gives us an opportunity to formally compare and contrast the views, expressed attitudes, strategic approaches, and management styles of the managers or management teams of units with different performance levels.

THE INFORMAL OR CONVERSATIONAL INTERVIEW

The informal interview is characterized by its much more spontaneous nature and its lack of structure. We use the informal approach to add depth of understanding to things observed or learned in other ways. It serves to tap opinions of a broad range of performers and provides us with quotes and thoughts for enriching data gathered other ways. For example, during a study of sales representatives for a nationwide purveyor of manufactured goods, we observed sixty salespeople making almost a thousand sales calls. Between calls we mostly listened, but we made a point of drawing out from the reps their views about new rep training, calibre of management, and fairness of compensation. On one set of calls, a rep volunteered that she could "do a lot better if her territory was laid out better." We added a query about territory layout to our conversations during the rest of the study and found that a significant number of sales reps were concerned about their travel patterns and the map of their territories. The organization used this piece of input to invest some effort and time in a mathematical modeling study of sales rep travel patterns and found out that territory layout and travel patterns could indeed be made more efficient.

The informal interview is structured in the sense that we are listening for certain kinds of verbal behavior from the respondents. There are some general probes or questions we will be sure to ask every member of the class of employee we are dealing with. At the same time, we keep the interview agenda open to change so we can be surprised by the discovery of attitudes, opinions, issues, and facts not anticipated beforehand.

ANATOMY OF THE STRUCTURED INTERVIEW

The structured interview consists of five steps:

1. Preparing for the interview

2. Starting the interview

3. Conducting the interview

4. Concluding the interview

5. Compiling and analyzing results

1. PREPARING FOR THE INTERVIEW

► Learn the local language.   As consultants, we are forever strangers in a strange land, struggling with the language. So is the in-house trainer who bounces from marketing to data processing to service. If you can speak—or at least understand—the local jargon, your credibility is immeasurably increased. DP handbooks, banking dictionaries, and even organizational glossaries are readily available. Find one. You at least should be able to nod intelligently when the VP of DP says, "Our biggest problem to date is convincing our users that real-time interface has a better mini/max than remote processing or current micro/mini capacities for ROMI in this configuration."

► Hold an introductory meeting.   If you are going to work in a central location, hold a brief informational/introductory meeting with the people you will be interviewing in depth. At that meeting, you *and* the supervisor of the people you will be interviewing can clarify the objectives for the interviews and make a pitch for candor and guarantee anonymity.

► Make an interview schedule outline.   The first top-management interview is the toughest to set an outline for, but even a sketchy one is better than none. We approach that initial interview with three inputs: (1) the Mager/Pipe questions (see page 0033); (2) some idea of the problem parameters, based on phone contacts and whatever else precipitated the need for this informational meeting; and (3) the upshot of at least one discussion with the company, division, or department liaison person. After the first management interview, the questions and topics to cover become more apparent. But even in a structured interview, you have to leave room for the informant to shape the agenda.

► Don't structure your interview around yes or no questions, even if you think you need yes or no answers. Asking open-ended, problem-solving questions—just as in a performance improvement interview—gets more information and commitment than asking yes/no questions.

► It is more appropriate to let the informant ramble than to try to force your personal ask/answer outline on him or her. Often you will be the first person who has asked the interviewee to explain the job or problem in standard English. That means he or she will be generating information on the spot and will be as interested in the resulting remarks as you are. Give interviewees room to roam in their heads. You get longer answers but better information.

► The face-to-face interview differs from the focus-group interview in a number of ways that we will discuss later. But, for now, be aware that you can't get away with as many vague or naive questions or "tell me about it" queries as you can in a focus group. It is better to be overprepared with questions and not need them than to be caught short with a recalcitrant interviewee.

► Bounce your questions off some neutral and knowledgeable source before the interview. You need to know that you are asking the right questions of the right person and that the questions make sense. Having to explain a pointless question to a safe source may save you time and face when you encounter a key management person.

► Cluster your questions topically. By organizing your questioning, you keep the interviewee focused where you want him or her, and you increase the likelihood that he or she will elaborate on the topic at hand.

► If your questions pertain to reports, published data, production charts, and the like, gather these sources together and have them with you. The other person may not have those things at hand or may never even have seen the data.

► Always conclude with an open-ended question. "What haven't I asked about that I should have?" is pretty good. So is "You know quite a bit about the problem of _____. What aspect might I be overlooking?"

► If the interviews are to be at a mid-level in the organization, you might want to prepare a list of items for an interviewee to rate from most to least important, a questionnaire to work through with you aloud, or a card-sorting task, wherein items of interest are sorted into categories of examples or non-examples of problems, ideas, and so on.

Not long ago, during a problem-clarification meeting with the president of a bank with eighteen branches, we were able to persuade the interviewee to rank his branches from "best" to "worst" by arranging on a long table three-by-five cards on which we had typed each branch name and performance statistics. We had him arrange the cards so that those branches that performed similarly were close to each other on the table and those that differed were placed farther apart. Later in the interview, we were able to pinpoint key characteristics of "successful branch management" by using the visual scale he had built as a frame of reference.

► The meeting should be scheduled at their convenience. The more you push to have the meeting at your convenience, the less credible you become.

A TRUE STORY   A line manager of our acquaintance, a man with responsibility over several hundred equipment installers, truck drivers, and repair people for the installation and repair division of a computer company, related the following exchange between himself and a would-be in-house HRD helper.

Mr. Process:	Mr. Big Shot, I'm Mr. Process Consultant. I have a commission from internal OD to meet with all key managers to set a schedule of meetings with you and your direct reports.
Mr. Big Shot:	My calendar is pretty full. It will have to be later this month.
Mr. Process:	Oh, that won't do. Mr. Top Dog insists that we meet with all key managers by the 15th.
Mr. Big Shot:	Let's see. I have a Wednesday sunrise prayer-group meeting, but if Mr. T.D. is going to be on your neck, I'll skip the meeting and see you here in my office at 5:45 this Wednesday morning.

Mr. Process: (silence)

Mr. Big Shot: Hello?

Mr. Process: Gee, I come in on the bus. I'd have to leave home at. . . . Oh gosh, I don't think so.

Mr. Big Shot: Okay, pal. Let's put 'em on the table. You don't want to see me anymore than I want to see you. Doesn't sound like you're as convinced as T.D. that this deal is necessary. So you come here, ask me your questions on Friday from 3:30 to 4:15, and we're done. Got it?

The point? Simple. The consultant went out on a limb to create a sense of urgency and importance about his assignment. When the line manager rose to the bait and called his bluff the consultant's credibility went up in smoke.

SOME SCHEDULING TIPS.

► Schedule a specific time.

► Leave at least forty-five minutes between interviews.

► Try not to schedule interviews late in the day or just before lunch.

► Avoid meet-and-eat interviews if possible, but be flexible.

► Leaving messages is fine, but keep calling. Many people throw away phone messages from callers they don't know.

► Arrive five minutes early.

► Don't interrupt a person while he or she is occupied with another person or agenda.

2. STARTING THE INTERVIEW

A face-to-face interview is not a mini focus-group discussion. There are differences in the preparation necessary: face-to-face requires more subtlety in question design and in the way you direct the focus.

We believe that one-to-one interviews differ from group interviews in both content and process. In focus-group work, the presence of peers usually gives the group members a sense of power and protection. If the group members don't like or are bored with what you're doing, they'll tell you—usually by moving the group away from your topic and toward theirs.

In face-to-face interviewing, there's neither protection nor autonomy. To say that interviewees are often "tensed up" about the interview is an understatement. We've had interviewees cancel out, get sick during the interview, show up stoned, bring in tape recorders, and ask to have a witness present. Focus groups tend to treat the whole get-together as a large coffee break and a lot of fun.

So, rule 1 for face-to-face interviewing has to be: *Don't touch content until you've built a trusting relationship with the interviewee.* Larry Wilson, at Wilson Learning Corporation, counsels salespeople who sell one-on-one to be aware that there are two types of tension in a face-to-face sales interview: *task tension* and *relationship tension.* Before an interview can move to a task plane, the relationship problem must be attached.[1] Interviewees tend to ask three sorts of questions about unknown interviewers:

1. *Intent questions.* "What is this person's reason for interviewing me?" "What is he or she going to do to me?" "How will talking to this person affect me and my job?" Notice the *me* focus. Real "bottom of the pyramid" stuff, to borrow from Maslow.

2. *Competency questions.* "Is this person qualified to talk with me on this subject?" "Does he or she understand our business well enough not to misunderstand what I'm saying?" "Can this person be trusted to interpret and convey my opinions and ideas correctly?" Here the focus is less defensive because it's on *you.*

3. *Propriety or commonality questions.* "Can this person understand 'where I'm coming from?' " "Are we—the interviewer and I— enough alike to have real communication?" "Is this a peer-to-peer, person-to-person interview, or is it a one-up, one-down thing?" *Us* and *we* questions are the least emotional and are fairly easy to handle. Dress, body language, and the peripherals make a big impact on propriety.

Salespeople used to be told that the best way to handle initial interview tension was to develop chitchat: ask about hobbies, family, nontask stuff. So they were advised, "If you see a bowling trophy on the client's bookshelf, say, 'You like bowling, do you?' " We don't know about you, but we're always tempted to answer those kinds of questions with, "No, I hate bowling, but I like trophies. I stole that one from a little old lady in Encino." Anyway, this synthetic approach to opening the interview led to the "Three Relation Questions and Go for the Throat" technique of *not* establishing communication. For example:

Q1 How's the wife, Charlie?
A1 Ran away with my best buddy last week.
Q2 Good, good. How's the boy at State doing?
A2 Terrible. Flunked out last quarter and is working in a diner to save money for a sex-change operation.
Q3 Do *you* ever see old Sam Smart from ABC Corporation? The guy who rolled that 300 game?
A3 Not since he ran off with my wife last week.
Q4 Great, great! Say, maybe we'd better do a little business. We always get carried away, don't we? Have you had a chance to run that proposal by your boss?

Our point is pretty obvious: If you have to fake it, forget it. With a group, you can simulate interest and concern; one-on-one, it's hard to pull off.

---

[1]The technical name of this "time-tension" model is the Yerkes-Dodson Law.

Rule 2 is: *Be prepared, but admit to knowing a lot less than the interviewee.* The interviewee is the only subject matter expert in the area of your concern. Attempting to treat an interviewee as a testee—someone who knows less than you, someone you're testing—blocks content communication and shuts off the information-gathering process.

After the relationship matters are taken care of, position yourself relative to the interviewee and clarify your expectations of the interview. We do that by reviewing the purposes of the meeting. After all, we asked to see the interviewee, so we must make clear why we need the time and then restate and clarify the purpose. Here is an example of one opening statement we used for a series of face-to-face interviews with regional sales managers:

> Mr. _____, I work for _____. a consulting company that has been retained by Mr. _____ of the national training center. We are looking at the effectiveness of current training with an eye toward making it more responsive to the fields needs. To do that, we need to talk to people like yourself who are in the best position to evaluate the people who do the selling. So, the purpose of this discussion is to get your feelings about current training programs and to tap your insights into problems that can effect field sales performance.

3. CONDUCTING THE INTERVIEW

Now it's time to let the interviewee focus on the topic. Don't jump right into the interview: move in slowly and calmly so the interviewee has a chance to get his or her bearings. Here are some tips, tricks, and topics to keep in mind when doing the actual interview.

A. FOCUS YOUR ATTENTION.

It takes considerable energy to be *focused* on the interviewee 100 percent of the time. A full day of interviewing is more tiring than a full day of hod hauling. But when you've done your homework and scheduled the interview for a time when you won't be too tired or hungry to hear, you will have the necessary energy. Some helpful focusing hints are:

- ► Use "extra" mind-time to evaluate what the speaker is saying. People hear faster than they speak, so a wandering mind is a continual danger.
- ► Form more than one conclusion. As you listen, write "possible hypothesis" statements and reminder questions next to your interview notes.
- ► Ask for concrete examples when the theory, concept, and jargon jungle get especially thick.
- ► Ask key questions more than once and more than one way.
- ► If your mind does wander or if you don't understand, ask the person to repeat what was said. "Could you say that another way? I'm not sure I followed you." works for us.

B. SEQUENCE THE QUESTIONING. When asking questions, sequence from general to specific. Keep your questioning upbeat, and maintain your interest, genuine or otherwise in the answer. Sometimes people need time to think about a question. Give it to them in the form of respectful silence. Summarizing the answer or ideas in a long statement gives you a double-check on what you heard and encourages elaboration. Above all, be flexible. Follow the twists and turns the interviewee wants to take. What look like blind alleys are sometimes short cuts to new, unexplored avenues.

C. ASK FOR CONSTRUCTIVE CRITICISM. While emphasizing that names and blames aren't of interest to you, be sure your interviewee understands the realities of the problem you are being paid to explore. If you are chasing after a supposed training-problem need but there are factors mitigating against it—for instance, an antitraining value in the field that nobody in home office wants to acknowledge—you need the information. However, criticism or "ain't it awful ing" can run on forever if encouraged and reinforced. Ask for it and note it, but don't agree with it, amplify it, or even repeat or rephrase it. Simply ask: "Are there political or other issues around the topic of _____ that I should know about? I'm not asking you to criticize the company, name villains, or point the finger, but are there any special factors about this problem that I should understand?"

D. PUT ANSWERS IN PERSPECTIVE. While you want mostly to gather opinions and ideas in a face-to-face, you do need a context for those opinions. Ask for specific examples. Ask what opinion *others* might hold; try to determine if other managers would agree with the interviewee's assessment of the situation. Ask for definitions or at least the intent of such loaded words as disaster, impact, urgent, important, hardheaded, vital, critical, uncooperative.

Be careful not to misinterpret opinion as fact. If someone says, "Hell, half our people come in late every day," ask later if literally half the staff comes to work late. Be as wary of the *absence* of criticism as you are of an excess. Asking a person what his or her experience has been with a program, product, or promotion gets him or her off the *critic* hook a bit. Six types of answers should raise a caution flag in your mind and on your note pad:

- ► Sweeping generalizations
- ► Convoluted answers peppered with complex terms you scarcely understand
- ► Answers that fit your preconceived notions too well or that line up too well with head office or the guy-next-door's view of the issues
- ► Confidential just-between-us replies
- ► Sentences beginning with "It stands to reason," "As you well know," "We can all agree," and other assumptive openers

E. AVOIDING
DISAGREEMENT.
When someone demands "What do *you* think the problem is?" or "How do they view it in head office?" you could be in for trouble. Toss the money back with "I guess if they thought they knew better than you, I wouldn't be here." By admitting that you aren't an expert and clarifying that you need confidential input, you usually can win people over to your side. Keep them there by:

- ► Avoiding sarcasm
- ► Playing "Can you top this?"
- ► Correcting facts or dates
- ► Contradicting an opinion
- ► Admitting an error if you make one
- ► Effecting reconciliation if you somehow offend or step out of line

When you find yourself in one of those uncomfortable and occasionally unavoidable personality conflicts, terminate the interview and look for another route of information gathering. Above all, remember you are working with a human being who has a right to good treatment from you and who can do you good or bad later.

F. MANAGING THE
INTERVIEW TIME.
Meeting time costs money, your's and their's. So maximize it by:

- ► Avoiding arguments over facts, opinions and trivialities.
- ► Changing the focus when the interviewee lapses into a monologue about how it was done in the old days
- ► Shifting the topic if the interviewee starts selling you his or her opinion or pressing you for agreement
- ► Above all, keep the small talk in balance. Some people need small talk to establish trust. Some abhor it. Some hide behind it. Keep your antennae sharp for what's going on in the exchange of small talk.

G. NOTE-TAKING.
How do you capture the data from a face-to-face? The most common approach is to take notes. Tape recording and questionnaire completion can also bring order to the interview process, but note-taking seems to be the most flexible and usable approach to capturing the data.

Too much note-taking, however, can get in the way of the interview. Edward Price Bell, a 1920s reporter who was as famous as the heads of state, captains of industry, and stars he interviewed, never took a note, preferring to reconstruct "a piece at a time from memory"; of course, he often took a fortnight to reconstruct a 5,000-word interview. Truman Capote trained himself to remember long passages of conversation with the help of a tape recorder; his spellbinding *In Cold Blood* was largely researched that way. Many a hard-bitten newspaper reporter takes pride in the ability to cover and write up a news conference from memory, using notes to confirm facts and references.

Since note-taking is the province and paycheck skill of the professional reporter, consider the following ten tips from Ken Metzler, a reporter and author of *Creative Interviewing: The Writer's Guide to Gathering Information.*

- ▶ Record names, dates, spellings, ages, percentages, and figures.   Quotes, quips, and anecdotes might lodge in your memory, but figures are elusive.
- ▶ Note major conceptual points, and follow up with a facts-and-figures probe.   Some reporters split their notebooks down the center, using one side for ideas and the other for data. For instance:

Part of turnover problem	← 18%
related to low pay	\$ 4 85 ABC
compared to market.	5. 25 vs. makt.
Supervisors are	
primarily males and no	
females promoted —	
females w/ambition turn	22% ♀
over quickly	11% ♂

- ▶ Develop a personal shorthand.   Getting a direct quote verbatim is a major note-taking problem. One solution is to train your mind to hold a quote in memory until you can write it down. Another is to take a speed-writing or shorthand course or to develop your own system. One simple trick is to drop the vowels and use symbols for common words: "ths hlps u gt ur inf wrd 4 wrd."

▶ Slow the pace.   Asking clarifying questions lets you catch up. So does saying, "That's a good way to say that. Let me get that verbatim." Or "Just a moment. That's an important idea. I want to get it down right."

▶ Discipline the conversation.   If the interviewee tells you that there are three reasons for something, scribble down "3 rsns" and number each point. If he or she only mentions two, ask for the third point.

▶ Use nonverbal reinforcement.   Note-taking encourages talk in the direction of the most pencil movement. So do head-nodding and noncommittal verbal clucking and "uh-huh-ing." Caution: Some people panic when you take notes in a flurry; to reduce tension, explain what you're writing.

▶ Memory training.   With a bit of practice, you can learn to include in your notes "recall cues," those simple sentences or phrases that bring back longer strings of conversation and ideas. A colorful phrase or unusual incident can be a good cue.

▶ Type up your notes.   Regardless of how good your notes and memory are, both fade. Typing your notes for file gives you a chance to flesh out what you have while it's fresh and to add impressions and suspicions. If you are working on an hypothesis, put relevant confirmation or negative instances in the typed notes. Note time, date, and names of those interviewed. If you are security conscious or just a bit paranoid, code the notes you might use—for example, LM1 for "first manager of low-performing unit interviewed." Just remember to write the code down somewhere.

4. CONCLUDING THE INTERVIEW Don't bring the interview to a sudden halt. Ease it to a stop. Summarize what you learned, but emphasize that you need time to pull everything together. Tell the person what you intend to do with the information and what actions it may precipitate. Don't *promise*, but do explain what you will be doing with the data.

Be sure to thank the person graciously for his/her time and for the open way you were treated. It doesn't hurt to lay it on a bit. If the person seems to be prolonging the meeting, be aware that he/she may want to tell you something of a sensitive nature. Probe gently.

If the interview is a high level, preliminary problem-identification, promise a follow-up action. A memo or letter reiterating the problem explanation, a second meeting, or an action proposal are typical follow-up to this sort of meeting. If you are doing field management interviews, *do not* promise a report of findings or a specific follow-up action. If a follow-up seems needed, simply write a "bread and butter" memo that once again thanks the interviewee for the time and candor. *Do not* review key points in your letter; doing so might cause a case of "cold feet."

5. COMPILING AND ANALYZING RESULTS

One approach to compiling and analyzing interview results is simply to sum key opinions across interviews. In some instances, we've simply gone back over our typed notes, looking for common complaints and speculations about the problem under review. Our summaries then take this form:

EMPLOYEE ABSENCES AND LATENESS.

Eight of the eleven first-line supervisors interviewed mentioned employee absence and lateness as factors affecting the production of their units. Typical of their comments are these:

> "How can I meet standard when I haven't got enough people to start the line when the shift starts?"

> "By the time they all straggle in or I can get a utility, I've lost 6½ to 10 manhours."

> "These people don't seem to care much about being here or not. Why be on time when nothing bad happens? I got no control here."

When asked to suggest remedies, four of these supervisors suggested that *policies and procedures* should be changed. Four others said they weren't sure what might change the situation. When pressed, two of the four suggested that central personnel would have to be "more consistent" and "overrule management" if the lateness and absence problems were to be solved.

When the good guy/bad guy framework is used, responses can be sorted and structured this way:

ABSENCE CONTROL.

Supervisors in high-performing units tended to differ from supervisors in low-performing units in their approach to *absence-control* techniques.

► Low-performer approach. In the low-performing units, supervisors either had no personal approach to absence control, believed that absence control is not possible with today's work force, or stressed the company's three-step discipline procedure.

> "These people don't want to work. There isn't much you can do but warn 'em and then try to fire 'em."

> "You should try to let someone go around here! All you get is grief. The best deal is to try to talk to 'em, but that doesn't help."

► High-performer approach. Supervisors of high-performing units tended to emphasize clear statement of expectations, performance discussions, and some form of positive recognition for attendance.

> "It's not easy to get people to work on time or even here these days. I just emphasize what is expected around here and once in a while, I let 'em know I'm glad they're here."

> "I set up this early-warning thing. I told 'em I have to know when they are going to be gone or late because we can't start up. Now they know I won't get crazy as long as I know in time. When they don't let me know, we sit down and have quite a talk!"

Obviously, the "four out of five supervisors" and the good guy/bad guy report formats won't do for your Statement of the Problem report. That one is based on the management interviews you held to determine the problem indicators or why management thinks there is a problem. That interview or set of interviews and your summary memo are simply the first cut at your problem analysis, not a separate findings report. A more interesting use of upper-management intuition and interview time is the structure we eluded to in Chapter 2, the "how do you know one when you see one" interview. As you may recall, we asked a senior bank manager these questions: "What would a well-run branch look like? When you picture a 'good branch' in your mind's eye, what do you see?" We boiled the answer to that question down into seven key elements. We then compared our notes from interviews with this senior manager's branch managers to see how much commonality there was between elements in the senior manager's mind's eye model and the branch manager's replies to the question: "What kinds of things are you trying to accomplish with this branch?"

We simultaneously compared the same senior manager's "best" branch to "worst" branch rank ordering to see how adherence to the boss's mental model affected branch performance ratings *and* to determine exactly what factors went into a good performance rating that might not be in the senior manager's verbalized "good" branch model. As you might guess, we found that management expectations—the top person's model of what a good branch *should* look like—correlated highly with branch performance rankings.

In addition, the interviews with managers of the high-performance-rated branches yielded fairly concise descriptions of what these managers were doing. So we ended up with:

1. Management's "performance theory"

2. The behavioral manifestation, or critical element, of that performance theory

3. A description of the things low-performing units were doing that *did not* exemplify the model

And all that critical data came from interviews with one very senior manager, six of of his key staff managers, and ten branch managers (managers of five high- and five low-performing units).

The statisticians in the crowd will recognize what we did as a sort of *degree-of-concordance* procedure. And we did, in fact, do some statistical testing but only for the purposes of publishing what we learned. Originally, we simply (1) listed the senior manager's seven key points on a large note card, (2) listed the key points from branch managers' interviews on smaller note cards, and (3) aligned the manager interview cards across a table in performance-rank order as shown in Fig. 9-1. Then we looked at the arrangement and read, reread, and re-reread the cards until an agreed-upon pattern of key points was obvious to us.

Fig. 9–1 The Concordance Procedure for Analyzing Interview Data.

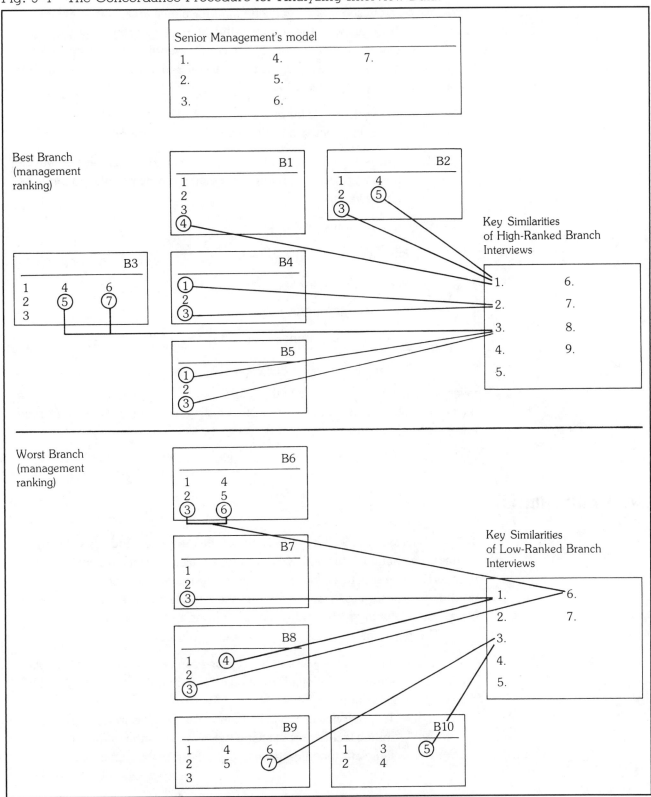

There are still other approaches to interview analysis. You could *post facto* develop a questionnaire over certain performance areas and use your interview notes to "answer" the survey as the interviewee probably would (or could) have, based on your interview. Easier still is sending the survey back to the people you interviewed as well as to others ranked the same way your interviewees are ranked. This technique:

1. Verifies the key differences that seemed to separate high- and low-ranked interviewees in the review of interview notes

2. Verifies the extent to which those same factors discriminate between others who were high/low ranked in the same population but not interviewed

While this sequence of

interviewing,

analyzing interviews,

developing a questionnaire,

sending a questionnaire, and

analyzing a questionnaire

takes *time and money*, it is one of the safest and surest approaches to capturing the key cognitive factors and behaviors that distinguish high and low performers and performance units.

LIMITS AND THINGS

The personal face-to-face interview is one of the most used and abused techniques for gathering data about performance problems. When the interview process is highly structured beforehand and is systematically implemented, it can be one of the best ways to gather performance-problem information. But as with every data-gathering technique, there are pluses and minuses.

The personal interview has a number of pluses:

▶ If the interviewer and interviewee can establish a congenial relationship, a lot of information can be shared in confidence within a short time.

▶ The interviewer can use rating scales, questionnaires, and card-sorting techniques to shape the interview and to relax and stimulate the interviewee.

- ► If the interview is especially fruitful, the length can be adjusted without having to consider other participants.
- ► The interviewer can shift and change interview style and question types to meet the style and comfort needs of the interviewee.

There are, however, at least four drawbacks to the personal interview:

- ► The one-on-one interview is definitely the most expensive—and slowest—way to gather information.
- ► Because interviewees may doubt that the interview will be held in confidence—especially if a tape recorder is used—they may not answer the interviewer's questions candidly or fully.
- ► Often the people selected for interview purposes within an organization are chosen because of their verbal skills or a reputation for candor rather than because they are representative.
- ► It is difficult to control the one-on-one interview to the extent that the structured questions get answered. An interviewer might get carried away with some tangential lead in the interview, and the interviewee may need more time than the interview allows to consider one or more of the interview questions.

CHAPTER 10 LET YOUR FINGERS DO THE WALKING: GATHERING INFORMATION OVER THE TELEPHONE

All of us have received at least one of those calls. They tend to come right around dinner-time or between halves of the Sunday football game. The voice at the other end asks, "Can you give me a minute to answer a few questions?" Intrigued, one in four of us acquiesces and then proceed to do the best we can to recall the last time we "purchased a quart of motor oil," "tasted an oleomargarine product" or "heard long-distance telephone call advertisement." The person calling is a telemarketing specialist—often a college student hired to call people to collect information about products, services, or advertisements for a market research or advertising firm.

You, too, can use methods and procedures the telephone market researcher employs to gather information. Ma Bell's intimate little communication device offers some distinct advantages over other forms of data gathering. According to A. M. Brown, training manager for American Cynamid Company in Princeton, New Jersey, there are five benefits to dealing with people over the telephone:

- ► Difficult to contact people, those not willing to schedule you for a face-to-face, are often amenable to a phone call, especially long distance.
- ► You can take notes, audiotape, refer to job aids, and use a script without the interviewee knowing or being distracted.
- ► The telephone commands attention and privacy. People seldom let a phone go unanswered, nor do they let a third party butt in when they're talking on the phone. People also tend to be more candid on the phone; it's like talking in the dark.
- ► The phone has immediacy. It is easier to establish a businesslike climate and come quickly to the point without the interviewee feeling rushed.
- ► The respondent can't read your body language. Your clothing, facial expressions, and any nervous mannerisms are hidden from the customer. You can concentrate on one vehicle, your voice.

We have used the telephone successfully to gather evaluative information about just-completed training, attempts to apply skills in self-study courses, managers' views of people who went through a program intended to improve productivity, and users' views of technical update materials. We have also used the phone exactly the way market researchers do—to gather information from consumers. But in these cases, we are interested in how the people who work for the client are perceived, not in the product consumed or purchased. We've found that telephone interviewing is faster than face-to-face and permits a fine degree of control. If you are talking to the wrong person or a marginally helpful informant, you can cut it short, hang up, and dial an alternate. Costwise, that beats the heck out of making a futile day trip to Dayton.

There are of course, some drawbacks, or at least limitations. You'll never get the same amount of time and attention over the phone you receive face-to-face. The topics you can cover are also somewhat limited. You won't get long, thoughtful, reflective ramblings over the phone either. Most people can't deal with abstract questions in the telephone format. In our experience, the topics best suited to the telephone interview seem to be:

- ► Reactions to a recently completed training program, workshop, or seminar experience.
- ► Data retrieval. When you need numbers, they can come quickly and easily over the phone, but it usually takes two calls, one to state the need and a second to get the data.
- ► Experiences with a company's customer-service or salespeople. In the same vein, the telephone respondent can give you candid information about appropriateness of a sales rep's call frequency, call preparation, and time utilization.

The *telephone interview* is a cross between a one-on-one interview and a mail survey. Since questions are written out and answers recorded and coded in some quantitative fashion, researchers classify the telephone interview as a survey technique. Calls are made to a random selection of the population in question—job incumbents, ex-trainees, or consumers—and interviews are conducted via a structured interview guide. The guides we've seen range from open-ended questions to questionnaires with specific choices. The typical telephone interview last 10–15 minutes. (About 20 percent of the people contacted by telephone give you 20 to 25 minutes.)

James J. Hubbard and Brenda K. Miller of Hubbard and Associates in Wheaton, Illinois, specify four pluses and four minuses for telephone interviewing.

The pluses are:

1. Telephone interviewing is the least expensive live interview you can conduct.

2. Interviews can be monitored and evaluated. And, because fewer interviewers are necessary, there's less chance for interviewer bias.

3. About 80 to 90 percent of those called agree to be interviewed.

4. People tend to be more candid over the phone than face-to-face. Hubbard and Miller have found, for example, that 70 to 80 percent of those interviewed over the phone will divulge household income figures; this is a much higher percentage than other methods yield.

The minuses are relatively minor:

1. Telephone interviews tend to be shorter than other kinds of interviews.

2. There is no possibility for "show and tell" or for any of the loosening-up exercises possible with the face-to-face interview.

3. The interviewer must work with a structured interview form that typically requires developmental time and pilot testing.

4. Not everyone succeeds at telephone interviewing. Good interviewers must be skilled at "breaking the ice" with total strangers over the phone.

In short, if you need to probe in-depth in order to make judgements about the respondents or if you have to refer to visual displays (books, graphs, charts, sales records, etc.) forget the telephone routine. However, if you need a fast sample of real people, and if quick responses rather than lengthy explanations are sufficient, and if the matter under investigation is concrete and fairly uninvolved conceptually, dial away.

THE QUESTIONS ARE THE THING

The key to the success of the phone survey is a good questionnaire. The introduction to the survey—the preamble the question askers present to the interviewee to elicit his or her cooperation—should be short and to the point and should help the interviewers establish rapport almost immediately in order to retain the listener as a respondent. Generally, a very brief explanation of what is being sought and whom the interviewer represents is all that precedes the first question. The big hurdle is to get the respondents to start answering questions. Once started, they tend to keep it up, but there is no absolute guarantee. Therefore, the questionnaire builder has to ensure a steady flow of simple, straightforward questions and has to be sure that the survey isn't a memory test. That is, questions must be short and easy to comprehend and don't depend on one another to be answerable. In other words, skip questions on this order: "Farmer Brown has three cows. He tethers one to the southeast corner of the barn with a twelve-foot rope, one to the northeast corner with a fifteen-foot rope, . . ."

And, don't for heaven's sake, think you have to get through every question with every person. Remember, only 20 percent will give you more than fifteen minutes. A hostile respondent is worse than none at all. So stop at the ten-minute mark, and ask if you could ask a few more, or would the interviewee like to stop.

Figure 10-1 is a sample of a telephone survey form.

The algorithm format of the Wingover survey, with its direct computer entry feature, typifies contemporary telephone survey instruments. This questionnaire is the end product of an extensive development process. In fact, the first version of the Wingover survey was a pretty basic affair, something like this:

The open-ended "scramble-and-write" survey format in Fig. 10-2 gives you the input for developing the final sophisticated instrument. You *could* get a lot of the developmental information for the survey from a focus group, but people do respond differently over the phone. So even if you use a group to start development, you will have plenty of revising to do once you turn to the telephone. Using the fill-in form for half a dozen or so calls can give you enough information to do a good job on the more sophisticated version. You essentially develop a survey the same way you develop a training program: write, try out, revise, try out, revise, revise, revise, revise. No secret to it, just an idea of where you want to go with the survey design and a couple of days on the phone.

In *Market Research: A Short Course for Professionals,* Bertram Schoner and Kenneth Uhl offer the following advice for constructing and using a telephone survey:

1. Since telephone surveys are typically short in duration and use highly structured questions, the interviewer must establish rapport immediately and move quickly to the questions.

2. A very brief explanation of what is being sought should precede the first question. The listener should be given little opportunity to withdraw from the conversation.

3. Early questions should be ice breakers, simple to answer and non-threatening. Respondents who feel they will look foolish need both encouragement and easy-to-answer questions.

Fig. 10-1 Adaptation of an Actual Airline Telephone Consumer Survey. This particular survey was a direct CRT entry affair.

Wingover Airlines Commercial
Travelers Survey

Precall

Phone #_____
Tickets 1st 10 mos._____
Last Wingover trip_____
Order placed by_____
Attempts_____

Intro

"Hello, is this _____? I am Joan Smith calling from Airline Survey Services. Our records indicate that you purchased a ticket for _____. Was that a ticket for you or for someone else?

1 __self   __office personnel   __boss   __other

Was the trip:

2 __business   __personal   __other
                                                        → to page E
                              → to page D

How frequently do you arrange business air travel for _____?

(pause—accept answer—probe)

3 __one trip a month   __two trips a month

     1 2 3 4 5 6 7 8 9 ____ trips a week

Of the last 10 trips you arranged, how many were on:

4 __Wingover   __Transamerica   __Americana   __Big Bird   __Agonized Air   __Southworst

I appreciate the time you've given me. Could I ask you just a few more questions?

No ———   Yes

    xxxxxxxxxxxxxx   Well fine. Could you give me
    xxxxxxxxxxxxxx   some idea why you chose Wingover
    xxxxxxxxxxxxxx   on the _____?

Exit

                    Personal   Travelers   Company
5 ☐ Route ☐ Time ☐ Preference ☐ Preference ☐ policy   ☐ _____

    Page F   Page G   Page H   Page I

              Could you tell me a little more about that?

Fig. 10-2 The Preliminary Wingover Survey.

Wingover Survey

Phone:_____
TrP TK:_____
Date:_____

1. Who made the reservation?

2. What sort of trip was it (business, pleasure, etc.)?

3. What is the person's air travel frequency? On which carriers?

4. Why did they pick Wingover for this trip?

5. Any comments about treatment during ticketing or on the trip?

4. In all surveys, some questions are less intimate, less difficult to pose, and less boring to answer than others. These kinds of questions should be asked up front. And if none of your questions qualify as a starting point, contrive one that does.

5. Questions may be difficult to answer because of: (1) respondents' poor memory; (2) a necessity to search for records; (3) a necessity to compute; (4) lack of knowledge, or (5) thinking or writing requirements. Such difficulties present impasses unless respondents are permitted honorable D.K.'s (don't know's).

6. Easy-to-answer questions are those that: (1) require short yes or no or check-mark answers, (2) do not demand much thinking and recall, and (3) do not make the respondent feel either right or wrong in answering them.

7. Once the flow of information starts, the questions should be sequenced to maintain an accurate and unambiguous informational flow. Remember, answering questions about someone else's training, services, and problems may not be particularly interesting for your respondents, unless those questions involve a very recent or unusual experience. Occasionally, you won't be able to get everything you need in less than fifteen minutes. Good luck! It takes creativity to build on instinct. And definitely remember to KISS!

8. A logical flow of questions aids recall and respondent thinking and generally encourages respondent cooperation. An investigator seeking to know the sequence and the time over which respondents have owned various makes of cars should not start by asking, "Have you ever owned a Ford? If so, when?" and so on for each car brand. More accurate answers would result if the interviewer worked backward, present to past, and also from the general to the more specific.

9. The best way to determine whether or not a sequence of questions is appropriate, once general rules and intuition have been exhausted, is simply to test instruments under realistic conditions. Such tests may point out structural, sequential, and other unnoticed flaws. Test and revise, test and revise—sounds familiar, doesn't it?

ANALYSIS OF RESULTS

Telephone Survey results can be analyzed the same way questionnaire results are analyzed, or if your survey doesn't use quantitative items, you can analyze the responses the same way you analyze face-to-face interview or focus-group results. A tape recorder attached to a telephone is an enormous help in gathering information. There are suction cup mounted microphones, as well as special rigs that become a permanent part of your telephone. Take your choice, but remember, the law says you have to tell the interviewee that you are taping.

Beyond statistical analysis, the results of the telephone survey—or any other survey for that matter—have to meet the tests of reasonableness.

Schoner and Uhl make the following suggestions for common sense testing of survey results:[1]

1. Even factual questions need some verifying. For instance, a famous test-retest-retest study found that when a group of people was asked the same single question, "Do you own a car?" at three different times over a period of a few weeks, the respondents gave consistent answers only 86 percent of the time. In another study, people who were asked if they had read *Gone With The Wind* somehow accounted for many more books than had been sold. When retested with, "Do you *intend* to read *Gone With The Wind?*" and then "Have you read it?," the proportions shrank back to something more reasonable.

---

[1]Adapted from Schoner and Uhl's *Market Research: A Short Course for Professionals* (New York: Wiley, 1976).

Those who collect information—over the phone, face-to-face, or any other way—must constantly be aware of the need to provide the proper environment and encouragement to respondents to obtain accurate information. People are inaccurate reporters—either they don't understand the questions, don't really have an answer, or don't want to tell you what you want to know. Whatever the reasons, we have to be in the double-check, accuracy-patrol business when we ask people for information.

2. One solution is to ask for essentially similar information at two different times in the interview. For example, to discern persons' ages, ask respondents how old they are. Or, if you don't want to be that forthright, ask them what year they graduated from high school. Unfortunately, the investigator may not be able to identify which of the responses are correct. Also, if a flow of answers seems inconsistent, suspect inaccurate responses.

3. Another way to check accuracy is to request immediate verification of some of all of the responses. Ask respondents for example who have indicated use of, say, Everready flashlight batteries to send their old batteries to the interviewer for new long-life ones.

4. A simpler check involves comparing findings from the study with what was previously known. For example, in a market where premium-priced beers hold a 25 percent market share, a market-wide study indicating 65 percent would be suspect. Respondents' ages clustering around final digits of 0s and 5s are suspect; equal last-digit distribution between 0 and 9 would be much more likely.

AVOID THESE MISTAKES WHEN USING THE TELEPHONE

Telephone selling expert Thom Norman of Scottsdale, Arizona, says that ten common snafus inhibit clear communication over the telephone. Teaching salespeople to handle these bugaboos goes a long way toward improving their teleselling success. The same advice seems to apply to you and us when we use the telephone to gather information.

1. *Using inappropriate tone of voice.*   Friendly and conversational is best. Your mood and physical condition show in voice tone. When you feel bad, tired, or hung-over don't do telephone polling.

2. *Speaking at the wrong speed.*   We tend to talk too fast when we are prepared and too slow when unprepared. Matching the prospect's conversational speed often reveals his or her listening comfort zone.

For most people, 140 words per minute is a comfortable listening pace.

3. *Talking to the wrong person.*   You should establish the credentials of the person you're talking to. Interviewing the mailboy can really be punishing—to both parties.

4. *Calling for the wrong purpose.*   "If you don't know where you're going, any road will get you there" applies to phone calls as well as face-to-face. Establishing the credentials of the person you are speaking to over the phone is tougher than face-to-face, but it's just as critical.

5. *Giving too much information.*   Just tell enough to put respondents at ease and start them answering questions.

6. *Not giving the person a reason to listen.*   The opening pitch is critical. You have about forty-five seconds to stimulate interest and establish your reason for being listened to before the respondent freezes you out.

7. *Not probing for answers.*   You have to discover things over the phone just as you do face-to-face. That means asking fact-finding/feeling-finding questions.

8. *Assuming you understand the prospect.*   Rarely can you establish complete rapport over the phone, but that's not your goal. You want permission to do fact-gathering. Don't assume you know everything from one phone call.

9. *Assuming the person understands you.*   One phone call is seldom enough to make yourself completely understood. Understanding comes later, as he or she learns of your product or service through experience or more communications with you.

10. *Failing to check person's availability to talk.*   Just asking for a minute of the prospect's time usually isn't enough. You have to be sensitive to what's going on at the other end of the phone. Do you hear conversation in the room? Is the prospect speaking in an unnatural, guarded way? If you pick up clues that it's a bad time to talk, make an appointment to call back.[2]

KEEPING YOUR BALANCE

Because telephone interviewing can be as psychologically draining as telephone selling, we offer some suggestions for keeping your sanity during a tele-surveying cycle.

> ► Keep a log of number of calls you've made and number you have to go. Charting progress toward the total number of contacts you need helps you remember the madness will soon end.
> ► Doing rehearsals and simulations with a friend helps you hit the ground running.
> ► Maintain a well organized work space.
> ► Set a by-the-hour contacts goal; stop for relaxation and reward when you make your numbers.
> ► Track calls, as well as contacts made. A busy signal, a wrong number or an "out to lunch" requires a certain amount of time and effort too.
> ► When you sound enthusiastic, fresh, and up-beat, the person on the other end is more likely to cooperate. Expectations again. But to sound that way, you have to *be* fresh and up.
> ► Take care of yourself. Interviewing people, face-to-face or over the phone, is hard, trying work. Don't burn yourself out the first day.

SATISFACTION ALMOST GUARANTEED

Telephone surveys lack something very important to us trainer and HRD types: you don't make eye-to-eye and handshaking intimate contact with the individuals. People may reveal a lot, but they still remain somewhat distant over the wires. That can make us uncomfortable and hesitant to pick up the receiver. But telephone surveying is a cheap, quick, reliable way to gather information. We have been very pleased with this technique for finding how people feel about recent training experiences, internal communications programs, and special incentive or content innovations. On the other hand, looking for feelings about how the individual is being managed or rapping about approaches to the selling game with salespeople hasn't worked very well; these interviews seem to lack the depth and texture of a face-to-face contact. In many other instances, though, we've obtained reliable results when we let our fingers do the walking and left the flying to somebody else!

SECTION IV PLAYING TWENTY QUESTIONS

People know a lot about behavior. Every focus group and interview series we conduct reconfirms this simple truth. But often that great wealth of people knowledge is locked beyond our reach, lacking both vocabulary and structure. This strange illiteracy explains, perhaps, the popularity of talk show psychologists and their books and the fact that neutral witnesses often give seemingly divergent accounts of the same observed event in a court of law. It certainly explains the wide variety and idiosyncratic nature of the information we obtain from different experts on the same subject.

This interesting human peccadillo makes for infinitely colorful and entertaining literature and performing arts but decidedly difficult communication among and between peoples. Perhaps the reason so many performance-review systems fall into disuse is that we are uncomfortable trying to force the richness and complexity of human behavior onto a sheet of paper or represent it justly on a five-point rating scale. Somehow, checking the box "☑ *Shows Average Amount of Initiative*" demeans the knowledge and behavioral potential of the evaluator and the individual being evaluated.

But to accomplish all the people-development things we are called upon to accomplish in organizations, we need reliable and valid, repeatable and accurate descriptions of *very* complex behaviors. Fortunately, with a bit of coaching and coaxing, we *can* structure and communicate what we know experimentally about human behavior. That, of course, is the big trick we must perform when we are wearing our performance-problem-analyst hats.

In this section, we look at three systems or methods of helping knowledgeable informants tell us what they know about behavior. The first, *critical incident technique,* uses small groups of such informants to develop what are sometimes referred to as Behaviorally Anchored Rating Scales (BARS). The second, *consensus techniques,* is really a set of methods for getting agreement from disagreeing—and sometimes disagreeable—subject matter experts. The final tactic is the time-honored *questionnaire/survey* method of getting information. These three approaches all share two common themes: (1) people know a lot about behavior, their own and other people's, and (2) we can tap that information *if* we ask the right questions in the right way.

Because we are dealing here with behavior and opinion-measuring scales and techniques, we don't have the problem of prematching groups of performers to work with. The good guy/bad guy, high performer/low performer structure is built into each of the methods. Of course, we *now* have the problem of finding informants who are certifiably competent to act as informants for us. And that can send you certifiably around the bend.

CHAPTER 11 TELL ME A STORY: THE CRITICAL INCIDENT TECHNIQUE

The critical incident approach is another one of those remarkable military-training inventions. The inventor, John C. Flanagan, a World War II military psychologist, was faced with the problem of improving military flight training. Specifically, too many trainees were cracking up training planes, and someone in the War Department suggested that perhaps the training wasn't emphasizing the right things. The key word here is *emphasis*.

Flanagan, who later founded the American Institute of Research, did something deceptively simple. He asked pilot trainees, the ones who were able to walk away, to describe—in terms of behavior—what exactly they had done incorrectly. This technique of soliciting "war stories" is the core of the critical incident process.

Later, Flanagan (1954)[1] formalized the process and defined it as a method of ". . . identifying critical job requirements . . . those behaviors which are crucial in making the difference between doing a job *effectively* and doing it ineffectively."

Critical incidents are reports or descriptions of things people in the studied population report having done or have been observed doing by others. These incidents are classified by supervisors or other knowledgeable subject matter experts as effective or ineffective in achieving the desired job results. These descriptions can take the form of stories, anecdotes, reports, or observations related by superiors, peers, subordinates, or by qualified observers. The incidents can be analyzed bit by bit, collectively, or both.

There are, of course, some parameters on the acceptability of these war stories. Critical incidents are facts, specific reports of observed behavior from qualified sources, not generalizations or opinions.

---

[1]Flanagan's article, "The Critical Incident Technique," is reproduced here as Appendix B. We didn't just include it to fatten the book or prove to you we knew where to find it. It is an important and well-written article. So read it, please.

Dr. Charles E. Watson, Miami (of Ohio) University, suggests critical incidents must address the questions:

1. What was done that led to effective job performance?

2. What was done that detracted from effective job performance or led to ineffective job performance?

3. What, if done differently, would have been more effective?

4. What attitudes, values, abilities, knowledge, skills (present or absent) *seemed* to lead to success or failure?

Consider, as examples, two incidents from a nursing training program Flanagan worked on in the late 1950s.

Effective Incident: A student nurse, double-checking the patient's name against the name on a medication card, catches an error on the card.

Ineffective Incident: A student nurse fails to chart consistent elevation of a patient's temperature when the doctor's decision to operate depends on the patient's temperature at 8:00 a.m. that day.

After the analyst collects many such incidents, a panel of experts sorts them into groups or factors. The first nursing example—the student catching the medication-card error—was sorted into a pile of similar incidents that eventually were given the collective factor name *Checking*. The second example—the student failing to chart a temperature—was sorted into a pile of similar incidents eventually called *Observing, Reporting* and *Charting*.

As a device for gathering data for building training materials and evaluating the performance of employees in the unit or units where the performance problem exists, critical incident is a thing of beauty. The trainer analyst literally ends up with a box full of great information for making case studies, video vignettes, and role-play situations. In addition, the resultant performance appraisal scales can be used to measure and evaluate both end-of-training and on-job behavior.

THE HOW-TO'S

Dr. Marvin Dunnette, of the University of Minnesota, has used the critical incident approach to develop highly sophisticated and reliable performance-review instruments called Behaviorally Anchored Rating Scales or BARS. His small-group technique for gathering incidents and developing these performance-measurement scales is fairly simple and most effective in sorting the wheat from the chaff of such large and nebulous jobs as "managing" and "selling." The critical incident process, as Dunnette has refined it, has six steps:

1. Gather two groups of subject matter experts (SMEs).

2. After amenities are exchanged, have them describe, in writing, specific job incidents and the results produced.

3. After editing, have the SMEs sort the incidents into factors and then name the factors.

4. Have the SMEs sort the incidents for "goodness" and "badness" along a seven-point scale.

5. Have SMEs fill any gaps in the scales with additional incidents.

6. After both groups have finished these five tasks, bring the two groups together, let them look at each other's handiwork, and reconcile their differences.

Flannagan, Dunnette, and others have applied versions of this process to jobs ranging from grocery clerk checkout to navy recruiting officer.

Figure 11-1 is an example of a behaviorally anchored rating scale developed by Dunnette and some colleagues.

It was developed as a performance evaluation tool for one skill cluster in the job of U.S. Navy recruiter. It describes the specific Navy recruiter skill/duty area salesmanship and gives examples of good and bad salesmanship behavior. On this particular scale, "9" is good and "1" is very poor. The recruiter's superior reads the description of the behavioral factor and the incidents laid out along the scale; then, based on observations of the recruiter in action, the superior gives the recruiter a score on salesmanship.

It takes eight such BARS to completely represent the important behaviors of the recruiters. All were developed using the six-step process just described.

Even though the scale in Fig. 11-1 was developed as a performance-rating instrument, its training implications are obvious:

► The eight examples of the behavior in question can be used for generating role plays, video examples, and the like.
► Distribution of such a scale to the trainees clearly communicates the objectives of the program and the expectations being placed on the trainees.
► Trainers and fellow trainees can give valuable feedback using the scale.

Fig. 11-1

Salesmanship Skills

Skillfully persuading prospects to join the Navy; using Navy benefits and opportunities effectively to sell the Navy; closing skills; adapting selling techniques appropriately to different prospects; effectively overcoming objections to joining the Navy.

9 —

A prospect stated he wanted the Nuclear power program or he would not sign up. When he did not qualify, the recruiter did not give up; instead, he talked the young man into electronics by emphasizing the technical training he would receive.

8 —

The recruiter treats objections to joining the Navy seriously; he works hard to counter the objections with relevant, positive arguments for a Navy career.

7 —

When talking to a high school senior, the recruiter mentions names of other seniors from that school that have already enlisted.

6 —

When an applicant qualifies for only one program, the recruiter tries to convey to the applicant that it is a desirable program.

5 —

When a prospect is deciding on which service to enlist in, the recruiter tries to sell the Navy by describing Navy life at sea and adventures in port.

4 —

During the interview, the recruiter said to the applicant, "I'll try to get you the school you want, but frankly it probably won't be open for another three months, so why don't you take your second choice and leave now."

3 —

The recruiter insisted on showing more brochures and films even though the applicant told him he wanted to sign up right now.

2 —

When a prospect states an objection to being in the Navy, the recruiter ends the conversation because he thinks the prospect must not be interested.

1 —

This is one of eight BARS developed by Dunnette et al. for evaluating the performance of incumbent U.S. Navy recruiters. Notice that some of the edited incidents don't line up with any specific numbered point on the 1-9 scale line. That is as it should be since the rater is looking for *behavioral examples*, not specific behaviors.

Figure 11-2 is a page from a nursing-trainee evaluation guide developed by Flannagan and his AIR colleagues. It was designed to be used by nurse trainee supervisors to evaluate the performance of nursing trainees during on-job training stints. The supervisor: (1) reads the generic description of the performance to be rated—in this case, *Judgment Regarding Professional Values;* (2) reads the examples and incidents of behaviors to be encouraged or discouraged; and (3) records and rates any similar incidents that were observed during the shift. Again, the training implications are clear.

Fig. 11-2 A Critical Incident-Based Description of Appropriate and Inappropriate Nursing Behavior.*

9. Judgment Regarding Professional Values

This area encompasses behaviors exemplary of both personal and professional values. Honesty, forthrightness, acceptance of personal responsibility for errors, awareness of ethical codes, and respect for the confidence of others are some of the specific values to be developed in this area.

Behaviors to be Encouraged

9. *Judgment Regarding Professional Values*

A. Called attention to own error which was otherwise unnoticed.
B. Reported situation accurately despite reflection on self.
C. Kept information confidential despite pressure to divulge it.
D. Maintained ethical standards in a difficult situation.

Incident: The student reported she had inadvertently used gauze squares (4 × 4's) from a jar that had been contaminated. No one saw her use these squares for a surgical dressing, but she was seriously concerned about the danger to the patient's welfare. She reported the incident promptly despite her concern about possible repercussions.

Behaviors Needing Improvement

9. *Judgment Regarding Professional Values*

a. Tried to cover up or denied obvious error.
b. Made exaggerated statements about nursing care given.
c. Used poor judgment about releasing confidential information.
d. Used questionable judgment in ethical matter.

Incident: The supervisor was making her 4:00 p.m. check on patients. She asked Miss Marks if she had catheterized Mrs. Jones. Miss Marks said she had done so "recently." At 4:30 p.m. the supervisor found Mrs. Jones in great discomfort. She had not been catheterized since early morning.

*Developed by Flanagan et al. The description is used for rating on-job behavior of trainees.
From John C. Flanagan, Angeline C. Marchese, Shirley A. Tuska, and Grace Fivars, *The Clinical Experience Record for Nursing Students: Instructor's Manual,* 1960 Psychometric Techniques Associates, Pittsburgh, Pennsylvania.

USING THE CRITICAL INCIDENT TECHNIQUE

The critical incident technique isn't for the study of every job. It seems most appropriate for analyzing jobs with a flexible or undefinable number of "right" ways to behave. Salespeople continually work on new ways to "close," but they must master the generic factor of "asking for the order." A critical-incident study of selling would generate a bundle of good and not-so-good closing statements for trainees to learn from but would not necessarily reveal the "best close" in any absolute sense. The trick is to teach the trainee to generate good closes in unpredictable situations.

The same criteria apply to nursing, police work, and similar jobs that entail considerable discretionary behavior. The same logic applies to certain skill clusters, such as written and verbal communication. A keyboard-skills expert or even a moderately competent performer can look at a typed page and judge it to be good or bad. Misspellings, erasures, smudges, and the like are well-defined, narrow criteria. But judging the content of the writing on that the typed page is a different matter calling for an evaluation by one or more experts who are guided by various criteria and multiple examples. Figure 11-3 shows a BARS scale that might be used for judging a trainee's communication skills.

DETAILED HOW-TO'S

The following is a description of the steps we took to develop a set of BARS for a sales-effectiveness study. The scales were eventually used to evaluate incumbents, anchor a training program, and evaluate both training and trainee effectiveness.

STEP 1. We assembled eight sales managers and made the following contract with them:

> "We need your input in developing measures of sales effectiveness for use in the training and evaluation of new salespeople. We will need about six hours of your time over the next two days—if all goes well."

The sales managers were then split into two groups of four and put into two separate rooms.

STEP 2. For about an hour, each group's facilitator conducted a mini-focus group around the topic "What makes a good sales rep?"

Fig. 11-3 A Critical Incident-Based Rating Scale Developed to Assist in Judging a Student's Communications Skills.

```
┌─────────────────────────────────────────────────────────────────┐
│              Written and Verbal Communication Skills              │
│                                                                   │
│  Writes and speaks clearly, fluently,  7  Student uses creativity │
│  and with imagination.                    and imagination in      │
│                                           written assignments.    │
│                                                                   │
│                                        6                          │
│                                                                   │
│                                           Student follows         │
│                                           guidelines provided     │
│                                        5  regarding assignments   │
│                                           (such as footnote form, │
│                                           paper formats, etc.)    │
│                                                                   │
│                                           Student participates in │
│                                           informal peer group     │
│  Usually gets the point across but is  4  discussions.            │
│  sometimes confusing                                              │
│                                                                   │
│                                        3                          │
│                                           Student doesn't         │
│                                           proofread papers        │
│                                                                   │
│                                        2                          │
│                                                                   │
│                                           Student isolates        │
│                                           him/herself from peers  │
│  Confusing presentation of ideas or no 1                          │
│  communication at all.                 ↓                          │
└─────────────────────────────────────────────────────────────────┘
```

From Borman, Dunnette, and Hough (1976).

STEP 3. When the groups had "wound down" a bit, the facilitators passed out Instruction Sheet I (see Fig. 11-4) and a pad of incident-recording forms.

STEP 4. When the group members seemed to have exhausted their store of *effective incidents,* we took a break. Then we reconvened and passed out Instruction Sheet II (Fig. 11-5) and more pads.

Fig. 11-4 Instruction Sheet and Blank Incident Pad for Use in Step 3.

Instruction Sheet I	What I Observed the Salesperson Doing:

Instruction Sheet I

The purpose of this get-together is to develop a body of meaningful information about sales performance for use in the development of job descriptions, performance appraisals, and training programs. We are working on the premise that *you* are the best and most reliable source of information about the sales force. *You*, because of your unique position in the company and your depth of experience. You have, at your command, worthwhile information about *effective* and *ineffective* job performance. Information about incidents you have observed, evaluated, and remembered and your judgments about the effectiveness of those actions are especially valuable. Let's begin with your recollection of examples of effective performance.

Directions:

1. Sit back for a minute or two and think about *specific examples* of effective performance you have seen on the part of salespeople. (Don't limit your recollection just to Super Star performance. We are interested in competence, not world records.)

2. Beginning on the next page, write down what you *observed* and what the *outcome* of the performance was.

3. Write out as many of these scenarios as you can remember.

4. Limit your stories to things you have observed salespeople do. Do not include stories about computer salespeople, etc. If you have had an opportunity to observe other learning-company salespeople perform, include those stories but label them as such.

The Outcome of What They Did:

Fig. 11-5 Instruction Sheet II Used in Step 4 of the Sales Rep Critical Incident Study.

Instruction Sheet II

What I Observed the Salesperson Doing:

When you have exhausted your supply of stories about effective performance, move on to examples of *ineffective* performance. The same general directions apply to the development of scenarios of ineffective performance as applied to the effective-performance examples.

Directions:

1. Take a minute or two to reflect upon examples of ineffective performance you have seen on the part of salespeople. Include examples of things that "just didn't seem to go very well," as well as examples of those disasters you would forget if you could.

2. Beginning on the next page, write down what you observed and what the outcome of the performance was.

The Outcome of What They Did:

3. Write out as many of these scenarios as you can remember.

4. Limit your stories to things you have observed people do.

Fig. 11-6 Samples of Raw Critical Incident Stories of Effective and Ineffective Sales Behavior.

a. What I Observed the Salesperson Doing:

This sales rep started the meeting by finding out what each person in the room was responsible for and how they were interfacing with computer printouts or terminals. During the presentation he mentioned a benefit of our product that related to each of those responsibilities and areas of need.

The Outcome of What They Did:

The client team decided to let us design a system plan and make a bid.

(Effective Performance Incident)

b. What I Observed the Salesperson Doing:

I was making a presentation at _____ with _____ _____ . They had four people in the room and we had two. _____ was on the other side of the table next to one of their people. The guy kept asking questions to ___ and _____ kept answering them. Pretty soon I wasn't sure what I had said and what I hadn't and where I was going next. I could have killed _____ .

The Outcome of What They Did:

They weren't very impressed with us.

(Ineffective Performance Incident)

STEP 5. When the groups had done their best at generating incidents, the sales managers adjourned for golf, leaving us with several dozen incidents (like those in Fig. 11-6) to edit.

STEP 6. We distilled and edited incidents far into the night. By *edit*, we mean that we took stories, such as the two in Fig. 11-6, and reduced them to a less wordy, more succinct form. The two incidents in Fig. 11-6 were edited into these three statements.

- ► Salesperson conducted distracting side conversation during another rep's presentation.
- ► Identified the roles and responsibilities of each person attending before beginning formal presentation.
- ► Mentioned a benefit of product to needs of each in room during presentation.

STEP 7. The following day, all 150 edited incidents had been typed on cards, and we gave a set to each group. The groups were instructed to sort the edited incidents into piles of *like behavior*. This sorting took about an hour.

Team A came up with five piles of cards representing factors they called:

- Preparation
- Greeting and putting at ease
- Questioning
- Making the pitch
- Closing

Team B took a more cerebral approach to their sorting and developed seven piles of incident cards they called:

- Prospecting
- Relating to client
- Uncovering needs
- Asking for action
- Presenting the proposition
- Answering objections
- Researching the client

STEP 8. After lunch and another nine holes, the two teams met as one big group, presented their results to one another, and then combined the results. Eventually they merged the twelve piles into seven and named the resultant factors:

- Finding prospects and leads
- Getting in front of the client
- Opening the call
- Uncovering the need
- Presenting the solution
- Overcoming objections
- Closing the sale

STEP 9. The next day, the salesmanagers arranged the cards in each pile along a seven-point scale we had attached to a table in the meeting room. Figure 11-7 shows one of the scales from this exercise.

STEP 10. Once the seven scales were laid out, taped down, and agreed upon, the salesmanagers and facilitators wrote new incidents either to fill in gaps on the scales or to better illustrate the extremes of a given scale. (The prose description of the factors represented by the scales was generated later and mailed to the managers for approval.) Once the scales were full, *everyone* went off for a few hours of fun in the sun.

SUMMARY

In a sense, the critical incident technique is an automatic application of Alfredo Paredo's Law of Disproportionate Distribution. Italian mathematician Paredo discovered that 20 percent of the Italian population controlled 80 percent of the country's wealth. The principle also applies to other situations: 20 percent of a

Fig. 11-7 A Rough Scale for Evaluating the Finding-Prospects Skills Developed from Sales Manager Critical Incidents.

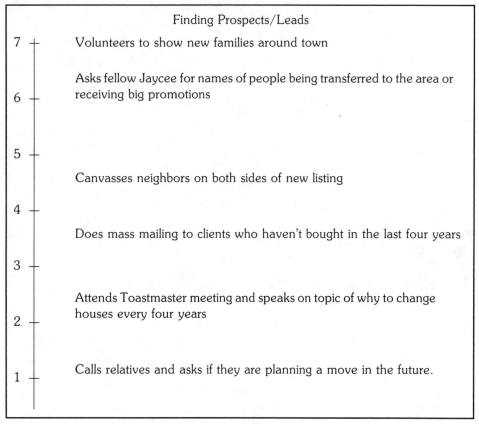

Finding Prospects/Leads

7 — Volunteers to show new families around town

6 — Asks fellow Jaycee for names of people being transferred to the area or receiving big promotions

5 —

4 — Canvasses neighbors on both sides of new listing

3 — Does mass mailing to clients who haven't bought in the last four years

2 — Attends Toastmaster meeting and speaks on topic of why to change houses every four years

1 — Calls relatives and asks if they are planning a move in the future.

company's salespeople make 80 percent of the sales; 20 percent of the sales generate 80 percent of the profits; and 20 percent of the effort yields 80 percent of the output. The critical incident approach tries to point out what that critical 20 percent of effort looks like.

When used to capture the critical behaviors of jobs and tasks that allow a high degree of individuality, it is an excellent tool. When used to capture the elements of very simple, highly repetitive, and procedurally limited jobs, it is somewhat disappointing. The task then is to apply the 80/20 rule to the use of critical incident techniques. Apply it to those 20 percent jobs when behavior is 80 percent discretionary, and don't use it for the 80 percent that are regularly regulated and predictably repetitive.

CHAPTER 12 MAKING ORDER FROM CHAOS: USING CONSENSUS GROUPS

Sometimes you can't get anyone to agree on anything. Even during the most straightforward, routine task-analysis assignment, you can get caught between subject matter experts (SMEs) who would debate sunrises and sunsets, not their time or quality but their actual existence. We have seen vehement disagreement arise over such issues as the "best" way to remove and replace a broken electric typewriter powershaft, the most "effective" and "efficient" way for tellers to count money, and the "proper" method of conducting an examination for heart disease. Regardless of the cause, disagreeing SMEs can vest quite a lot of ego in the argument. And, left unmanaged, such situations can quickly degenerate into a lose-lose struggle.

The trainer caught in a vise between unbending experts, has three options: (1) run like heck, (2) take sides, or (3) precipitate consensus. The first has considerable merit, but most of us lack the panache necessary to make a hasty retreat look like victory. The second option has a number of obvious drawbacks, the least of which is that your training program will be unacceptable to—and probably unused by—those you side *against*. The only real option is to grit your teeth and try to bring the opponents to some sense of agreement.

First of all, you are going to have to display a neutral, nonthreatening air of objectivity and some fair-to-middling conflict resolution/facilitation skills. In addition to keeping an honest disagreement manageable, you will need some techniques for helping your SMEs take an objective look at the knowledge and skill the population under consideration must master if it is going to succeed in the SMEs' sphere. Fortunately, there are a number of structured problem solving/decision-making techniques available for helping us help our disagreeing SMEs bring consensus out of chaos.

An old Russian proverb says, "If nine sober men tell you you're drunk, lie down." The social psychologists have a more elegant expression for this "Rule of Nine" approach to agreement: they call it *consensual validation*. And that is what these techniques, the consensus techniques, are about—bringing knowledgeable people together, jury fashion, and tapping their collective wisdom to guide our training and development decisions. Techniques ranging from such very formal approaches as the Kepner-Tregoe system, Brainstorming and Synectics, to such informal approaches as analogy and WAG, the good old wild guess, have application.

The technique you choose will depend on the situation. One important deciding factor is the complexity of the job under study. A second major situational variable is the degree of agreement or disagreement among the experts.

Most of the situations we encounter fall into one of three categories or situations:

> *Situation 1:*   Few tasks, low disagreement among experts
>
> *Situation 2:*   Many tasks, low to moderate disagreement
>
> *Situation 3:*   Complex and unclear tasks, high disagreement or probability of disagreement

We'll look more closely at the characteristics of each situation and the resolution techniques we've found useful in each.

SITUATION 1:
FEW TASKS, LOW DISAGREEMENT

In these situations, there aren't a great many skills or skill groups to be mastered, but experts seem to disagree about the relative importance of the skills. Typical of Situation 1 is the struggle between sales experts over which is more important for beginning salespeople to learn—product knowledge, prospecting skills, closing skills, fact-finding, or making written proposals.

In a technical training vein, we've seen disagreement over the relative importance of general troubleshooting skills, standard repair techniques, assembly/disassembly of equipment, and identification of common breakdown symptoms. We've even refereed disagreements over the skills a new trainer must have in a given organization. In some organizations, *trainer* is synonymous with "stand in front of class and lecture." In others, the term might mean material writer, computer programmer, or any of a dozen things. Only the people who run the department know; and when they disagree, some sort of consensus technique is called for.

A simple *priority matrix*[1] will help the SMEs in most of these situations develop a priority list or ranking of skill importance. The matrix was developed by

---

[1]The priority grid is also referred to as the method of decomposable matrices by Nobel Prize-winning mathematician Herbert Simon and is based on his extensive research into human problem-solving processes.

the problem-solving, decision-making people to help managers decide among a limited number of possible options. The steps are actually quite simple:

1. List all options. Here, these would be the job skills or skill clusters.

2. Set the factors, clusters, or skill names against each other in a matrix.

3. Weigh the factors against each other, one at a time.

4. When all factors have been compared one by one and the matrix is completed, count the number of times each factor was chosen.

5. The skills or factors with the most entries on the matrix are those that training should emphasize.

An example might help. Suppose you need a new car. Prudence and sanity require you have at least some idea of what you want before you start looking. As Dr. David Campbell cautions, "If you don't know where you're going, you're liable to end up someplace else." So you and your board of directors meet and decide that you need something big enough for two kids, a rubber raft, a large dog, and at least six pairs of skis—snow or water. In addition, you want something with "good gas mileage," a decent repair record, and it better be blue. That makes four criteria:

▶ acceptable/pleasing color
▶ low repair cost record
▶ adequate internal space (probably a station wagon)
▶ estimated gas mileage of 18+ in the city and 22+ in the country

Now we can put these in a priority matrix or consensus grid, a beast that looks like this:

Item	A. Pleasing color	B. Low repair cost	C. Station wagon	D. Good gas mileage	
A. Pleasing color		1	2	3	
B. Low repair cost			4	5	
C. Station wagon				6	
D. Good gas mileage					

Now the task is to weigh the factors against one another on the matrix. It works like this:

> *Question:* Which is more important, the car be (A) a pleasing color or (B) have low repair costs? If you eventually decide the answer is A, then A goes in box 1 on the grid. The next task is to compare items A and C; then A and D. This is followed by comparing B and C, B and D, and finally C and D and putting the "winning" factor number in the appropriate matrix box. The crossed-out boxes are comparisons that don't make sense—for instance, comparing A to A, or asking "Which do you prefer, a pleasing color or a pleasing color?" Equally pointless is asking, "Which do you prefer B or A?" after you have already asked, "Which do you prefer A or B?"

Suppose the following grid is the result of your pondering all the factors in pairs, one against one:

Item	A. Pleasing color	B. Low repair cost	C. Station wagon	D. Good gas mileage		
A. Pleasing color	✕	B	C	D		
B. Low repair cost	✕	✕	C	D		
C. Station wagon	✕	✕	✕	C		
D. Good gas mileage	✕	✕	✕	✕		

Now add up the number of A's, B's, C's, and D's:

A = 0   B = 1   C = 3   D = 2

The tally gives you a priority of features to evaluate when looking for your new car:

C Station wagon/styling is most important characteristic

D Low gas mileage is second most important

B Low repair cost is next

A Pleasing color is in last place

When you go out auto shopping, you can put together a form like this:

New Car Evaluation Form			
Factor	Acceptability	Rank	Score
Interior space (wagon)	(1 2 3 4 5) ×	(3) =	_____
Low gas mileage	(1 2 3 4 5) ×	(2) =	_____
Repair costs	(1 2 3 4 5) ×	(1) =	_____
Color acceptability	(1 2 3 4 5) ×	(1) =	_____
		Total	_____

Suppose you look at three cars—a Bugle, a Yavool, and a Hiku. As a result of your fact finding, you give the Bugle a 4 on interior space, a 3 on gas mileage, a 3 on repair costs, and a 5 on color. That's a total score of 26. The Yavool gets 4 on space, 4 on gas mileage, 3 on repair costs, and 4 on color for a total of 27 points. The Hiku gets 3 on interior space, 5 on gas mileage, 4 on repair costs, and 4 on color for a total of 27 points.

Now, on the basis of objective logic, your choice is between the Hiku and the Yavool. But suppose you have a guilty conscience, feel some stirrings of "buy American," and would feel unpatriotic driving a foreign car. Seems you've just discovered a new criterion for choosing a car that you didn't know was important until now. So buy the Bugle! Or keep looking! The point is, you have reduced the chaos of the car-buying decision to a manageable size.

This simple prioritizing system works just as well for choosing among job applicants or sorting out the relative importance of job skills for a training program. Figure 12-1 is a simple priority or consensus grid we use to choose among good alternatives and ideas. For practice, sit down with one or two colleagues and do a consensus ranking of these two sets of criteria.

SET 1 Objective: To set priorities for choosing a new trainer for the department

- ► Good platform performer
- ► Can evaluate program cost effectiveness
- ► Develops good student materials
- ► Can direct a video production
- ► Can use small-group techniques

SET 2 Objective: To set the order of importance among topics for a training program for managers at ABC Corporation

- ► How to handle seventy-five or more people
- ► How to manage by objectives

Fig. 12-1　Simple Consensus or Priority Matrix.

I. Goal of Task:	A	B	C	D	E	F	G	H	I	J
A.	X									
B.	X	X								
C.	X	X	X							
D.	X	X	X	X						
E.	X	X	X	X	X					
F.	X	X	X	X	X	X				
G.	X	X	X	X	X	X	X			
H.	X	X	X	X	X	X	X	X		
I.	X	X	X	X	X	X	X	X	X	
J.	X	X	X	X	X	X	X	X	X	X

Using the Simple Consensus Grid or Priority Matrix:

1. List each factor to be weighed (features, skills, skill clusters).
2. Set factors against one another in the grid.
3. Weigh factors against each other, one at a time.
4. When completed, count the number of times each factor was chosen.
5. Factors with most entries receive most emphasis in decision being made.

	Weight	(×)	Scale (1-5)	(=)	Value Score
II. a.	_____	×	_____	=	_____
b.	_____	×	_____	=	_____
c.	_____	×	_____	=	_____
d.	_____	×	_____	=	_____
e.	_____	×	_____	=	_____
f.	_____	×	_____	=	_____
g.	_____	×	_____	=	_____
h.	_____	×	_____	=	_____

Total

_____

- ► How to write confusing status reports
- ► How to conduct flattering performance reviews with minorities and women
- ► How to return calls
- ► How to steal only pens and paper clips
- ► How to walk on water

SITUATION 2:
MANY TASKS, LOW TO MODERATE DISAGREEMENT

Frequently, when a task, needs or organizational analysis yields pages and pages of detail, the trainer/analyst lacks guidance for determining which is "nice to know" and which is "need to know" information and skill content. This is also a situation in which we often find disagreeing SMEs. Solution? The *consensus survey group*—a cross between what Robert Bramson (Bramson, Parlette, Harrison and Associates) calls a *nominal group* and a standard questionnaire/survey administration.

Though you will have to do some scrambling while running a nominal survey group, the process is relatively straightforward.

1. Convene a panel of six to eight SMEs, bona fide experts who have the authority to set content specs for the program. Preferably, you have been working with these people during the course of the study.

2. Have the group review the documentation you have compiled for completeness and accuracy. If the SMEs discover any holes or inaccuracies in the documentation, ask them to help filling in and correct them.

3. Assemble the job description information into logical chunks and procedural clusters.

4. Attach "critical" rating scales to the groupings and sub-elements (see Fig. 12-2).

5. Have SMEs rate the groupings of job skills according to their criticality for the level of trainee to be addressed in the training.

6. Compile the SME ratings. Since this part of the procedure will take some time, arrange the session so that compiling can be done while the SME panel is lunching.

Fig. 12-2 A Sample Page from a Questionnaire Designed for Use by a Survey Group of Bank Operations Officers.*

Ratings

A = This is extremely critical. A starting teller *must* be able to do this alone without errors the first day on the job.

B = This is *very* important but not critical. A new teller must be able to do this, but occasional errors can be tolerated until a starting teller gains experience.

C = A starting teller must understand the requirements of this task and must be able to do this with help the first day on the job.

D = A starting teller must understand the requirements of this task but doesn't have to be able to do this the first day on the job.

E = A starting teller is *not required* to do this on the first day or on any subsequent days.

Teller Duties	*Circle One*
6. Given a payroll check to be cashed (customer does not have a savings account), a starting teller will cash it *only* after doing all the following: 1. determined that there is a check-cashing privilege on the check; 2. verified the customer's signature.	A B C D E
7. Given a check to be cashed against a savings account, a starting teller will cash it *only* after doing all the following: 1. verified the customer's signature; 2. determined that the available balance in the account will cover the check.	A B C D E
8. Given a check that can be cashed against a savings account, a starting teller will correctly place holds against that account.	A B C D E
9. Given a 1st Class card and a house check to be cashed, a starting teller will cash the check *only* after doing all the following: 1. verified the customer's signature under black light; 2. determined that the amount of the check can be paid.	A B C D E

*The goal is to trim to a manageable number the tasks a teller trainee must master at the A level of competence during training. The entire questionnaire has forty such items.

7. Give each SME a photocopy of the compiled results and his or her original rating sheets.

8. Go over the composite ratings one at a time with the panel.

9. Where there is a substantial diversity of ratings, ask for discussion, and negotiate agreement if possible. If discussion and negotiation fail to bring the panel closer to agreement, suggest resolution through a majority vote. As a last resort, suggest that the remaining disagreements be arbitrated by a third party whose opinion the SMEs agree to accept. (We have yet to see an instance where the disagreement actually went to arbitration. We have, however, been in situations where the *discussion* of bringing an arbitrator into the disagreement has moved the disagreement off "dead center".) After the panel has completed the criticality ratings and negotiated consensus, it should adjourn, knowing there will be a follow-up.

10. During the follow-up, reiterate the final agreed-upon priorities, and the way the information will be used to set priorities for training program emphasis. This follow-up procedure gives panelists a last chance to recant if they have any second thoughts.

SITUATION 3:
COMPLEX AND UNCLEAR TASKS,
PROBABILITY OF DISAGREEMENT HIGH

In situations where the tasks have never been performed, the job does not yet exist, or there is a variety of possible ways to conceptualize the job, a fair consensus must be reached. Doing a task analysis of the skills and knowledge for the first astronaut to be sent to Mars or trying to develop a skill inventory for the marketing manager of the 1980s are typical situations that demand a tightly controlled consensus procedure, such as the Delphi technique.

The Delphi technique dates back to the early days of World War II, when the U.S. government asked the Rand Corporation to determine which U.S. cities would be attacked by enemy bombers and what the consequences would be. Because there was no precedent for the answers, the "think tank" people knew that surveying military specialists would produce a muddle of different responses, all based on individual observations. Certainly there could be no consensus—and no forecast.

What emerged as the solution to this forecasting problem was the Delphi technique, conceived by Rand specialists to allow individuals to focus their opinions on an unknown in hopes of reaching a discernable convergence of opinion. The effect, then as now, is to lend direction to difficult, complex questions for which there are no absolute answers.

The technique was named after the Oracle at Delphi, who held forth in the sixth century B.C. People who wanted to look into the future submitted written questions to the Oracle's temple. These were answered by a priestess, who uttered mystical sounds from a deep trance. These sounds were then interpreted to the questioner by a priest who spoke in verse. The Oracle was considered the most powerful of Greece's prophets and forecasters.

In the organizational problem-solving context, the Delphi can be used for planning strategies, forecasting future situations, planning and developing new products and generating probable cause lists for specific performance problems. We have used it to get agreement on the skills service technicians would need to develop when a company's major product line switched from electromechanical to electronic. While the Delphi is splendid for focusing energies toward a desired end, its highly structured nature and the time it takes to complete such a study may sorely test an organization's will or, at least, its patience.

The Delphi technique can involve a handful or a hundred informed panelists. A critical factor is that each participant be genuinely interested in solving the problem. A single panelist performing in a perfunctory manner can create distortions. But despite this dependence on good intent, a well-done Delphi is always more accurate and reliable than the opinions of a single individual.

HOW IT WORKS IN THEORY   First, Delphi panelists review a series of scenarios, future-tense descriptions of events that haven't yet occurred. Each scenario, a combination of reality and science fiction, falls somewhere between a forecast, whose interrelationships have not yet been examined, and a mathematical model, whose internal consistency is demonstrable. Panelists then judge the relative likelihood and ultimate desirability of the scenario event. The end result is both a predictive answer and an indication of conviction.

Each scenario is presented at least two and sometimes four times to panelists. Feedback is offered after each presentation. Thus, diverse groups, such as a corporate sales department and a corporate engineering department, begin to reach a convergence of thought. Though feedback is computed and reported to all panelists, the panelists themselves are not identified. The feedback shows both the group average or median and the presence of agreement and disagreement.

Used within an organization or company, the Delphi can uncover breakthroughs in new ideas and techniques, solve long-term planning problems, and generally impinge on all the issues of the managerial process.

Van de Ven and Delbecq conducted a study involving both nominal groups, something similar to our consensus survey group, and Delphi groups. Participants in the Delphi groups not only generated more alternatives to problem situations, they generated more innovative alternatives. The researchers concluded that creative thinking is more likely to flourish when individuals within a group setting work somewhat independently. The Delphi is the height of working independently.

In one Delphi situation, we had first-line supervisors speculate on causes of absences until a consensus list of five most-likely causes emerged. We then proceeded to use the Delphi approach to have the same supervisors speculate on solutions to these absence problems. The process took four weeks, during which management became increasingly anxious. But the first-line supervisors eventually produced some pretty good—and outrageous—solution ideas; what's more, they were able to avoid the macho posturing that had interfered with their effectiveness in a face-to-face, problem-solving group. For example, one of the top solutions was the institution of flextime in a few departments where work wasn't sequential. No one felt it would be "safe" to suggest flextime in an open meeting, but the anonymity of print was reassuring. Once the suggestion appeared on paper, others were free to endorse and promote it.

This same Delphi group provides an example of the spin-off benefits that can result from a Delphi. One supervisor commented on the bottom of one of the surveys, "Absences aren't nearly as big a problem as people standing around waiting to get the equipment up and running in the mornings." This tidbit went into the hopper the next round and out popped the suggestion: "Why not pay someone an hour overtime to come in early and get the gear warmed up?" Putting this notion to work led to a savings of about twenty-two more hours a week; that's an ROI of just about 3:1.

CONDUCTING THE PRIORITY GRID
AND CONSENSUS SURVEY GROUP MEETINGS

The Delphi technique is essentially a blind man's bluff affair. Nobody meets, and all opinions pass in the mail. But the consensus survey group and priority grid procedure are small group activities, the dynamics of which require some control. By *control,* we simply mean a need to keep people focused on the problem and using the procedural structure.

Harvey J. Brightman, author of *Problem Solving: A Logical and Creative Approach,* suggests that flexibility in leadership style is the key to orchestrating a consensus problem-solving meeting, which is exactly what a priority grid or consensus survey group meeting is. The problem to be solved in this case is either to prioritize the importance of skills to be learned or to determine which of two or more opposing opinions will prevail in the matter of which skill sequence will and which will not be taught. When six of seven SMEs rank "ability to repair ten most common faults" as more important than "ability to apply a general problem-solving model to machine breakdown," an important difference in approaches to training repair people has been resolved. The trick is to get that resolution through reasoning rather than politics or intimidation.

Norman R. F. Maier, a brilliant small-group-process theorist, has formulated ten principles of good consensus leadership. These apply to problem solving sessions in general but are applicable to specific consensus tasks as well. Even the simple job of setting priorities, task or training-program objectives can generate conflict if the group is misled. Poor leadership can also stymie a discussion of the various options to be put on the matrix.

Principle 1: Overcome barriers by stressing the possible.

Keep the group focused on the problem. Where are we? Where do we want to be? What barriers separate us from where we want to be? Anything else is superfluous. If you find your group doesn't have the necessary authority, convene one that does.

Principle 2: Don't reinvent the wheel—but recognize that all problems are not alike.

Respect old ways and means, but also acknowledge that new times require new solutions. So what if all the tellers hired in 1955 could add, subtract, multiply, and divide? If the available 1981 work force doesn't have any of those in it, don't get bogged down in a discussion about the good old days. Keep the focus on the here and now.

Principle 3: What's in a name? Seek multiple definitions of the problem.

Encourage your group to generate multiple definitions of the problems and/or solutions. Don't get hung up on terms. Once a problem is defined, we begin to solve *that* problem, oblivious of possible alternative definitions. A problem of "how to reduce conflict" can also be defined as "how to channel the conflict into productivity." Urge or allow the group to explore different problem definitions.

Principle 4: Be problem-minded—not solution-minded.

Keep the group (and yourself) from premature closure. Encourage alternative problem definitions or solutions. People are uncomfortable with unsolved problems. But solution effectiveness increases when there's no pressure for closure. Don't ask for a vote until the question has been debated.

Principle 5: Encourage creative discontent.

Discontent can lead either to hard feelings or innovative behavior. Keep the discontent channeled. Submerged discontent may surface as group-think pathology. Encourage minority opinions, and protect those who see the problem differently. Avoid the tyranny of the majority!

Principle 6: Separate idea generation from idea evaluation.

Discourage arguing over ideas during the initial phases of the session. Eventually, it will be necessary to barter and compromise, but to do so prematurely is to be solution- not problem-solving centered.

Principle 7: Don't let a single member dominate the discussion.

Everyone in the decision group is there by virtue of his or her expertise. Therefore, their thoughts, experiences, and feelings are all valid. Make sure everyone is heard.

Principle 8: View problems as choice situations.

People have a low tolerance for ambiguity; they prefer making a decision to understanding the problem. When you are simply trying to generate a discussion of why a particular item on the consensus survey has earned a split vote, people may want to change their votes or politically force their opinions. Encourage the group to generate logical arguments for supporting their positions, but contain and discourage attacks on others' arguments.

Principle 9: View choice situations as problems.

When the discussion narrows to one or two solutions, it may be appropriate to re-examine and redefine the problem. Instead of voting on either solution A or solution B, encourage the group to take another look at the problem. A new problem definition might generate solutions C, D, and E. This is especially crucial when generating items for the priority grid. Better too many features to weigh than not enough.

Principle 10: Prohibit power trips.

Everyone in a problem-solving consensus group is equal; as leader, however, you occasionally are viewed as more equal than others. Because you have more power, your suggestions will tend to carry more weight, regardless of their quality. It is important that you do not enter the session with preconceived solutions. If you really feel that all trainees absolutely must master Basic Electronic Principles 101 to do the job, you're entitled to that opinion, but you are also obligated to *sit on it* when the discussion on Basic Principles 101 is in progress. On the other hand, you should not abdicate your responsibility as a professional problem solver. If you don't participate at all, the group may lose an effective resource. Thus, you should view your job as that of problem-solver *and* facilitator, not to mention professional clarifer.

Obviously, some of these ten principles are more applicable either to the priority matrix or consensus survey group techniques. The idea-generating suggestions, for instance, are more germane to the listing activity in the priority matrix. But protecting minority opinion is harder to do—and more important—when discussing differences in criticality or ranking of skill items on the consensus survey. They all, however, relate in some way to problem-discussion leadership. Remember, the priority matrix and the consensus survey are *structural* devices to help focus and direct a consensus discussion; they are not substitutes for democratic rational argument and debate.

A QUICK REVIEW

Consensus techniques are methods for synthesizing data already known about the tasks in question and getting agreement among subject matter experts on that data. They come into play when there is more than one way to do a job or to approach the learning—in other words, when experts are in conflict. Conflicts among the experts usually arise when the task in question has:

- ► Alternative methods or sequences
- ► Many influences that contribute to an effect
- ► Many skills of differing importance

The priority matrix method is useful when there are relatively few factors and relatively little disagreement. The consensus survey group method is useful when there are many details that are difficult to sort out into "nice to know" and "need to know." The Delphi technique is used when the data to be organized are highly speculative and futuristic; for example answering the question, "What skills should we emphasize in the 1980s?" might require using the Delphi.

Regardless of which technique you use, the biggest barrier to consensus development is poor problem-solving group leadership. Only *you* know for sure what information and agreement you need from a specific group of subject matter experts, so only you can guide the SMEs toward successfully supplying these commodities.

CHAPTER 13 USING SURVEYS AND QUESTIONNAIRES

The most widely used, and roundly abused, information-gathering technique is the survey study. When carefully conceived and conducted, survey or questionnaire study can expedite your task, needs, or organizational analysis. Ideally, it will yield information about needs, problems, potential problems, and organizational obstacles—as well as employee perceptions, attitudes, and options.

Too often, however, the survey or questionnaire study is used to ". . . avoid the responsibility of in-depth confrontation of the issues being addressed," says survey critic Dr. Harry Levinson, of the Levinson Institute. Levinson further believes that "no single 'fill in the blank' or multiple-choice question or group of questions can adequately plumb human insight and opinion." Levinson is especially critical of organizational opinion polls. He suggests that questions are usually biased toward the sponsor's hoped-for outcome, and results are never as clear-cut as the analysts would have us believe.

Questions like the following, taken from actual published and disseminated questionnaires, do little to dispel the complaints of Levinson and others:

► Which are you?
_____ American
_____ Indian
_____ Black
_____ Chicano
_____ Female
_____ Foreign National

► Do you believe that our nonsales employees should not receive incentive pay as opposed to hourly or monthly salary schedules?
_____ Yes
_____ No

If the experiences of public opinion pollsters of the Harris, Roper, Gallup variety are any indication, a large segment of the general public shares Levinson's distrust of surveys and polls. One indicator is a widespread decrease in response rate. Shortly after World War II, survey people talked about return rates of 80 to 95 percent as average. Today, the return rate of a through-the-mail survey is more likely to be in the 15-to-35 percent range. And people aren't just ignoring requests for information; they are often downright hostile to them. The following letter, expletives deleted, came back to a survey group in one of their stamped, self-addressed envelopes:

> Dear Sirs:
> I received your third mailing today. Thanks for the other two stamps. I don't intend to send this survey back either. First of all, I don't think the things you asked are any of your business. Number two, your questions are obviously slanted and biased toward your viewpoint. Should you ever come up with a reasonable, un-slanted questionnaire, I might answer it.
>
> > Yours very truly,

And here are some choice comments directed at us, that were of a supervisory-needs-assessment questionnaire:

> My boss handed these out to all the supervisors at our staff meeting and told us to fill them out now. He thinks I'm filling this one out, too. But I am not. How nuts do you think I am to rat on myself to a computer that will screw it all up anyhow. I hope nobody answers these stupid questions and you get fired instead.

And there's always the pollster's classic snafu in the Truman-Dewey election of 1948. Ask a group of people what they think of polls and surveys, and somebody invariably brings up that old embarrassment.

SO WHY BOTHER?

Despite the skepticism and hostility expressed toward surveys and polls, the opinion research business is a growth industry. This year, more than $3 billion will be spent by government, business, and industry on polls ranging from consumer-satisfaction studies to employee-job-satisfaction studies. Why?

1. *Cost.*   Surveys are the cheapest form of information gathering yet devised. A medium-sized focus-group study (four to six groups) will cost anywhere from $11,000 to $18,000. Face-to-face interviews tally up to $30 to $75 per head, depending on the complexity of the study. Telephone polls are slightly cheaper: $5 to $30 per head. Questionnaire studies, with follow-up and contingency plans and multiple mailings, seldom exceed $10 per head.

2. *Ease.* Questionnaires are easy to administer and easy to take. People you could never reach by phone are likely to answer questionnaires. Compilation and analysis are also relatively painless. Computers and good pocket calculators have taken most of the drudgery out of survey work and turned a whole generation into poll takers.

3. *Standard conditions.* All respondents are asked the same questions in the same way, usually in the same general time frame. And, their answers aren't susceptible to any of the face-to-face interview biases.

4. *Familiarity.* People are familiar with questionnaires, and they usually know how to respond candidly.

5. *Number.* Many more people can be contacted by paper and pencil questionnaires than by any other currently used surveying method.

There are, of course, some drawbacks to surveys as well.

1. GIGO (*Garbage In, Garbage Out*). Surveys are extremely vulnerable to the charge of untranslatable results. Ambiguous and even unanswerable questions confound the surveyed. Here's an extreme example:

Do you still beat your spouse?

_____ Once a week or less
_____ Bread
_____ Only during Lent
_____ San Francisco
_____ No, I'm French

Computers compound rather than simplify the situation in at least three ways:

► They hide poor questioning under impressive numbers, percentages, and correlation statistics.
► Questions are forced into computer scorable formats such as true/false, yes/no, and multiple guess.
► Easy analysis encourages "fishing-expedition" type questions.

2. *Hostility and misinformation.* Questionnaires are cold and impersonal. People can react unfavorably to the medium and skew their responses accordingly. Anonymity cloaks such deceit and misinformation and, of course, gives no opportunity for clarifying questions the reader can't understand. One disturbing study found that

10 percent of all mail questionnaires are answered by someone other than the person intended. A salesmanagers survey that is filled out by the sales manager's secretary, spouse or three-year-old kid may have some curiosity interest, but that's hardly what we're after.

3. *Low response rate.*   A small percentage return makes one doubt the validity and representativeness of the information received. We never really can answer the question: "What do the non-respondents look like?" After all, they didn't respond. It is feasible to argue that 12 angry truckers can seriously bias a questionnaire on speed limits and ICC regulations if only 20 or 30 "bull haulers" out of 2,000 take the time to respond.

4. *Survey results lack meaning.*   Surveys are subject to overinterpretation unless they are anchored in reliable baseline or comparison data. And such is unlikely to be the case for an in-house survey. A finding that "20 percent of our salesmanagers say they need time-management training" could lead to erroneous training activity if you don't know that time management is and always has been the number-one expressed training need of sales managers. In fact, 20 percent is much lower than the figure found in a recent national survey of salesmanagers.

All things considered, though, the survey is and will continue to be a most useful and most used information-gathering tool available for tapping the thoughts, opinions, and needs of large populations. Better to know the problems and allow for them than to use surveys inappropriately or to dispense with them altogether.

Our approach to making the most of surveys in service to organizational needs and task analysis revolves around three fairly conservative propositions. These propositions assume that we trainers tend *not* to be statistical analysis geniuses, and we usually don't have access to the resources of a statistical consultant or a computer. Our only—and in the long run—best resources are a clear head, a true heart, and a decent pocket calculator.

EFFECTIVE SURVEY RESEARCH BEGINS WITH LEG WORK, NOT PENCIL WORK

Survey research expert Steve Mayer of Rainbow Research agrees that most survey studies suffer from a lack of front-end analysis, or, to be blunt, plain old leg work. The result, he suggests, is indicated by items that don't ask the right questions and by surveys that are too long. Both these flaws are obvious to would-be respondents and serve to depress survey return rates.

The remedy is plain, old-fashioned homework. Interviews, focus groups, site visits, and reviews of performance data all help clarify and define the goal of your study and give you a context for explaining the obtained results. Survey experts Douglas R. Berdie and John F. Anderson, principals in Anderson & Berdie Research and authors of *Questionnaires: Design and Use*, suggest the following four questions as a sort of quick litmus test of preparedness:

1. Can you state the purpose of your proposed study in 25 words or less?
   ► What do you want to know?
   ► Why do you want to know it?
   ► What will happen as a result of answering the research question? (Both plus and minus information)
   Question: When you have described the goal of the study, ask yourself, "Is this study *really* worth doing?"

2. Are *you* familiar enough with the topic and the people you will be surveying to keep subject matter experts in line when they start carping about your survey?

3. Do you have a sponsor who will push the project? Fund it? Utilize the results? Stand behind you when things foul up?

4. Are you sure you can reach the necessary population? Have you anticipated their reasons for possibly *not* responding? Can you follow up with them? Assure them anonymity?

If you can't pass this test, you're certainly not ready to begin building a survey study of a particular problem. Back to the homework part.

FOLLOW THE KISS PRINCIPLE (KEEP IT SIMPLE, STUPID)

Everyone of us has looked at a sophisticated climate/attitude survey or Census Bureau beauty and marveled at its complexity. And we amateurs are frequently tempted to emulate these productions when we design our own questionnaires. Consequently, we often err by developing survey items that are "tricky" and thus open to misinterpretation and over analysis; by developing clever response scales when they're not needed; and by going for a larger sample of the population than is necessary.

We try to follow three KISS guidelines when designing questionnaires that will provide easy-to-analyze responses and useful results.

A. *Use yes/no and data-reporting items rather than scaled items whenever possible.*   We're all addicted to Likert-like scales. Writing and interpreting questions attached to "strongly agree to strongly disagree" scales is kind of fun in a beard-plucking, navel-contemplating way. And then sitting around asking each other "What do these results really mean?" Making tea leaf explanations to management about the hidden meanings in a set of responses shrouds our work in a cloud of expertise and mystery. Unfortunately, we often end up writing items like this one just for fun and power:

I am a supervisor.

Strongly Agree	Agree	Neither Agree Nor Disagree	Disagree	Strongly Disagree
1	2	3	4	5

Another reason for avoiding scaled items is the temptation to average the results. These 1-through 5 scales *look* as though they measure something in an orderly, ruler-like fashion. But the distance between a 1 and a 2 response is not necessarily the same as the distance between a 4 and a 5 response. So computing a *mean* of the four responses (2, 3, 5 and 8) and concluding that 4.5 is the average answer, the mean opinion, is a shakey practice.

How you ask do the "big guys," the climate survey people, get away with averaging? Easy: they don't necessarily assume that their scales have equal intervals. They make their interpretations, instead, by comparing XYZ Company's answers to the answers given by hundreds or thousands of previous respondents. Our homemade surveys don't have that *normed baseline data* for comparison purposes.

B. *Use the smallest sample possible.*   We all tend to oversurvey. But the more surveys we send out, the more we are obliged to get back or account for as "missing in action." For example, suppose we send out 100 surveys and receive 75 back. Seventy-five percent is a fair-to-middling rate, *but* we can only guarantee our results are accurate plus or minus 25 percent. As we mentioned earlier, a small percentage return makes one doubt the validity and representativeness of the returned information. We never really can answer the question "What do the nonrespondents look like?," and a minority of especially sensitized respondents can throw the results in a cocked hat. Better to send out 30 surveys and work like heck to get them all back.

The following abbreviated table (Fig. 13-1), adapted from *Hays' Statistics for the Social Sciences*, gives you an idea of the number of people you need information from to assure that your survey represents the views and thoughts of the population you are studying.

Fig. 13-1*

| A Sample Size Table for Proportions | | | | | |
| Degree of Accuracy = ±.05 | | Proportion of Sample Size = 0.5 | | Confidence Level = 95% | |
Population	Sample	Population	Sample	Population	Sample
10	9	230	144	1400	301
15	14	240	147	1500	305
20	19	250	151	1600	309
25	23	260	155	1700	313
30	27	270	158	1800	316
35	32	280	162	1900	319
40	36	290	165	2000	322
45	40	300	168	2200	327
50	44	320	174	2400	331
55	48	340	180	2600	334
60	52	360	186	2800	337
65	55	380	191	3000	340
70	59	400	196	3500	346
75	62	420	200	4000	350
80	66	440	205	4500	354
85	69	460	209	5000	356
90	73	480	213	6000	361
95	76	500	217	7000	364
100	79	550	226	8000	366
110	85	600	234	9000	368
120	91	650	241	10000	369
130	97	700	248	15000	374
140	102	750	254	20000	376
150	108	800	259	30000	379
160	113	850	264	40000	380
170	118	900	269	50000	381
180	122	950	273	60000	381
190	127	1000	277	70000	382
200	131	1100	284	120000	382
210	136	1200	291	160000	383
220	140	1300	296	1,000,000	383

*This table tells you the number of people you must survey to accurately represent the views of the population under study. Accurate here means reliable at the .005 reliability level. In other words, the chances of the results being funky is 5/100.

Hand in hand with the idea that you need the *right* sample size and *right* return rate is the concept of asking the *right* people. Call that concept *randomization*. Most statistics are based on the assumption that we have a *chance* or *random* selection from the population under study. Doug Berdie believes that this is the most frequently violated statistical principle. If you decide to do a 100 percent sample of the sales force or supervisors or female employees, your only problem is response rate. You must ensure that you get all the surveys back—or enough of them to rule out unrepresentativeness. If you decide that a sample of thirty people will suffice, you must ensure that the thirty people are randomly selected and don't just represent men or people who can be depended on to fill out and send in the questionnaires. They must truly be a random sample.

To avoid getting distorted and unreliable results, sample small and randomly and work hard at getting a good return rate.

C. *Use the simplest statistic possible.*   Dr. Michael Scriven, an expert in program evaluation, suggests that any statistical test you can't do with a simple hand calculator may be too complex to yield practical results. We tend to agree, though there are occasions—say, when you have 250 surveys to compile and analyze—when a computer might be an expedient.

Generally, we feel we can do a rather good job of problem analysis using simple *descriptive statistics;* some appropriate adding, subtracting, multiplying, and dividing; some tips and tricks for looking at descriptive data; and a clear head. It has been our experience that being able to build good charts, graphs, and tables is a valuable skill. So is the simple skill of being able to calculate mean, median, mode, range, and standard deviation. Conceptually, we only need an understanding of the ideas of normal data, skewed data, and cross-tabs to see us through 90 percent of all the studies we have been called upon to conduct. Appendix C has a quick review of what these measures and terms mean. Appendix C also has a quick review and how-to of three ways of testing statistical significance: chi-square, the t-test and nomographic testing.

You'll probably never use any of the three, but they are there just in case—like a security blanket or back-up parachute. When and where to use them are included in the same appendix, as well as an example of each used in a survey study. Actually, the nomograph *may* be of use to you from time to time to check out your hunch that two percentages are significantly different. But that, too, is really a security-blanket function.

Overall, we feel that statistical tests of significance are valuable, pure research tools, but *most* HRD situations rarely demand them. Instead, use the "Inter-Ocular Trauma Test": If the results hit you between the eyes, they probably have practical import. Don't confuse significance with importance. Results can be *statistically significant* but trivial nonetheless.

PILOT TESTING A SURVEY TO AVOID PITFALLS

We pilot test new products, work systems, and training programs, so why not questionnaires? There's nothing more embarrassing than a phone call informing you that "there's no box to check for my department" or "I can't figure out how I'm supposed to answer question 7." And how does it feel to receive a return mail survey with four pounds of red-penciled grammar and syntax corrections? According to John Anderson, pilot testing a survey often shows you ways to shorten and simplify the final instrument, just as pilot testing a programmed text or workshop shows you where the fat and skinny areas are.

We use a three-step pilot test. First, we photo copy our finished masterpiece and test it one-on-one with three specially selected people: (1) a member of the client's staff, (2) a member of our own staff, and (3) a member of the population under study. We ask these guinea pigs to read the survey aloud and talk their way through the answers. That way, we pick up any ambivalences or misinterpretations of meaning and can use the testee to help correct the problem on the spot. Second, after appropriate wailing and gnashing of teeth, the survey is cleaned up, and a small sample goes out to the target group. Third, when these come back, we do a dry run on the scoring, compiling, and interpreting. This is where we find out that our instruction to "pick the one answer that best represents your . . ." was completely ignored, and most of the ungrateful wretches pick *three* items from the list. Though this debugging process is a pain, it saves us from the ignominy of having to throw out cases, invent silly scoring protocols to compensate for bad questions, and generally lose confidence in our own results.

THE CASE OF XYZ MANUFACTURING, INC.

Rather than talk any more rules and guidelines, let's work up a specific survey for a specific case application.

Sam Gumball is training director of XYZ Manufacturing, Inc. The divisional personnel director of the Energy and Power Division of XYZ, calls Sam and orders a supervisory training program. Sam asks what that program might discuss and is told, "Give 'em everything. They don't know from hunger about management." Sam then gives the personnel director the two-minute "if you don't know where you're going" speech. The personnel director concedes that a *little* research won't hurt, but "Make it quick. We've got to do something now!" You see, the president of the division, the chairman's grandson, was at an international convention, where he heard this nationally-known management expert espousing the glories of management development for the masses. Now he's decided that Energy and Power's performance problems will be cured by a good dose of supervisory training for all hands.

Because the franchise is broad and the coins are rattling loudly in the would-be sponsor's purse, there is a temptation to do one of those "What sort of training do you think you need?" surveys. Instead, we opt to travel a more conservative route.

STEP 1. FIGURE OUT THE PROBLEM. The best bet is to ignore the panic and work with the division management on identifying causes of their specific problems and developing specific solutions. Step One is to see what problem the requesters—the *real* requesters, not the personnel director—think they are trying to solve. David M. Schiff, publisher of *Consultants Digest,* a monthly newsletter for HRD consultants, calls this get-together an *alignment meeting*—an attempt to determine what the client perceives the problem to be.

Once everyone is comfortable and coffeed, the first question to ask in the alignment meeting is: "What's the problem, and who's hurting because of it?"

Thanks to Sam's brilliant questioning and incisive use of reflective listening, the client is finally able to state, "Productivity in the assembly area of the battery plant is consistently below time-study standards, and labor costs are rising. But beyond that, productivity in the entire battery plant and the entire Energy and Power division is lower than we budgeted for this year."

More leg-work follows, and Sam finds:

- ► Production records verify low productivity in the battery plant.
- ► Supervisors gripe a lot about commitment, morale, and the reluctance of "the kind of people we hire today" to really work.
- ► According to the personnel director, salary reviews and performance reviews are linked; (that is, performance-review ratings determine salary-increase increments).
- ► Quality control and production data are closely guarded—for management's eyes only.
- ► There are 61 supervisors in the battery plant and 210 in the division.

Sam now has enough information to develop an idea worth focusing on via a survey study. Sam's working hypothesis for the study is:

First-line supervisors in XYZ's Energy and Power division battery plant *do not* provide adequate performance information to the people who work for them. The problem of insufficient performance feedback is especially critical in battery assembly areas and leads to low productivity and employee morale and turnover problems.

A working hypothesis gives Sam a concept to use for building survey items. It does not, however, provide a license for ignoring other needs of the population. The hypothesis is just Sam's starting point for working with the division; Sam's educated guess about where the 20 percent that will yield the 80 percent happens to be in the Energy and Power division.

STEP 2. DESIGN, PILOT, AND ADMINISTER THE SURVEY. Here is where the first signs of trouble usually creep in. There's always pressure to rush the job. After all, we've spent one, two, three, and maybe even eight or nine days getting the parameters of the sponsor's problem in focus. Now he or she is terribly anxious for us to solve that problem. Never mind that it's taken one, two, three, or maybe ten years for things to get so bent out of shape. And never mind that, once you tell 'em what the problem looks like and what it will cost to start solving it, they will take one, two, three, maybe even ten weeks to give you a go/no go decision. All that is irrelevant when the heat's on.

It takes concentration to dig in your heels, play patient counselor, and do the job right. By "right" we mean that you take the time to design a survey that will yield analyzable results, pilot test the bugger till it is idiot-proof, and set an administrative strategy that will maximize return rate and give you a decent data-processing turnaround.

In order to build a survey that will gather meaningful information about the problem, Sam needs think-time and test-time. When you (we or Sam) rush the job, you end up with two problems. The first is a survey like the one in Fig. 13-2 that smacks of shallow thinking and poor preparation.

And Sam's would-be respondents are sensitive to such signs of schlock. Surveys that have no place for a respondent's department code, lack a response category for the respondent's answer, and contain "hard to understand and interpret" items often end up where they belong—in the circular file.

We can't give you an entire course on questionnaire item design, but we can pass along some guidelines.

SURVEY DOs

► Begin with a few nonthreatening, easy-to-answer items. This ensures that respondents will continue to complete the questionnaire with a positive attitude. Threatening items at the beginning of a questionnaire can cause defensive—and frequently invalid— responses.

► Make your items as brief as possible. Filling out questionnaires can be a bore. Sometimes respondents will automatically turn off when they encounter tediously long items.

Fig. 13-2 Excerpts from the Bad News XYZ Manufacturing Survey.*

PART I: ME AND MY DEPARTMENT

1. How long have you been with XYZ Manufacturing?
   __under 2 years   __8 to 15 years
   __2 to 8 years   __over 15 years

2. How long have you been a supervisor?
   __under 2 years   __8 to 15 years
   __2 to 8 years   __over 15 years

3. How long have you been in your current assignment?
   __under 2 years   __8 to 15 years
   __2 to 8 years   __over 15 years

4. How many people do you have responsibility for?
   __less than 10   __15 to 25
   __10 to 15   __over 25

5. In which department are you a supervisor?
   __manufacturing   __administration
   __sales   __other_____
                                    (specify)

PART II: ABOUT THE PEOPLE WHO WORK FOR ME

1. To answer this question, consider the *job knowledge* of the people who work for you.

   At this point, how knowledgeable are your people about their jobs?

   | 0%   10%   25%   50%   75%   90%   100% |
   | No   Average   Know |
   | knowledge   everything |
   | at all |

2. To answer this question, consider the *performance level* of the people who work for you.

   At this point, how *efficiently* do you think your people perform their jobs?

   | 0%   10%   25%   50%   75%   90%   100% |
   | Not   Average   Complete |
   | efficient   efficiency |
   | at all |

3. Which of the following courses would you say would help your people most improve their performance? (pick three)

__a. Working with others

__b. QXM spot-weld techniques

__c. Quality control for operators

__d. Understanding standards

__e. Reading blueprints

__f. Personal time management

__g. Safety, the drill press, and you

__h. Industrial health and hygiene

__i. Other_____
   _____

4. In your opinion, how good a job is the company doing at complying with our EEO/Affirmative Action goals?

   __very good __good __normal __poor __very poor

PART III: ABOUT YOU AND YOUR OWN TRAINING NEEDS

This part of the survey will help you assess your own training needs.

1. How good are you at doing performance appraisal?

Very Good	Good	About Average	Need Improvement	Not Very Good
5	4	3	2	1

2. How good are you at giving your people day-to-day performance feedback?

Very Good	Good	About Average	Need Improvement	Not Very Good
5	4	3	2	1

3. Which of the following courses would help you improve your supervisory performance? (pick three)

   __a. Time management   __f. Positive employee discipline

   __b. EEO compliance   __g. Delegation

   __c. Job instruction training __h. Conducting better meetings

   __d. Human relations   __i. Budgeting

   __e. Hiring procedures   __j. Safety, first-aid, OSHA

4. Comments:_____
   _____
   _____

---

*The survey that won't tell Sam anything he wants to know about the problem.

► Emphasize the crucial words in each item. If certain words might change the entire meaning of the item when misinterpreted, italicize or underscore them.

► Leave adequate space for respondents to make comments. Although unstructured comments are often difficult to analyze, they can provide valuable information that might not otherwise be collected. Plenty of white space also makes the form appear less cluttered and more professional.

► Group items into coherent categories. This makes the respondent's job easier because he or she won't constantly shift mental gears, become fatigued, and make a mistake. Categories don't have to be labeled, but similar items should be grouped together.

► Provide some variety in the type of items used. This keeps respondents from becoming fatigued and bored and is particularly important for long questionnaires. Alternative types include: multiple-choice, true-false, short-answer, open-ended items, ranking items, and items that are contingent upon previous responses.

► Include clear, concise instructions on how to complete the questionnaire. Heed Murphy's Law here, too. Be sure that your instructions will inhibit any attempts (conscious or otherwise) to complete the questionnaire incorrectly.

► Specify what to do with the completed questionnaire. The return address should be clearly identified on the cover letter and on the form itself. Should the questionnaire be returned in a self-addressed envelope? What's the deadline for completing it? (By the way, deadlines increase questionnaire response rates.)

► Provide incentives for a promptly completed questionnaire. This doesn't mean you should "bribe" respondents, just that you should make every effort to motivate them to respond. Help respondents realize the importance of collecting this information, and explain how it will be used to benefit them. Sometimes the clout of a questionnaire signed by a highly credible person can promote responses. This device should be weighed against that of an anonymous questionnaire, one that will encourage more candor on controversial items.

► Use professional production methods. The more professional your questionnaire looks, the more likely you will get a high response rate. A printed questionnaire is easier to read and respond to.

► Provide a well-written personal cover letter. Questionnaires should always be sent with cover letters explaining their purpose and the reasons respondents were selected. Personal letters are best; if this isn't feasible, have the letter printed to match the type in the address and salutation. Never use a form letter.

► Include other experts and relevant decision makers in your questionnaire design. This helps assure that your questionnaire is comprehensive and technically correct. It will add credibility to the project and will give you a head start toward utilizing the completed data.

► Plan how to analyze and use the data when designing the questionnaire. Consider the analysis and use of data from the start. What might be a good question can result in meaningless data. Consider the nature of responses as carefully as you design the questions.

► Be prepared to handle missing data. Invariably, there will be incomplete responses and missing data on the returned questionnaires. Unless you have a plan for dealing with this missing data, you'll be stymied. Anyone who has used a five-point (or seven-point) rating scale knows that missing data cannot always be treated as though they were 3s or 5s (the midpoints of the scale).

► Test your questionnaire on representatives of the target audience. You may be surprised how many serious errors went undetected during the most careful and systematic design process. Perhaps the best way to test a questionnaire (without involving complex statistics) is to watch a few respondents complete it. If they're having difficulties, question them in detail to determine the source. Questionnaire designers frequently find that a single ambiguous word can invalidate even the best questionnaire item. A little time spent in pilot testing can eliminate lots of problems later on.

► Number and include some identifying data on each page. It's possible that the pages of the questionnaire may come apart, causing problems for the respondent. Avoid this by numbering and identifying each page.

SURVEY DON'Ts

► Don't use ambiguous, bureaucratic, technical, or colloquial language. It can confuse or alienate respondents. Don't give Murphy's Law an opportunity to sabotage your study. Pilot testing the questionnaire can help avoid this error.

► Don't use negatively worded questions unless absolutely necessary. Negatively worded items can easily be misinterpreted or clue respondents into a "desired" response. Most negative-sounding items can be reworded positively.

► Don't use double-barrelled items that ask respondents to respond to more than one statement or question. Such items can be confusing, especially when the respondent feels differently about each part. Instead, make each item a simple, discrete question or statement. When in doubt, make two items out of one.

► Don't bias respondents by hinting at a "desired" response. For questionnaire results to be valid, respondents must not be biased by the way the items have been written. Again, pilot testing is the best way to avoid inadvertently biasing respondents.

► Don't ask questions to which you already know the answers. Don't waste respondents' time—and your own—by including items with only one realistic response. The inclusion of such items will bore respondents, needlessly increase the length of the questionnaire, and cause more work for those analyzing the data. The only exception to this rule is when you need documentation for the item in question.

► Don't include extraneous or unnecessary items. Make sure all the items on your questionnaire will yield useful data. Otherwise, you may overwhelm or unnecessarily fatigue the respondent. Check for this error by practicing tabulating and analyzing the data yourself.

► Don't put important items at the end. Items at the end of a questionnaire rarely get the same kind of attention that earlier items get. Save the least significant items for the end.

► Don't allow respondents to fall into "response sets." When a great many questionnaire items call for similar responses, respondents tend to continue responding in the same way. Item variety will counteract this tendency, as will a conscious decision to vary response formats and probable responses for consecutive items.[1]

---

[1] This list of Survey Do's and Don'ts leans heavily on an article written for TRAINING Magazine (May 1979), p. 34, by Dr. Dean Spitzer, an American educational psychologist, currently teaching at Western Australia Institute of Technology. It was abridged with permission of Lakewood Publications, Minneapolis, Minnesota (612) 333-0471. All rights reserved.

Even this extensive list of do's and don'ts doesn't cover the whole waterfront of designing, piloting, and administering a survey study. Rather than reiterate what we've gleaned from friends, colleagues, and our old college texts, we prefer to give you some references.

The single best source of tips and tricks on survey building is:

► *Questionnaires: Design and Use*
by Douglas R. Berdie and
John F. Anderson

The Scarecrow Press, Inc.
Metuchen, New Jersey, 1974

Two other good resources for survey design are:

► *Organizational Surveys: An Internal Assessment of Organizational Health*
by Randall B. Dunham and Frank J. Smith

Scott, Foresman and Company
Glenview, Illinois, 1979

    This is a fairly complete how-to for doing your own survey design, administration, and analysis. The emphasis is on job-satisfaction studies, which we designated earlier, but don't let that stop you. There is good advice here.

► *Questionnaire Design and Attitude Measurement*
by A. N. Oppenheim

Basic Books, Inc.
New York, New York, 1966

    Don't let the date fool you—this is one of *the* standard survey texts and just as relevant today as when it was written. There's more emphasis here on Likert-type scales than we think is necessary, but there's also plenty common sense and good guidance.

Meanwhile, back at XYZ, Inc. Sam has to get the act in gear and take it on the road. Figure 13-3 shows a sample of items from Sam's final survey. It represents our concept of what a useful needs survey should look like and the way it should be built to facilitate easy data collection, organization, summarization, analysis, interpretation, and presentation.

STEP 3. ORGANIZING, SUMMARIZING, ANALYZING, AND INTERPRETING RESULTS.   The first task is to pull the results together so Sam can visually inspect them. The simplest approach is to take a clean copy of the survey and enter the raw numbers, percentages, and measures of central tendency on it. Figure 13-4 is an example of what we mean.

Fig. 13-3 Excerpts from XYZ Manufacturing's *Good News* Needs Survey.

PART I: YOU AND THE UNIT YOU SUPERVISE

1. How long, *to the nearest year*, have you worked for XYZ Manufacturing? _____

2. How long, *to the nearest year*, have you been a unit supervisor at XYZ Manufacturing? _____

3. How long, *to the nearest year*, have you been supervising the unit you now supervise? _____

4. How many years, *to the nearest year*, of supervisory experience do you have; count both years as a supervisor at XYZ *and* years as a supervisor elsewhere. _____

5. How many people are you currently supervising? _____

6. How many people are you budgeted for? _____

PART II: ABOUT THE PEOPLE YOU SUPERVISE

1. How many absence days—both excused and unexcused—did your people take between January 1, 1980 and April 1, 1980? _____

2. How many *overtime hours* did your unit work between January 1, 1980 and April 1, 1980? _____

3. How many *overtime hours* was your unit budgeted to work between January 1, 1980 and April 1, 1980? _____

4. How many people did you hire for your unit between January 1, 1980 and April 1, 1980? _____

5. How many people did you *release* from your unit between January 1, 1980 and April 1, 1980? _____

6. How do you train your new people?

   a. We have a formal—away from the work station—training program. ____yes____no

   b. I break in all the new people myself. ____tes____no

   c. I have a written training routine I follow for new people. ____yes____no

   d. I have one specific person assigned to train in new people. ____yes____no

   e. I assign one of the experienced people to show new people the job. (Who that is depends on who's available.) ____yes____no

7. What is the length, *to the nearest week*, of the probationary period in your unit? _____

8. Of the people you hired between January 1, 1980 and April 1, 1980:

   a. How many people did *not* meet minimum production standards by the end of their probationary period? _____

   b. How many people did you *release* because they did not meet minimum production standards? _____

9. How many of your people fall into each of the following four performance categories?

   a. Usually exceeds 100% of standard. _____

   b. Usually meets, sometimes exceeds 100% of standard. _____

   c. Usually meets 100% of standard. _____

   d. Falls below 100% of standard more often than most. _____

10. How many of your people did you conduct performance reviews with between January 1, 1980 and April 1, 1980? _____

11. The following question asks you to tell us how you feel about the performance review process. Please be as candid as possible in your answers.

    A formal performance review should be conducted:

	Agree	Disagree
a. Once a year.	_____	_____
b. Twice a year.	_____	_____
c. Every quarter.	_____	_____
d. Whenever a person s performance seems to be slipping.	_____	_____
e. Seldom. They are a waste of time.	_____	_____

PART III: ABOUT YOUR TRAINING AND DEVELOPMENT NEEDS

1. Have you attended a formal supervisory training program within the last five years? ____yes____no

2. *If you have attended* a formal training program, where, when and under what circumstances? (For example, night school, when working for another company, in college, several years ago at XYZ, etc.) _____

   _____

   _____

3. Please rate yourself in the following supervisory skill areas. Put an "X" in the space that represents your skill level.

	I do this well	I am about average	I could use some improvement
a. Assigning work	_____	_____	_____
b. Keeping workflow going	_____	_____	_____
c. Telling employees how they're doing day to day	_____	_____	_____
d. Controlling absences	_____	_____	_____
e. Conducting performance reviews	_____	_____	_____
f. Training new employees	_____	_____	_____
g. Disciplining employees	_____	_____	_____
h. Controlling line machine downtime	_____	_____	_____
i. Getting people to perform at standard	_____	_____	_____
j. Making employees understand what I want them to do	_____	_____	_____

Fig. 13-4   Excerpts from XYZ Manufacturing's *Good News* Needs Survey.

PART I: YOU AND THE UNIT YOU SUPERVISE

	Mean	Median	Mode	SD
1. How long, *to the nearest year*, have you worked for XYZ Manufacturing?	9	10	8	1.5
2. How long, *to the nearest year*, have you been a unit supervisor at XYZ Manufacturing?	3	4	4	2
3. How long, *to the nearest year*, have you been supervising the unit you now supervise?	2	4	3	1
4. How many years, *to the nearest year*, of supervisory experience do you have; count both years as a supervisor at XYZ *and* years as a supervisor elsewhere.	2	4	3	1
5. How many people are you currently supervising?	23	19	21	12
6. How many people are you budgeted for?	28	28	25	15

PART II: ABOUT THE PEOPLE YOU SUPERVISE

	Totals		Median	Mode	SD
1. How many absence days—both excused and unexcused—did your people take between January 1, 1980 and April 1, 1980?	920	17	19	18	2.5
2. How many *overtime hours* did your unit work between January 1, 1980 and April 1, 1980?	170 10,370		150	160	8.2
3. How many *overtime hours* was your unit budgeted to work between January 1, 1980 and April 1, 1980?	4,880	80	80	80	—
4. How many people did you hire for your unit between January 1, 1980 and April 1, 1980?	_____				
5. How many people did you *release* from your unit between January 1, 1980 and April 1, 1980?	_____				
6. How do you train your new people?					

b. Usually meets. sometimes exceeds 100% of standard.   _____

c. Usually meets 100% of standard.   _____

d. Falls below 100% of standard more often than most.   _____

10. How many of your people did you conduct performance reviews with between January 1, 1980 and April 1, 1980?   _____

11. The following question asks you to tell us how you feel about the performance review process. Please be as candid as possible in your answers.

A formal performance review should be conducted:

	Agree	Disagree
a. Once a year.	_____	_____
b. Twice a year.	_____	_____
c. Every quarter.	_____	_____
d. Whenever a person s performance seems to be slipping.	_____	_____
e. Seldom. They are a waste of time.	_____	_____

PART III: ABOUT YOUR TRAINING AND DEVELOPMENT NEEDS

1. Have you attended a formal supervisory training program within the last five years?   ____yes____no

2. *If you have attended* a formal training program, where, when and under what circumstances? (For example, night school, when working for another company, in college, several years ago at XYZ, etc.) _____

_____

The next task is to start moving the numbers about, looking for interesting peculiarities. Even the demographic or "Who are these people anyway?" information can be informative. Take a look at Fig. 13-5, a table of demographic data Sam plucked off the survey.

Though demographic data are usually used to cross-tab or make comparisons of the "supervisors with large departments have more turnover than supervisors with small departments" sort, the demographics themselves tell some interesting tales—*if* Sam knows how to look at numbers.

Fig. 13-5 Part I. Demographics—Training Needs Survey
E and P Supervisors.

	Mean	Median	Mode	Standard Deviation
1. Years with XYZ	9	10	8	1.5
2. Years as supervisor	3	4	4	2
3. Years this unit	2	4	3	1
4. Years sup. total	2	4	3	1
5. No. of people supervised	26	19	21	12
6. No. of people budgeted	28	11	25	15

For instance, a glance at Fig. 13-5 reveals at least three significant findings.

1. On the average, most departments are *under* their budgeted manpower. They may be understaffed for the production demands. (Item 6 is larger than item 5.)

2. The standard deviations for items 5 and 6 are large numbers. A standard deviation equal to or greater than 25 percent of the mean is a large standard deviation. This means that only some units are understaffed. It also suggests Sam may want to look closely at differences in turnover, absences, and so on between understaffed and fully staffed department.

3. The mean, median, and mode calculations for questions 1 through 4 aren't terribly different, so the skew of the numbers is probably slight. But, the mean, median and mode of item number 5 are different enough to merit special attention. Some may want to graph the data from items 5 and 6 to see just how skewed the numbers are.

Notice that these demographics say nothing about age, race, sex, eye color, or tongue length. Sam is doing a training-needs analysis of first-line supervisors, not an EEOC inventory or a psychological study. A dime will get you a dollar, though, that every other time you or Sam start doing a survey study, some joker will suggest, "Hey, why don't *we* ask some questions about how they feel about left-handed Pazeneian Pirates?" Best bet is to cut the jokers from the deck. If the joker is your boss, just try to minimize the amount of garbage he or she insists on stuffing into your study. Every bit of garbage that goes into a survey increases the likelihood of garbage outcomes, and you'll end up holding the garbage bag every time.

Figures 13-6 and 13-7 give you an idea of how rich Sam's data really are. All this information comes from five items in Part II of the survey.

Figure 13-6 shows overall absence data and an overview of department-by-department performance. Units with exceptionally high absence records, unit 2, and units with exceptionally low absences, unit 61, can be separated out and given special attention in the survey analysis. It's called shrinking the problem to a size you can get your arms around. By looking at the extremes of absence rate, you may see critical differences emerge.

Fig. 13-6 Absence Analysis—From Part II Items.

Unit Code	Absence Days	Number of Employees	Absences per Employee
01	16	17	0.94
02	30	12	2.50
03	14	11	1.27
|	|	|	|
60	18	25	0.72
61	8	22	0.36
61	920	1,037	

Mean no. of employees/unit = 17.00
Mean no. of absences/unit = 15.10
Mean no. of absences/emp. = 0.89

Fig. 13-7 Overtime Analysis—From Part II.

Unit Code	O.T. Worked	O.T. Budget	% of Budget
1	80	85	94
2	120	70	171
3	300	100	300
|	|	|	|
60	95	80	119
61	70	60	117
61	10,370 hrs.	4,880	212.5

Mean O.T. budget/unit = 80 hrs.
Mean O.T. worked/unit = 170 hrs.
Mean O.T. worked/person = 10 hrs.
Mean O.T. work/person/mo. = 3.33 hrs.

Figure 13-7 shows the overtime worked compared to planned or budgeted overtime. While it's obvious that overbudget overtime is out of hand for many departments, there are important differences by department. Unit 3 is much higher in overtime than are units 1 and 61. It's important to find out why and how *else* these units differ. Unit 3, for instance, is also one of the highest absence-rate departments. If unit 3 also turns out to have high turnover, we know we should examine it closely for critical differences in environment, management, and other factors that may help account for the divisional performance problems.

Figure 13-8 shows that all departments tend to be under-staffed by one person, which may account for the overtime glut in Fig. 13-7. In addition, some—but not all—units have gone through a lot of people, which explains more about the overtime problem. And as the disparity in central tendency suggests, some departments are contributing more than their fair share to the churn.

We won't go any further with the analysis of Part II results, but it is obvious that Sam's survey, simple and straightforward as it is, has garnered some important information. And Sam's analysis, simple as it may seem, is developing some subtle implications about the real locus and nature of the problems and their causes.

The table in Fig. 13-9 suggests that most supervisors have had no formal training in supervisory techniques; those who have had some training received it in a variety of places, so a uniform supervisory approach is doubtful.

In addition, many supervisors have identified (1) getting people to perform at standard, (2) telling employees how they are doing day to day, and (3) controlling absences as areas where they need improvement. Sam originally hypothesized that supervisors were weak in these areas.

Fig. 13-8 Turnover Analysis—From Part II.

Unit	No. of Employees	No. of Employees Budgeted	Percent of Budget	No. Hired This Quarter
1	17	17	100	1
2	12	16	75	3
3	11	16	65	9
|	|	|	|	|
60	25	27	93	2
61	22	25	88	5
61	1,037	1,098	94	488

No. of employees/unit = 17
Mean of budgeted employees/unit = 18

No. of employees hired this quarter:
Mean = 8 Median = 2 Mode = 2

Fig. 13–9 Self-Report of Training Needs—Part III.

		Yes	No
1.	Have you attended a formal supervisory training program in the last five years?	37%	63%
2.	Circumstances		
	▶ Several years ago at XYZ Co.	28%	
	▶ Other company	11%	
	▶ Night school	18%	
	▶ College	20%	
	▶ Service	13%	
	▶ Other (single related courses, books)	10%	
		100%	

	3. Behavior	Do Well	Average	Need Improvement
a.	Assign work	12 (20%)	38 (62%)	11 (18%)
b.	Keep work flowing	23 (38%)	32 (52%)	6 (10%)
c.	Day-to-day feedback	7 (11%)	29 (48%)	25 (41%)
d.	Absence control	13 (21%)	28 (46%)	20 (33%)
i.	Maintain performance standards	13 (21%)	18 (29%)	30 (49%)
j.	Make employees understand	28 (46%)	22 (36%)	11 (18%)

Though we haven't looked at all the responses to all the questions in the survey, you should be getting a pretty good feel for our look-and-think approach to survey-data analysis.

CROSS-TABS

There's only one other operation you must be able to perform to do a full survey-centered needs analysis. That operation is referred to as *cross-tabs*. Very simply, a cross-tabs instruction to a computer tells the computer to make a table out of the answers to two or more questions. To do that, the survey information has to be cut into categories. And that, of course, is why surveys are often designed in a "check one of the following" format.

But that system makes more assumptions than we trainers need to deal with. Instead, you can do your own cross-tabs by sorting the questionnaires into piles and making your own table. Figure 13-10 is a sample of two handmade cross-tabs Sam performed on the survey data.

Fig. 13–10

	Cross-Tab A		
	Years of Supervisory Experience vs.		
	Number of "Need Improvement" Areas		
Experience	*No./* *Percent*	*Items* *Checked*	*Items/* *Person*
4 years or less	21 (34%)	39 (44%)	1.86
More than 4 years	40 (66%)	49 (56%)	1.23
Totals	61 (100%)	88 (100%)	

	Cross-Tab B				
	Years of Supervisory Experience vs.				
	Unit Absence Rate				
Experience	*No./* *Percent*	*No. of* *Absences*	*No. of* *Employees*	*Employees/* *Supervision*	*Absences/* *Employee*
4 years or less	21 (34%)	462	326	15.5	1.86
More than 4 years	40 (66%)	458	711	17.7	0.64
Totals	61 (100%)	920	1037		

Figures 13-3 through 13-10 are reprinted with permission from the September 1980 issue of TRAINING, the magazine of Human Resources Development © 1980, Lakewood Publications, Minneapolis, Minnesota. All rights reserved.

Cross-tab A addresses the question "Do less experienced supervisors perceive that they have more need-for-improvement performance areas than do other supervisors?" The table tells us quite a bit. First, about one-third of the supervisors fall into Sam's less-experienced (four years or less) category. Secondly, the less-experienced supervisors accounted for a slightly greater proportion (44 percent) of needs-improvement areas than we would expect from their relative proposition in the population (34 percent). Sam can even conclude that they *do* tend to say the "need improvement" in some areas by roughly 50 percent (1.86 ÷ 1.23).

So the answer to the original question is an unequivocal "somewhat." Three more flamboyant findings come from the cross-tab B in Fig. 13-10.

1. Supervisors with less than four years experience tend to supervise somewhat smaller departments than do more experienced supervisors. No big deal, but interesting.

2. Supervisors with less experience account for a greater proportion of absences (50 percent) than you would expect, based on their proportion in the population of supervisors (34 percent).

3. And here's a big "aha!" Absences per employee are 290 percent higher in departments run by less experienced supervisors (1.86 ÷ 0.64).

This sample cross-tab gives you something to dig into. Fifty percent of the absences came from 31 percent of the employees and 34 percent of the departments. And these latter departments are run by people with less than four years supervisory experience. Question: What are the two-thirds doing that the one-third isn't? What are the managers of the one-third doing about their supervisors' absence rates?

Because Sam wondered if the amount of supervisory experience had anything to do with the division's problems, he decided to look at the survey results in pieces and he was encouraged to do that wondering because he noticed that the standard deviation for the question "How many total years of supervisory experience do you have?" was rather large.

We can not leave Sam and XYZ, Inc. You get the picture, we're sure.

BOTTOM LINE:
OBSERVATION, IMAGINATION, AND A POCKET CALCULATOR

We've been trying to make two points:

► A well-designed survey gives you good information.
► A well-designed survey can be analyzed without a computer or a Ph.D. in statistics.

These are the principles we suggest you consider. Look at the information your respondents supplied—really look at it, table it, play with it, ask questions, and look for hints as to where the important relationships are hiding. Use your imagination and intuition. If you've been around more than a week or two, you've probably developed a genuine gut feel or clinical sensitivity to the problems of your organization. Use that gut feel to guide your analysis. And last but not least, take your pocket calculator and do some adding, subtracting, multiplying, and dividing of raw numbers.

We won't lie to you. Analyzing survey results is highly clerical and detailed, requires immense concentration, is boring as hell, and is almost impossible to delegate. But it is definitely "bread upon the waters" work as well: that little bit of pain-in-the-neck effort that *winners* invest up front reaps big results at the bottom line.

A survey, according to Webster, is a "careful examination for some specific purpose." Organizational surveys are a reasonable way to tap attitudes, opinions, perceptions, reactions to specific events, and information on developmental needs. Survey information can help you understand organizational problems, garner information on training needs, and even gain insight into tasks to include in training. Surveys say, "We care, and we want to know what you think and what you want."

SECTION **V** ODDS AND ENDS

As we reached the end of our sorting and sifting task, we found that we had some very useful FTO techniques left over; that is, techniques that do not fit within the observational, discussion, or instrumental categories. However, these are highly useful and usable techniques.

Chapter 14, *Looking at Performance Information,* is primarily a tribute to Dr. Thomas Gilbert, who has taught us all some very good lessons in looking at performance data. We have time and again found valuable performance problem data just lying around in file folders and in printouts just waiting to be analyzed by a sharp-eyed trainer. Gilbert's wise words and our cases may convince you that the best data is often the data you already have at your disposal.

Chapter 15, *Fault Tree Analysis,* is a common engineering and computer systems troubleshooting technique that is finding a home in our human factors arena. We're still learning its intricacies, but, thanks to Dr. Dean Spitzer, we've been convinced that it will eventually become one of our most used approaches to thinking our way through performance problems.

Chapter 16, *Pyramid Power,* is an explanation of how we use Robert Gagne's hierarchy of learning to analyze subject matter and turn it into learning materials. There are other taxonomies and learning hierarchies now, but Gagne's was first, and remains the best developed.

CHAPTER 14 LOOKING AT PERFORMANCE INFORMATION: READING THE OTHER PERSON'S WATCH

When it comes to analyzing performance problems, there's more than a grain of truth in the old barb: "a consultant is someone who borrows your watch and then tells you what time it is." Very often the people closest to the problem can't see the signs an outsider can see. No stupidity implied, just the invisibility of the everyday, the overfamiliar. Sometimes just digging in a "wastebasket" or two can turn up important performance-problem clues that people who see them daily tend to overlook. The client's computer or accounting files or the walls of the supervisor's work station can provide rich data for the study of existing productivity and performance records.

By analyzing the bottom-line figures on productivity, turnover, complaints, absences, wastes, cost, and other regularly recorded measures of company results, you can significantly advance your study of a performance problem. These performance records do not immediately focus on the behaviors that make up high performance. Rather, they focus on the bottom-line *results* of behaviors. For example, they focus on revenue generated rather than on techniques used for generating revenue. Or they focus on levels of scrap rather than on employee behaviors that produce scrap. But properly recast and examined, they can be extremely illuminating.

Managers typically do not understand the analytical value of the bottom-line information that they so earnestly gather. That's because they gather the records for managerial purposes, not for performance-problem analyses. Among their data aims are:

1. Obtaining an overview of the organization's status. To do so, they total the results of various performers so they can say: "This year we produced so many units." Then they compare these totaled results to previous totals in order to determine a gain, a loss, or a trend. This information is further compared to determine the needs of the organization and to make decisions about budgets, manpower, and additional financing, among other things.

2. Paying incentives. In this case, management looks at the results of the individual performers, compares them to the standard and awards bonuses and merit increases accordingly.

3. Conducting individual performance reviews. Again, management looks at the results of the work of individual performers and compares them to a standard. Based on their findings, they make decisions about an individual's placement and training and motivation needs.

As investigators of performance problems, we tend to look at these same records from a different perspective. We're looking for clues as to how performance improvement among certain *groups* of employees will have a maximum impact on the bottom-line results. Managers concentrate on totals and on individuals; we concentrate on groups of individuals in between these two extremes.

NEEDS ANALYSIS

For our purposes, performance records can be used initially to answer the question: "Is there a performance problem?" Or, "Are there groups of persons in this organization whose performance needs improvement?" As we said earlier, these are the questions the investigator should answer *before* launching a lengthy and expensive study of what the performance is and how performance might be improved.

According to Thomas Gilbert, author of *Human Competence,* "We have no need to measure behavior until we have measured accomplishments . . . There can be no purpose in measuring deficiencies in rifle handling until we have established deficiencies in hitting the target." Gilbert, one of the field's most original thinkers, has made many valuable contributions to the theory and practice of performance analysis. His concept of PIP, or "Potential for Improving Performance," is extremely useful in needs-analysis work and in looking for the human-factors indicators in performance data. Gilbert believes we get the most mileage out of an organization's performance records by "comparing the very best instance of that performance with what is typical." A need is revealed when we discover a significant difference between the average performer and the high performer or "exemplar" who proves that a high level of performance is, indeed, achievable.

This may seem elementary until we realize that most managers do not do this. They tend to assume that the results of the average performer's work are the standard and that the results of the exemplar's work are exceptional. In many workplaces, it is typical to assume that the high achiever is some kind of hyperactive eccentric, is lucky, or possesses a unique talent. Gilbert's assumption, however, is that the exemplar is not a fluke, and is simply one of the high-performing "good guys" we have been talking about. The exemplar establishes an ideal that demonstrates a *possible* standard of performance, and raises the question: "What if everyone could perform at that level?"

Let's accept that assumption while we explain the concept of PIP. Then we will consider its application under less optimistic assumptions. The PIP is simply a measure of opportunity. It is a ratio of exemplary performance to typical performance that can be expressed mathematically as:

$$PIP = \frac{Exemplary\ performance}{Typical\ performance}$$

Let's say, for example, that ten performers exhibit the following production results:

Benson	131
Boyd	117
Collins	91
Everson	139
Halstead	192
Lerner	125
Owens	110
Santoro	125
Taylor	133
Watson	106
Total	= 1,269 (126.9 average)

By adding everyone's results (over the same time period), we get a total of 1,269 units. We also observe that Halstead is the highest or exemplary performer with 192 units. We plug this information into the PIP formula this way:

$$PIP = \frac{192}{126.9} = 1.51$$

By dividing the highest performance (192) by the average performance (126.9), we get a PIP of 1.51. This means that if *everyone* were to perform at Halstead's level, the organization would realize a performance improvement one and a half times what it is getting now. Or, in other words, it is *possible* to improve performance by as much as 50%.

Clearly, this indicates a pretty strong *need* for improving performance. The beauty of the PIP method for conducting a production-data needs analysis is that it is extremely fast and simple. There's no need for an extensive survey, a long series of interviews, or exhaustive travel to observe in a dozen locations. You simply walk into the manager's or accountant's office, spend an hour or so learning how to read their computer printouts or company records, and then put in another hour or two with a hand calculator to the exemplar and the averages. The hard part of this kind of study is not *doing* it; the hardest part is getting access to the records in the first place.

There are some ways to expedite your study. It's usually a good idea to sit with someone who can interpret the readouts for you. To be sure you are comparing apples to apples, you may need some help determining which sets of figures are relevant for your purposes. You don't have to add all the numbers to get an average. Random selections will do, at least for a first cut. But you *must* find the highest performer. Also it's a good idea to get a list of the several highest performers—the top ten for example. Then ask your friendly assisting manager to tell you about these people. It could be that the numerically highest performer is exceptional in some other way (such as being the president or having an unusual IQ). Settle on an exemplar who is in *every* other respect like the average performer.

Finally, before you go through all the data, ask management if they really know what you're looking for. Maybe they are aware of who is average and who is the exemplar, but they probably have never made the PIP comparison.

If you are something of a cynic and you don't put much credence in the assumption that average mortals can improve their performance to the level of the exemplar, there are other ways to compute the PIP from performance records. The "counter-exemplar" method is one. This method does *not* identify the absolute performance bungler and compare him to the average. There is little to be gained from picking on one person like this, even if you could make a positive exemplar out of him or her. No, the counter-exemplar method consists of computing the PIP of a low-performing *segment* of the population, such as the lowest 10 or 20 percent, and comparing it to the average. For example, we found in one sales organization that 20 percent of the sales force was producing only $75,000 in sales per year versus an overall average of $120,000 per year. This amounted to a PIP of 1.6 for that population.

$$\text{PIP} = \frac{\$120,000}{75,000} = 1.6$$

Another variation is to compare the averages of high and low subgroups, for example, the average of the bottom 50 percent versus the average of the top 50 percent. In the same sales force study, we came up with a PIP of 2.6 when we compared the bottom 20 percent with the top 20 percent, which was producing an average of $197,000 per annum.

$$\text{PIP} = \frac{\$197,000}{75,000} = 2.6$$

ASSESSING THE VALUE OF AN INTERVENTION

The second use we can make of information taken from performance records is in assessing the *economic* value of the interventions we might make to improve the performance of the lower-performing group. After all, the PIP is a measure of potential or opportunity. It can tell us in dollars and cents how much the performance improvement will be worth. This is done simply by multiplying the PIP ratio by the economic value of the performance of the average performer (in the exemplar method) or the lower-performing group (in the nonexemplar method).

Let's go back to our example of ten performers who produced 1,269 units among them. Remember that we came up with a PIP of 1.51 with Halstead as the exemplar? Let's say that the units sell for $13 each. At 1,269 units a month, the current month's production by the ten people totals $16,497. The PIP tells us that if everyone produced at Halstead's rate, the company would produce 1,916 units (1269 × 1.51). Assuming all units could be sold for $13, sales would amount to $24,910 per month—or an additional $8,413. In other words, the potential economic value of making an intervention that might bring everyone's performance up to Halstead's is $8,413 per month.

In our example of the sales force with a low-performing 20 percent, we had a PIP of 1.6 compared with the average. Multiplying the low performers' $75,000 by 1.6 would increase the average sales figure to $120,000 per year—or an additional $45,000. We further calculated the economic benefit to the company by multiplying $45,000 by the number of people involved. This particular company had a sales force of 3,000 persons; the 20 percent involved amounted to 600 persons (20 percent of 3,000). Thus, the economic potential for intervening and improving the production of the 600 low performers and bringing them just up to the average was $27 million!

When you're armed with figures like these, it's not difficult to justify an intervention based on performance-record data. Nor is it difficult to cost-justify the additional research that should be performed to determine the exact reason for the performance differential.

But before you go rushing off with a green pencil to calculate all the dollars you can save for your in-house clients, remember that we are talking about a *potential*—that is, the maximum possible that could be achieved by bringing the lower-performing group up to the standard of the higher-performing group. This ideal level of improvement is rarely achieved, and experience has taught that a PIP of less than 1.5 is rarely worth the effort. This is the figure that Gilbert uses, and we have found out—the hard way—that he didn't just pluck it out of the air.

This does not mean that having a PIP of 1.5 + is the only rationale for justifying an intervention. There are fields of interest and areas of performance where using ROI figures to justify change would be ludicrous. Would you go to a doctor if you knew his or her technical PIP was greater than zero? There are many ways to make a judgment about the value of instituting changes in an organization. For example, in a fast-moving, rapidly growing company the sheer will of management or the requirements of a changing technology may demand performance changes—and training and development activities. But when your performance records are *valid criteria* for making a go/no go decision, 1.5 is a good standard to work with.

IDENTIFYING HIGH AND LOW PERFORMERS

The third use of performance records is to identify high and low performers for subsequent studies. This is a critical use of the records. Whether or not we use one of Gilbert's PIP methods to assess the need and/or value of an intervention, we must use these records as an anchor for the decisions we make about whom to call high and whom to call low when stratifying the population. Very often, we won't have access to a company's performance records; nor will we have the opportunity to select participants for the study. Too often the persons responsible for deciding who is "high" and who is "low" will name individuals who fit their own criteria, which may be contaminated by other issues. The client who has *carte blanche* to nominate people for us to study may think this way: "Send 'em to D.C. to work with Bert. That old S.O.B. can sell the pants off anybody. Don't know how he does it, but by golly he'll give 'em an earful." As we said in the chapter on surveys, randomization is critical. We need a random sample of high performers and a random sample of low performers to work with and study.

To avoid this problem, insist that the study be *objective*. On that basis, the high and low performers must be identified against an indisputable, agreed-upon set of performance criteria. Whenever possible, make the criterion a performance number from already existing performance records. Remember, these are the numbers people are currently being rewarded, chastised, fired, reviewed, and promoted for. They are a vital part of the system and a key to understanding. Selection of the actual number above which one is considered a high performer and below which one is considered a low performer must be made by the client's management. This is one of those examples of Tactic #5 from Chapter 2: "Let management make management decisions." If you have access to the records yourself, you can make some suggestions about what the numbers should be. In any case, insist on numerical criteria that can be verified in existing performance records by someone who has access to them.

When suggesting cut-off numbers for stratifying high and low performers, include a "buffer" between the cut-off points of the high and low. For example, when we conducted field studies on the sales force, we could have picked a number like $100,000 per year as a cut-off between the $75,000 average lower group and the $120,000 higher group. The trouble with this is that you get some people near the border who could be in either group. To avoid this kind of border dispute in our study, we required a high performer to be generating at least $110,000 per year and a low performer generating less than $90,000.

If that makes your people crazy, go with three groups: highs, lows, and middles, but concentrate your analysis time and money on the highs and lows. That's where you'll find most obvious contrasts. Simply use the middles as a double check. Nine times out of ten, middles look like an amalgam of highs and lows, a cross-breed. If they don't, there may be important demographic differences other than gross sales or number of widgets produced. Check the middles' "stats" against the highs and lows immediately. But unless you find something interesting there—for instance, an unusual age, sex, education, or previous employment profile—just leave the puzzle alone. To do otherwise, can be diverting, expensive, and at cross-purposes with your performance-problem study.

MAKING HYPOTHESES ABOUT WHAT THE PERFORMANCE PROBLEM IS

Performance records are constructed out of individual and local time sheets and production reports. They can also contain interesting demographic data. The wealth of data available from performance records can be analyzed to determine patterns that may give clues to the cause(s) of the performance problems. The key question to ask when you have access to these sorts of records is: "What are the common denominators of the high performers and how do they differ from the common denominators of the low performers?"

The production records of one sales force, for example, showed sales totals as well as subtotal figures for several product lines. When we first looked at the data, it seemed that the higher-performing group had a better product mix (sales in each product line) than the lower-performing group. This would have led to the conclusion that trainees should be drilled in selling across the whole product line. But, on further investigation, we noticed that experience also made a difference. The higher-performing experienced salesperson was selling the whole product line. His low-performing, less-experienced counterpart tended to sell fewer lines. On the other hand, the higher-performing new person was concentrating on one or two lines, contrary to company desire. And the low-performing new person, apparently trying to do what was expected and sell all product lines, had sales in all of the product lines, but the numbers in each were low. This told us that it might be appropriate to argue that new people first should be taught how to sell just one or two products, and then gradually be taught more about the other product lines. This was the hypothesis we formed from looking at the production data and that we later tested by interviews in the field and surveys.

There are several useful categories you can almost always look for in analyzing performance records this way. One of these is *experience* in the job. If performance increases with experience, its pretty clear that the problem falls in the training area; that is, how to speed up the acquisition of the knowledge and skill needed to do the job at higher performance levels. If low performers level off or even decrease with experience, that's a tip-off to some kind of nontraining issue, such as a lack of feedback or incentive; or perhaps the existence of a high-stress situation. In the first case, you want to build your hypotheses around training; in the second case, around other issues.

In one case, we found that salespeople averaged very low production volumes in the first two years of their employment. Turnover was also high during that period. Yet after two years of experience, their production was very good. This was a good indicator of a training need. The data were even more convincing when we noticed that some of the newer people were performing at very high levels after only four to six months on the job. This told us they might know or somehow be learning something that the current training was not giving to the others. This hypothesis indicated a need for some kind of discussion-type research in which we would ask people fairly open-ended questions about how the training they received had helped them. To finish the story and show you how bloody smart a little elbow grease can make you look, we discovered that the high performers were very critical of the training they received and had modified it for themselves in some way. In one branch, new trainees had joined forces to write an applications algorithm to overcome the confusion they felt when they left training. Low performers, on the other hand, praised the training program, saying that they wished they were better able to put it into practice.

Another interesting factor to look for is the *location* of high and low performers. "Old Bert" in D.C. may have a very special captive market sub-segment no one else has access to; he may simply be the right person in the right place at the right time and not a useful exemplar at all. This is usually pretty easy data to find, since most records are kept by region, district, plant, or work station. There are two patterns to look for here. If the high and low performers tend to show up only in certain groups, the problem may lie more with the managers than with the actual performers. On the other hand, if the high and low performers are distributed equally throughout the organization, the problem probably lies with the individuals. In the first case, you should test hypotheses concerning managerial practices; in the second case, try hypotheses about lack of knowledge and skill among the employees.

This is also where PIP information can be of great value. Thomas Gilbert presents the following case (Fig. 14-1) in *Human Competence*.

DETERMINING THE MOST OPPORTUNE LOCUS FOR AN INTERVENTION

This final use of performance records is related to the use of records for hypothesis making. If the performance records show greater variations among management groups than among individuals within management groups, we should consider shifting the focus of the whole study and our intervention effort to the managers.

Fig. 14-1*   A PIP Example.

Supervisor A		*Supervisor B*		*Supervisor C*	
Clerk	*U/hr*	*Clerk*	*U/hr*	*Clerk*	*U/hr*
1	65	11	62	21	141
2	65	12	61	22	137
3	63	13	61	23	137
4	60	14	60	24	134
5	60	15	59	25	130
6	58	16	50	26	130
7	56	17	50	27	126
8	54	18	50	28	121
9	51	19	45	29	120
10	48	20	40	30	119
Average	58.0	Average	53.8	Average	129.5

The average for all 30 clerks is a productivity of 80.4 units per hour. The *clerical* PIP is then (assuming quality and costs are constant):

$$\text{PIP Clerk} = \frac{141}{80.4} = 1.75$$

This is an appreciable PIP.

Of much greater significance, however, is the supervisory PIP (calculated here by taking the average of all groups *except*[2] the highest):

$$\text{PIP Super.} = \frac{129.5}{55.9} = 2.32$$

Clearly, the difference between ordinary supervisors and the exemplar is much more significant than that between the ordinary clerks and the exemplary clerk. The largest clerical PIP *within* a group is 1.15. This tells us immediately that what we should do to improve clerical performance is look first to the supervisors. Two of the supervisors are relatively incompetent. But Supervisor C is doing something right, and we should find out what it is.

*From *Human Competence: On Engineering Worthy Performance,* by Tom Gilbert. Copyright 1978 by McGraw-Hill, New York. Used with permission of the McGraw-Hill Book Company.

This can mean getting beyond the level of first-line supervisor. The trick is to look at the data in strategic terms. What about the performance differences among plants, districts, regions, or even national groups? What about the differences among employees trained in one school or another or by one method or another? As Gilbert puts it, "It makes the most sense to begin the program of improvement at the highest level where a significant PIP exists."

In one sales organization, we found the following demographic anomaly:

	Service with Company	Years in Sales	Mean Sales Last Year	Range of Sales	Model Sales	Median Sales	Standard Deviation	Number of People
A.	4 years or less	10+ yrs.	$60,000	$ 0–200K	$40,000	$75,000	$40,000	52
B.	9 years or more	10+ yrs.	$112,000	$30–500K	$100,000	$96,000	$60,000	30

Apparently, five years prior to our study, a decision was made to bring some "fresh blood" into the sales force. A senior officer was worried that the sales force was "too inbred," an understandable concern. So he sent a mandate and hired a recruiting firm to help design a program for selecting experienced salespeople, not an appropriate response. Had the worried warrior taken an experimental approach, he wouldn't have ended up with the problem indicated in our chart. The performance data and some simple question-asking revealed what might be a strategically caused, rather than a training-and-development performance problem. In this case, a T&D solution would have been a bandaid for a broken leg.

On the other hand, you have to remember that you can't teach the world to sing in one easy lesson. You may not be in a position to say, "The real problem around here is top management." Even if it is, you may have to get there by degrees, starting first at the level where you are able to operate.

In summary, you can get a wealth of useful information from the "waste-basket" of performance records. These records tell you what results the organization is getting from the performance in question. Some rapid calculations via the PIP technique can tell you whether a change in performance is needed. A PIP of more than 1.5 means that a high payoff will result by improving the performance of the target group.

Performance records are absolutely essential in tying your selection of high and low performers to verifiable, objective criteria. Furthermore, the records can provide useful insights into what may be causing the performance problems, new people who need training, older people who need motivation, or all people who need better management.

CHAPTER 15 FAULT TREE ANALYSIS: MAKING PROGRESS WORKING BACKWARDS

Not too long ago we thought Fault Tree Analysis was something only a botanist might use. But thanks to Dr. Dean Spitzer of Western Australia Institute of Technology, we now know that FTA is a time honored method of analyzing breakdowns in the function of diode and other solid-state and digital equipment. Spitzer found that the Fault Tree Analysis process can be used to figure out human performance problems. What follows is Spitzer's explanation of Fault Tree Analysis for trainers, as it appeared in the February 1980 issue of *Training* Magazine.

Fault Tree Analysis, or FTA, is a systems safety engineering technology that can be used effectively in organizational and human resources development. Originally developed by Bell Laboratories scientists and refined by Boeing Company engineers, Fault Tree Analysis was first used to identify potential causes of failure in the Minuteman Missle launch system. For many years, FTA has been a significant tool for troubleshooting hardware systems of all types and determining where critical faults might exist. FTA has frequently resulted in the redesign of unsafe systems or the development of back-up mechanisms. It's not difficult to imagine the potential use of such a technology in examining possible causes of failure in organizations.

Fault Tree Analysis is so named because the process results in the construction of a tree-like logic diagram. This diagram graphically displays the complex interrelationships among events that ultimately can lead to system failure. One reason FTA is so powerful is that it helps managers understand the complexity of the organizations they manage, recognizing that relatively insignificant events at a low level of organizational activity can, through a complex chain of events, lead to more general and more serious failures at higher levels. This is the essential rationale behind the FTA technique.

Fault Tree Analysis is the reverse of usual task analysis approaches, which analyze systems in terms of success. FTA analyzes systems in terms of failure. There is some evidence that this approach represents a considerable advance, particularly psychologically. Apparently it's easier for people to undertake a comprehensive analysis in terms of failure than it is for them to analyze in terms of success. Managers who could not generate a task analysis from a vantage point of success often have no trouble doing so in terms of failure. In addition, agreement among analysts is easier to obtain in failure analyses than in success analyses. More research is needed to explain these observed phenomena.

Fault Tree Analysis begins with a clear mission statement for the organization or part of the organization to be analyzed. Based on this mission statement, an *undesirable event* is postulated, usually the failure of the mission (or some part of the mission). This undesirable event (or UE) is the object of the subsequent analysis. From this point, the analysis proceeds downward, in a tree-like fashion, at each level determining "the most probable and immediate causes of the higher level failure."

USING LOGIC CONCEPTS

One of the most critical features of Fault Tree Analysis is the use of *logic gates* to represent the relationship between failure events. Two types of logic gates are typically used in FTA, the *AND gate* and the *OR gate*. The AND gate, depicted in Figure 1, describes a situation in which each of the contributory failure events must occur in order for the more general event to happen. In other words, events B and C must occur together before event A will result. Such situations tend to contain a natural element of safety, since the probability of both contributory failure events occurring at the same time is remote.

The OR gate, depicted in Figure 2, describes a situation in which the more general failure event will occur if only one of the contributory failure events occurs at the same time. That is, failure event A will occur if either contributory event B or contributory event C occurs. This situation is characteristic of unsafe systems. Research has shown that organizational systems tend to have a preponderance of OR gate relationships among potential failure events. This makes Fault Tree Analysis that much more relevant to organizational analysis and problem solving.

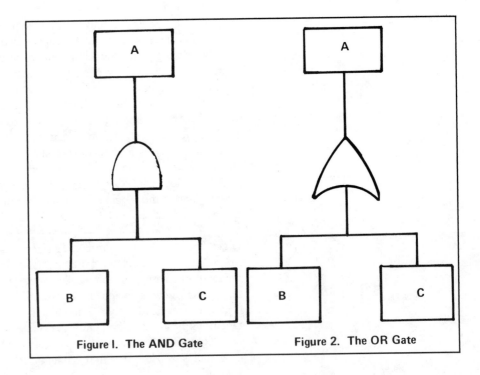

Figure I. The AND Gate   Figure 2. The OR Gate

USING LOGIC GATES

The use of logic concepts in Fault Tree Analysis permits the quantification of the Fault Tree through the use of Bayesian probabilities and Boolean algebra. More about this shortly. A number of other symbolic notations—the event symbols—are also important. *Rectangles* symbolize events that result from the combination of more specific (lower-level) failure events through a logic gate. *Circles* symbolize a basic failure event that does not require further development in the Fault Tree. *Rhombuses* symbolize events that are not developed further in the tree due to a lack of information or resources. And *houses* symbolize events that occur normally within the system but can contribute to a more general failure when linked to another failure event. These symbols, together with the logic gates, make up the language of Fault Tree Analysis. An illustrative Fault Tree Diagram is presented in Figure 3.

An interpretation of the tree depicted in Figure 3 might read as follows:

Event A can be caused by the occurrence of failure event B *or* failure event C. Failure event B can result from the occurrence of failure event D *or* failure event E. Failure event C will only occur as a result of the joint failure of failure event F *and* normal event G. Event E will result from the joint occurrence of failure event H, failure event J *and* normal event I.

Although this explanation might seem strange and convoluted at first reading, to the experienced Fault Tree Analyst such an explanation makes con-

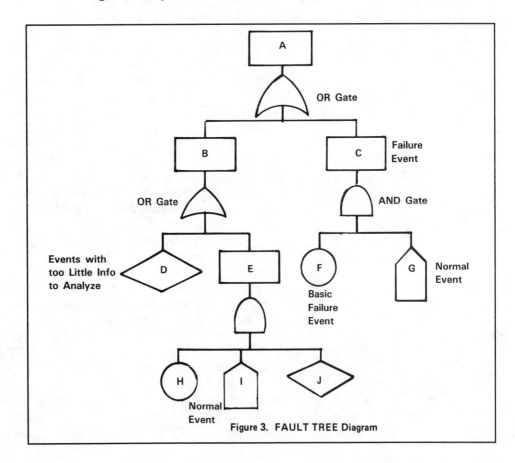

Figure 3. FAULT TREE Diagram

siderable sense. Like any new language the symbolic language of FTA takes time and practice to learn. The language and syntax of Fault Tree Analysis provide the real potency of the tool.

The first step in Fault Tree Analysis is the development of the logic diagram; this is called "qualitative analysis." The Fault Tree Analyst must make good use of key people within the organization to identify failure events and recognize their relationships. Successful qualitative analysis depends on the effective collection and utilization of both objective and subjective data acquired from members of the organization. Experience with FTA has shown that the development of the qualitative tree can occur through the work of individuals or groups. The most effective approach is to assign persons to work on areas of the tree that correspond most closely with their areas of expertise within the organization. Since the process depends upon the utilization of expertise, much of it subjective, the selection of experts is particularly critical to the success of the analysis.

Fault Tree Analysis usually proceeds in sequential steps. First, failure events are generated on index cards in order to facilitate creativity and the rearrangement of events. These cards also make it easy to add events that appear to be missing and eliminate unimportant or redundant events. Once these cards have been validated by members of the organization, a printed version can be produced. And this document can be validated again to ensure accuracy. Then, the Fault Tree Diagram can be produced, either manually or by computer. The decision concerning whether to use a computer depends on the complexity of the analysis and the resources of the organization.

Once the qualitative tree has been developed, the relevant decision makers can decide whether to stop at this stage or to continue on to "quantitative analysis." Quantitative analysis is the process of placing numerical values on failure events in terms of their *probability of occurrence* and their *relative contribution* to more general failure events. This rather complex process requires considerable expertise. In hardware systems, relative contributions and probabilities can be determined objectively by using project specifications and test data. In organizational systems, Fault Tree quantification tends to be more subjective, depending upon the expertise of experienced members of the organization. However, the use of subjective probabilities is reliable when effectively collected through the use of appropriate instrumentation.

In quantitative analysis, probabilities and relative contribution values can be combined through Boolean algebra techniques to yield a set of critical path values for each of the logic gates of the tree. This computation is usually done by computer since manual computation can be extremely time-consuming, except for the simplest trees. A Fault Tree Analyst can trace the critical path values from the top of the tree downward, following the highest value at each gate, to determine one or more critical paths. A Fault Tree Diagram with critical path values and a critical path tracing is depicted in Figure 4. Of course, this represents only a very small segment of an actual Fault Tree.

Although quantitative analysis represents an extremely powerful tool, it is not essential for obtaining real benefits from Fault Tree Analysis. In fact, the process of FTA may, in some cases, provide greater benefits for an organization than the product. FTA is indeed a potent organizational development technol-

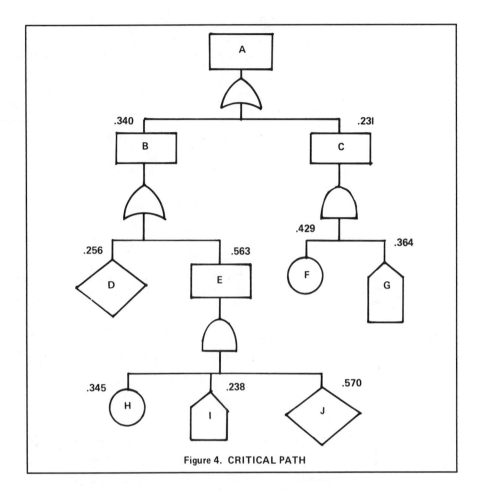

Figure 4. CRITICAL PATH

ogy that can serve to involve members of an organization in problem solving. The process of FTA tends to increase commitment to organizational goals, to clarify roles and tasks and to show the relationships and interdependencies among people who work in the same organizations. The result is almost always improved cooperation and communication. For managers, FTA can identify major weaknesses in the design of the organization as well as in its operation. Simply by eyeballing the diagram, managers can determine where problems are most likely to arise and where failure might most likely occur. The analysis diagram can serve as a useful document in facilitating communication between managers in different departments and uniting them in common pursuits of the achievement of the organizational mission.

Quantitative analysis can provide an accurate identification of organizational problems. It also provides the analyst and the manager with potent ammunition for effecting organizational change. The tracing of critical paths throughout the organization can provide objective evidence of problems that is difficult to refute, especially since quantification is based on the estimates of a large number of "experts" within the organization.

Fault Tree Analysis is an exciting new technology that may have extremely promising applications to the analysis of organizational systems. Hardware engineers have used it successfully to ensure systems safety. It can be used effectively by OD practitioners to help managers improve the "safety" of their departments or organizations and increase the likelihood that goals will be achieved. However, like any other OD technique, Fault Tree Analysis can be abused. The potential of the technique must be tempered with caution. The expression "garbage in, garbage out" is particularly relevant in discussing Fault Tree Analysis. And the warning must be implicit in these words remembered when FTA is applied to HRD situations.[1]

When we present Fault Tree Analysis in seminars and workshops, people either hate it or love it. If you hate it or think it is just too analytical, skip to the next chapter. If you want to take a whack at understanding Fault Tree Analysis in more depth, continue on.

The following FTA is one attempt at putting into perspective a number of study findings to see if we could at least sort out the possible causes of a selling problem. As you will note, we haven't followed Spitzer's subjective probability advice, but the FTA system helped us perceive possible causes nonetheless.

We've just put the example into the same format as Spitzer's Figure 3 to avoid some confusion and to allow for some simplification of the actual tree we drew.

In words, the tree reads like this:

1. The West Coast division of LPO Electronix has seen a significant steady sag in the sales-to-calls figures over the last ten months.

2. Field research says two facts are influencing the slump. Sales reps are making mighty sloppy calls (from observational studies) and managers say their people are reporting a lot of installations of new Japanese equipment in their old accounts. Service confirms the return of old equipment through dealers.

3. On the competition side, we know that two Japanese companies have been opening outlets rapidly, and six months ago marketing at LPQ decided to hold off all new products for one year.

4. On the people side, we have a rumor that the "big hitter" salesmen are being wooed by the new Japanese competitors. We also have focus-group and survey data indicating that a ceiling has been put on sales compensation. No more $200K years for heavy hitters.

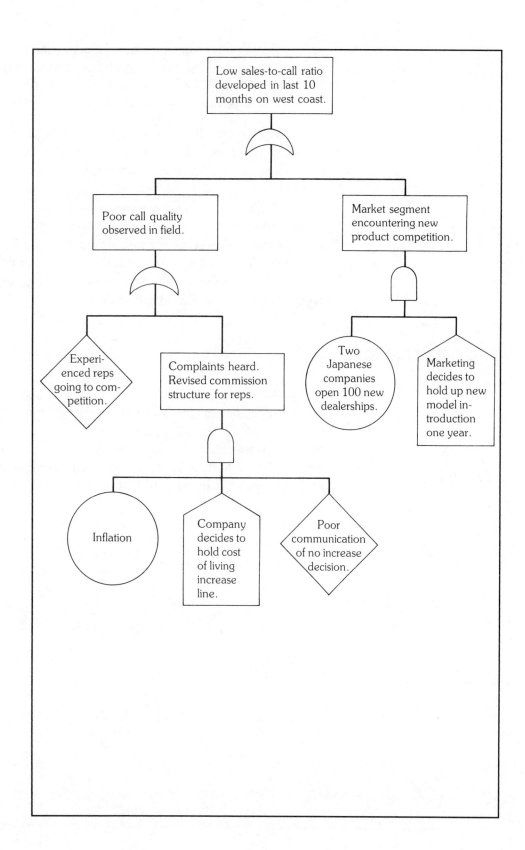

5. We know for sure that inflation is a factor in current pay dissatisfaction and that the personnel department is determined not to pay any $60 to $70K bonus checks this year. Also, the decision on the pay ceiling was very poorly communicated.

When we line these factors up, we see that there are a lot of possible solutions. Our client voted to do three things at once: bring that held-up product out of the closet, discount some current prices, and elevate the sales-compensation ceiling a bit.

No training? Actually, we were called in to look for training problems and found nothing of much consequence in comparison with the factors in the fault tree. We did, however, recommend some "asking for the order" and need-finding training for the salespeople, as well as some orientation related to the competition. When the new equipment came out of the marketing closet, new-product training was also introduced.

TO BE CONTINUED . . .

We are just learning how helpful Fault Tree Analysis can be to us. From our current vantage point, it appears that FTA will become a major task, needs, and organizational performance-problem analysis tool. Just as the technique of "fishbone" problem analysis has become a standard piece of Quality Control Circle training, FTA is likely to become a standard technique to be mastered by trainers and OD specialists in "high tech" organizations.

CHAPTER 16 PYRAMID POWER: USING LEARNING HIERARCHIES IN TASK ANALYSIS

Gagne, a psychologist from Princeton University, was contracted by the military in World War II to improve the army's training procedures. In particular, he was asked to find a more effective way of training bomber aircraft gunners to increase their accuracy. Much to his surprise, he found that all the good things he knew about learning—all that pre-World War II work on massed versus spaced practice, the effect of knowledge of results on performance and meaningfulness of tasks—didn't help that much with this most important assignment. But wartime ingenuity being what it is, he rolled up his sleeves and found a new tactic—namely, that all jobs could be broken into pieces and the pieces broken into small pieces and those small pieces broken into smaller pieces. Gagne found, in fact, that mastering most jobs required a mastery of the pieces and parts in some orderly fashion.

He discovered that tasks, such as gunnery, are made up of lots of different kinds of component skills: for example, handling the gun, recognizing targets, and tracking a target. Some of these components, he found, were difficult to master, others were not, but all had to be mastered before the performer could become a competent gunner. He found that mere practice in *handling* the gun was far less important for achieving competency than was understanding the principles of tracking. Therefore, he claimed, a good gunnery training program should emphasize tracking over shooting, and the current practice of squeezing off thousands of rounds of ammunition at a target was simply a waste of training time, money, effort and hearing.

Gagne also discovered that most tasks *presuppose* other tasks. For example, "being able to recognize a target" is presupposed or must be mastered before the performer is able to "shoot at target." And the tasks "recognize and shoot at target" are in turn presupposed to "being able to track the target."

GAGNE'S HIERARCHY

During his work on breaking jobs into small tasks, Gagne noticed similarities among the task breakdowns. From this he developed a hierarchial list of the kinds of skills a task can be analyzed into. There are higher and lower levels of skill within a task, and the higher order skills presuppose the lower. The higher-level skills usually cannot be mastered until the lower-level skills are mastered. As a simple example, the task "driving a car and making a right-hand turn" cannot be performed until such mundane behaviors as "starting the car," "shifting car into gear" and all the other subbehaviors or subtasks of "making a right-hand turn" are mastered.

As straightforward as the idea of a pyramid of tasks seems today, it was quite extraordinary in 1962. The idea that a trainee might need to be taught to "identify the red warning light," "locate the overload switch," and "move the overload switch from the OFF to ON position" before the trainee could master the task: "activate the overload system when red warning light is lit" was a big "Aha!" to a lot of Ph.D. military trainers.

This insight led Gagne to the generalization that all tasks can be classified by type or level, and these types of tasks can be displayed in a hierarchial model where each type is made up of, and presupposes, the types below it.[1]

We won't attempt to explain the whole Gagne approach here. He has written a number of books on the topic, and they require pretty careful reading for complete digestion. But we do want you to get enough of a feel for the Gagne system so you will see when and where it can be useful to you.

According to Gagne, the most complex tasks or job element anyone can be asked to perform, at the top of his pyramid, is *problem solving.* The least complex or lowest level on his pyramid, is *stimulus recognition.* An example of the former might be "troubleshoot a malfunctioning clock radio" and the latter, "identify a malfunctioning clock radio."

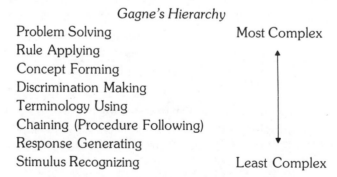

Gagne's Hierarchy

Problem Solving	Most Complex
Rule Applying	
Concept Forming	
Discrimination Making	
Terminology Using	
Chaining (Procedure Following)	
Response Generating	
Stimulus Recognizing	Least Complex

---

[1]Gagne's seminal article, "Military Training and Principles of Learning," *American Psychologist,* vol. 17 (December 1962), is a good primer to Gagne, so we have included it as Appendix A.

Following Gagne's own bottoms-up principle, let's take a look at his hierarchy. We'll begin with the smallest of the small, the first half of the basic Gagne unit, the stimulus/response pair. The stimulus is the trigger or cue that sets off the performer's action; the response is the action itself.

According to Gagne, each must be learned before it combines with others to form a unit.

STIMULUS RECOGNIZING

Stimulus here refers to the simplest form of cognitive action or perceived environmental change that can trigger the performer's action. It is the "when you see this . . ." part of the "when you see this, do that" formula. The stimulus could be a warning light going on, a superior's command, a particular movement of a machine part, or any other cue that is to be obeyed. This concrete, sensory signal is at the bottom of the hierarchy because it is presumed in any action or response of the performer. It is the most primitive initiator of a task. For example, an unskilled manual laborer may receive only the following stimulus training: "sweep there." That's all the training that may be needed. The action of sweeping is not taught because it is already presumed to be in the worker's repertoire of behavioral responses. All he needs to learn is the cue.

RESPONSE GENERATING

The *response* is the action the performer should take on cue from the stimulus. It is the "do that" part of "when you see this . . . do that." When the warning light goes one, turn off this switch. When your superior says, "Present arms," hold your rifle like this. When the flange moves completely to the left, pull this lever. When the customer says, "I wouldn't do business with your chicken company if it was the last vendor on earth," say, "Oh? Could you tell me more about that?" The focus at this level of learning or training is on adding a new behavior or response to the repertoire of the trainee.

The response always presupposes that the stimulus has been learned. For training, this means you cannot simply teach the performer the response or action you desire. You must make sure that he is first able to recognize the stimulus that triggers that action. In other words, response learning is more complex than mere stimulus learning. It usually occurs in a stimulus-response (S-R) pair.

From a task and training analysis point of view, you often need to decide which part of the S-R pair requires the greatest training effort. For example, if the trainee is not supposed to pull the lever until the flange has returned to a precise spot on the machine, it will probably be more important to train him to recognize the stimulus than to execute the response. That's because the simple action of pulling a lever is probably already in the trainee's repertoire, but the ability to recognize the precise configuration that makes up the stimulus is new. He doesn't need to practice pulling the lever, but he does need to practice timing his action or recognizing the precise cue. For practice purposes, it wouldn't make any difference if he pulled the lever himself or just snapped his fingers while watching another operator. On the other hand, if the lever has to be pulled in a very specific way, it may be very important to practice "pulling" until he can do it right every time.

For purposes of task analysis, this means it is not enough merely to describe a performer's action. You also have to inquire about the stimulus that triggers that action. And you have to judge which of the two—if not both—needs to be emphasized in the training.

CHAINING (PROCEDURE FOLLOWING)

Chaining is a step up from producing a response. It is the act of producing a series of responses. The performer of a chain takes several steps in a definite sequence in order to complete a procedure. By definition, a *procedure* is a task composed of two or more steps that follow each other in a definite sequence. Changing a flat tire is an example of chaining. When you notice the flat (stimulus): first, stop the car (response #1). Second, open the trunk (response #2). Third, remove the jack (response #3). And so on until you close the trunk and drive off again (response #n). The whole series (from response #1 to response #n) is the chain. As Fig. 16-1 illustrates, a chain is a box full of interlinked stimulus-response elements.

Fig. 16-1   A Behavioral Chain.

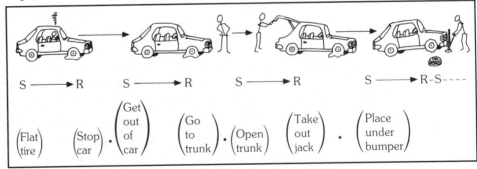

Note that any of the S-R units could potentially be broken into even smaller units.

In anyone's view of task analysis, it is important to capture all the steps in the chain or procedure. This is evident from what we said earlier (Chapter 4) about "task listing" being the most common concept people have about what task analysis looks like.

In Gagne's point of view, it is also important to notice that the procedure or chain is made up of many individual actions (responses), the mastery of which is presupposed to the performer's success with the whole chain. Thus, in doing task analysis, Gagne would advise determining which steps in the procedure may need prior treatment or emphasis in the training program before expecting the trainee to master the whole procedure. For example, trainees in a "do it yourself" auto mechanics class may need some practice turning a tire wrench to find out just how tight they have to make the tire lug nuts for the wheel to stay put while driving.

TERMINOLOGY USING

In some jobs, the performer doesn't have to be able to describe what he or she is doing. Just see the stimulus and perform the response or chain required. In these cases, it is not necessary to teach the trainee the proper terminology of the tools and materials of the task. It is a step up the hierarchy to be required to describe the elements that one is dealing with. For example, to be able to tell a customer, a supervisor, or the person on the next shift what you have accomplished or to be able to go to a parts desk and ask for what you need by proper name or identification number is a fourth-level task that requires specific training.

In reality, of course, language is used before, during, and after the performance of most tasks. So it is, in a way, academic to fit the special class of "terminology using" into the hierarchy. Essentially, Gagne is saying that you can't assume terminology is being learned if it isn't consciously being taught.

Conversely, learning terminology should not be assumed to be critical or important unless your task analysis specifies a need for learning some sort of terminology. How many sales-training courses have you seen that teach the trainee to say the words "feature advantage benefit" or "selling to the need" but never teach *how* to develop FAB statements or identify buyer needs? It used to be a fairly common error, teaching the buzz words but not the concepts and applications underlying them.

Gagne himself inserts terminology-using (or "verbal association") in the hierarchy at this point because he sees it as a higher form of chaining, that is, the linking together of proper utterances to form the right names or labels of things. For our purposes, the idea is simply to ask ourselves during a task analysis, "Is using proper terminology important to accomplishing this task?" If it is, it should be given proper treatment in the training program. If not, then there is little to be gained from making sure the trainees are expert in attaching the right names to things. Treating names of things, as stimuli requiring some sort of general response, is often enough.

Another reason why terminology-using fits into the hierarchy at this point is that it is necessary (or at least highly useful) for all the higher-order tasks. And, as we indicated, it is often not necessary for the lower-order tasks. This is also sort of the borderline between the purely behavioral/reflexive task components and the cognitive, or thought, components of a task. As we move on up the hierarchy, verbal mediation becomes more a part of the task and the training for that task.

DISCRIMINATION MAKING

A task can become more complex (and thus move up the hierarchy) in two ways. One way is by increasing the number of steps that have to be taken. This is why, for example, chaining is more complex than response producing. The other way is to add *variables,* changeable conditions that make the task performance an "it depends" or conditional matter. Sometimes you do it and sometimes you don't, sometimes you do it this way, and sometimes you do it that way. Having variable values in the stimulus side of the equation of a task brings us to the next higher level in the learning hierarchy and introduces the need for making discriminations.

If stoplights were red_1 red_2 red_3 instead of red yellow green, and if there was only one light bulb, then learning to discriminate between shades of red would become a critical driver-education skill. Or, if the Department of Natural Resources requests an employee to count the bird population at a spot in the forest the individual will need to discriminate between the different kinds of birds observed. There are many different species, so keenness of discrimination is key to the job. Now all this presupposes the lower order of tasks: ability to follow department procedures for taking a bird census; a thorough knowledge of the terminology names and characteristics of the various species; and stimulus recognition (knowing one when you see it).

In analyzing any task, you have to ask if there is ever any difficulty in picking out the triggering stimuli among trainees. If there is a possibility of stimulus confusion, then the higher-level skill of *accurate discrimination* is part of the task to be mastered, and the trainee will have to learn to distinguish the right stimuli from a number of possible look alikes.

CONCEPT FORMING

Forming a concept is the next higher level of task in the Gagne system. It is related to discrimination-making in that it is a cognitive skill of being able to recognize something amid variables, but it is a step higher since it requires the performer to generalize from an incomplete or changing set of variables. Discrimination is the skill of being able to identify a concrete item (a species of bird, a defective part, or an enemy aircraft) from other concrete variables in the environment. Concept forming is more complex because it is more abstract. It is the skill of recognizing a task variable from a set of partial clues. In making a discrimination, the performer says, "Uh-huh, that's definitely an X, not a Y." In forming a concept, one says, "Based on a couple of clues, we probably have a Z."

The police officer who observes your car's erratic motion is trying to form a concept: "Do I see enough clues to call this reckless driving?" The geologist trying to determine potential mineral exploration sites is forming a concept. So is the medical diagnostician trying to read the meaning of darker and lighter shades on your x-ray. They begin to see a pattern in the variables. The pattern matches a certain type or category. The technician or doctor may in some sense be thinking, "Even though this x-ray is different in many ways from all other x-rays, it still belongs to this kind or category of problem."

Another example of a task that requires concept formation is recognizing customer attitudes. What a customer says or may say in any specific instance is unique or idiosyncratic. But based on a number of clues in the customer's statements, body language, and tone of voice, a pattern emerges, and the salesperson forms an impression that this customer is really suspicious, or dissatisfied, or whatever.

Sometimes concept forming is the highest level needed for a task—as in the case of the geologist or the x-ray specialist. In most cases, however, it is simply the first step in a higher order of performance; the second step is called *rule applying.*

RULE APPLYING

All jobs have rules, but "rules" in this context don't refer to conduct or standards. They are, rather, the logical rules that govern the technology of a task. We are talking about the *rules* of estimating, the *laws* of physics, or the *principles* of accounting. These rules are, of course, implicit in every task. But in some tasks, the performer is not required to know or be able to state the rules; he is only required to carry out some predetermined application of them. It is a higher-level task when the performer is required to know the rule *and* to decide how and when to apply it. For example, a policeman needs to know enough about a law to determine when it is apparently being broken. A lawyer needs to know the intricacies of the law in question to be able to argue the merits of his or her client's case.

This is the kind of task that requires an employee to handle two or more concepts simultaneously. The first concept is the rule itself: for example: "All weak points should be reinforced." The second concept is a recognition that the rule does apply in this case: "These points are weak and should be reinforced." Gagne calls this a "chain of concepts." It is best expressed in the "if . . . then . . ." format: (*If* a point is weak, *then* reinforce it).

A rule-applying task is made up of a number of variables. *If* condition B occurs, the performer is to do C instead of D. This level of task normally requires concept forming as a prerequisite, because the performer has to make judgments about which of many possible conditions is occurring. The sales process is a good example of this kind of task. The salesperson realizes that the customer must go through a series of perception-changing experiences to be able to make the buying decision. Since the buyer rarely tells the seller where he or she is in the process, the seller has to make judgments on a set of behavioral clues, and then act on the rule that says, "*If* this is what the buyer is thinking, *then* this is what I should say or do next." Rule following means taking the most appropriate action for the circumstances within the context of a complex process.

Sometimes the cognitive component that triggers the action of following the right logical rule is a simple discrimination. The insurance underwriter, for example, who has a complete application with all the necessary information is able to select a policy by applying the rules to simple discriminations. "If the applicant is between the ages of 25–30, then. . ." "If the applicant has such and such an illness, then. . ." And so forth.

The point is that rule applying is a complex task that presupposes certain lower-order tasks. From the point of view of task analysis, it is important to ask what kinds of tasks are presupposed.

- ► Does the performer have to form concepts?
- ► Does the performer have to make discriminations?
- ► Does the performer have to execute chains of procedures in order to carry out the application of the rule?
- ► A combination of the above?

In a sense, the rule-applying concept in the Gagne system is the material that goes in the decision boxes of the algorithm method, and that is where we've found it most helpful. Gagne has a lot to say about the teaching of rules, learning to do the behaviors in the rules and, making the judgments that are so integral to the well-oiled algorithm.

PROBLEM SOLVING

Problem solving is what you do when the logical system of rules breaks down (otherwise known as troubleshooting) or when the logical system doesn't quite apply (otherwise known as thinking creatively). The main characteristic of problem solving is the act of *projecting an hypothesis*. It's when the performer has to say, "What if we tried this?" Or, "Maybe this is what's wrong." Or, "How might this work?" In other words, there's no clear stimulus in the work environment that defines what action to take or what rule to apply. Problem solving is a fundamentally generative act.

In troubleshooting, a very strong, logical system, or set of rules exists in the work material. The trouble is the mechanism that embodies the system just isn't operating. The machine is broken. Everyone can see that it doesn't work, but nobody knows why. So they call in the troubleshooter whose job is to apply the presupposed rules of the system to the disabled mechanism. He mentally dismembers the mechanism into its subsystems. He forms an hypothesis about which subsystem is probably at fault. And, he applies some form of test instrument to verify his hypothesis. If the test shows the right condition, then he knows what to fix. If not, he forms another hypothesis and tests it, always working off the logic of the underlying system.

In more creative problem solving, where there is no known logical system of rules just under the surface, the performer is still able to do the job consistently only if he or she is working off an analogous system—some relevant experience, pattern, or metaphor. An engineer who is expected to come up with a new design will try out some new combinations of old elements in his mind. He is constantly forming hypotheses based on these elements. For example, "What would happen if we put the support structure of the building on the outside instead of the inside?" He is accepting some existing rules—the need for a supporting structure—but changing others.

A story teller is another example. He or she creates new material during the telling, but this new material comes from new ways of looking at previous experience and other stories he or she has heard. Eventually the story forms itself in a recognizable pattern—a novel, which is not like every other novel but not so different that you couldn't recognize it as a novel.

There is a supposedly true story about Apollo 13 that puts some perspective on problem solving. As you recall, Apollo 13 was the mission that had trouble in flight. The good news was that everyone came back alive. The near-tragedy was averted not because the crew had a prelearned response to the malfunction but, in the words of Flight Commander Jim Lovell, because "We had practiced solving so many problems in training that we just went into the problem-solving mode and figured it out." The point, of course, is that for some kinds of complex jobs, where the unexpected is to be expected, the only appropriate training is problem-solving training. But aside from professions of astronaut and surgeon, there may not be too many jobs so critical that the training expense is justified.

A sort of sub-issue that surfaces from the Gagne conceptualization is that of determining how much training (and at what level) is appropriate for a given job. Intrinsic to Gagne's system is the implication that appropriate levels of learning are knowable and justifiable—and inappropriate levels are not.

Some critical characteristics or indicators tell you when a task is of the problem-solving type:

- ► Different high performers do it differently.
- ► There are many unpredictable elements in the task.
- ► The performer is expected to define, fix, create, or re-examine the rules.

There are, of course, problems in everyone's work, not all of which are worth noting in a task analysis. Our concern is with the job that consists primarily of problem-solving activities. In attempting to analyze the job so we can help someone learn it, we will proceed to look for the lower-level tasks that are presupposed to solving the problems—primarily the rules and concepts that are recombined in the problem-solving process. These are the lower-order or presupposing tasks that must be mastered before practice in problem solving can sensibly be used as a training step.

FIRST APPLICATION — TEACHING STRATEGIES

As we have implied, there are two kinds of applications for Gagne's hierarchy of tasks. The first application is developing teaching strategies (primarily Gagne's intended application), and the second is the use of the task-analysis mode (primarily our application).

A good teaching strategy will take the hierarchy into account when sequencing instruction and make sure the learner has mastered the presupposed lower-order tasks before expecting him or her to perform the higher-order tasks. This may seem self-evident, but it is often violated in practice. For example, trainees are often expected to perform case-study role plays (essentially problem-solving activities) without first having been drilled or even instructed in the specific behaviors they have to exhibit to succeed in the role play. Frequently, they have been instructed in the logical rules that are needed to solve the case, but they have not been instructed or been able to practice the verbal behaviors, such as question asking, that are necessary to apply the rules in the interpersonal arena where the problem really occurs.

A second teaching application is that each type of task on the hierarchy is best taught by using certain methods. Or, as Gagne would have it, by being attentive to certain "conditions." Paraphrasing Gagne:

1. *Stimulus learning* is accomplished by pointing out the environmental cue. It is tested by observing if the trainee responds in its presence.

2. *Response learning* occurs by instruction and demonstration. It usually requires a lot of drill to make sure the action occurs on cue and in the desired manner.

3. *Chaining* is learned in the same way, but repetition is even more necessary to help the learner remember the entire sequence. Often additional or supplementary cues are needed during the training to help the learner's memory. Then these cues are gradually withdrawn until the learner can do the entire sequence without prompting.

4. *Discrimination* is important to provide a lot of practice in picking out the desired item from a multitude of look-alikes. Audiovisual material can be quite effective for this purpose. The drill should make the look-alikes more and more similar until they are practically identical.

5. *Concept learning* is accomplished by clarifying the concept with lots of examples. The examples both illustrate the concept and fill it with some content.

6. *Rules* are learned the same way as concepts, since they are types of concepts. In addition, the trainee should be shown how that concept applies in certain situations and should be required to apply the concept in given examples or cases.

7. *Problem solving* is taught by pointing out that one has to select the right rule for a problem, that only one of several may apply. The process should be illustrated. Then the trainee should be challenged to solve a series of relevant problems, progressing from easy to difficult.

SECOND APPLICATION — TASK ANALYSIS STRATEGIES

The hierarchy is also a useful tool for analyzing tasks. And the task analysis application is necessary in order to apply the teaching application. Throughout our discussion of the hierarchy, we have pointed out some of the task analysis applications. For example, we gave you some tips on how to identify each of the various levels of a task. Now we would like to bring all this together into a *strategy*, an organized set of questions to keep in mind as you approach the analysis of any task. The set of questions related to the hierarchy may be asked in the course of applying any of the methods we discussed in previous chapters. It is not so much a method as it is a structure to guide the questions you ask or the analysis you make.

Let's assume that we are interviewing a subject matter expert, the tools of whose trade may or may not be present. We are asking for a description of the task as she sees or performs it. We have no particular reason to put the task anywhere on the hierarchy.

Our strategy is to work from the bottom of the hierarchy to the top. Actually, we begin at the response-producing phase, since this is what she is most prepared to tell you about. So the first question is, "How do you normally do this job?"

Then, as the information comes out, double back to pick up the stimuli that trigger each of the steps she tells you about: "How do you know when to do that?"

Chains do not normally require a special question. They just flow out as the SME talks, especially if he or she has the tools at hand and is showing you during the interview. Otherwise, just ask: "Could you give me the details on that? What are all the steps?"

"Whom does he or she (the performer) interact with?" is the key question to getting at the need for terminology using. And the follow-up questions are: "What do they talk about?" and "How accurately does he or she have to name things?" After that, you're into specifics.

A key question to determine if the job is near the bottom or the top of the hierarchy is: "Does it always happen this way, or do you sometimes do it differently?" The answer to that question tells you whether or not you are dealing with a simple procedure (low on variables) or a complex process (high on variables). If the SME says that it pretty much goes the same all the time, then you can just check out some discriminations and stop going up the hierarchy. This means checking out how good the performer has to be at picking out the triggering stimuli. A good question to ask is: "Can you ever be fooled about when to do it?"

If the SME says the task does not always go the same way, then you have to move all the way up the hierarchy. We find it's most convenient to jump two steps ahead at this point and inquire about the rules that have to be followed. The top of the hierarchy is aimed at servicing some kind of logical system, so it's best to find out first what the system is before trying to figure out what concepts make it up or what problems have to be solved around it. A good question to ask is "How does the whole system work?" followed by "What key ideas is the whole thing based on?" Once the big picture starts to come into focus, go after the variables: "What are the exceptions? Why do you do it this way instead of that way? How do the other people do it? How else could you do it? Why?"

Once you know what the alternative methods are, you should get more refined information about the kind of knowledge needed to decide which alternative to take, such as which rule to apply. As we said earlier, sometimes this will be a simple, concrete discrimination, and sometimes it will be a more abstract conceptual judgment. The questions to ask here are: "How can you tell? How can you be sure? and Does everybody always see it the same way?"

Finally, you can ask about the problem-solving dimension: "Do you have to know how to fix it if it breaks down? How much guesswork is involved? What do you have to do that they don't ever tell you about? or Where do the new ideas come from?"

By arming yourself with these questions and keeping the hierarchy itself in the back of your mind, it's not too hard to ferret out the principal hierarchial components of a task.

A final application of Gagne's hierarchy to the business of doing a task analysis is the guidance it provides for selecting the right task-analysis method. Assuming that you have a good idea or hypothesis about where the task fits on the hierarchy, the hierarchy can steer you toward the most fruitful investigative technique. Some of the techniques we discussed in Chapters 4 through 7 are more appropriate to tasks at different levers of the hierarchy.

If the task seems to be at the low end of the pyramid, you can probably fall back and apply S-R tables or task listings to the observable jobs. This is because you are dealing mostly with response production and chaining, which have low variability and can be captured by these tools. Also, because you have low variability, interviewing one or at most, a few SMEs will probably give you all the information you need.

If the task is at the high end of the hierarchy, you will probably want to use some kind of algorithm to capture the logic of the process and all its alternatives. When you have a lot of decision variables (high in concept forming or problem solving) and many SMEs are likely to have various ways of sizing up the situation, you would do well to apply focus-group or critical-incident techniques to gather various perceptions of what to do under differing circumstances. These methods will also give you some idea of how a group of specialists would judge the quality of various types of solutions or applications.

SUMMARY

Learning hierarchies, such as our adaptation of Gagne's, have an important application to the business of task analysis. True, you can succeed in the business without this concept. But this is the kind of subtlety that separates a wooden analysis from one that will help you plot an effective and efficient training solution.

SECTION **VI** MATCHING TECHNIQUES AND PROBLEMS

So far, we've described the strategies, tactics, and techniques we use in our task, needs, and organizational analysis work. It's time now to be more specific about when each technique is appropriate or inappropriate for a specific investigation. But a word of caution: Our guide for this section is our experience. We've seen no research that indicates, "Technique A uncovers 'the truth' in situation Omega, while Technique B does not." We are simply reporting our own personal success and failure experiences.

For instance, we've found in our experience the simple behavioral-observation approach isn't that effective in studying some kinds of managerial behavior. The S-R table below, for example, doesn't help us understand managerial behavior or determine what to train managers to do or think. We also know that some esteemed management researchers, such as Henry Mintzberg, Fred Luthans, and Tim Davis, don't necessarily agree with our assessment.

Luthans, for example, believes straight behavioral observation is invaluable in breaking the logjam of management theory and placing a functional behavioral perspective on the management role. He is a good researcher who makes some valid points, but we think for the kind of work we do as trainers, the simple, task-listing type of behavioral observation is a minor tool.

One other caveat: We have been and will be discussing the strengths and weaknesses of each analysis technique somewhat in isolation. But tactic four

Stimulus (S)	Response (R)
1. Picks piece of paper from in-basket	1. Frowns at paper
2. Picks up telephone receiver	2. Yells into telephone receiver
3. Slams telephone receiver on cradle	3. Swears at paper
4. Crumples up paper	4. Throws paper
5. Picks piece of paper from in-basket	5. Frowns at paper

(discussed in Chapter 2) still holds: "Never use just one technique." Regardless of how well a given technique may seem to fit the problem you're investigating, distortion and subjectivity can creep into your results when only one technique is applied. The validity and incontestability of your results can be greatly strengthened by using at least two techniques. So, your task is not to pick *the* best technique, but rather the best-matched *set* of techniques for zeroing in on the performance problem you are trying to figure out.

CHAPTER **17** DECIDING WHEN TO USE WHAT: ORGANIZATIONAL CRITERIA

The techniques described in this book are all methods of getting answers to questions that have been useful to us at one time or another. The most important factor to consider in selecting a method is to choose one that gathers information on the kind of question you need to answer. As discussed in the early chapters, our strategic preference is to follow a variation of the Deden-Parker three-phase model and work down the organization: first identifying the big picture problem(s) at the organizational analysis level; next tackling the performance discrepancy in quantitative and behaviorally specific terms at the operations analysis level; and, finally building a competence sketch or performance model out of data from the two preceding phases and the final individual analysis phase.

In essence, we are trying to find answers to a series of questions. So the technique we choose depends on the level or phase of our analysis and the specific question we are trying to answer. Here are some of the specific questions we are called on to answer in an FTO study.

Question 1: Is there a training need?

In the strict training-needs sense, this is really a two part question: "Does a performance problem exist? If so, what are the training-related parts?" This is the training-needs-analysis question in its narrowest sense. Someone has hollered, "Teach 'em to do it better!" And, you are trying to determine whether they really are failing the 45-caliber test. Sometimes this first step is easy, sometimes it isn't. You may be able to walk up to the low performers in question, ask for a demonstration of skill, and resolve the issue. Sometimes it's more subtle. You might have to take check rides with a dozen sales reps before you begin to see the subtle behavioral differences between high and low performers.

Of course, there are times when your prerogative to investigatively answer questions such as "Is there an important performance problem?" and "Can training make it go away?" has been usurped. We've all run into situations wherein management opinion, government edict, or organizational politics has mandated that training is the answer, never mind the question. Our advice is to test the waters gently; if important minds have already been made up and funds allocated, don't fight city hall. Sure, you might get lucky and become a hero for showing management how to save all that time and money by implementing a more appropriate non-training solution, but the odds are that you'll be stoned as an obstructionist for trying to stop the party after the noisemakers and hats have already been distributed. No amount of good FTO work will get you points for raining on the wrong person's parade. Only do FTO research when it is wanted and when the results will be a factor in the decision to intervene or not intervene and how that intervention will be conducted. In short, don't try to drive the wagon when you've only been asked along for the ride.

Most of the time, though, opinions are split over the cause or causes of the performance problem you're being asked to help solve, and solutions are far from obvious to anyone. Often key groups, such as the performers themselves (especially the low performers), won't even agree that there is a performance problem.

It's not unusual for an organization to have performance blind spots. Many organizations regularly conduct customer satisfaction, share of market, comparison shopping, and organizational-image studies just to see if there are performance problems or market needs the organization is unaware of or has been pretending didn't exist. These often become preliminary performance-problem indicators, stimulus points for HRD, and training development activities. One of our clients recently conducted a study of its largest and most profitable product to find out why people buy it. When the research found significant differences between company opinion and marketplace reality, there was suddenly a need for a lot of new sales training. This type of situation welcomes the suggestion that FTO research is needed.

Question 2: What are the parameters of the problem, need, and task?

Once the existence of a performance problem has been verified, it's time to look for first-order causes. We've yet to find a performance problem without a mixture of causes. While Mager and Pipe's flowchart is great for helping us sort out possible performance-problem causes, it can give the impression that most performance problems have single causes. They don't.

We recently worked on a "teach 'em to make better quality widgets" problem that had a "feedback to machine operator" component, a "change the quality control inspection procedure" component, and a "train the supervisors to reinforce good performance/correct poor performance" component. So by first-order causes, we mean the 20 percent components that will give us the most bang for the buck. In this little widget-manufacturing problem, we started with feedback posting and then moved on to changing the quality-control inspection procedures. The supervisory training component is still untouched, but the quality problem is under enough control so the training can wait another budget cycle. No need to overkill on the solution side.

The key to finding first-order causes is concordance—getting agreement on causes from a number of different avenues. When observations of high and low performers tell us that high-performing salespeople *make more cold calls* and *ask for the order more frequently* and when managers complain in one-on-one interviews and on surveys that salespeople spend too much time with existing accounts and don't seem to know when to ask for the order, we've pretty much surrounded a probably first-order cause for low sales performance. We have concordance from three relatively independent data sources: our observations, management interviews, and survey data.

Question 3: What do we solve first?

Once we've isolated first-order causes to a problem, we're still not ready to start implementing solutions. We need consensus on, and prioritization of, the first-order causes. It is incumbent on management and/or subject matter experts to make the final decisions about importance and priority. No statistical method can take the place of management's decisions about priorities and importance. Only management has enough information about new products, budget concerns, and the like to decide which problems must be attacked immediately and which can be postponed.

Also, management and SMEs often have different views of the same problem, different performance philosophies and solution preferences, and different senses of priority. We can, and should, facilitate resolution of these disagreements, but we can't co-opt those decisions. First of all, resource allocation is a management prerogative; and second, it is an act of commitment. For instance, when management decides implementation of quality-control circles is a number-one priority for the organization, the organization successfully implements circles. When management treats quality-control circles as a nice but not necessary idea, they go nowhere. The same applies to the kinds of problems we uncover in an FTO study. If management decides the problem(s) is top priority, the giant green light suddenly shines on implementing just about any solution you can reasonably defend.

And, as we discussed in chapter 12 on consensus techniques, there are plain old content-area priorities that only subject matters experts can decide upon. So, in a sense, there are two questions here:

3a. What problems should be attacked first?
3b. What are the most important content areas to deal with?

And as Tactic Five in Chapter 2 suggests, it is best to let management do management's thing—that is, decide.

Question 4: What goes into the training component?

When we're finally down to a point where training makes sense as a solution, we need to figure out what goes into the training. In essence, this is what the content management and SMEs must decide in question 3b. As for technique, here we have to go back to the technical and political basics of: "Which technique is most appropriate for a specific kind of job?" "Which technique do we have the time and money to use?" and "Which technique will garner the visibility—or lack of it—appropriate to the situation?"

Table 17-1 is one of the decision-making tools we've designed for helping select the right analysis method for the multitude of situations and questions to consider before starting an FTO study.

ADDITIONAL CRITERIA FOR SELECTION

Table 17-1 presents a number of other criteria that may influence the choice of technique. The first distinction—which is also implied in earlier chapters of this book—is whether or not the data you seek are observable. If they are, then observation methods can be applied. If not, other methods such as the *talking about performance* or *20 questions* techniques have to be used.

BUY-IN. Another important factor, and a somewhat political one, to consider in choosing a method of analysis is whether or not employee buy-in is important to the conduct of the study or the resultant training or performance-improvement program. "Employee" in this sense is defined as anyone in the organization who will be affected by the program. It may include persons from all authority levels of the organization. People need to feel they have been consulted about changes affecting them. In some instances, you will be well advised to advertise loud and clear how profoundly this research and any subsequent programs have been created "in response" to employee requests, opinions, and surveys.

COST. Every budget is limited. Frequently, your choice of a data-gathering tool will be influenced by budget considerations. We have provided some indication of cost differences in Table 17-1. Each square is divided into three relative cost categories: high, medium, and low. And each method in a box is listed from highest to lowest in price. The high-cost category, including focus groups, interviews, and critical-incident studies, takes large numbers of employees away from production and involves a considerable amount of "think work" in collating, analyzing, and interpreting the information. Low-cost methods take the time of a few people and they are easy to put together and interpret. The middle group is simply a mean on the continuum of being long on employee man-hours but short on analysis, or vice versa.

Fig. 17-1 Technique Selection Criteria.

Question/ considerations	Cost	Do we have an FTO need at all?	What are the behavioral, attitudinal, and skill/knowledge specifics?	What items bear the most weight on the problem?
Task or Information Is Observable	High			
	Med.		Algorithm (6) Time/motion (6) Stimulus/resp. (6) Task list (5) Freq. count (5)	Freq. count (5)
	Low	Records (2)	Artifact (4)	
Task or Information Is Not Observable	High	Cust. focus (8) Cust. interview (8) Cust. telephone (6)	Critical Incident (7) Focus (8) Interview (8)	
	Med.	Mgmt. focus (8) Mgmt. interview (5) Mgmt. telephone (6) Questionnaire (5)	Questionnaire (5) Simulation (4)	Telephone survey (5) Intercept survey (5) Questionnaire (5) Survey group (4)
	Low	Mgmt. mandate (1)	Delphi (10)	Delphi (10) Priority grid (2)
Employee Buy-in Is Important (Political)	High	Emp. focus (8) Emp. interview (8)	Focus (8) Interview (8)	
	Med.	Questionnaire (5) Telephone (5)	Questionnaire (5) Telephone (5)	Questionnaire (5) Telephone survey (5) Survey group (3)
	Low	Quick question. (3)		

The methods are listed in order of cost from high to low.

The number after each method indicates the amount of time consumed on a scale from 1-10 (10 = high time-consumption).

All the above comparisons of time and cost assume that the study is done on an adequate sample of in-house personnel in one location (except customer studies). Additional costs may include travel, long-distance charges, incentives, fees, and materials.

ELAPSED TIME. A final consideration is how much time you have to do the study. In our opinion, all the methods we have described (with the possible exception of the Delphi method) can be applied in a reasonable amount of time—the 20 to 60 days we consider normal for 99.8 percent of the projects we do. Nevertheless, some go faster than others. Table 17-1 provides our estimate of the relative time needed to use each method. The number next to each method is taken from a scale of 1 to 10. A "10" indicates high time-consumption. A "5" is about the time it takes to design, distribute, and tabulate a good questionnaire. Depending on your level of skill and the approval characteristic of your organization, that figure can vary from two weeks to a month.

In making both our time and cost estimates, we assume that all the studies are being conducted at a single location and that an adequate sample of company personnel (or close-by customers) is being used. Decentralization means an increase in both time and cost. Incentives and fees for non-company personnel should also be considered. Also, the cost of time and materials for some simulations can be astronomical.

DOES OR DOESN'T AN IMPORTANT PERFORMANCE PROBLEM EXIST?

Let's look at the classic meaning of needs analysis, determining whether or not a problem or need exists in the first place and evaluate the methods we've described in terms of how appropriately they answer the question, "Is there a legitimate human performance problem?" Then we'll assess the appropriate ones against some of the secondary criteria just mentioned.

PERFORMANCE RECORDS. By far the easiest, quickest, and surest way to answer the question is to dig around in the wastebasket and look at such performance records as productivity, turnover, absences, customer complaints, grievances, profit levels, and other readily available data that are collected regularly and that can be differentiated into high- and low-performing sectors. Somewhat less readily available but equally revealing are documents such as exit interview reports and performance appraisal summaries. The needle to look for in this haystack is: "Some of our people (teams, branches, plants) are doing a better job than others." If so, this could mean the good ones know something the others don't know; do something others don't do; or are selected, managed, or developed differently. A deeper study, employing the techniques we've been pushing here, should be applied to find out who, what, when, where, and why the differences exist.

CUSTOMER STUDIES. Sometimes company performance records do not reveal any needs for change. A company's production, sales, and complaint levels could be in the same "fat and happy" range they've been in for years. So what's the need for change? Perceptive organizations—interested in marketing improvements, new product development, or sensing potential problems and trends—regularly check their beliefs against their customers' perceptions and satisfaction levels.

Customer focus groups, interviews, and telephone surveys are excellent ways to get new information about what customers are thinking or feeling in response to your product and/or your people. The three types of studies in this group are relatively expensive, but they provide early-warning information about areas of unsuspected dissatisfaction and potential need for change. If your company or client looks good in all its important internal performance indicators but wise heads suspect a need for "something more," one of these customer-study techniques is probably right for you. As far as we're concerned, Peter Drucker was right on the mark when he said, "The business of management is selling jobs—careers—to employees." Researching the employee population as carefully as one researches the external consumer market is a worthwhile effort.

MANAGEMENT FOCUS GROUPS AND INTERVIEWS. A key step in any needs analysis is to determine how much fever management feels on the subject and how it views the performance problem. Remember Tactic Five from Chapter 2 "Let line managers make critical decisions." This applies at least as much to initial needs assessment as it does to the kinds of final details that demand consensus. If your management doesn't agree there is an organizational problem to be solved and doesn't sanction your study, then the results of the study, no matter how excellent, will probably end up in the dark spaces under executive credenzas.

Focus groups and interviews are effective tools for bringing together management thought. After all, if you were a highly placed, effective manager, you naturally would galvanize the energies of your management team by conducting meetings and interviews that would require its members to focus their attention on certain problems. If you do this as an effective manager, why not do the same thing when researching a performance problem? Focus groups and interviews are simply ways of helping people find the time, space, and stimulus to focus on a problem and express their perceptions of it. As a trainer/researcher, you not only have the ability to do this, you also have the license to write up and issue a research report. As we said in Chapter 2, when we presented our optimal strategy for organizational research, nothing happens till management buys in. And that strategy can be actualized in several ways.

Some organizations go to great lengths to formalize these kinds of techniques for involving management in needs analysis. Whole buildings have been turned into corporate "assessment centers." Other more modest efforts have gone into establishing quality-control committees, management seminars, and plain old meetings. All these are strategies for need awareness. Why not take an effective medium-cost approach to this? When you require management input or energy for initial needs assessment, set up a research project that includes a series of interviews or focus groups. If you feel comfortable and credible running the groups, great. If you think an outsider would be a better bet and would add to your internal political status, so be it.

TELEPHONE INTERVIEW. Calling up key people and asking them what they think or how they feel about a problem is an effective and relatively inexpensive way to test the waters quickly. It also allows you to ask for their help in planning what else should be done to get the endorsement of others on the issue. Another advantage is that the telephone can get you to a relatively representative sample—employees and managers in various plants, departments, or branches of an organization. It doesn't hurt to call a couple of opinion-leading customers as well. The key, of course, is having the predeveloped influence to make those calls. If you are part of the team, an equal among equals, you can get away with the informal telephone gambit. Otherwise, go with a more formal approach.

Again, your purpose dictates how to do this. If you wish to gather some information or crystalize an existing concern *and* if you have the clout, a simple set of telephone interviews will suffice. On the other hand, if your purpose is to count noses, a more formal and sanctioned telephone survey—in which you ask the same set of questions and keep score of the responses—would be appropriate.

QUESTIONNAIRES. When someone asks, "Do we need to do any training around here?" the frequent reaction is to send out a questionnaire asking how many people think so. And for good reason. This method has the advantage of being both democratic and quantitative. It's hard to argue with a majority of both managers and employees who agree that "we need to do something about Blue Widget productivity." Besides, it's a relatively low-cost and painless way to get the information. More often than not in our consulting work, we are given a set of questionnaire results that prompted our client organization to call us in the first place. But all the surveying in the world will be for naught if the questions and sampling strategies are poorly conceived and executed. Remember, a survey or questionnaire is not a needs analysis; it's simply a *part* of a needs analysis.

MANAGEMENT MANDATE. The question "Do we have a need?" has often been answered long before the trainer or consultant is called in. It is implied in a management decision to increase performance, implement a new technology, or "get with" some trend or change in the industry. For example, if a competitor is eating into a traditional market share with a product that is technically similar and equally priced, someone in marketing is going to conclude, "*They* know something about selling or customer service that our people don't." And we all have had plenty of phone calls from worried marketing managers and sales vice presidents who say, "Our biggest competitors have been giving their people that new 'Sell Like Hell or Else' training program. Have you got something we can counter it with?"

Maybe you're saying this is not so much a strategy or method of doing a needs analysis as it is admitting to a *fait accompli*. True enough. And from a strategic point of view, it tells you when further study or *any* FTO sort of study won't move the ball along in a desirable direction.

One trouble with management decrees, statistical performance information, and even customer studies is that they don't necessarily arouse the home troops' enthusiasm. People often respond positively only when they feel they've been consulted. Several of the techniques we've examined for gathering performance information have the added benefit of involving employees in the needs-identifying process. Key among these are focus groups, interviews (face to face and on the phone), and questionnaires.

INTERVIEWS AND FOCUS GROUPS. Though effective, these two approaches to answering the questions, "Do we have a problem?" and "What might be causing it?" are far from quick and dirty. There are much less costly and time-consuming ways to answer these questions, but conflicting opinions and rumors frequently cloud consensus, and sometimes little reliable hard data exist. That's when these costly methods serve to clarify issues and give some firm leads on the nature and genesis of the performance problem.

They are also politically useful. One-on-one interviews or focus groups are highly visible and draw attention to the subject at hand. When every foreman or sales manager is interviewed about productivity improvement, you can bet that productivity improvement will suddenly go to the top of the list of every interviewee's to-do list. And as we have said before, both approaches give you a lot of leads to follow when designing questionnaires and making behavioral observations. They also reveal a lot about the performance theories that govern various employees. When a manager of a low-performing unit tells you, "You have to be tough. Too much of that 'good job' kind of talk makes 'em think you're weak," you know you've got your work cut out for you. If that manager's unit and the units of like-minded managers are also performing below standard, behavioral observations and interviews with line people probably will unearth a lot of employee punishment, discontent, and just plain fear and loathing.

QUESTIONNAIRES. When sparingly and precisely built and administered, questionnaire surveys can gather good information and promote employee buy-in. But even if your only reason for doing a survey is to promote buy-in and raise some expectations, you can't risk a bad study. First of all, employees know a mediocre survey when they see one. Secondly, the sponsor will want to look at results and have them explained.

As time passes and money gets spent, the results of the most blatant buy-in survey have a way of becoming a serious part of the study. One of our clients wanted to survey the entire field—over 4,000 people—so that "everyone could feel they were contributing some input." We took the survey seriously, and, sure enough, six weeks later the client had forgotten the "survey study as a buy-in" theory and had assembled a blue ribbon, top management panel to hear and question the findings of "this very expensive study you've been conducting." Had we not taken the study seriously and done our best to make it first-rate, we would have ended up wearing the "sucker of the month" badge.

In summary, then, when you are working in the early stages of a needs study, at the organizational-analysis level, and are trying to convince management-team members that a legitimate performance problem exists, use fairly visible, interactive methods to underscore the existence and urgency of the problem. That translates as focus groups and one-on-one interviews. But don't fool yourself. Management generally needs more than its own words and data parroted back to convince them that the problem exists and is important. So give yourself a back-up. Generally, performance-record or personnel-record analysis data make a good evidential double team for a senior management group. Direct behavioral observations of performers also help sway management.

At the operational level, your methods should be less intrusive and should match the organizational climate, type of job under study, and nature of the problem. At this level, focus groups with performers, supervisors, and high/low performance groups; good guy/bad guy behavioral frequency studies; and attitude/skill surveys are appropriate—also, the old one-to-one interview in one of its infinite varieties. The goal at this level is to look for organizational obstacles, from lack of tools and training to wrong marketing strategy, and to look for critical behavioral differences between high and low performers. Consistently anchor your good guy/bad guy and high performer/low performer contrasts to significant performance data and to performance models that are appropriate to the culture.

At the *individual or job content level,* the classic task analysis level, you will need task listings, S-R tables, algorithms, critical incidents, and all the other job-descriptive information you can pump from your certified subject matter experts. At this level, too, consensus techniques survey data, and behavioral-frequency-study results are useful for setting priorities and understanding exactly which knowledges and skills are demanded of performers. The Gagne sort of analysis comes into play as an instructional strategy aid once the tasks to be learned are agreed upon and the level of learning specified.

Earlier, we discussed how to get management to agree that a problem exists. We then discussed briefly what should be done at the operational and individual levels of analysis. If that cursory treatment was enough for you, jump ahead to Chapter 20. If, on the other hand, you want more information on when to use what criteria, go on to the next page.

CHAPTER **18** DECIDING WHEN TO USE WHAT: TECHNICAL CRITERIA

From here on, we'll skip the political criteria and get more technical. But the question is the same: "How do you know when to use what?" The answer is generally the same: "From our experience, it looks like this . . ." But this time through, let's look at the techniques by group and talk about the technical strengths and weaknesses of each as an information-gathering tool.

There are some tactical matters to take care of first, such as specifying the goal we are working toward and matching the means or techniques at our disposal to it. Many variables can influence the judgment of what the right technique is for a given situation. Therefore, it is important to cull out as many of the unimportant variables as possible before beginning. In particular, it is important to clarify certain assumptions and roles with line management. This usually can be done in a series of interviews. The key questions to answer when you are trying to help management specify the problem as they see it are these:

1. What is the mission of the organization and/or the work unit under study?

The answer to this question determines the relevance of everything else in the study. For example, if the mission of the work unit is to develop a new line of products, there may be little relevance to methods that examine the most effective ways of producing the old products.

2. What are the responsibilities of various persons in the study?

This breakdown of the previous question establishes the purpose and relevance of the specific jobs of each category of persons in the work unit. It also helps sort out whom to study. For example, management of a particular finance institution told us it was the responsibility of company representatives to sell heavy-equipment dealers on the use of their credit packages. What we found out was that none of the reps were carrying out this primary responsibility. Instead, they were spending their time policing the dealers and collecting from the dealers' customers who had fallen behind in their payments. When credit was sold at all, it was being sold by the reps' supervisors. This affected our research strategy quite profoundly. It meant we had to study the supervisor's job to determine why the supervisors were essentially doing the reps' jobs for them. *Then* we could go back and figure out what the reps should be doing and what obstacles to performance existed—other than the fact that their bosses were doing their jobs. When we say "go back," we mean that we simply reversed our interview schedule so we talked to supervisors before we went out on calls with the reps. Two factors were involved in the problem. First, the rep job was more interesting than the supervisor job. Second, policy about who was to do what had changed, but no effort had been made to change line-level expectations or to train anyone for the new strategy.

3. What question are we going to try to answer in the study?

Different methodologies are better suited to answering different kinds of questions. We need to select the method that helps answer the question for which management holds us accountable. For example, if managers of the finance institution just mentioned simply wanted a list of the skills necessary to sell credit, that would require one kind of research technology. But since they wanted to know why the reps weren't selling credit, a different technology was required.

4. What will the study be used for?

It makes a considerable difference whether the information is going to be used for training, management selection, performance appraisal, or some other purpose. For example, if the purpose of the study is to develop a set of scales for selection of performance appraisal, it will require an analysis that can pick out a relatively small number of key skills readily observed and measured by a supervisor. To this purpose, a critical-incident or prioritizing technique might be more appropriate. If, on the other hand, the purpose of the study is to train new recruits in the step-by-step performance of a simple job, an analysis that captures more items and lays out the information in a sequential fashion (first do this, then do that, and so forth) will be required. In this case, a task listing, S-R table, or algorithm might be more appropriate.

MATCHING TECHNIQUE TO TASK

Now the stage is set for matching techniques to tasks. As we've said a couple of ways, the first important discriminator is *observability*. If the majority of the important task behaviors can be observed, you should consider techniques in the S-R table, task listing, time and motion, frequency counting, algorithm, and artifact analysis cluster. But where the most important parts of the task tend to take place in the performer's head or tend to depend on the verbal behavior of others, the weapons of choice are interviews, focus groups, critical incident, simulation, Delphi technique, and questionnaire.

This is, of course, a gross first cut, not a cut-and-dried, inviolable rule. As you have already seen, we often use counting to study selling. But we generally consider selling both an in-the-head and interpersonal set of tasks. The point is, there are both *observable* and *non-observable* chunks to all jobs, but if most of the tasks are observable, start there.

CHOOSING THE RIGHT OBSERVATIONAL TECHNIQUE If the actual performance can be observed under natural conditions and, if most of the information you need is visible to the eye or can be obtained through simple questioning, you can apply one or more of the observational techniques. Table 18-1 summarizes our approach to deciding which observational technique to use when, but let's elaborate a bit.

TASK LISTING. Task listing is most appropriate when the task occurs repeatedly. As soon as the operator has to make choices, the task-listing method becomes cumbersome. When in doubt, start with task listing and see how far you can go before you have to start branching.

Table 18-1 Selecting Observational Techniques.

	Criteria (If . . . .)	Methods (. . . . Then)
The task is highly repetitious, and the operator makes few choices	Speed of operation is not important or not under performer's control	Task Listing
	Speed of operation is important and under performer's control	Time/Motion
The task is only moderately repetitious, and the operator makes choices based on specific conditions	Moderate number of choices	Stimulus/Response Tables
	High number of choices	Algorithm
The task is not very repetitious (Behaviors do not necessarily follow from specific conditions)		Frequency Count
The task involves visible artifacts—tools, products, etc.		Artifact

TIME-AND-MOTION. This variation of task listing simply adds information about how long it takes to perform the steps on the list. It is appropriate when you're training people to match or exceed performance standards at certain speeds, which, of course, must be under their control. We don't suggest you become an expert in conducting time-and-motion studies. But if your organization uses such studies for costing purposes, do become an expert in reading and interpreting their results.

STIMULUS RESPONSE TABLES. Once the task starts to branch and is no longer a strictly repeatable process, it is necessary to use a method that records the stimuli the performer must respond to. The S-R table method is effective when the choices are relatively few and easily recognizable.

ALGORITHM. The algorithm method can be used to describe the steps of almost any task, even one that is not highly visible (such as rules of logic). But it is most appropriate—even essential—in describing tasks involving a high degree of discrimination, that is, when the performer has to make many choices.

FREQUENCY COUNT. Some observable tasks take place without a high degree of evident logic or necessary conditions. When this is so, or at least seems to be so, the frequency count method can be quite effective. It helps you see which behaviors are indeed repeated and at what rate, and what their effect is.

ARTIFACT STUDY. This method can be applied to any task, whether or not the behaviors of the task are visible. It is most useful as a supplement to other methods. All that is required is some visible tool, product, stimulus, tracking device, work record, or other artifact to examine.

CHOOSING THE RIGHT TECHNIQUE FOR ANALYZING THE NONOBSERVABLE If important parts of the performance cannot be observed under realistic conditions or if the information you need is not visible to the eye (for example, the performer's reasons or motives), you can apply several of the techniques we have categorized as "Talking about Work" and "Playing 20 Questions." Table 18–2 should help you decide which of these techniques is most appropriate for your specific purposes.

All non-observational methods are essentially an indirect analysis; therefore, we are usually dealing with human opinions. The key to selecting the right method is knowing whose opinion is needed and for what purpose. The variables that determine this are:

- ► How well you personally know the content of the task
- ► Whether or not the task exists at this point in time
- ► The degree of difference in people's opinions

Table 18-2 Selecting Non-Observational Techniques.

	Criteria (If . . . .)		Methods (. . . Then)
The researcher does *not* know the content of the subject	The task itself exists and the differences in the opinions of the performers are likely to be . . .	Low	Interview
		Moderate	Focus Groups
		High	Critical Incident
	The task itself does *not* exist and the differences in the opinions of the subject matter experts are likely to be . . .	Low to Moderate	Simulation
		High	Delphi
The researcher does know the content of the subject	But the population's degree of feeling or demographic distribution is not known		Questionnaire

CONTENT VERSUS QUANTITATIVE RELATIONSHIP. The first question you have to ask yourself in choosing the right non-observational technique is whether your purpose is to gain *qualitative* information about what makes up the task or *quantitative* information about measurable variables in the task. In our opinion, you must have the former before you can do anything about the latter. For example, if you are trying to discover why customers are complaining about "rude" employee performance, you would do well to interview some employees and some complaining customers first to find out what *kinds* of behaviors are considered "rude" before sending out a questionnaire to find out how these behaviors correlate with other organizational, personnel, or managerial changes.

If your purpose is to gain a large body of qualitative information, then some form of discourse is needed—interview, focus group, and so forth. If your purpose is to gain quantitative information—to determine exactly how many people feel a certain way, how their opinions distribute demographically, or how their opinions correlate with other variables, such as sales or time with company or type of management—then some form of questionnaire is more appropriate.

WHETHER OR NOT THE TASK EXISTS. This factor determines whom you talk to. If the task exists, then you have performers and/or their managers to talk to. If the task does not exist, then you have to talk with subject matter experts. This factor also determines the method you use to talk to these groups. When the job exists, you are able to talk to people about their actual experiences—what they did, what someone else did, and what happened as a result. When the job does not exist, the discussion becomes much more speculative and imaginative, and it is necessary to use techniques that invite the experts to create possible experiences and reactions.

THE DEGREE OF DIFFERENCE The techniques needed for dealing with widely divergent opinions are
IN THE OPINIONS. much more elaborate than those for dealing with similar opinions. They
take more time, and they are usually more expensive. Sometimes people in the
training business tell us their program is based on a "critical incident" study—as if
this gives the program some special validity. One colleague, for example, used that
technique for a conflict-resolution program. But we felt that wasn't necessary. The
skills of conflict resolution are relatively well-known to begin with. And, a series of
interviews with high performers to see how the skills are applied in the shop in
question probably would have sufficed. That is to say, the good performers probably were all doing about the same thing. You may find you have to use an elaborate technique because it is the only one your audience will accept or find "impressive." But if your performers are likely to agree with one another, a simpler method
of doing the analysis would be technically more appropriate.

Let's review the non-observational methods for task analysis and comment on the appropriateness of each.

INTERVIEWS. Interviews are usually the easiest way to tap a person's thoughts, opinions,
and feelings about a job. The advantage is that you can control the flow of information and zero in on the areas you need to know about. The key criterion for using
this technique is that the interviewee must be very representative of the opinions
likely to be held by an entire group of performers or supervisors of performers.
When in doubt, conduct at least three interviews. If the story begins to repeat itself,
stop; you have completed your objective. If the stories seem very different, stop
again and consider changing methods; if you stick with one-on-one interviews in
this situation, you will find yourself with a lot of conflicting information, no budget
or time left, and few convenient ways of putting the pieces together.

There are, of course, exceptions. If one of your FTO study objectives is to
find out how much similarity or difference exists in branch managers' understanding of the organizational mission; or if you are chasing attitudinal differences between managers of high- and low-performing departments or branches,
you would interview all managers, regardless of how the interviews are going. In
these situations, you would analyze the interviews according to some concordance measure.

FOCUS GROUPS. Focus groups are most useful when a certain amount of diversity is expected in the performers' opinions. The group interaction at once stimulates
people to contribute diverse points of view and to attempt to resolve any apparent strong differences.

CRITICAL INCIDENT. This method is most appropriate when performers are unable to describe
any kind of pattern in their work. Their opinions differ widely—not so much on
whether this or that action is good or bad—but as to whether it is necessary or

when it should be done. In this situation, you are dealing with *instances* of be-havior rather than logical and necessary *patterns* of behavior. Encourage the performers to generate and sort out these instances until you see a "pattern" that says, "Do more of these kinds of things and less of those kinds of things."

SIMULATION. Simulation in the context of non-observational techniques refers to talking with experts about the probable steps to take in a future task. It is part interview, part role play, and part study of existing documents, models, or pieces of equip-ment. It is the appropriate method to use when you and your subject matter ex-perts seem to have a good handle on all the variables that will have to be accounted for in a job that doesn't yet exist.

DELPHI. If your subject matter experts disagree with one another on what the job is going to entail or what is important, you should have them project their different thoughts by means of the Delphi technique. You don't want to undertake this rather tedious exercise unless it's pretty obvious the experts are having trouble getting together intellectually, emotionally, or geographically. By the way, if you are surprised to see the Delphi technique sitting here alone without the other consensus techniques, don't be. The Delphi serves a dual purpose: it can be used to gather information about job content—especially for controversial and not yet existing jobs—just as easily as it can be used to resolve conflict among SMEs or to priortize tasks and duties. Actually, the Delphi was originally in-vented for that purpose. Just recently, Patricia McLagan of McLagan Associates in Minneapolis conducted a Delphi study among a number of training directors and consultants to build a competency model for trainers.

QUESTIONNAIRE. Though survey studies often promote buy-in for a training program, the strongest technical reason for using the questionnaire is to gather quantitative in-formation. The survey tells us how many people believe a certain way or believe they have a certain need. Actually, the term *needs analysis* has often been used synonomously with survey, as in the ubiquitous and misleading article title, "How to Write a Needs Analysis Survey That Really Gets at Needs."

The questionnaire answers these questions: "How many people agree that this idea, problem, task, or obstacle exists and is important?" and "How much overlap is there between the opinions of group A and group B?" For example, if supervisors and subordinates or older and younger employees appear to have very different ideas, thoughts, or perceived needs, the survey can tell us whether these differences do indeed exist and how extensive they really are. The questionnaire is also a super tool when used to query a large group about opinions and ideas expressed in a focus group, though the temp-tation is to skip the survey and go with the focus-group study results.

THE PROBLEM OF PRIORITIZING TASKS

To reiterate, the FTO study can be seen as an attempt to answer three questions:

1. Is there a real human factors problem or need?

2. What are the specifics of the problem, need, or task?

3. What are the most important aspects of the problem, need, or task?

Answering the third question sometimes requires agreement of consensus among "experts," and sometimes all those involved with the problem have to be polled to figure out what the most important elements are.

Earlier we discussed three "pure" consensus techniques or strategies. But in the matter of getting agreement, there are a number of other options. For instance, if a simple majority rule seems appropriate, questionnaire or survey results will answer the question at hand. Table 18–3 conveys the conditions and circumstances, the criteria, we use for choosing the appropriate prioritizing technique.

BEHAVIOR FREQUENCY COUNT. Sometimes the decision to be made concerns observable behavior. In these cases, the behavior-frequency-count technique can be used to great advantage, especially if the disagreement is about which behavior is most important. In those instances, the behaviors high performers do more often than low performers can be identified as most significant.

OPINION SURVEYS. In other instances, priority decisions cannot be made on the basis of observable information, and it becomes a question of sorting out opinions. One group of methods for deciding among opinions is the opinion survey, which is appropriate when the decision is to be made quantitatively, depending on which opinion has the numbers on its side. It's rather like voting, except that the voters may be a sample group of employees, customers, managers, or the public at large.

The selection of one survey technique rather than another can be a matter of logistics, what is easier and quicker or what is less costly. Guests in a hotel, for example, may be easier to survey by phone than face-to-face at the check-out desk. Customers of a retail mall may be easier to survey in person than by mailing them questionnaires. When the population to be polled is known by name and address, it may be easier to survey by mail.

It makes sense to use a questionnaire, regardless of the logistics, if the items themselves are quite lengthy or require the respondent to look up information or think about his or her response. On the other hand, the need for spontaneity or timeliness may be a good reason for choosing the telephone survey, even if it means looking up the person's number in a directory. For example,

Table 18-3 Selecting the Right Prioritizing Tool.

	Criteria (If . . .)		*Methods (. . . Then)*
Disagreement concerns observable behavior			Behavior Frequency Count
Disagreement concerns nonobservable feelings and opinions	The matter can be settled by counting noses or surveying relevant opinions	Items to be prioritized are numerous or require thought	Questionnaire
		Items require spontaneity or timeliness	Telephone Survey
		Population is not identified by name	Intercept Survey
	The matter must be solved by subject matter experts or people with insight to future strategy	Moderate disagreement about a few items	Priority Grid
		Moderate disagreement about many items	Survey Group
		Considerable disagreement	Delphi Technique

customers or employees suspected of having had a bad experience with an organization are more likely to respond to a caller who shows interest in them than they are to send back a form to the company that may have offended them.

CONSENSUS TECHNIQUES. Quite often, the matter of determining the priorities for your training material or management intervention requires the cooperation and commitment of several people who approach the situation with strong, or at least divergent, opinions. In this case, the decision requires a process of reaching consensus.

We suggest you consider using one of three tools for reaching consensus. The first is the *priority grid,* which is relatively quick, easy, and inexpensive to use. It is only applicable, however, when there are relatively few items to choose among.

The *survey group* is more appropriate when there are several items to choose among. For example, if a task involves a large number of steps, a survey group can pare down the list for you.

Finally, the *Delphi technique* is useful when there is considerable disagreement. It allows the parties to present their arguments and change their minds without having to endure a confrontation.

SUMMING UP

Deciding when to use which FTO technique isn't as complex and technical as it may seem, especially if you keep in mind the three questions an FTO study aims to answer:

> "Is there a people problem?"

If there *is,*

> "What is causing it?"

If training is part of the problem cause,

> "What should they be doing that they aren't doing now?"

The techniques we've explored and the criteria we've specified in this chapter can help you answer these three questions and prioritize the factors involved with the answers.

CHAPTER 19 A FLOW CHART APPROACH TO SELECTING THE RIGHT TECHNIQUE

If the preceding discussions of when to do what seem too complex for your particular working situation, this chapter should be more to your needs and/or liking. We have developed a basic flow chart that can help you select the right tool for the right problem. This algorithm, which admittedly reflects many of our biases, concentrates on the purely technical factors that make one method more appropriate than others for a particular kind of job. In order to develop a simple, illustrative algorithm, we have left many conditions out of consideration. In particular, we have disregarded conditions of time, cost, and politics. So, put aside your budget worries and other constraints, and refer to the following flow chart (Fig. 19-1) for help in answering the technical questions that determine the right investigative technique.

The first consideration is whether or not you *need* to use any of these techniques. If the task in question is fully described and the description is fully agreed upon by the subject matter experts, then the investigative phase of your job is complete, and you can proceed to the intervention phase—your report, your recommendations, or writing objectives for your training program.

If the task is not fully described and agreed upon, then you have to select the right investigative tool. First, ask yourself, "What is missing—the description or the agreement?" If you already have a good description of the elements that make up the task but can't get your SMEs to agree on their priority, then you will want to apply one or more of the consensus or decision-making techniques. On the other hand, if you don't even have a list of the elements yet, then you need to apply one or more of the job-description techniques: task listing, S-R tables; frequency counts, and so on.

Fig. 19-1   Technique Selection.

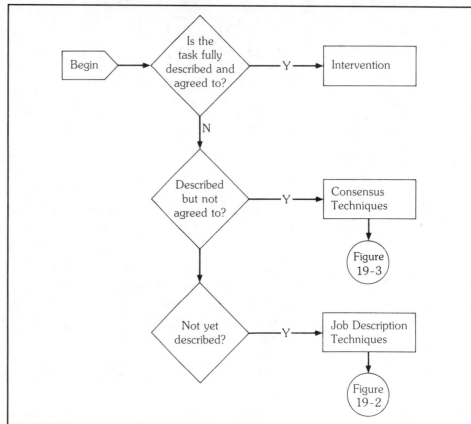

JOB-DESCRIPTION TECHNIQUES

Let's go first to the algorithm for job-description techniques, since you would encounter these first if you were starting from the ground up.

This flow chart (Fig. 19-2) is not as complicated as it looks. Its advantage is that it forces you to make the right technical choices at the beginning and thus avoid flirting with techniques inappropriate to the job.

The first critical question concerns the *existence* of the performer. If the performer is observable in real conditions, then and only then does it make sense to apply any of the observation techniques. If not, you must take a more indirect route.

The very existence of the performer is often an issue for, say, a job that has never been done before. In this case, you have to try some kind of simulation (physical or imaginary) or even the Delphi technique, if the task is highly complex, futuristic, and subject to several interpretations. In the case of jobs-to-

Fig. 19-2 Job Description Techniques.

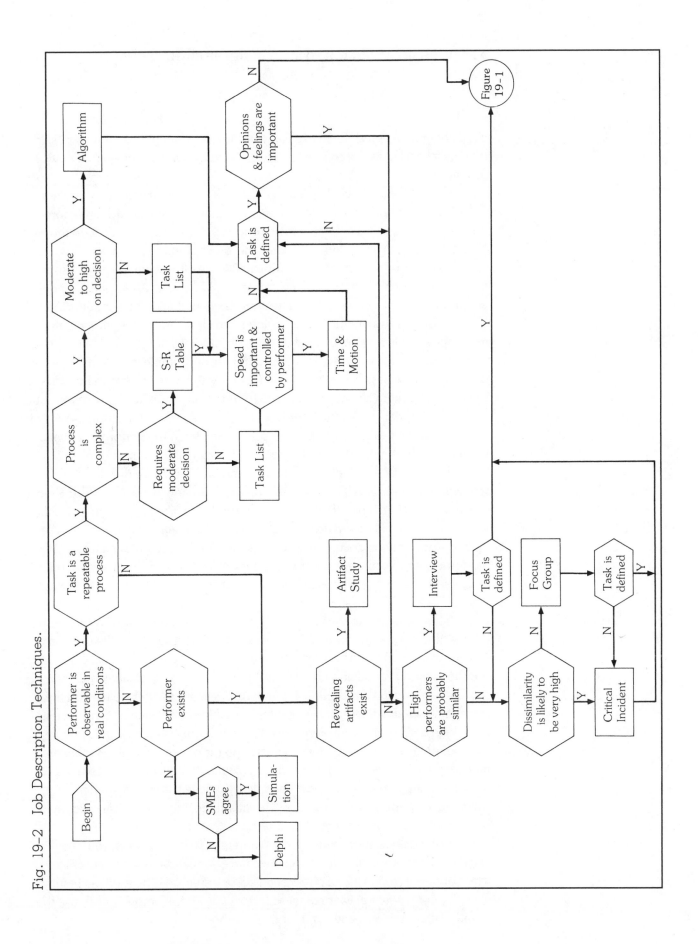

be, a committee or task force usually writes up job descriptions for new positions that must be filled as the company expands into a new technology or a new product line.

But let's say you've decided that the task is observable in real conditions. Before you head off with a clipboard and hardhat, you should ask one more question: "Is the task a set, repeatable process?" If not, forget the trip to the field. You'll get more mileage out of one of the other studies.

Okay, so it's observable and repeatable. The flow chart gives you some clues about which observational technique would be most appropriate for different purposes and circumstances. The *complexity* of the job makes some difference. Mostly it rules out the S-R technique, which is sometimes cumbersome to use when studying complex jobs. But complexity does not discriminate against task listing, which can be used for both complex and simple jobs. What does discriminate against task listing is a job that requires the performer to make *decisions*. An algorithm can always be used for observing repeatable processes, but it is most appropriate when the performer has to make a lot of decisions. And, of course, time-and-motion studies are appropriate when the performer's *speed of operation* is both important to the task and under his or her control.

Let's go back to the left side of the chart and say we've decided that the task was not an observable, repeatable process. So now what do we do? Before automatically launching off into interviews and focus groups, we like to ask if there are any *revealing artifacts* we can look at. If there are, we'll want to scare up and study various documents, records, or objects and ask ourselves: "What did someone have to do in order to produce this?" If that doesn't answer our question completely, it at least gives us a lot of clues about what to ask in the follow-up "talking about" study.

There are two reasons to undertake a "talking about the job" study. One is because the job is a nonobservable process; the other is because the opinions or feelings of the performers are important to the job. The key technical criterion for selecting among the talking-about techniques is the degree of *similarity or dissimilarity* among the performers. If the performers are all likely to tell you the same thing, interview only a few of them. But if they are likely to exhibit a relatively high degree of dissimilarity, select a focus group, which would encourage the unearthing and airing of these different points of view. Finally, if there are many differing opinions and explanations of what the desired performance should be, and there are respected people who have firsthand experience watching the performers in question "do their thing," then a critical incident study might be your best bet.

In choosing between face-to-face and telephone interviews, you have to consider some factors that aren't on the chart—for example, time, access and whether or not some kind of physical object or visual aid is needed in the interview. By now, you are aware of these factors and should know how to use them to make the decision between interview methods.

Fig. 19-3 Techniques for Agreement.

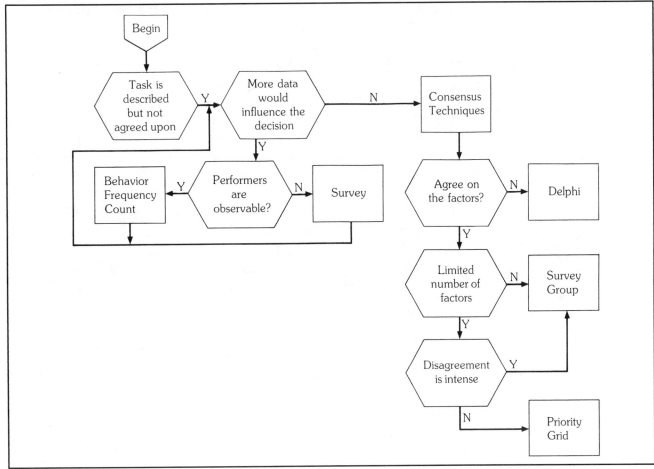

Let's focus again on the consensus techniques box (Fig. 19-3). If the performer's task is fully described but you are unable to get agreement upon which elements in the task are paramount, then consider using one or more of the consensus or decision-making techniques. This is the second criterion that requires the input of a gaggle of SMEs.

The first question to ask when deciding which consensus technique to use is whether or not there are some *data* that would influence the decision. We find that the most persuasive data come from frequency counts taken in live observations. So, if your performers are observable, do a behavior frequency count and include the results in the data you present to the consensus group.

If the performers are not easily observable, a survey would be your next-best method for getting some objective data to influence the decision. Whether you do a telephone, questionnaire, or intercept survey will depend on such logistical factors as: access to the population, time, and cost.

Let's assume that you've gathered all the possible data, and you have nothing more to tell your decision makers. Now you simply have to help them decide on the priorities of the job. Enter the concensus techniques.

The difficulty of the decision governs your choice among these techniques. The first thing to consider is whether or not the decision makers are going to accept your definition of the factors involved in the decision. If not, then you have to apply some kind of Delphi technique in which they work alone or in small groups to define their own set(s) of factors.

If, however, they agree that all the elements of the decision are present, then you can use either the survey group or priority grid to reach actual consensus. The priority grid is useful under two conditions: the number of factors is limited, and disagreement is not too intense. The advantage of the priority grid is that you don't have to assemble a group to execute it. You simply ask everyone to make his or her choice, you compile the results, and you announce them.

Use the survey group when the choice is more difficult. Through the use of various instruments (surveys, straw votes, even priority grids) and discussion, you pare down the choices, facilitate the trade-offs, and negotiate the final decisions.

SECTION **VII** IN SUMMARY

We come to the place where the rubber hits the road, as it were. We've found that all the research and analysis in the world is worthless unless somebody buys the result you are selling; unless you can convince others that you have found out something important. Facts do not speak for themselves; truth does not win in the end. Facts and truth have to be sold. An FTO study is a way of gathering objective data. Using that data effectively is another matter. Data simply gives you a power base from which to suggest solutions to problems.

As we all have seen, all to often, it is the size of the voice raised that gets one heard, rather than the value of what is said. Data gives you some of the equalizers you need—a good presentation and a set of acceptable solutions. And, as we have found out the hard way, the skill, thought, and care we bring to presenting results to the people who give the nod, may be the most important part of an FTO study.

CHAPTER **20** REPORTING RESULTS TO MANAGEMENT

The most important part of any needs, task, or organizational effectiveness study is delivering the results to management. You may have performed the best study in the history of the organization. The results and findings may be overwhelming in implication. But if your presentation of those results is poorly positioned and lacks persuasive power, nothing—but *nothing*—will change in your organization.

There is an old adage about the infinite number of slips possible twixt the cup and the lips. The slip we've observed trainers make most frequently—and most unnecessarily—is that of presenting the results of a professionally done, first-rate study in a lackluster, amateurish fashion.

But don't results speak for themselves? No way! As consultants, we are hypersensitive to the image we project to our clients. We are always striving for credibility in the clients' eyes. In a sense, we are always selling. What we don't understand is why organizational staff people, who are also consultants, internal consultants, totally neglect *their* client image. As an in-house trainer, you have to compete for organizational resources with not only outsiders but other staffers as well. You must be able to sell your ideas and study findings to gain the resources you need to solve the problems you find.

Like it or not, the results of a mediocre study persuasively presented are more likely to generate management action than are results of an excellent study poorly presented. Our guiding principle is: *The quality of a results presentation is more important than the quality of study that produced the results.* To be blunt, we are convinced, as are others we know who make a living doing organizational research, that it is the quality of our results *presentations,* not the quality and thoroughness of our *work,* that gains us kudos and repeat business from our clients. Experience has taught us that we must put as much thought and cleverness into the communication of results as we put into the design and conduct of the study itself.

Toward that end, we have developed ten guidelines to bear in mind when attempting to communicate and *sell* results to management.

RULE 1: DEFINE THE PURPOSE FIRST

You may be getting tired of this line, but it's as true for presentations as it is for anything else: If you don't know where you're going, you'll probably end up somewhere else. You wouldn't start a task analysis, a needs study, or an organizational-problem study without defining your goals. The same applies to a results presentation.

John F. (Jack) Anderson, of Anderson & Berdie Research, puts it this way:

> When you're commissioned by an organization to do an evaluation or any kind of program or personnel research, it's because someone wants an answer to a question. But beyond that, they are usually anticipating the need for some course of action. So we have an obligation to present the results of our work in a way that allows the decision makers in the audience to determine that course of action. If, six months after you've presented your findings nothing has changed, you haven't really done the job you were commissioned to do.

Though some we've talked to have said it differently, the essence is usually the same. To be precise, *the purpose of any presentation of field research findings—be they findings from an evaluation study, a needs analysis, or a climate study—is to communicate so that others can formulate and instigate a course of action. When we report findings to a sponsor or client, our pervasive goal should be to cause someone to do something.*

Until you can answer the question "*Who* do you want to have do *what,* and *how* do you get them to do it?," you can't start planning a presentation. At least not a presentation that will communicate something specific and dynamic to the intended audience. Even if you are reporting that everything is okay in a program, work group, or system, there is still an implied action goal. The desired action may be to gain consensus that the program should continue unchanged or uninterrupted. It could also be that your goal is to keep the program funded. It might even be that you want to demonstrate your competency and worth. Regardless of specifics, every presentation needs a clearly conceived action goal.

Anderson and Berdie suggest that you try to state, in 25 words or less, the action you want the study sponsor to take as a result of your presentation of results. If you can't, we question whether you began your study by asking, "What is the problem I'm looking at, and why is it important enough to warrant this study?" And we question as well whether you took time to sit back when the study was finished and answer the questions, "What did I learn that explains the cause of the problem?" and "What did I learn about ways the problem might be eliminated?"

RULE 2: KNOW THY AUDIENCE

When you develop a training program, you do your best to make it audience-sensitive. Educational level, vocabulary, background, and experience, among other factors, are seriously contemplated when designing training. The same treatment applies to designing a results presentation. Among the important audience questions to ask are these:

1. Will the audience for the presentation be decision makers, technical people, or a mix of both?

2. What kinds of results presentations have they favored in the past?

3. Do they prefer written results to oral presentations?

4. How do they respond to charts and graphs?

5. Have they ever totally panned a presentation of results?

We used to believe that you could psyche out an audience at arms length. We accepted, for instance, the assumption that decision makers are more receptive to big-picture results presentations than to reams of charts, correlations, and printouts. However, a mortifying misread of one of those rare data-cruncher decision makers—the type who likes to impress the room with his or her mastery of Statistics 201—cured that bad habit. Don't try to outguess your audience. No one expects the fry cook to guess how you want your eggs; so don't try to guess how the powers that be want their results cooked and served.

Generally, the best source of this sort of intelligence is the study sponsor. After all, he or she authorized your work and is on the line with you. So ask. And ask your liaison as well. The person who has been helping you connect with the right people and generally expediting your work is likely to know the sensitivities and preferences of the decision makers.

RULE 3:
COMMUNICATE AS
YOU GO

Communicating results is *not* a one-shot affair. Douglas R. Berdie, the other half of Anderson & Berdie, believes that part of the communication job is to keep the client posted on everything that's happening. Send the sponsor and/or key decision makers copies of surveys, work schedules, and your routine field communiqués about the project. Pen some sort of FYI on their copies. As results accumulate, share bits and pieces with your key person(s).

Why this emphasis on communicating as you go? Five reasons:

1. The sponsor is paying for your time and effort, and needs to see energy being expended. Call it a need for positive feedback. But it is also true that communication and observable effort build credibility and trust. Your sponsor is your best friend, *if* you keep him or her abreast of what you are doing and learning.

2. The results of your work will be more easily accepted by those who have ownership feelings toward the study. Asking the sponsor for advice and making brief, informal interim reports help build that sense of ownership.

3. The sponsor and some of the key decision makers can give you valuable feedback when you have questions about findings. An unexpected, unusual, or especially damning revelation needs validation. A sympathetic sponsor can tell you if your findings make sense in light of his or her experience and intuition. And sponsors often have access to other research, studies, or problems that they can use to judge your unusual findings.

   Note: We aren't suggesting you give the sponsor veto power over your findings. We simply believe the sponsor is a great sounding board.

4. The sponsor knows who should see your results, who will need to concur with them before problem-solving action can take place, and how you should package that information for those key decision makers. They can tell you, for instance, who needs a private preview beforehand and who must be catered to during a public presentation.

5. Sponsors *don't* take kindly to public surprises, especially disagreeable surprises. By giving sponsors and key decision makers a sneak preview of the bad news, you give them time to accept it, think about implications and ramifications, hypothesize causes and remedies, and generally plan a response strategy they can unleash when you publicly present the bad news. Sponsors and key decision makers want to be on your side. After all, they are asking you to look at their programs and/or problems and give them a reading about how things are going. A tactical information leak gives them the lead time they need.

RULE 4: TAILOR THE MEDIA STYLE TIME MIX FOR THE AUDIENCE

When you read *presentation of results,* what do you think of? A written report? A group of people sitting around a walnut conference table? A presenter with flip charts, overheads, and grand graphics?

We've noticed that most results presentations follow the rule of tradition. If our client organization traditionally writes 200-page results reports, *we* write 200-page results reports. If most results presentations are delivered orally to small groups, we follow this organizational formula as well. If the folks like those long reports or cozy meetings, great. But remember, a two-day presentation and a 200-page report may be too little for some groups and studies; while, a two-hour presentation and a 20-page report may be too much for others.

The trick is to tailor. If you plan to present your findings report to six people, find out as much as you can about the communication styles and organizational and personal needs of those individuals. What issues are they sensitive to? What vested interests do they have that relate to your study? What outcomes do they expect and what results will be rejected out of hand? What are the "we tried that" or "oh, no, we don't" issues? What are the local taboo words, ideas, concepts?

Regardless of the particular needs, expectations, and communication confort zones of your clients there are some generally accepted givens for effective client communication.

▶ If you find you must prepare a written report, do so in unadorned English. The object is to communicate, not to overpower.

▶ In both written and oral communications to mixed audiences of decision makers and technical people, use the *Wall Street Journal* or pyramidal format. Organize the report in this order: (a) a brief statement of the problem under investigation, (b) findings, and (c) if appropriate, conclusions and recommendations. In written form, this "executive overview," as it is sometimes dubbed, will be two to five pages long. In oral presentation, it should take less than an hour to establish rapport, set a workable climate, and get to the punchline. The subsequent parts of the report simply elucidate the executive overview and, if necessary, explain study methods, data reduction procedures, and the like.

▶ Most audiences prefer a *descriptive* results report as opposed to correlational or complex tabular presentations. If you are an in-house or trusted investigator, you are probably accepted as a competent expert. So spare your audience the details of your design and analysis steps, and keep your computer runs to yourself.

▶ Clearly separate findings, interpretations, conclusions, and recommendations. Dr. Darwin Hendle, of the University of Minnesota Measurement Services Center, suggests that while clients want to hear your ideas on possible problem solutions, they need to know what is supportable fact or finding and what is your own informed conjecture. Separate the two so you don't dilute the impact of the facts and findings.

▶ Accuracy is another key to credibility. Spelling and organizational title errors, tables that don't total 100 percent, wrong dates and misattributions, all these undercut your credibility with the audience. When in doubt, use phrases such as "It is our understanding," or "It is our perception of the situation," rather than "The problem is . . ." or "Since the goal of your division is to . . ." Acknowledging that you might be wrong is always preferable to being overly self-assured.

► Think your way through the media and choreography of the presentation. Use the same media-method savvy you use when designing a training package, a sales presentation, or any sort of media show. "Why," Jack Anderson asks provocatively, "do we assume that a report is a written mini-thesis or that an oral presentation requires an armful of unreadable tables on mylar sheets? How about presenting results in skit form or as poetry or in a cartoon or slide show format? People somehow have the idea than an evaluation-results report should be dull to be legitimate."

RULE 5: PILOT TEST THE PRESENTATION

We pilot test training, don't we? Isn't a problem-analysis study or a needs analysis just as important to your success? Get your research team, your department's two biggest nit-pickers, and the coordinator from client department together, for a dress rehearsal. Only during a dry run will you realize that your findings aren't as crystal-clear as you thought or that *MBO, TA,* or *Behavior Mod* are taboo expressions in the client organization but that *goal setting, interpersonal communication* and *performance management* are acceptable. You'll also get a reaction to the "sell power" of your presentation from the client rep, as well as some thoughts about who will react negatively to the presentation and how to mitigate that response.

RULE 6: DELIVER BAD NEWS FIRST

Research by Linda Marshall and Robert Kidd of Boston University suggests that people prefer to hear bad news first, then good news. Though they aren't sure, they suspect that this placement of the bad and the good makes the good seem better and the bad seem less so. Whatever the case, bad news is still bad news and must be delivered with care. Don't begin with "Good morning. Your course really stinks. Now for the good news . . ." If you still prefer to give good news first, ease your way into it. Good news first, mixed results second, and bad news last is a formula some still prefer.

Steve Mayer of Rainbow Research in Minneapolis, also cautions that bad news should be delivered directly and not unnecessarily minimized or sugar-coated. "If you minimize bad news, you rob your sponsor of an important learning opportunity," he says.

Jack Anderson advises not to overblow the good news either. "You might get away with saying, 'This is the finest program of its kind we've ever had the inestimable pleasure to evaluate,' once or twice, but people get awfully suspicious of that sort of syrup," he contends.

A good model for delivering bad news is the fine arts review. People who review books, movies, plays, art shows, and the like know that a bad review is more difficult to write—and often more interesting to read. The reviewer must compare and contrast, use examples and analogies, and generally construct a more persuasive argument than is necessary for complimentary reviews.

Edward F. Kelly of the Center for Instructional Development, Syracuse University, believes that a literary-criticism approach to program evaluation and research reporting is useful because it demands a public justification on two fronts. The literary critic must *evaluate* and *explain* what standards were used for particular judgment. When a fine arts critic writes, "I thought I'd be moved by this brave new symphony, but it was only a gentle breeze compared to the hurricane of emotional experience I had been led to anticipate by pre-performance publicity," we know what he or she felt and why. In our more mundane FTO world, the same end is achieved this way:

> A number of sales experts believe and a few well-done research studies substantiate the belief that the more times a salesperson asks for an order during a face to face sales call, the greater the probability of consumating a sale. Therefore, our finding that low performers tend to ask for the order one-third fewer times per sales call seems significant.

When you clarify your criteria and your judgements, your audience has a context for understanding your findings and for personally judging the limits of the results. It gives them an intuitive answer to the question, "But how important *is* important?"

RULE 7: LEAVE NOTHING TO CHANCE
Nit-pick both your presentation and written material relentlessly. You may have conducted the best study in the world and developed strong, compelling results and findings, but a third-rate presentation can make a mockery of all your hard work.

Use sharp, word-processed copies of written materials instead of poor photocopies or mimeos. Package written materials in attractive binders. Use professionally prepared visuals. These little things gain you important credibility points. Making certain that presentation rooms are clear and comfortable, that appropriate audio-visual equipment is on hand and functioning, and that chairs and tables are suitable for the group, are examples of thoughtfulness that can gain still more credibility points. Reports peppered with misspellings or smudges, malfunctioning overhead projectors, and a pile of party hats and empty champagne bottles in a corner of the presentation room are unfortunate little touches that do not gain you credibility points.

Your professionalism is being tested during a face to face results presentation. You'll be questioned about your findings and occasionally challenged. How you react will affect the reception of your report. You only have one chance to make a positive, credible impression, so don't leave that impression to chance.

RULE 8: EXPECT TO
BE REJECTED

A client once did us a great favor by explaining that we should be prepared to have his group reject our findings. "We won't believe much of what you tell us right now," he said. "But a few months from now, you'll see a lot of action." This same client was a bank senior vice president who had seen the results in preview—the tactical leak at work—and knew them to be potentially unsettling. He went so far as to compare a client's acceptance of bad news results to Dr. Elizabeth Kubler-Ross's stages of death acceptance. How right he was!

In the intervening years, we have observed about seven steps or stages in the "Acceptance of Bad News Syndrome."

Stage 1: You're wrong. The client believes your findings are wrong and should be dismissed summarily.

Stage 2: You're right, but you took a bad sample. The client believes *you* believe your findings, but they are based on bad sampling and are a statistical accident.

Stage 3: You're right, but your results are trivial. The results and findings are right, but they are out of context. Seen in the proper perspective, the insider's perspective, the bad news results are merely trivial.

Stage 4: You're right, but we like it this way. The results are correct and important. However, we don't consider this situation bad. On reflection, we really like things this way.

Stage 5: You're right, but we can't change. Okay, so things are bad. But that's the nature of our business [bureau, organization, or whatever], and we would have to change all of society to alter our situation.

Stage 6: Okay, you're right. Let's do something. The problem is real and probably manageable. Let's do something about it.

Stage 7: Problem! What Problem? The client accepts the problem, solves it, and goes on. In instances of especially sensitive organizational problems, the client represses or denies the existence of the resolved problem; this is rather like the ex-smoker who can't really remember having any difficulty quitting.

Awareness of this seven-step syndrome may help you over some rough spots, come presentation time. The client who's familiar with these seven steps can also maintain a measure of composure when his or her team starts taking one or more of them.

RULE 9: KEEP
THE BALL IN
THEIR COURT

Your job as investigator and results presenter can't be overruled by your natural inclination to nurture. Sure, you should counsel and be empathetic if the client starts bemoaning your findings, but focus your counseling on the meaning and implication of results. Direct challenges to your methodology should be answered in a calm, rational way. Any show of impatience with the client's questioning can only make matters worse. It might even be wise to assume a fairly unemotional, detached manner during the entire results-presentation period. If you appear too "high" on your results, you might be misinterpreted as a lightweight.

For sure, avoid prolonged discussions about why things turned out as they did. *Everybody* has a story to tell and a rationalization to make. You erode your findings by sympathizing with those "If you worked here, you'd understand" stories.

If you've done your work carefully and well and presented your report competently and confidently, you're on solid ground. You have nothing to be defensive about, explain away, or react emotionally to.

RULE 10: EVALUATE

One way to evaluate an FTO study is simply to stand back and watch. If you see activity taking place around the neighborhood of the problems you elucidated, that's a nice indicator. Or, after some time has passed, you might want to come right out and ask what happened as a result of the study, report, and presentation. If the answer is, in so many words, "Not much," you have just inherited a new study. That's the one you are going to have to do to find out why the results of your original study didn't produce the results you planned, or any results at all. After all, if your study was on target and your presentation followed these guidelines, it should have had an effect.

When crystal balling an old study that went sour, there are two important questions to ask and answer for yourself.

> **1.** Did I study the wrong problem, come to the wrong conclusion, or recommend the wrong course of action?

If your answer to all or any of the above is yes, then your best bet is to simply shake it off, learn from your error, and try again. If the answer is no then ask this second question.

> **2.** Is it possible that, regardless of what I find or recommend, nothing will *ever* happen around here?

If your answer to this testy little query is affirmative, you would be well advised to keep your resume up to date. And your head down.

CHAPTER 21 BEYOND FIGURING THINGS OUT: SOLUTIONS STILL PAY THE RENT

Those of us in the training and human resources development profession are on retainer to solve performance problems and to strategize ways of helping our sponsoring organizations help other people in the organization do the right job well. In short, solutions still pay the freight, and the call to "do a little research first" is usually anathema to a manager saddled with a difficult problem. We can't help but remember the client of a few years back to whom we proposed a complete package: a needs- and task-analysis study, program development, and a results evaluation. "Great little proposal," he said, "but I can't really afford it. So skip the research part; I'll tell you what to put in the program. And forget the evaluation; I'll know whether it works or not." We ended up walking away from that one.

Beyond, or perhaps within, that would-be client's assertions that he didn't need any research was a very erroneous assumption that you should consider when you're told to "forget that research stuff, *we* know what the problem is; what *they* really need; and how to handle this." Applied organizational research, which is what a Figuring Things Out study really is, is not a passive, invisible occurrence. It takes place in time and space, involves people, and has an effect on the very things you are observing; it is an active intervention and a "solution" in its own right. Remember the Heisenberg Principle we borrowed from physics? Just as the act of measuring the temperature of a volume of water changes the temperature of the water by virtue of the presence of the thermometer, so, too, does the act of studying organizations and people change the people and organizations being studied.

Going out into the field and asking managers to verbalize their operating/managing philosophy: asking engineers or doctors or technicians to express the thoughts running through their heads while they work; and listening to salespeople tell how they decide whether a prospect is a good or a bad bet are interventions. By their occurrence, these activities change the behavior of the action objects—the performers themselves. We've seen instances where low-performing sales branches and high-absence assembly lines have reversed course just because we were nosing around asking "why" questions. We are *not* simply in the pure and pristine information-gathering and analysis business. We are, always and forever, in the change business.

The first behavioral observation study you conduct can teach you that. Standing about with a clipboard, stopwatch, and white coat, making copious notes, and muttering, "Tsk, tsk, tsk," can have a walloping effect on the behavior of the people you are trying to observe au naturel. And as we said in chapter 4 on behavioral-observation studies, there are both pluses and minuses to that problem. On the plus side, if the performers in question know you are there, but still can't do the job correctly or if they do it according to a set of norms that are contrary to organizational expectations, you've learned something very important. On the other hand, we stand to lose something by our very visibility. But, as we said in that same chapter, the obtrusive effects of observational approaches can be minimized and managed, if not eliminated.

Intervention at this level of thought and effort has minimal organizational impact. In the scope of an organization's overall operations, one little observational study in the Fort Wayne branch or a series of one-on-one interviews with supervisors in Boise is small potatoes. The real interventional impact of a Figuring Things Out study originates at a much higher level in most organizations. This becomes clear when you start asking yourself and others, "Why are we looking at this problem in the first place?" The answer is always that someone is thinking about changing the organization and needs information to check out his or her hunches, either about the need for change or to further his or her strategy for pulling off a desired change.

In other words, we are almost always caught up in *someone's*, sometimes even our own, scheme to change things. This doesn't give us any ethical-dilemma nightmares either. It simply confirms how inextricably we as investigators are enmeshed with the change business. Our ultimate, unstated Figuring Things Out study mission is almost always to provide information that will help guide some form of organizational change.

To do the job well, we must be good technicians, and we must be aware of the myriad changes going on around us; those we are caught up in and those that our activist/researcher roles and activities expose us to.

FOR INSTANCE . . .

We once did a study for a highly profitable, established manufacturing organization with a large national and international sales force. The company had a centralized sales-training function and a head-office training staff commissioned to prepare new hires to sell a large, diverse, and sophisticated product line. As you might reasonably guess, there were factions and frictions and countless unresolved conflicts among marketing, sales, management, and training personnel over course content imperatives, centralization versus decentralization of sales training, and curriculum control. It happens in every organization and has as many healthy as unhealthy ramifications.

A need for major change was well established before we were retained to look for and gather data on key issues. The actual sales job had been growing geometrically in complexity as new products and technologies were introduced. A job that once had consisted of putting two samples in the car trunk and then knocking on doors from sunrise to sunset had become a bid proposal, systems-selling proposition. The training had grown in parallel complexity. A simple "features advantage benefits" training program had become a semi-automated, multi-media 'business' owned by professional instructional technologists, most of whom had never carried a sales kit.

But Big Company was justly proud of the "state of the art" of its sales-training program. Still, there was widespread dissatisfaction over performance in the field. Salespeople weren't producing up to expectations, and it seemed that everyone in sales, marketing, and training was pushing a favorite solution. Better some tension over solutions than no comprehension of a problem!

We entered the picture to help the people running the training add yet another level of sophistication to what they were doing. Our familiarity with modeling theory, video, and the like brought us the call. The only research the vice president who hired us had in mind was the kind that would help us learn enough about the population, products, and current standard operative procedures to build a new version of the old program.

Discussions with the vice president, directors, peers, and subordinates made it painfully obvious that without a real figuring-things-out effort we might end up holding—or being in the bag. If the directors' idea of a cure for the current gripes—packaging the old shoe in a new razzle-dazzle box—worked, he won; if it failed to quell the palace revolt, *we* could lose. Greed, of course, dictated that we hang in there and find a way to give the client both what he *wanted* and what he *needed*.

Our break came when we discovered that lack of "field acceptance" tended to undercut any solution that came out of headquarters. Both the training director and his vice president realized that if we went through the motions of doing some research, field personnel might accept the new program because it was based on their input. As this point, no one who hired us had the slightest concern about the data we might turn up. Obviously, it would simply show that field sales management was failing to reinforce the training. Our research, which was santioned for political reasons, was seen as "simply good marketing."

The vice president was convinced that we would exonerate the current training. The training director, though committed to the worth of his training, was nonetheless curious about what else our spade work might turn up. He arranged conditions and saw to it that our studies were conducted objectively. But he was more than sure he had his finger on the corporate pulse and knew that sort of change events were going on in the field.

We received a warm welcome once we reached the field. "At last they are going to listen to us," said field sales managers. The subjective feeling of a need for change was palpable, and we never had any difficulty getting the subjects to express their views, fill out surveys, or let us ride along with high- and low-performing sales reps. The immediate effect of the research was a burst of energy by local and regional supervisors to motivate the troops. This reaction was partially catalyzed by a supplementary, ad hoc training program that the chief sales manager himself had sent out and also by an incentive-motivation call program instituted by an obscure part of the marketing group.

This raised an interesting question: Were these programs going to come out anyway at this time? Or did the research project flush them out? After all, wouldn't it be smart to put on a push or publish a performance solution before our research made it obsolete? Or, even better yet, to institute solutions eventually proved right by the research? We'll never know the answers to these questions. But we are no longer surprised when the appearance of solutions coincides with the beginning of a research project. We are more surprised when this *doesn't* happen.)

At the conclusion of our figuring-things-out study, we had three major findings:

1. The training was not being reinforced in the field. On that score, headquarters had been correct.

2. The current training was aimed at developing only a small percentage of the behavior characteristic of the high performers.

3. Within the organization, we found at least eight fundamental controversies and/or disagreements about the nature, mission, roles, tasks, and training of new reps. These controversies were strongly polarized. And because the new field salespeople felt torn between head-office and field-management expectations, performance suffered.

Round three: As our results pot began to boil, the marketing vice president and training director noticed an odd smell and came to investigate. This time, there was little talk about "research as a political tool" but a lot of noise about using "basic field-generated performance data" to institute change. The training director, in particular, became very interested. And, as more data condensed into findings, another change occurred: he started using them. At one point, he photocopied pages of a preliminary findings report on high-performer observed behaviors and passed them out in class. The target was moving. And it moved fast. By the time we'd completed our two months of field work, the new rep training had been modified to reflect about 90 percent of the behaviors that separated high and low performers. At the same time, carping about field efforts to reinforce training died out, *despite* our findings that there was merit to the claim.

The marketing vice president took the results of our field research very seriously. He could see that the study was not merely political and had turned up some interesting problems, not of all of which related to changing the training program. We had also uncovered some fundamental problems in the way the sales organization conceived of its mission and structured the tasks people performed. But these problems were outside of the vice president's purview and would have to go back to the senior sales managers themselves.

In no time at all, we found ourselves in the consensual validation business going to task force meetings, clarifying findings and issues, and refereeing discussions and votes on various proposals, alternatives, and behavioral blueprints. A recounting of one of the issues under debate, and its resolution will suffice to remake the point that research is an *intervention*.

The scene was one of the task force meetings called to resolve one of the issues that surfaced in the field data-gathering phase. The issue was the confusion among different experts about how reps should be selling. We spent half a day raising each viewpoint and refereeing the discussion. At the half-way point, we wrote eight resolution statements and then spent the last half of the day with our SMEs, who voted on the merits of each of our propositions. Each task force member could vote "yes," "yes but," or "no and here's why." On each proposition, overnight we tabbed and showed them where they were in agreement.

Another day of horse-trading and bargaining, but with a difference: A task force committed to fighting it out to the death was laughing, cajoling, negotiating, and problem solving. When the smoke finally cleared, task force members sauntered arm-in-arm off to bar and golf course and we collapsed. This final meeting had removed the philosophical roadblocks to developing an effective training program. The participants went home knowing that the battle was over and that they had no choice but to support the program when it came out.

Only after all that did we begin to use the research to fulfill our original contract determining what new training interventions should actually be developed and in what new media method combinations. Once the controversial assumptions were clarified, we were able to help plug the research details into the client's program design grid and come up with all the objectives, tests, and teaching points necessary for new programming that would improve field performance.

That's a very long but very true story. It's not a story of heroism but one of change and using figuring-things-out research as a facilitating force in change.

Recap the events and you'll see even more clearly the pattern of change that decent field research—an FTO study—can precipitate.

1. The research was commissioned by someone who had a desire for *change* and who was looking for leverage.

2. By its presence, the act of research stimulated a *change* in the level of activity in the field.

3. Those who had been contemplating some independent, curative action suddenly did an about-face and introduced the courses and programs they had been contemplating. More *change*, stimulated by the presence of the research.

4. As parts of the new selling model began appearing in the research findings, headquarters training people made temporary *changes* in existing programs.

5. Controversial issues were focused clearly for the first time—another intervention, another change.

6. Issues that had heated, cooled, hardened, and became obstacles over the years were forced to resolution—intervention, solution, change.

7. Consensus was forced out of a stubborn group, and the members resolved to buy in to their own consensus—intervention, solution, change.

8. The training director got the content he needed for his new, improved high-technology training program; in fact, he ended up with a mandate for *more* programming than ever before. And he had more approval and commission and mandate than ever before. Again, intervention, solution and change.

The moral of the story is that solutions to problems come in a variety of trappings. Our sponsor in the Big Company case really believed that training was going to solve his problems. Eventually, training was a big part of the solution. But the "figuring-things-out" investment was every bit as important and played just as crucial a role in changing things that needed changing as did the fine sales training programs that eventually were developed. To truly handle Big Company's performance problems, both the research and the training were critical; like horse and rider, they needed each other to get from point A to point B, from where they wanted, needed, to go.

The point we've been hammering on is that applied action research—attempting to figure things out—is a very powerful intervention. Never apologize for doing it or expect to do it in an environment free of politics and/or hassles. Action research is an activity that stimulates other activity. Change stimulates change. Sometimes, as in the Big Company case, the change happens so fast you can hardly tally it. Sometimes it takes a sundial to perceive the movement. But that's the way most interventions are—unpredictable and maddeningly individualistic. Patience and a firm grasp on the reality of the change process are necessary if you want to manage action research meaningfully. But manage it you must. Every "figuring-things-out" study, every piece of organizational action research you undertake, precipitates change and must be managed. Done correctly, competently, and compassionately, a "figuring-things-out" study is both an information-gathering activity and a vital part of the organizational change process we are ultimately paid to help facilitate.

APPENDIX A GAGNE DEFINES TASK ANALYSIS

MILITARY TRAINING AND PRINCIPLES OF LEARNING*

Robert M. Gagne
Princeton University

The subject chosen for this address is one which I think I can view with a certain perspective. Stated very briefly, this circumstance arises from the face of my changes in occupation, from that of an investigator of learning principles in academic laboratories, to a research administrator of programs of military training research in government laboratories, and back again to an academic laboratory. In making the remarks to follow, I claim nothing more than this perspective, which perhaps carries with it a certain detachment, or freedom from involvement with particular learning theory, as well as with particular training problems.

What I should like to talk about are some general impressions concerning the applicability of learning principles to military training. In the time available to me, I cannot really do more than this. It would be satisfying to think that I could review and marshal the evidence from military studies of training in a truly systematic manner. I am not sure that this can be done even with unlimited time. But at any rate, my aim is much more limited than this. Perhaps it can be stated in the following way. Suppose that I were a learning psychologist, fresh out of an academic laboratory, who was to take a new job in charge of a program of research on some type of military training. What principles of learning would I look for to bring to bear on training problems? What kinds of generalizations from laboratory studies of learning would I search for and attempt to make use of in training situations? The answers I shall suggest for these questions require first a consideration of what kinds of principles have been tried, and how they have fared.

---

*Presidential address delivered at the annual meeting of the Division of Military Psychology, 69th Annual Convention of the American Psychological Association, New York, NY, September 5, 1961. Supported in part by Contract AF 49(638)-975, with the Office of Scientific Research, U.S. Air Force. The opinions expressed are those of the author. Copyright 1962 by the American Psychological Association. Reproduced by permission of the publisher and the author.

SOME REPRESENTATIVE MILITARY TASKS

First, we need to have in mind certain representative military tasks for which training either is or has been given, in order that we can consider in detail the kinds of learning principles that are applicable. Here are three which will serve well as examples: (1) flexible gunnery; (2) putting a radar set into operation; (3) finding malfunctions in an electronic system.

FLEXIBLE GUNNERY. The gunner of a now obsolete type of bomber aircraft was typically located in the waist or the tail of the plane, and aimed and fired a gun at fighter aircraft attacking on what was called a "pursuit course." To do this he looked at the attacking fighter through a reticle containing a central dot, which he lined up with the target by rotating his gunsight horizontally and vertically. At the same time, he had to "frame" the aircraft within a set of dots arranged in a circle whose circumference could be varied by rotating the round hand-grip by means of which he grasped the gunsight. This is the kind of task the psychologist calls "tracking," on which a great many laboratory studies have been carried out. It was, of course, tracking simultaneously in the three dimensions of azimuth, elevation, and range. To perform this task, the individual had to learn a motor skill.

PUTTING A RADAR SET This kind of task is typically what is called a "fixed procedure." That is, the
IN OPERATION. individual is required to push buttoms, turn switches, and so on, in a particular sequence. Here, for example, is a set of steps in a procedure used by radar operators to check the transmitter power and frequency of an airborne radar (Briggs & Morrison, 1956):

1. Turn the radar set to "Stand-by" operation

2. Connect power cord of the TS-147

3. Turn power switch on

4. Turn the test switch to transmit position

5. Turn DBM dial fully counter-clockwise

6. Connect an RF cable to the RF jack on the TS-47

There are 14 more steps in this procedure. Notice that each of the steps by itself is easy enough; the individual is quite capable of turning a switch or connecting a dable. What he must learn to do, however, is to perform each step in the proper sequence. The sequence is important, and doing step 5 before step 4 may be not only an error, it may be dangerous. What must be learned, then, is a sequence of acts in the proper order.

FINDING MALFUNCTIONS IN COMPLEX EQUIPMENT. This is in many respects a most complex kind of behavior. There are of course some very simple kinds of equipment in which this activity can be reduced to a procedure; and when this is true, the task is one that can be learned from that point of view. But the major job, for complex equipment, is one of troubleshooting, a problem-solving activity that has considerable formal resemblance to medical as well as other kinds of diagnosis. Suppose this is a radar set, again, and that the initial difficulty (symptom) is that no "range sweep" appears on the oscilloscope tube face. Beginning at this point, the troubleshooter must track down a malfunctioning component. He does this first by making a decision as to how he will check the operation of subordinate parts of the system, next by carrying out the check and noting the information it yields, next by making another decision about a next check, and so on through a whole series of stages until he finds the malfunctioning unit. In each of these stages, he presumably must be formulating hypotheses which affect his actions at the next stage, in the typical and classically described manner of problem solving. What does the individual have to learn in order to solve such problems? This is indeed a difficult question to answer, but the best guess seems to be that he must acquire concepts, principles, rules, or something of that nature which he can arouse within himself at the proper moment and which guide his behavior in diagnosing malfunctions.

Here are, then, three types of activities that are not untypical of military jobs, and which are aimed at in military training: a motor skill like flexible gunnery; a procedure like putting a radar set into operation; and troubleshooting, the diagnosing of malfunctions in complex electronic equipment. Each of these tasks has been examined more or less intensively by military psychologists and learning specialists. Among other things, each of these tasks can be shown to be not entirely unique, but to represent a rather broad class of tasks, in its formal characteristics, which cuts across particular content or occupational areas. For example, flexible gunnery is a tracking skill, which formally resembles many others, like maneuvering an airplane, sewing a seam on a sewing machine, hovering a helicopter, and many others. As for procedures, these are common indeed, and may be found in jobs such as that of a clerk filling in or filing forms, a cook preparing food, a pilot preflighting an airplane. Diagnosing difficulties is certainly a widely occurring kind of activity, which may be engaged in by the leader of a group who detects the symptom of low morale, as well as by a variety of mechanics who "fix" equipment of all sorts. Accordingly, one should probably not consider these particular examples as peculiar ones; instead, they appear to be representative of a wide variety of human activities.

LEARNING

How are these kinds of tasks learned? What is it that the learning psychologist can say about them which will enable anyone (the teacher, the curriculum builder, the training manager) to undertake to arrange the external conditions in such a way that the desired performances will be acquired with the minimal expenditure of time, money, and wasted effort?

Suppose that you were, in fact, a psychologist who had studied learning, both animal and human, from the standpoint of experiment and theory and that you were faced with this problem. How can scientific knowledge of learning be used to improve the process of training? Notice how I've stated this question. I am not asking, how can scientific approach be applied to the study of training. Nor am I asking, how can experimental methodology be applied to the study of training. There are certainly answers to these questions which have been provided by several people, notably Crawford (1962). The question is, rather how can what you know about learning *as an event, as a process*, be put to use in designing training so that it will be maximally effective?

The psychologist who is confronted with this question is likely to appeal, first, to a basic point of view towards learning which is so highly ingrained it may be called an *assumption*. Beyond this, and secondly, he looks for certain *principles* which have been well established by experiment. These are principles which relate certain variables in the learning situation, like time intervals between trials, sequence of trials, kind of feedback after each trial, and so on, to such dependable variables as rate of learning or goodness of performance. Let us try to see what can be done both with the basic assumption and with some of the more important principles.

THE ASSUMPTION. The assumption that many learning psychologists would bring to the problem of designing training is something like this: "The best way to learn a performance is to practice that performance." I should like to show, later on, that this assumption is by no means a good one. But before I do that, I want to consider the question, where does this assumption come from, anyhow? First, it seems to have a cultural basis, by derivation from the writings of John Dewey, preserved in the educational catch-phrase "learning by doing." Second, it appears to come by unwarranted generalization from laboratory prototypes of learning, such as the conditioned response. In conditioning, classical or otherwise, one observes learning only *after* the animal has made the first *response*. Thus performance comes first, and learning is often considered to result from practice of this performance. Third, the assumption comes from theory which deals with conditioning, and which conceives of what is learned as either a response or an association terminating in a response, in either case established by *practicing the response* (with reinforcement). Without going into the matter further at the moment, the basic reason that generalization of this notion to the learning of the human tasks I have mentioned seems questionable is simply that the responses required (turning switches, inserting plugs, moving handles) do not have to be learned at all—they are already there in the human's repertoire.

PRINCIPLES

Beyond this assumption that learning comes about when performances are practiced, what *principles* can the learning psychologist depend on? What kinds of conditions have been found to affect the rate of learning? What findings can he bring to bear on the problem of designing training to be maximally effective?

Let me mention some of the best-known of these principles, not necessarily all of them, using various sources. In part, I shall depend on an excellent article by Underwood (1959). First of all, there is *reinforcement,* the principle that learning will be more rapid the greater the amount of reinforcement given during practice. Other principles include *distribution of practice, meaningfulness,* increasing the *distinctiveness* of the elements of a task, and *response availability.*

These principles would appear to provide the learning psychologist with a fairly adequate bag of tricks with which he can approach the job of designing effective training. There is much evidence in the experimental literature that one can in fact alter the rate of learning by manipulating these variables in the learning situation, whether one is working with single conditioned responses or with verbal material having a somewhat more complex organization. Each of these variables, so far as is known, can be manipulated to make a dependable difference on learning, in the direction of increased as well as decreased effectiveness.

USING THESE ASSUMPTIONS AND PRINCIPLES IN TRAINING DESIGN

How does one fare if he seriously attempts to use this basic assumption and these principles to design effective training situations? *Not particularly well.* The assumption that the most effective learning is provided by practice on the final task leads one astray on many occasions. As for the principles, sometimes they can clearly not be applied, that is, there is no way to manipulate the training situation in the manner suggested by the principle. In other instances, the evidence simply fails to support the principle. When this happens, there may be good theoretical reasons for the event, but this still does not restore one's faith in the usefulness of the principle.

It will be possible here only to give a few examples of military training situations in which these assumptions and principles failed to work, but I have
chosen them to be as representative as possible. Let me emphasize again that I
do not maintain that these examples demonstrate that the principles are invalid. I
simply want to show that they are strikingly inadequate to handle the job of designing effective training situations.

MOTOR SKILL. First, let's consider what is perhaps the most difficult case, the learning of
a motor skill like gunnery. What happens if we try to employ the assumption that
the best way to learn gunnery is to practice gunnery? Using the kind of task required of a flexible gunner, a number of studies were made of the conditions of
learning for this performance. One of the earliest ones, during World WAR II,
reported by Melton (1947), showed that different amounts of practice in firing at
sleeve targets during one through ten gun-camera missions made no significant
difference in the measured proficiency of gunners. A number of other studies of
gunnery also indicate the very small and often insignificant effects of practice
continued beyond the first three trials or so (Rittenhouse & Goldstein, 1954).
Furthermore, several such studies confirm the finding that the major improvement in this performance comes as a result of informing the learners of the correct picture to be achieved in ranging (i.e., so that the dots just touch the wing
tips of the target aircraft) (Goldstein & Ellis, 1956). In other words, to summarize
the finding very briefly, the evidence is that simple practice on the gunnery task is
not a particularly effective training method; instructions about the correct sight-
ing picture for ranging is much more effective in bringing about improved performance. Perhaps there are good theoretical reasons for this. But the fact remains
that practicing the performance is *not* the best way to learn.

What about the principles of learning? Well, let's consider the one which a
learning psychologist might be inclined to think of first—reinforcement, or the introduction of knowledge of results during practice. Translated into a form applicable to motor skills learning, the principle is that the more adequate are the
knowledge of results, the more rapid the learning. This variable, too, has been
tried out in a number of studies. Typically what was done was to augment the
knowledge of results that come to the gunner through his observing his own
tracking performance on a screen, by providing an extra cue, such as a buzzer,
which sounded whenever the gunner was exactly on target in all three dimensions. The effect of this extra cue, it was found, was to improve the performance
during learning. But did this mean that the learning itself was more effective, or
simply that the buzzer "propped up" the performance? One seeks the answer to
this question by comparing the performance of buzzer-trained and non-buzzer-
trained groups on a standard criterion task without the buzzer. When this was
done, the findings in several studies were negative (df. Goldstein & Ellis, 1956),
and one (Goldstein & Rittenhouse, 1954) actually showed that learners who

had the advantage of augmented knowledge of results (reinforcement), exhibited a lower performance on second gunnery task.

Other learning principles were unconfirmed in training situations. For example, a carefully executed study could find no evidence for changes in learning as a result of alterations in conditioning of practice and rest periods (Rittenhouse & Goldstein, 1954). Still other variables simply cannot be used in the training situation. For example, the meaningfulness of the task is set by the task itself, and cannot be altered by changing the conditions of training. Similarly, the internal similarity of the elements of the task are fixed by the task; one cannot, for example, change the degree of resemblance of the aircraft or of the track they follow by simply redesigning the training without setting about to change the nature of the task itself. (I omit here a discussion of the transfer effects of training with an easy discrimination to performance on a hard discrimination, and vice versa. This is a different principle than the one under discussion, and the evidence about it is not clear-cut.) What about response availability or familiarity? From the evidence on practice previously cited, as well as studies on part-training (Goldstein & Ellis, 1956) it seems fairly clear that the responses in this task (turning knobs, moving the gunsight up and down with a handle) were highly familiar in the first place. No one, so far as I know, ever seriously proposed that they were not.

Perhaps these examples are sufficient to at least raise doubts about the usefulness of the learning psychologist's assumptions and principles, when he attempts to apply them to the practical job of designing training for motor skills. On the whole, it may fairly be said, I think, that the assumption was often wrong and the principles were seldom useful in bringing about training improvement. I caution you again that I am not saying the learning psychologist was unsuccessful in improving training. In many instances, he was very successful. What I am trying to answer is the question of when he was successful, what knowledge or set of principles was he using?

PROCEDURES.   There are not many analytical studies of the learning procedures. Perhaps the reason for this is that learning procedures is relatively such an easy matter, and the methods used to train them seem relatively so obvious, that little work was done on them. Consequently, I shall have to base my arguments primarily on these obvious features, rather than on a great deal of experimental evidence.

Suppose one is faced with the task of training someone to "turn on" a radar set by turning and pushing a series of fifteen switches in a particular sequence. (This is taken to be a simplified version of a representative procedural task.) How does one go about it? If one proposes to conduct training simply by "practicing the task" it becomes obvious almost immediately that this is an inefficient method to use. What is usually done is this: the learner is provided with a *list*, which states, in effect, "First, turn on power switch; second, depress voltage switch; third, set voltage knob to reading 10k etc." (e.g., Briggs & Morrison,

1956). Now the individual may be required to commit the list to memory first, and then proceed to the task; or, he may be allowed to use the list while he practices going through the sequence. The important thing is, however, that it is the *learning of the list* that contributes most to the performance of the task, not the practice of the switch-pressing responses, another example contrary to the principle that the best way to learn is to practice the required performance. I do not say that the performance should never be practiced, simply that something other than direct practice of the final task is more effective for learning procedures, just as is true for motor skills in the example previously described.

Learning principles applied to the training of procedures do not fare very well, either, although again I must note the absence of experimental evidence. One cannot alter meaningfulness, and in most cases the responses required are highly familiar. When they are not, as may be the case when a single step requires the use of an unfamiliar tool, this principle may actually have some limited usefulness. Someimes the principle of increasing the distinctiveness of the elements of the task can be used, and one would indeed expect it to work. For example, one could put distinctive cues or labels on each of the switches in the 15-switch procedure, and this might be expected to speed up the rate of learning. However, it may be noted that this becomes a matter of changing the task (i.e., the equipment), rather than of changing the conditions of learning. From evidence on the learning of nonsense-syllable lists, one would not expect a variable like distribution of practice to make much difference as a training variable, as Underwood (1959) has noted. Again, a review of learning assumptions and principles has indicated limited usefulness.

DIAGNOSING MALFUNCTIONS. When we turn to a consideration of troubleshooting complex equipment, even the most theoretically dedicated learning psychologist is forced to recognize, almost from the start, that the idea of learning to troubleshoot by simply practicing troubleshooting verges on the ridiculous. The most obvious reason is that one cannot identify a single *task* to be practiced. The troubleshooter is faced with a great variety of initial problem situations, each of which may have a great variety of causes. He cannot possibly practice solving all of them. In fact, it is clear that he must learn not a single task, but a *class of tasks*, or perhaps even several classes of tasks. Yet, people do learn to do them, quite successfully, without ever doing anything that can legitimately be called "practicing the final performance."

What they do learn, among other things, is an elaborate set of rules pertaining to the flow of signals through a complex circuit. To a large extent, they learn these rules by looking at and responding to a circuit diagram which is a representation of the equipment rather than the equipment itself. And they use the rules in thinking about the signal flow, that is to say, in making successive decisions leading to a solution of the problem (finding the malfunction).

Since, as I have said, it is impossible to define a single task to be practiced in learning troubleshooting, it is just about equally difficult to apply the principles of reinforcement, meaningfulness, internal differentiation, and so on, to the design of training. If one accepts the task of "learning the rules" as what must be done, it is of course possible to ask the question as to whether such learning variables would apply to that task. This is a job that may some day be done by those interested in research on "learning programming." But it has not been done as yet. The evidence to date (such as it is) has not indicated strong effects, or even significant ones, for the variable of reinforcement in connection with learning programs (Goldbeck & Briggs, 1960). Other variables have not yet been investigated in relation to the learning of rules and principles.

WHAT IS APPLICABLE TO THE DESIGN OF TRAINING?

Does this mean that the psychologist has virtually nothing to offer to the problem of designing effective training? Have the results of psychologists' efforts to improve training been entirely negative? Quite to the contrary, it seems to me that efforts can be identified which were quite effective in producing significant improvements in training, and which led to some demonstrably useful designs for training. But the principles which were found to be effective for such purposes were not those that have been mentioned.

Here are the psychological principles that seem to me to be useful in training:

1. Any human task may be analyzed into a set of component tasks which are quite distinct from each other in terms of the experimental operations needed to produce them.

2. These task components are mediators of the final task performance; that is, their presence insures positive transfer to a final performance, and their absence reduces such transfer to near zero.

3. The basic principles of training design consist of: (a) identifying the component tasks of a final performance; (b) insuring that each of these component tasks is fully achieved; and (c) arranging the total learning situation in a sequence which will insure optimal mediational effects from one component to another.

These statements certainly imply a set of principles which should have very different names from those we are now most familiar with. They are concerned with such things as *task analysis, intratask transfer, component task achievement,* and *sequencing* as important variables in learning, and consequently in training. These principles are not set in opposition to the traditional principles of learning, such as reinforcement, differentiation of task elements, familiarity, and so on, and do not deny their relevance, only their *relative importance*. They are, however, in complete opposition to the previously mentioned assumption "the best way to learn a task is to practice the task."

It should also be pointed out here that I am unable to refer to any well-organized body of experimental evidence for these newly proposed principles. They come instead by inference and generalization from a wide variety of instances of learning and military training. I do not claim more for them than this. But they have to be stated before any systematic experimental work can be done on them.

Let me try now to illustrate a definite meaning for these principles with some examples. Consider first the procedural task described previously. "1. Turn radar set to 'standby' operation; 2. Connect power cord of the TS-147; 3. Turn power switch on; 4. Turn test switch to transmit position, etc." The first step to be undertaken here is to analyze this task; and (with certain minor assumptions on our part), this is seen to be, first the learning of an order series of responses to things; and second and subordinate to this, the locating of these things. These two *component tasks* have a hierarchical relationship to each other and immediately suggest the proper *sequencing* for the arrangement of the learning (or training) situation. That is to say, what must first be undertaken is that the learner learn what and where the "things" are (the "standby operation" switch, the "TS-147," the power switch, the test switch, and so forth). This is a matter of identification learning, which has considerable resemblance to the paired-associate learning of the psychological laboratory. Having achieved this subordinate task, it is then possible for the learner to undertake the second, or "serial order of things" task. According to the principle proposed the maximal positive transfer to this task would be predicted following completely adequate performance on the subordinate task of identifying the "things."

Laboratory experiments which have undertaken to test such a hypothesis seem to be scarce. It is possible, however, to make reference to two studies (Primoff, 1938; Young, 1959) which have some suggestive findings. Generally speaking, when one learns a set of paired associates first, and then undertakes the learning of these units serially, there is high positive transfer; but when one learns units serially first, the amount of transfer to paired associate learning is very low indeed. These results strongly suggest that there is a *more efficient* and a *less efficient* sequence which can be arranged for the learning of a procedural task, and that this sequence involves learning one subtask before the total task is undertaken. A procedure is a task that can be analyzed into at least two component tasks, one of identification, and the other of serial ordering. The first is subordinate to the second in the sense that it mediates positive transfer to the second, provided it is first completely mastered.

Can this kind of analysis be applied to a more complex task like troubleshooting? Indeed it can, and those psychologists who thought about the problem of training troubleshooting came close to the kind of analysis I have suggested. Generally speaking, they recognized that troubleshooting some particular equipment as a final performance was supported by two broad classes of subordinate tasks. First, there was knowledge of the rules of signal flow in the system, and second, the proper use of test instruments in making checks. The rules of signal flow themselves constitute an elaborate hierarchy of subordinate tasks, if one wants to look at it that way. For example, if the signal with which the mechanic is concerned is the output of an amplifier, then it may be necessary that he know some of the rules about data flow through an amplifier. Thus the task may be progressively analyzed into subordinate components which support each other in the sense that they are predicted to mediate positive transfer.

The task of using test instruments in making checks provides an even clearer example, perhaps. Obviously, one subordinate task is "choosing the proper check to make" (presumably a matter of knowing some "rules"); another is "selecting the proper test instrument" (an identification task); still another is "setting up the test instrument" (a procedural task, which in its turn has components like those previously described); and another is "interpreting the instrument reading" (another task involving a "rule"). Even identifying these component tasks brings to troubleshooting a vast clarification of the requirements for training. If one is able to take another step of arranging the proper sequencing of these tasks in a training program, the difference which results is remarkable. This is the interpretation I should be inclined to make of the studies which have demonstrated significant improvements in troubleshooting training, such as those of Briggs and Besnard (1956); of Highland, Newman and Waller (1956); and of French, Crowder, and Tucker (1956). In providing training which was demonstrably successful, these investigators were giving instruction on a carefully analyzed set of subordinate tasks, arranged in a sequence which, so far as they could tell, would best insure positive transfer to the variety of problem situations encountered in troubleshooting. It was *the identification of these tasks and this sequence* which I believe was the key to training improvement.

A good deal of other work also proceeded along these lines, although not always with a terminal phase of measured training effectiveness. For example, a whole series of studies by Miller and Folley, and their associates, were concerned with what was called *task analysis*. They had such titles as these: Line maintenance of the A-3A fire control system: III. Training characteristics (Folley & Miller, 1955); Job anticipation procedures applied to the K-1 system (Miller, Folley, & Smith, 1953); A comparison of job requirements for the line maintenance of two sets of electronic equipment (Miller, Folley, & Smith, 1954). What was all this talk about task analysis? Did it have anything to do with training? My answer is that it had to do with training more than with anything else. These were thoroughgoing and highly successful attempts to identify the variety of tasks contained in a job, and the variety of subtasks which contributed to each task. There was in fact explicit recognition of the idea that successful final performance must be a matter of attaining competence on these subtasks. So here again was the noton that effective training somehow depended on the identification of these subordinate tasks, as well as on their arrangement into a suitable sequence to insure positive transfer to the final performance.

A third source of these ideas in military training research should be mentioned. This was the development of training devices applicable to such jobs as electronic maintenance. It came to be recognized that these devices were in some respects very different from the traditional trainers such as those for developing skill in aircraft maneuvers. They were called "concept trainers," and this, as Briggs' (1959) discussion of them implies, was another name for "teaching machines." As such, they were developed independently of Skinner's ideas, and they were in fact based upon an entirely different set of principles, as is clear from the accounts provided by Briggs (1956), Crowder (1957), and French (1956). Each of these training devices (or teaching machines), aside from its hardware engineering, was developed on the basis of a painstaking task analysis, which identified the subordinate tasks involved in a total task like troubleshooting a particular electronic system. The subordinate tasks thus identified were then incorporated into a sequence designed to insure maximal positive transfer to the final task. There were certainly some programming principles, but they bore little resemblance to those which are most frequently mentioned in recent literature; in my opinion, they were much more important than these.

Still a fourth area of effort in training research was related to these ideas. This was the development of techniques to provide behavioral guides, or "job aids" in support of performance in various technical jobs (Hoehn, Newman, Salts, & Wulff, 1957). In order to do this, it was found necessary to distinguish between those kinds of capabilities which could best be established by thorough training, and those kinds which could be established by minimal training plus the provision of a check list or handbook. Obviously, here again there had to be a detailed task analysis. Subordinate tasks had to be identified which would mediate transfer either to the kind of performance required without a handbook, or the kind required with a handbook. Besides the initial task analysis, it is again evident that this line of work was making use of ideas about component task achievement and intratask transfer.

SUMMARY

Now that I have conveyed the message, my summary can be quite brief. If I were faced with the problem of improving training, I should not look for much help from the well-known learning principles like reinforcement, distribution of practice, response familiarity, and so on. I should look instead at the technique of task analysis, and at the principles of component task achievement, intratask transfer, and the sequencing of subtask learning to find those ideas of greatest usefulness in the design of effective training. Someday, I hope, even the laboratory learning psychologist will know more about these principles.

REFERENCES

Briggs, L. J. "A Troubleshooting Trainer for the E-4 Fire Control System." *USAF Personnel Train. Res. Cent. Tech. Note,* 1956, No. 56-94.

Briggs, L. J. "Teaching Machines for Training of Military Personnel in Maintenance of Electronic Equipment. In E. Galanter (ed.), *Automatic Teaching: The State of the Art.* New York: Wiley, 1959, Ch. 12.

Briggs, L. J., and Besnard, G. G. "Experimental Procedures for Increasing Reinforced Practice in Training Air Force Mechanics for an Electronic System." In G. Finch and F. Cameron (eds.), *Research Symposium on Air Force Human Engineering, Personnel, and Training Research.* Washington, D.C.: National Academy of Sciences—National Research Council, 1956, pp. 48-58.

Briggs, L. J., and Morrison, E. J. An Assessment of the Performance Capabilities of Fire Control System Mechanics." *USAF Personnel Train. Res. Cent. Tech. Memo.,* 1956, No. ML-56-19.

Crawford, M. P. "Concepts of Training." In R. M. Gagne (ed.), *Psychological Principles in System Development.* New York: Holt, Rinehart and Winston, 1962, Ch. 9.

Crowder, N. A. "A Part-Task Trainer for Troubleshooting." *USAF Personnel Train. Res. Cent. Tech. Note,* 1957, No. 57-71.

Folley, J. D., Jr., and Miller, R. B. "Line Maintenance of the A-3A Fire Control System: III. Training Characteristics." *USAF Personnel Train. Res. Cent. Tech. Memo.,* 1955, No. 55-5.

French, R. S. "The K-System MAC-1 Troubleshooting Trainer: I. Development, Design, and Use." *USAF Personnel Train. Res. Cent. Tech. Note,* 1956, No. 56-119.

French, R. S., Crowder, N. A., and Tucker, J. A., Jr. "The K-System MAC-1 Troubleshooting Trainer: II. Effectiveness in an Experimental Training Course." *USAF Personnel Train. Res. Cent. Tech. Note,* 1956, No. 56-120.

Goldbeck, R. A., and Briggs, L. J. "An Analysis of Response Mode and Feedback Factors in Automated Instruction." Santa Barbara, Calif.: American Institute for Research, 1960 (AIR Tech. Rep. No. 2).

Goldstein, M., and Ellis, D. S. "Pedestal Sight Gunnery Skills: A Review of Research." *USAF Personnel Train. Res. Cent. Tech. Note,* 1956, No. 56-31.

Goldstein, M., and Rittenhouse, C. H. "Knowledge of Results in the Acquisition and Transfer of a Gunnery Skill." *J. Exp. Psychol.* 48 (1954): 187-196.

Highland, R. W., Newman, S. E., and Waller, H. S. "A Descriptive Study of Electronic Troubleshooting." In G. Finch and F. Cameron (eds.), *Research Symposium on Air Force Human Engineering, Personnel, and Training Research.* Washington, D.C.: National Academy of Sciences—National Research Council, 1956, pp. 48-58.

Hoehn, A. J., Newman, S. E., Saltz, E., and Wulff, J. J. "A Program for Providing Maintenance Capability." *USAF Personnel Train. Res. Cent. Tech. Memo.,* 1957, No. ML-57-10.

Melton, A. W. (ed.) "Apparatus Tests." *USAAF Aviat. Psychol. Program. Res. Rep.*, No. 4 (1947): 917–921.

Miller, R. B., Folley, J. D., Jr., and Smith, P. R. "Job Anticipation Procedures Applied to the K-1 System." *USAF Hum. Resources Res. Cent. Tech. Rep.*, 1953, No. 53-20.

Miller, R. B., Folley, J. D., Jr., and Smith, P. R. "A Comparison of Job Requirements for Line Maintenance of Two Sets of Electronics Equipment." *USAF Personnel Train. Res. Cent. Tech. Rep.*, 1954, No. 54-83.

Primoff, E. "Backward and Forward Association as an Organizing Act in Serial and in Paired Associate Learning." *J. Psychol.* 5 (1938): 375–395.

Rittenhouse, C. H., and Goldstein, M. "The Role of Practice Schedule in Pedestal Sight Gunnery Performance." *USAF Personnel Train. Res. Cent. Tech. Rep.*, 1954, No. 54-97.

Underwood, B. J. "Verbal Learning in the Educative Processes." *Harvard Educ. Rev.* 29 (1959): 107–117.

Young, R. K. "A Comparison of Two Methods of Learning Serial Associations." *Amer. J. Psychol.* 72 (1959): 554–559.

APPENDIX **B** THE CRITICAL INCIDENT TECHNIQUE

THE CRITICAL INCIDENT TECHNIQUE*

John C. Flanagan

During the past ten years the writer and various collaborators have been engaged in developing and utilizing a method that has been named the "critical incident technique." It is the purpose of this article to describe the development of this methodology, its fundamental principles, and its present status. In addition, the findings of a considerable number of studies making use of the critical incident technique will be briefly reviewed and certain possible further uses of the technique will be indicated.

The critical incident technique consists of a set of procedures for collecting direct observations of human behavior in such a way as to facilitate their potential usefulness in solving practical problems and developing broad psychological principles. The critical incident technique outlines procedures for collecting observed incidents having special significance and meeting systematically defined criteria.

By an incident is meant any observable human activity that is sufficiently complete in itself to permit inferences and predictions to be made about the person performing the act. To be critical, an incident must occur in a situation where the purpose or intent of the act seems fairly clear to the observer and where its consequences are sufficiently definite to leave little doubt concerning its effects.

Certainly in its broad outlines and basic approach the critical incident technique has very little which is new about it. People have been making observations on other people for centuries. The work of many of the great writers of the past indicates that they were keen observers of their fellow men. Some of these writers must have relied on detailed notes made from their observations. Others may have had unusual abilities to reconstruct memory images in vivid detail. Some may have even made a series of relatively systematic observations on many instances of a particular type of behavior. Perhaps what is most conspicuously needed to supplement these activities is a set of procedures for

*Source: From *Psychological Bulletin*, vol. 51 (July 1954), pp. 327–58. Copyright © 1954 by the American Psychological Association. Reprinted by permission.

analyzing and synthesizing such observations into a number of relationships that can be tested by making additional observations under more carefully controlled conditions.

BACKGROUND AND EARLY DEVELOPMENTS

The roots of the present procedures can be traced back directly to the studies of Sir Francis Galton nearly 70 years ago, and to later developments such as time sampling studies of recreational activities, controlled observation tests, and anecdotal records. The critical incident technique as such, however, can best be regarded as an outgrowth of studies in the Aviation Psychology Program of the United States Army Air Forces in World War II. The Aviation Psychology Program was established in the summer of 1941 to develop procedures for the selection and classification of aircrews.

One of the first studies (40) carried out in this program was the analysis of the specific reasons for failure in learning to fly that were reported for 1,000 pilot candidates eliminated from flight training schools in the summer and early fall of 1941. The basic source used in this analysis was the proceedings of the elimination boards. In these proceedings the pilot instructors and check pilots reported their reasons for eliminating the particular pilot. It was found that many of the reasons given were clichés and stereotypes such as "lack of inherent flying ability" and "inadequate sense of sustentation," or generalizations such as "unsuitable temperament," "poor judgment," or "insufficient progress." However, along with these a number of specific observations of particular behaviors were reported. This study provided the basis for the research program on selecting pilots. Although it was found very useful, it also indicated very clearly the need for better procedures for obtaining a representative sample of factual incidents regarding pilot performance.

A second study (13), which emphasized the importance of factual reports on performance made by competent observers, was carried out in the winter of 1943-1944 in the 8th, 9th, 12th, and 15th Air Forces. This study collected the reasons for the failures of bombing missions as reported in the Group Mission Reports. Although in the preparation of these reports much greater emphasis was given to determining the precise facts in the case, it was apparent that in many instances the official reports did not provide a complete record of all the important events. Even with these limitations, the information given was found to be of considerable value, and the systematic tabulations that were prepared provided the basis for a series of recommendations that resulted in important changes in Air Force selection and training procedures.

In the summer of 1944 a series of studies (74) was planned on the problem of combat leadership in the United States Army Air Forces. These represent the first large-scale, systematic effort to gather specific incidents of effective or ineffective behavior with respect to a designated activity. The instructions asked the combat veterans to report incidents observed by them that involved behavior which was especially helpful or inadequate in accomplishing the assigned mission. The statement finished with the request, "Describe the officer's action. What did he do?" Several thousand incidents were collected in this way and analyzed to provide a relatively objective and factual definition of effective combat leadership. The resulting set of descriptive categories was called the "critical requirements" of combat leadership.

Another study (74) conducted in the Aviation Psychology Program involved a survey of disorientation while flying.[1] Disorientation in this study was defined to include any experience denoting uncertainty as to one's spatial position in relation to the vertical. In this study pilots returning from combat were asked "to think of some occasion during combat flying in which you personally experienced feelings of acute disorientation or strong vertigo." They were then asked to describe what they "saw, heard, or felt that brought on the experience." This study led to a number of recommendations regarding changes in cockpit and instrument panel design and in training in order to overcome and prevent vertigo while flying.

In a project carried out in the Aviation Psychology Program in 1946, Fitts and Jones (12) collected descriptions of specific experiences from pilots in taking off, flying on instruments, landing, using controls, and using instruments. These interviews with pilots were electrically recorded. They provided many factual incidents that were used as a basis for planning research on the design of instruments and controls and the arrangement of these within the cockpit.

In addition to the collection of specific incidents and the formulation of critical requirements, as outlined above, the summary volume (13) for the Aviation Psychology Program Research Reports contained a discussion of the theoretical basis of procedures for obtaining the critical requirements of a particular activity. Perhaps the best method of describing the status of these procedures at the close of the war is to quote from the discussion in this summary volume, which was written in the late spring of 1946. In the section on techniques for defining job requirements, the present author wrote as follows:

> The principal objective of job analysis procedures should be the determination of critical requirements. These requirements include those which have been demonstrated to have made the difference between success and failure in carrying out an important part of the job assigned in a significant number of instances. Too often, statements regarding job requirements are merely lists of all the desirable traits of human beings. These are practically no help in selecting, classifying, or training individuals for specific jobs. To obtain valid information regarding the truly critical requirements for success in a specific assignment, procedures were developed in the Aviation Psychology Program for making systematic analyses of causes of good and poor performance.

---

1. This study was planned by Paul M. Fitts, Jr., who also contributed to the previously mentioned USAAF studies and planned and carried out the interview study with pilots described below on the design of instruments, controls, and arrangements.

Essentially, the procedure was to obtain first-hand reports, or reports from objective records, of satisfactory and unsatisfactory execution of the task assigned. The cooperating individual described a situation in which success or failure was determined by specific reported causes.

This procedure was found very effective in obtaining information from individuals concerning their own errors, from subordinates concerning errors of their superiors, from supervisors with respect to their subordinates, and also from participants with respect to co-participants (13, pp. 273-274).

DEVELOPMENTAL STUDIES AT THE AMERICAN INSTITUTE FOR RESEARCH

At the close of World War II some of the psychologists who had participated in the USAAF Aviation Psychology Program established the American Institute for Research, a nonprofit scientific and educational organization. The aim of this organization is the systematic study of human behavior through a coordinated program of scientific research that follows the same general principles developed in the Aviation Psychology Program. It was in connection with the first two studies undertaken by the Institute in the spring of 1947 that the critical incident technique was more formally developed and given its present name.

These studies were natural extensions of the previous research in the Aviation Psychology Program. The study reported by Preston (52) dealt with the determination of the critical requirements for the work of an officer in the United States Air Force. In this study, many of the procedural problems were first subjected to systematic tryout and evaluation. Six hundred and forty officers were interviewed, and a total of 3,029 critical incidents were obtained. This led to the development of a set of 58 critical requirements classified into six major areas. The second study, reported by Gordon (27, 28), was carried out to determine the critical requirements of a commercial airline pilot. In this study, several different sources were used to establish the critical requirements of the airline pilot. These included training records, flight check records including the specific comments of check pilots, critical pilot behaviors reported in accident records, and critical incidents reported anonymously in interviews by the pilots themselves. From this study, 733 critical pilot behaviors were classified into 24 critical requirements of the airline pilot's job. These were used to develop selection tests to measure the aptitudes and other personality characteristics found critical for success in the job. They also provided the basic data for the formulation of an objective flight check to determine the eligibility of applicants for the airline transport rating.

The third application of the critical incident technique by the staff of the American Institute for Research was in obtaining the critical requirements for research personnel on a project sponsored by the Psychological Sciences Division of the Office of Naval Research. In this study (20), about 500 scientists in 20 research laboratories were interviewed. These scientists reported more than 2,500 critical incidents. The critical behaviors were used to formulate inductively a set of 36 categories, which constitutes the critical requirements for the effective performance of the duties of research personnel in the physical sciences. This initial study provided the basis for the development of selection tests, proficiency measures, and procedures for evaluating both job performance and the research report.

Another project undertaken by the American Institute for Research in the spring of 1948 provided valuable experience with the critical incident technique. This study, reported by Nagay (48), was done for the Civil Aeronautics Administration under the sponsorship of the Committee on Aviation Psychology of the National Research Council. It was concerned with the air route traffic controller's job. One of the innovations in this study was the use of personnel of the Civil Aeronautics Administration who had no previous psychological training in collecting critical incidents by means of personal interviews. In previous studies all such interviewing had been conducted by psychologists with extensive training in such procedures. In this study, aeronautical specialists from each of the seven regions conducted the interviews in their regions after a brief training period. An interesting finding from this study was the clear reflection of seasonal variations in flying conditions in the types of incidents reported. The study also demonstrated the selective recall of dramatic or other special types of incidents. This bias was especially noticeable in the incidents reported several months after their occurrence. The incidents obtained in this study were used to develop procedures for evaluating the proficiency of air route traffic controllers and also for developing a battery of selection tests for this type of personnel.

In the spring of 1949 the American Institute for Research undertook a study to determine the critical job requirements for the hourly wage employees in the Delco-Remy Division of the General Motors Corporation. This study, reported by Miller and Flanagan (46), was the first application of these techniques in an industrial situation. Foremen who were members of a committee appointed to develop employee evaluation procedures collected 2,500 critical incidents in interviews with the other foremen in the plants. On the basis of these data a form was prepared for collecting incidents on a day-to-day basis as a continuous record of job performance.

Using this form, the Performance Record for Hourly Wage Employees (21), three groups of foremen kept records on the performance of their employees for a two-week period. A group of 24 foremen recorded incidents daily; another group of 24 foremen reported incidents at the end of each week; and a third group containing the same number of foremen reported incidents only at the end of the two-week period. The three groups of foremen represented comparable conditions of work and supervision. The foremen reporting daily reported 315 critical incidents; the foremen reporting weekly, 155 incidents; and the foremen reporting only once at the end of two weeks reported 63 incidents. Thus, foremen who reported only at the end of the week had forgotten approximately one half of the incidents they would have reported under a daily reporting plan. The foremen who reported only at the end of the two-week period appeared to have forgotten 80 percent of the incidents observed. Although it is possible that the findings may be partially attributed to the fact that the foremen making daily records actually observed more critical incidents because of the daily reminder at the time of recording, it is clear that much better results can be expected when daily recording is used.

Another analysis based on data collected at the Delco-Remy Division compared the number of critical incidents of various types obtained from interviews with those recorded daily by the foremen on the performance records. Although there were some differences in the relative frequencies for specific categories, the general patterns appeared to be quite similar. These results suggest that critical incidents obtained from interviews can be relied on to provide a relatively accurate account of job performance if suitable precautions are taken to prevent systematic bias.

In addition to the development of the performance record described above, the critical incidents collected in this study were used as the basis for constructing selection tests covering both aptitude (18) and attitude (2) factors.

STUDIES CARRIED OUT AT THE UNIVERSITY OF PITTSBURGH

A substantial number of studies have been carried out in the department of psychology at the University of Pittsburgh by students working for advanced degrees under the author's direction. Most of these studies had as their objective the determination of the critical requirements for a specific occupational group or activity. Many of them also included contributions to technique. In 1949 Wagner (66) completed a dissertation on the critical requirements for dentists. In this study, critical incidents were obtained from three sources: patients, dentists, and dental school instructors. The incidents were classified into four main aspects of the dentist's job: (a) demonstrating technical proficiency; (b) handling patient relationships; (c) accepting professional responsibility; and (d) accepting personal responsibility. As might be expected, the patients did not report as large a proportion of incidents for demonstrating technical proficiency or accepting professional responsibility as did the other two groups, and the instructors reported only a relatively small proportion of their incidents in the area of handling patient relationships.

On the basis of the findings from this study, a battery of selection tests was developed for use by the University of Pittsburgh School of Dentistry. A number of proficiency tests for measuring ability with respect to certain of the critical requirements were also developed using these results as a basis.

Another dissertation completed in 1949 was Finkle's (11) study of the critical requirements of industrial foremen. This study was conducted in the East Pittsburgh plant of the Westinghouse Electric Corporation. Critical incidents were obtained from foremen, general foremen, and staff personnel. A number of points pertaining to technique were studied.

One finding was in reference to the effect on the types of incidents obtained of the degree of importance or exceptionalness set up as a criterion for reporting or ignoring incidents. The incidents obtained from the use of questions that asked for incidents only slightly removed from the norm were compared with incidents obtained from questions intended to elicit more definitely effective or ineffective behaviors. Some examples of these questions are:

1. Think of a time when a foreman has done something that you felt should be encouraged because it seemed to be in your opinion an example of good foremanship. (Effective—slight deviation from norm.)

2. Think of a time when a foreman did something that you thought was not up to par. (Ineffective—slight deviation from norm.)

3. Think of a time when a foreman has, in your opinion, shown definitely good foremanship—the type of action that points out the superior foreman. (Effective—substantial deviation from the norm.)

4. Think of a time when a foreman has, in your opinion, shown poor foremanship—the sort of action which if repeated would indicate that the man was not an effective foreman. (Ineffective—substantial deviation from norm.)

The frequencies of incidents obtained in each of the 40 categories into which the effective behaviors were classified were compared for the questions requesting slight and substantial deviations from the norm, and the significance of the differences was tested by means of the chi-square test. Two of the differences were significant at the 1 percent level and one at the 5 percent level. Comparisons of the frequencies in each of the 40 categories for ineffective incidents failed to reveal any chi squares significant at either the 5 percent or the 1 percent level.

The questions involving only a slight deviation from the norm resulted in more effective incidents concerned with gaining the respect and loyalty of the workers and also in more incidents that involved making, encouraging, and accepting suggestions. They produced significantly fewer incidents regarding fitting men to jobs. The small number of significant differences—only three in 80 comparisons—suggests that the types of incidents obtained are not very greatly changed by variations in wording of the questions comparable to those shown above. It seems likely that this is at least partially due to the fact that the persons interviewed report only incidents that represent a fairly substantial deviation from the norm regardless of the precise wording of the question asked.

Another comparison made in this study related to the influence of asking for an effective or an ineffective incident first. About 10 percent more incidents were obtained from booklets requesting effective incidents first than from booklets requesting ineffective incidents first. This difference was sufficiently small so that it could reasonably be attributed to chance sampling fluctuations.

The incidents collected in this study were used, along with other data, in the preparation of a Performance Record for Foremen and Supervisors (23).

A study was conducted by Nevins (50) on the critical requirements of bookkeepers in sales companies. She collected incidents relating to applicants for bookkeeping positions as well as for employees working in this capacity.

For the collection of the information about the practicing bookkeepers, a modification in the critical incident technique was made. This was done because, in the bookkeeping profession, success and failure are usually defined in terms of persistent behavioral patterns. Occasional mistakes in adding and balancing accounts are expected, but repeated errors are considered serious. Instead of the single incident, therefore, many of the items included represented either a pattern of behaviors or a series of similar behaviors.

Weislogel (72) determined the critical requirements for life insurance agency heads. A principal feature of his study related to the comparison of two types of agency heads—managers and general agents. It was believed that the critical behaviors for one type of agency head might provide a different pattern than that obtained for the other. This hypothesis was not confirmed by the analysis of the obtained incidents. The patterns of critical requirements were found to be quite similar for the two types of administrators.

Smit (58) carried out a study to determine the critical requirements for instructors of general psychology courses. Perhaps the finding of most general importance in this study was the existence of substantial differences between the patterns of critical incidents reported by students and faculty. The faculty reported a significantly larger percentage of effective behaviors in the following areas: giving demonstrations or experiments, using discussion group techniques, encouraging and ascertaining students' ideas and opinions.

The students, on the other hand, contributed a larger percentage of behaviors in the following areas; reviewing examinations, distributing grades, and explaining grades; using lecture aids such as drawings, charts, movies, models, and apparatus; using project techniques; giving test questions on assigned material; helping students after class and during class recess; the manner of the instructor.

The faculty reported a larger percentage of ineffective behaviors concerning maintaining order. The ineffective behaviors that were reported in a larger percentage by students involved these areas: presenting requirements of the course, using effective methods of expression, dealing with students' questions, pointing out fallacies, reviewing and summarizing basic facts and principles, using project techniques, using verbal diagnostic teaching techniques, achievement testing students on assigned material, objective type achievement testing, using humor.

This is a good illustration of the problem of the competence of various types of available observers to evaluate the contribution to the general aim of the activity of a specific action. Examination of the reports from students indicated a somewhat limited sphere of competence. Apparently one of the principal reasons for this was the lack of perspective on the part of the students and their inability to keep the general aim of the instructor clearly in mind because of its divergence from their own immediate aims. In many cases, this latter aim seemed to be directed toward achieving a satisfactory grade in the course.

Eilbert (7) developed a functional description of emotional immaturity. The contributors of critical incidents included psychiatrists, psychologists, psychiatric social workers, occupational therapists, nurses, and corpsmen from a military hospital, plus 13 psychologists in nonmilitary organizations. The subjects of the incidents were primarily patients under psychiatric care.

The contributors were given a form that oriented them to the concept "emotional immaturity" by suggesting that it was revealed generally by childlike modes of behavior. The questions used to elicit incidents were: Have you recently thought of someone as being emotionally immature (regardless of diagnosis)? What specifically happened that gave you this impression? What would have been a more mature reaction to the same situation?

Because of the indefinite nature of the concept, it was felt that a check should be made on the contributor's understanding of his task. Twenty of the participating persons were asked to summarize briefly their interpretation of what they had been asked to do. This appeared to be very useful in developing the phrasing of the questions so that they were uniformly interpreted by the various observers.

The author of the study classified all the immaturities on the basis of a classification system developed from preliminary categorizations prepared by six of the contributors. This classification was submitted to 14 psychiatrists for review. They were asked to indicate which of the categories they were willing to accept as a type of immaturity as the term had been defined in an official document.

More than half the categories were accepted by at least 13 of the 14 judges, and none was rejected by more than 50 percent of the judges. It was felt then that the system was acceptable.

This study illustrates the application of the critical incident technique to the study of personality. It is believed that this study provides an excellent example of the possibilities for developing more specific behavioral descriptions.

Folley (24) reported on the critical requirements of sales clerks in department stores. The behaviors were abstracted from narrative records of individual shopping incidents written by shoppers who were relatively inexperienced in evaluating sales personnel. For various reasons, including the competence of the observers, their training, and their limited point of view, the resulting description must be regarded as only partial.

In the past few years, many other individuals and groups have made use of the techniques described above, or modifications of them, in a wide variety of studies. Some of these studies on which reports are being published will be reviewed briefly in the section on applications.

THE PROCEDURE IN ITS PRESENT FORM

From the foregoing discussion, it is clear that the critical incident technique is essentially a procedure for gathering certain important facts concerning behavior in defined situations. It should be emphasized that the critical incident technique does not consist of a single rigid set of rules governing such data collection. Rather it should be thought of as a flexible set of principles which must be modified and adapted to meet the specific situation at hand.

The essence of the technique is that only simple types of judgments are required of the observer, reports from only qualified observers are included, and all observations are evaluated by the observer in terms of an agreed upon statement of the purpose of the activity. Of course, simplicity of judgments is a relative matter. The extent to which a reported observation can be accepted as a fact depends primarily on the objectivity of this observation. By objectivity is meant the tendency for a number of independent observers to make the same report. Judgments that two things have the same effect or that one has more or less effect than the other with respect to some defined purpose or goal represent the simplest types of judgments that can be made. The accuracy and therefore the objectivity of the judgments depend on the precision with which the characteristic has been defined and the competence of the observer in interpreting this definition with relation to the incident observed. In this latter process, certain more difficult types of judgments are required regarding the relevance of various conditions and actions on the observed success in attaining the defined purpose for this activity.

It is believed that a fair degree of success has been achieved in developing procedures that will be of assistance in gathering facts in a rather objective fashion with only a minimum of inferences and interpretations of a more subjective nature. With respect to two other steps that are essential if these incidents are to be of value a comparable degree of objectivity has not yet been obtained. In both instances, the subjective factors seem clearly due to current deficiencies in psychological knowledge.

The first of these two other steps consists of the classification of the critical incidents. In the absence of an adequate theory of human behavior, this step is usually an inductive one and is relatively subjective. Once a classification system has been developed for any given type of critical incidents, a fairly satisfactory degree of objectivity can be achieved in placing the incidents in the defined categories.

The second step refers to inferences regarding practical procedures for improving performance based on the observed incidents. Again, in our present stage of psychological knowledge, we are rarely able to deduce or predict with a high degree of confidence the effects of specific selection, training, or operating procedures on future behaviors of the type observed. The incidents must be studied in the light of relevant established principles of human behavior and of the known facts regarding background factors and conditions operating in the specific situation. From this total picture hypotheses are formulated. In only a few types of activities are there both sufficient established principles and sufficient information regarding the effective factors in the situation to provide a high degree of confidence in the resulting hypotheses regarding specific procedures for improving the effectiveness of the results.

In the sections which follow, the five main steps included in the present form of the procedures will be described briefly. In order to provide the worker with maximum flexibility at the present stage, in addition to examples of present best practice, the underlying principles for the step will be discussed and also the chief limitations with, wherever possible, suggestions for studies that may result in future improvements in the methods.

1. GENERAL AIMS

A basic condition necessary for any work on the formulation of a functional description of an activity is a fundamental orientation in terms of the general aims of the activity. No planning and no evaluation of specific behaviors are possible without a general statement of objectives. The trend in the scientific field toward operational statements has led a number of writers to try to describe activities or functions in terms of the acts or operations performed, the materials acted on, the situations involved, the results or products, and the relative importance of various acts and results. These analyses have been helpful in emphasizing the need for more specific and detailed descriptions of the requirements of activities. Typically, however, such discussions have failed to emphasize the dominant role of the general aim in formulating a description of successful behavior or adjustment in a particular situation.

In its simplest form, the functional description of an activity specifies precisely what it is necessary to do and not to do if participation in the activity is to be judged successful or effective. It is clearly impossible to report that a person has been either effective or ineffective in a particular activity by performing a specific act unless we know what he is expected to accomplish. For example, a supervisor's action in releasing a key worker for a half a day to participate in a recreational activity might be evaluated as very effective if the general aim of the foreman was to get along well with the employees under him. On the other hand, the same action might be evaluated as ineffective if the primary general aim is the immediate production of materials or services.

In the case of the usual vocational activities the supervisors can be expected to supply this orientation. In certain other types of activities, such as civic, social, and recreational activities, there frequently is no supervisor. The objectives of participation in the activity must then be determined from the participants themselves. In some instances, these may not be verbalized to a sufficient extent to make it possible to obtain them directly.

Unfortunately, in most situations there is no one general aim which is the correct one. Similarly, there is rarely one person or group of persons who constitute an absolute, authoritative source on the general aim of the activity. In a typical manufacturing organization the foreman, the plant manager, the president, and the stockholders might define the general aim of the workers in a particular section somewhat differently. It is not possible to say that one of these groups knows the correct general aim and the others are wrong. This does not mean that one general aim is as good as another and that it is unimportant how we define the purpose of the activity. It does mean that we cannot hope to get a completely objective and acceptable general aim for a specific activity. The principal criterion in formulating procedures for establishing the general aim of the activity should be the proposed use of the functional description of the activity which is being formulated. Unless the general aim used is acceptable to the potential users of the detailed statement of requirements, the whole effort in formulating this statement will have been wasted.

The most useful statements of aims seem to center around some simple phrase or catchword which is slogan-like in character. Such words provide a maximum of communication with only a minimum of possible misinterpretation. Such words as "appreciation," "efficiency," "development," "production," and "service" are likely to be prominent in statements of general aims. For example, the general aim of a teacher in elementary school art classes might be the development of an appreciation of various visual art forms on the part of the students. The general aim of the good citizen might be taken as effective participation in the development and application of the rules and procedures by which individuals and groups are assisted in achieving their various goals.

With the aid of a form of the type shown in Fig. 1, the ideas of a number of well-qualified authorities can be collected. It is expected that in response to the question on the primary purpose of the activity many persons will give a fairly lengthy and detailed statement. The request to summarize is expected to get them to condense this into a brief usable statement. These should be pooled and a trial form of the statement of general aim developed. This statement should be referred either to these authorities or to others to obtain a final statement of the general aim that is acceptable to them. Necessary revisions should be made as indicated by these discussions. Usually considerable effort is required to avoid defeating the purpose of the general aim by cluttering up the statement with specific details and qualifying conditions.

Fig. 1   Outline for Interview to Establish the General Aim for an Activity.

---

1. *Introductory statement:* We are making a study of (specify activity). We believe you are especially well qualified to tell us about (specify activity).

2. *Request for general aim:* What would you say is the primary purpose of (specify activity)?

3. *Request for summary:* in a few words, how would you summarize the general aim of (specify activity)?

In summary, the general aim of an activity should be a brief statement obtained from the authorities in the field which expresses in simple terms those objectives to which most people would agree. Unless a brief, simple statement has been obtained, it will be difficult to get agreement among the authorities. Also it will be much harder to convey a uniform idea to the participants. This latter group will get an over-all impression and this should be as close to the desired general aim as possible.

2. PLANS AND SPECIFICATIONS

To focus attention on those aspects of behavior which are believed to be crucial in formulating a functional description of the activity, precise instructions must be given to the observers. It is necessary that these instructions be as specific as possible with respect to the standards to be used in evaluation and classification. The group to be studied also needs to be specified.

One practical device for obtaining specific data is to obtain records of "critical incidents" observed by the reporting personnel. Such incidents are defined as extreme behavior, either outstandingly effective or ineffective with respect to attaining the general aims of the activity. The procedure has considerable efficiency because of the use of only the extremes of behavior. It is well known that extreme incidents can be more accurately identified than behavior which is more nearly average in character.

One of the primary aims of scientific techniques is to insure objectivity for the observations being made and reported. Such agreement by independent observers can only be attained if they are all following the same set of rules. It is essential that these rules be clear and specific. In most situations the following specifications will need to be established and made explicit prior to collecting the data:

a. THE SITUATIONS OBSERVED.   The first necessary specification is a delimitation of the situations to be observed. This specification must include information about the place, the persons, the conditions, and the activities. Such specifications are rather easily defined in many instances. For example, such brief specifications as observations of "the behavior in classrooms of regularly employed teachers in a specified high school while instructing students during class periods," constitute a fairly adequate definition of a situation of this type.

In complex situations it is probably essential not only that the specifications with respect to the situation be relatively complete and specific, but also that practical examples be provided to assist the observer in deciding in an objective fashion whether or not a specific behavior should be observed and recorded.

b. RELEVANCE TO THE GENERAL AIM.   After the decision has been made that a particular situation is an appropriate one for making observations, the next step is to decide whether or not a specific behavior which is observed is relevant to the general aim of the activity as defined in the section above. For example, if the general aim of the activity was defined as sustained high quality and quantity of production, it might be difficult to decide whether or not to include an action such as encouraging an unusually effective subordinate to get training that would assist him in developing his ability in an avocational or recreational activity not related to his work. In this case, it might be specified that any action which either directly or indirectly could be expected over a long period of time to have a significant effect on the general aim should be included. If it could not be predicted with some confidence whether this effect would be good or bad, it should probably not be considered.

The extent of detail required to obtain objectivity with respect to this type of decision depends to a considerable degree on the background and experiences of the observers with respect to this activity. For example, supervisors with substantial experience in a particular company can be expected to agree on whether or not a particular behavior is relevant to the attainment of the general aim. On the other hand, if outside observers were to be used, it would probably be necessary to specify in considerable detail the activities that can be expected to have an effect on the general aim.

c. EXTENT OF EFFECT ON THE GENERAL AIM.   The remaining decision that the observer must make is how important an effect the observed incident has on the general aim. It is necessary to specify two points on the scale of importance: (a) a level of positive contributions to the general aim in specific terms, preferably including a concrete example, and (b) the corresponding level of negative effect on the general aim expressed in similar terms.

A definition which has been found useful is that an incident is critical if it makes a "significant" contribution, either positively or negatively, to the general aim of the activity. The definition of "significant" will depend on the nature of the activity. If the general aim of the activity is in terms of production, a significant contribution might be one which caused, or might have caused, an appreciable change in the daily production of the department either in the form of an increase or a decrease.

In certain specific situations, it might be desirable and possible to set up a quantitative criterion such as saving or wasting 15 minutes of an average worker's production. In some situations, a definition of significance might be set up in terms of dollars saved or lost both directly and indirectly.

Actions which influence the attitudes of others are more difficult to evaluate objectively. Perhaps the best we might be able to do is to state it in terms of a probability estimate. For example, one such criterion might be that the minimum critical level would be an action that would have an influence such that at least one person in ten might change his vote on an issue of importance to the company.

d. PERSONS TO MAKE THE OBSERVATIONS. One additional set of specifications refers to the selection and training of the observers who are to make and report the judgments outlined in the steps above.

Wherever possible, the observers should be selected on the basis of their familiarity with the activity. Special consideration should be given to observers who have made numerous observations on persons engaged in the activity. Thus, for most jobs, by far the best observers are supervisors whose responsibility it is to see that the particular job being studied is done. However, in some cases very useful observations can be contributed by consumers of the products and services of the activity. For example, for a study of effective sales activities, the customers may have valuable data to contribute. For a study of effective parental activity, the children may be able to make valuable contributions.

In addition to careful selection of the persons to make observations, attention should be given to their training. Minimal training should include a review of the nature of the general aim of the activity and a study of the specifications and definitions for the judgments they will be required to make. Where the situation is complex or the observers are not thoroughly familiar with the activity, supervised practice in applying these definitions should be provided. This can be done by preparing descriptions of observations and asking the observers to make judgments about these materials. Their judgments can be immediately confirmed or corrected during such supervised practice periods.

Fig. 2   Specifications Regarding Observations.

---

1. Persons to make the observations.
   a. Knowledge concerning the activity.
   b. Relation to those observed.
   c. Training requirements.

2. Groups to be observed.
   a. General description.
   b. Location.
   c. Persons.
   d. Times.
   e. Conditions.

3. Behaviors to be observed.
   a. General type of activity.
   b. Specific behaviors.
   c. Criteria of relevance to general aim.
   d. Criteria of importance to general aim (critical points).

In Fig. 2 is shown a form for use in developing specifications regarding observations. The use of this form in making plans for the collection of critical incidents or other types of observational data should aid in objectifying these specifications.

3. COLLECTING THE DATA

If proper plans and specifications are developed, the data collection phase is greatly simplified. A necessary condition for this phase is that the behaviors or results observed be evaluated, classified, and recorded while the facts are still fresh in the mind of the observer. It would be desirable for these operations to be performed at the time of observation so that all requisite facts could be determined and checked. Memory is improved if it is known in advance that the behavior to be observed is to be remembered. It is greatly improved if the specific aspects of what is to be observed are defined and if the operations to be performed with respect to evaluation and classification are clearly specified.

The critical incident technique is frequently used to collect data on observations previously made which are reported from memory. This is usually satisfactory when the incidents reported are fairly recent and the observers were motivated to make detailed observations and evaluations at the time the incident occurred.

The importance of obtaining recent incidents to insure that the incidents are representative of actual happenings was demonstrated in the study on air route traffic controllers by Nagay (48) reported above. However, as also discussed in that study, in some situations adequate coverage cannot be obtained if only very recent incidents are included.

Evidence regarding the accuracy of reporting is usually contained in the incidents themselves. If full and precise details are given, it can usually be assumed that this information is accurate. Vague reports suggest that the incident is not well remembered and that some of the data may be incorrect. In several situations there has been an opportunity to compare the types of incidents reported under two conditions (a) from memory and without a list of the types of incidents anticipated, and (b) those reported when daily observations were being made in a routine work situation, and the evaluations and classifications were made and recorded on a prepared check list within 24 hours of the time of observation. The results of one such comparison were discussed briefly above in connection with the American Institute for Research study of factory employees.

During the observational period a negligible number of incidents were reported by the foremen as not fitting into the general headings included on the list. Although the proportions of incidents for the various items on the list are not identical, they are reasonably close for most of the items. Items on such matters as meeting production requirements and accepting changes in jobs are higher in terms of the recorded than the recalled incidents. The fact that items such as wasting time and assisting on problems are lower for the recalled incidents suggests that part of this discrepancy lies in the interpretations of the category definitions. The classifying of recorded incidents was done by the foremen, while the classification of the recalled incidents was done by the research workers. In fairness, it should also be noted that the definitions used by the research workers were rewritten before they were incorporated in the foremen's manuals.

On the whole, it seems reasonable to assume that, if suitable precautions are taken, recalled incidents can be relied on to provide adequate data for a fairly satisfactory first approximation to a statement of the requirements of the activity. Direct observations are to be preferred, but the efficiency, immediacy, and minimum demands on cooperating personnel which are achieved by using recalled incident data frequently make their use the more practical procedure.

Another practical problem in collecting the data for describing an activity refers to the problem of how it should be obtained from the observers. This applies especially to the problem of collecting recalled data in the form of critical incidents. Four procedures have been used and these will be discussed briefly:

A. INTERVIEWS. The use of trained personnel to explain to observers precisely what data are desired and to record the incidents, making sure that all necessary details are supplied, is probably the most satisfactory data collection procedure. This type of interview is somewhat different from other sorts of interviews and a brief summary of the principal factors involved will be given.

(i) *Sponsorship of the study.* If a stranger to the observers is collecting the data, it is ordinarily desirable to indicate on what authority the interview is being held. This part should be as brief as possible to avoid any use of time for a prolonged discussion of a topic irrelevant to the purpose of the interview. In many instances all that needs to be said is that someone known and respected by the observer has suggested the interview.

(ii) *Purpose of the study.* This should also be brief and ordinarily would merely involve a statement that a study was being made to describe the requirements of the activity. This would usually be cast in some such informal form as, "We wish to find out what makes a good citizen," or, "We are trying to learn in detail just what successful work as a nurse includes." In cases where there is some hesitation about cooperating or a little more explanation seems desirable, a statement can be added concerning the value and probable uses of the results. This freqently takes the form of improving selection and training procedures. In some instances, it would involve improving the results of the activity. For example, the interviewer might say, "In order to get better sales clerks we need to know just what they do that makes them especially effective or ineffective," or "If parents are to be more effective, we need to be able to tell them the things they do that are effective and ineffective."

(iii) *The group being interviewed.* If there is any likelihood of a person feeling, "But, why ask me?" it is desirable to forestall this by pointing out that he is a member of a group which is in an unusually good position to observe and report on this activity. The special qualifications of members of this group as observers can be mentioned briefly, as, "Supervisors such as yourself are constantly observing and evaluating the work of switchboard girls," or, "Students are in an unusually good position to observe the effectiveness of their teachers in a number of ways."

(iv) *The anonymity of the data.* Especially for the collection of information about ineffective behavior, one of the principal problems is to convince the observer that his report cannot harm the person reported on in any way. Usually he also needs to be convinced that the person reported on will never know that he has reported the incident. Assurances are not nearly so effective in this situation as actual descriptions of techniques to be used in handling the data, which enable the observer to judge for himself how well the anonymity of the data will be guarded. Under no circumstances should the confidences of the reportees be violated in any way. The use of sealed envelopes, avoidance of identifying information, the mailing of data immediately to a distant point for analysis, and similar techniques are helpful in establishing the good faith of the interviewer in taking all possible precautions to safeguard the incidents reported.

(v) *The question.* The most crucial aspect of the data collection procedure is the questions asked the observers. Many studies have shown that a slight change in wording may produce a substantial change in the incidents reported. For example, in one study the last part of one of the specific questions asked was, "Tell just how this employee behaved which caused a noticeable decrease in production." This question resulted in almost all incidents reported having to do with personality and attitude behaviors. This part of the question was changed to, "Tell just what this employee did which caused a noticeable decrease in production." This second question produced a much broader range of incidents. To the question writer "how he behaved" and "what he did" seemed like about the same thing. To the foremen who were reporting incidents "how he behaved" sounded as if personality and attitudes were being studied. The subtle biases involved in the wording of questions are not always so easily found. Questions should always be tried out with a small group of typical observers before being put into general use in a study.

The question should usually refer briefly to the general aim of the activity. This aim might be discussed more fully in a preliminary sentence. It should usually state that an incident, actual behavior, or what the person did is desired. It should briefly specify the type of behavior which is relevant and the level of importance which it must reach to be reported. It should also tie down the selection of the incidents to be reported by the observer in some way, such as asking for the most recent observation, in order to prevent the giving of only the more dramatic or vived incidents, or some other selected group, such as those which fit the observer's stereotypes.

An effective procedure for insuring that the interpretation of the persons being interviewed is close to that intended is to request a sample of persons typical of those to be interviewed to state in their own words what they understand they have been asked to do. These persons should be selected so as to represent all types who will be interviewed. From a study of their interpretations, necessary revisions can be made to insure that all interviewees will be in agreement as to the nature of the incidents they are to provide.

(vi) *The conversation.* The interviewer should avoid asking leading questions after the main question has been stated. His remarks should be neutral and permissive and should show that he accepts the observer as the expert. By indicating that he understands what is being said and permitting the observer to do most of the talking, the interviewer can usually get unbiased incidents. If the question does not seem to be understood, it can be repeated with some reference to clarifying just what is meant by it. If the observer has given what seems like only part of the story, he should be encouraged by restating the essence of his remarks. This usually tends to encourage him to continue and may result in his bringing out many relevant details that the interviewer did not know the situation well enough to ask for. In some cases, it is desirable to have the interviews recorded electrically and transcribed. This increases the work load substantially, and trained interviewers can usually get satisfactory reports at the time or by editing their notes shortly after the interview.

Usually the interviewer should apply certain criteria to the incidents while they are being collected. Some of the more important criteria are: (a) is the actual behavior reported; (b) was it observed by the reporter; (c) were all relevant factors in the situation given; (d) has the observer made a definite judgment regarding the criticalness of the behavior; (e) has the observer made it clear just why he believes the behavior was critical.

In Fig. 3 is shown a sample of the type of form used by interviewers to collect critical incidents. Of course the form must be adapted to the needs of the specific situation.

Fig. 3   Sample of a Form for Use by an Interviewer in Collecting Effective Critical Incidents.

"Think of the last time you saw one of your subordinates do something that was very helpful to your group in meeting their production schedule." (Pause till he indicates he has such an incident in mind.) "Did his action result in increase in production of as much as one per cent for that day?—or some similar period?

   (If the answer is "no," say) "I wonder if you could think of the last time that someone did something that did have this much of an effect in increasing production." (When he indicates he has such a situation in mind, say) "What were the general circumstances leading up to this incident?"_____

_____

_____

"Tell me exactly what this person did that was so helpful at that time."

_____

_____

"Why was this so helpful in getting your group's job done?"_____

_____

_____

"When did this incident happen?"

_____

"What was this person's job?"

_____

"How long has he been on this job?"

_____

"How old is he?"_____

B. GROUP INTERVIEWS. Because of the cost in time and personnel of the individual interview, a group interview technique has been developed. This retains the advantages of the individual interview in regard to the personal contact, explanation, and availability of the interviewer to answer questions. To some extent it also provides for a check on the data supplied by the interviewees. Its other advantages are that the language of the actual observer is precisely reproduced and the time for editing the interviews is virtually eliminated.

The method consists of having the interviewer give his introductory remarks to a group very much as he would do in an individual interview. There is an opportunity for questions and clarification. Then each person is asked to write incidents in answer to specific questions contained on a specially prepared form. The size of the group which can be handled effectively will vary with the situation. If the group is fairly small, it is usually possible for the interviewer to read the responses of each member of the group to the first question and make sure that he understands what is wanted. There seems to be a certain amount of social facilitation, and the results in most situations have been excellent. In the report of the first use of this procedure by Wagner (65), the amount of interviewer time required per usable incident was 4.3 minutes for the group interview procedure as compared with 15.7 minutes for individual interviews. The quality of these incidents, obtained from officers in the United States Air Force, appeared to be about the same for the two situations.

C. QUESTIONNAIRES. If the group becomes large, the group interview procedure is more in the nature of a questionnaire procedure. There are, of course, all types of combinations of procedures that can be used. The one that is most different from those discussed is the mailed questionnaire. In situations where the observers are motivated to read the instructions carefully and answer conscientiously, this technique seems to give results which are not essentially different from those obtained by the interview method. Except for the addition of introductory remarks, the forms used in collecting critical incidents by means of mailed questionnaires are about the same as those used in group interviews.

D. RECORD FORMS. One other procedure for collecting data is by means of written records. There are two varieties of recording: one is to record details of incidents as they happen. This situation is very similar to that described in connection with obtaining incidents by interviews above, except that the observation and giving of incidents are delayed following the introductory remarks and the presentation of the questions until an incident is observed to happen.

A variation of this procedure is to record such incidents on forms which describe most of the possible types of incidents by placing a check or tally in the appropriate place.

As additional information becomes available on the nature of the components which make up activities, observers may thus collect data more efficiently by using forms for recording and classifying observations. In the meantime, because of the inadequacy of the information currently available regarding these components, it seems desirable to ask observers to report their observations in greater detail and have the classification done by specially trained personnel.

E. SIZE OF SAMPLE.   A general problem which overlaps the phases of collecting the incidents and analyzing the data relates to the number of incidents required. There does not appear to be a simple answer to this question. If the activity or job being defined is relatively simple, it may be satisfactory to collect only 50 or 100 incidents. On the other hand, some types of complex activity appear to require several thousand incidents for an adequate statement of requirements.

The most useful procedure for determining whether or not additional incidents are needed is to keep a running count on the number of new critical behaviors added to the classification system with each additional 100 incidents. For most purposes, it can be considered that adequate coverage has been achieved when the addition of 100 critical incidents to the sample adds only two or three critical behaviors. For jobs of a supervisory nature, it appears that between 2,000 and 4,000 critical incidents are required to establish a comprehensive statement of requirements that includes nearly all of the different types of critical behaviors. For semiskilled and skilled jobs between 1,000 and 2,000 incidents seem to be adequate to cover the critical behaviors.

Coverage of all or nearly all of the various critical behaviors is not the only criterion as to whether or not a sufficient number of critical incidents has been collected. If a relatively precise definition of each critical behavior category is required, it may be necessary to get at least three or four examples of each critical behavior. Similarly, if the critical incidents are to be used as a basis for developing selection tests, training materials, and proficiency measures, more incidents may be required to provide a sufficient supply of usable ideas for the development of these materials.

In summary, although there is no simple formula for determining the number of critical incidents that will be required, this is a very important consideration in the plan of the study; checks should be made both on the first hundred or so incidents and again after approximately half of the number of incidents believed to be required have been obtained in order to make it possible to revise the preliminary estimates, if necessary, with a minimum loss in effort and time.

4. ANALYZING   The collection of a large sample of incidents that fulfill the various conditions out-
    THE DATA   lined above provides a functional description of the activity in terms of specific behaviors. If the sample is representative, the judges well qualified, the types of judgments appropriate and well defined, and the procedures for observing and reporting such that incidents are reported accurately, the stated requirements can be expected to be comprehensive, detailed, and valid in this form. There is only one reason for going further and that is practical utility. The purpose of the data analysis stage is to summarize and describe the data in an efficient manner so that it can be effectively used for many practical purposes.

In the discussion which follows, it should be kept in mind that the process of description has been completed. The specific procedures to be discussed are not concerned with improving on the comprehensiveness, specificity of detail, or validity of the statement of the requirements of the activity. Rather, they are concerned with making it easier to report these requirements, to draw inferences from them, and to compare the activity with other activities.

The aim is to increase the usefulness of the data while sacrificing as little as possible of their comprehensiveness, specificity, and validity. It appears that there are three primary problems involved: (a) the selection of the general frame of reference that will be most useful for describing the incidents; (b) the inductive development of a set of major area and subarea headings; and (c) the selection of one or more levels along the specificity-generality continuum to use in reporting the requirements. Each of these problems will be discussed below:

A. FRAME OF REFERENCE. There are countless ways in which a given set of incidents can be classified. In selecting the general nature of the classification, the principal consideration should usually be that of the uses to be made of the data. The preferred categories will be those believed to be most valuable in using the statement of requirements. Other considerations are ease and accuracy of classifying the data, relation to previously developed definitions or classification systems, and considerations of interpretation and reporting, which will be discussed in a later section.

For job activities, the choice of a frame of reference is usually dominated by considerations of whether the principal use of the requirements will be in relation to selection, training, measurement of proficiency, or the development of procedures for evaluating on-the-job effectiveness. For selection purposes, the most appropriate classification system is a psychological one. The main headings have to do with types of psychological traits that are utilized in the selection process. For training uses, the best classification system follows a set of headings that is easily related to training courses or broad training aims. For proficiency measurement, the headings tend to be similar to those for training except that there is less attention to possible course organization and aims and greater attention to the components of the job as it is actually performed. For the development of procedures for evaluating on-the-job effectiveness to establish a criterion of success, the classification system is necessarily directed at presenting the on-the-job behaviors under headings that represent either well-marked phases of the job or provide a simple framework for classifying on-the-job activities that is either familiar to or easily learned by supervisors.

Similarly, in nonvocational activities the frame of reference depends on the uses planned for the findings. For example, if a study is being made to define immaturity reactions in military personnel, the frame of reference would depend somewhat on whether the functional description is to be used primarily to identify personnel showing this type of maladjustment or whether the principal use will be to try to prepare specifications for types of situations in which immaturity reactions would not lead to serious difficulties.

B. CATEGORY FORMULATION. The induction of categories from the basic data in the form of incidents is a task requiring insight, experience, and judgment. Unfortunately, this procedure is, in the present stage of psychological knowledge, more subjective than objective. No simple rules are available, and the quality and usability of the final product are largely dependent on the skill and sophistication of the formulator. One rule is to submit the tentative categories to others for review. Although there is no guarantee that results agreed on by several workers will be more useful than those obtained from a single worker, the confirmation of judgments by a number of persons is usually reassuring. The usual procedure is to sort a relatively small sample of incidents into piles that are related to the frame of reference selected. After these tentative categories have been established, brief definitions of them are made, and additional incidents are classified into them. During this process, needs for redefinition and for the development of new categories are noted. The tentative categories are modified as indicated and the process continued until all the incidents have been classified.

The larger categories are subdivided into smaller groups and the incidents that describe very nearly the same type of behavior are placed together. The definitions for all the categories and major headings should then be re-examined in terms of the actual incidents classified under each.

C. GENERAL BEHAVIORS. The last step is to determine the most appropriate level of specificity-generality to use in reporting the data. This is the problem of weighing the advantages of the specificity achieved in specific incidents against the simplicity of a relatively small number of headings. The level chosen might be only a dozen very general behaviors or it might be several hundred rather specific behaviors. Practical considerations in the immediate situation usually determine the optimal level of generality to be used.

Several considerations should be kept in mind in establishing headings for major areas and in stating critical requirements at the selected level of generality. These are listed below:

(i) The headings and requirements should indicate a clear-cut and logical organization. They should have a discernible and easily remembered structure.

(ii) The titles should convey meanings in themselves without the necessity of detailed definition, explanation, or differentiation. This does not mean that they should not be defined and explained. It does mean that these titles, without the detailed explanation, should still be meaningful to the reader.

(iii) The list of statements should be homogeneous; *i.e.*, the headings for either areas or requirements should be parallel in content and structure. Headings for major areas should be neutral, not defining either unsatisfactory or outstanding behaviors. Critical requirements should ordinarily be stated in positive terms.

(iv) The headings of a given type should all be of the same general magnitude or level of importance. Known biases in the data causing one area or one requirement to have a disproportionate number of incidents should not be reflected in the headings.

(v) The headings used for classification and reporting of the data should be such that findings in terms of them will be easily applied and maximally useful.

(vi) The list of headings should be comprehensive and cover all incidents having significant frequencies.

5. INTERPRETING AND REPORTING

It is never possible in practice to obtain an ideal solution for each of the practical problems involved in obtaining a functional description of an activity. Therefore, the statement of requirements as obtained needs interpretation if it is to be used properly. In many cases, the real errors are made not in the collection and analysis of the data but in the failure to interpret them properly. Each of the four preceding steps, (a) the determination of the general aim, (b) the specification of observers, groups to be observed, and observations to be made, (c) the data collection, and (d) the data analysis, must be studied to see what biases have been introduced by the procedures adopted. If there is a division of opinion as to the general aim and one of the competing aims is selected, this should be made very clear in the report. If the groups on whom the observations are made are not representative of the relevant groups involved, they must be described as precisely as possible. The aim of the study is usually not a functional description of the activity as carried on by this sample but rather a statement relating to all groups of this type. In order to avoid faulty inferences and generalizations, the limitations imposed by the group must be brought into clear focus. Similarly, the nature of judgments made in collecting and analyzing the data must be carefully reviewed.

While the limitations need to be clearly reported, the value of the results should also be emphasized. Too often the research worker shirks his responsibility for rendering a judgment concerning the degree of credibility which should be attached to his findings. It is a difficult task, but if the results are to be used, someone will have to make such a judgment, and the original investigator is best prepared to make the necessary evaluations either for the general case or for certain typical specific examples.

USES OF THE CRITICAL INCIDENT TECHNIQUE

The variety of situations in which the collection of critical incidents will prove of value has only been partially explored. In the approximately eight years since the writer and his colleagues began a systematic formulation of principles and procedures to be followed in collecting this type of data, a fairly large number of applications has been made. The applications will be discussed under the following nine headings: (a) measures of typical performance (criteria); (b) measures of proficiency (standard samples); (c) training; (d) selection and classification; (e) job design and purification; (f) operating procedures; (g) equipment design; (h) motivation and leadership (attitudes); (i) counseling and psychotherapy.

Space is not available here to describe these various applications in detail. However, a brief description of the types of application that have been made, along with brief illustrative examples and references, will be presented. Some of the studies involve several of the types of applications to be discussed. The presentation is not intended to be complete, but rather to give the reader interested in further study some orientation and guidance.

MEASURES OF TYPICAL PERFORMANCE (CRITERIA)

The simplest and most natural application of a systematically collected set of critical incidents is in terms of the preparation of a statement of critical requirements and a check list or some similar type of procedure for evaluating the typical performance of persons engaged in this activity. If an observational check list that includes all of the important behaviors for the activity is available, the performance of the individual can be objectively evaluated and recorded by merely making a single tally mark for each observation. Such records provide the essential basis for criterion data which are sufficiently detailed and specific for special purposes but at the same time can be combined into a single over-all evaluation when this is desirable. Such a procedure was first suggested and tried out in connection with developmental studies of the American Institute for Research. These included: Preston's study of officers for the United States Air Force (52); Nagay's study on air route traffic controllers for the Civil Aeronautics Administration (49); and M. H. Weislogel's study on research personnel for the Office of Naval Research (69). Another American Institute for Research study was reported by R. B. Miller and the present author (21). This was a performance record form for hourly wage employees developed in cooperation with personnel of the Delco-Remy Division of the General Motors Corporation, the Employment Practices Division of that corporation, and the Industrial Relations Center of the University of Chicago. The same authors have developed similar performance records for salaried employees, and foremen and supervisors (22, 23). The principles and procedures underlying this type of evaluation of performance have been published elsewhere (14, 15, 17).

A number of important contributions to the development of functional descriptions and standards of performance have been made by other groups using the critical incident technique. One of the most notable of these is the development by Hobbs et al. (3, 31), of *Ethical Standards of Psychologists*. More than 1,000 critical incidents involving ethical problems of psychologists were contributed by the members of the American Psychological Association. It is believed that this represents the first attempt to use empirical methods to establish ethical standards. Because of the importance of this study, and the generality of some of the problems involved, certain of the conclusions reported by the Committee on Ethical Standards for Psychology in their introductory statement will be quoted here.

> First, it is clear that psychologists believe that ethics are important; over two thousand psychologists were sufficiently concerned with the ethical obligations of their profession to contribute substantially to the formulation of these ethical standards. Second, psychologists believe that the ethics of a profession cannot be prescribed by a committee; ethical standards must emerge from the day-by-day value commitments made by psychologists in the practice of their profession. Third, psychologists share a conviction that the problems of men, even those involving values, can be studied objectively; this document summarizes the results of an effort to apply some of the techniques of social science to the study of ethical behavior of psychologists. Fourth, psychologists are aware that a good code of ethics must be more than a description of the current status of ethics in the profession; a code must embody the ethical aspirations of psychologists and encourage changes in behavior, bringing performance ever closer to aspiration. Fifth, psychologists appreciate that process is often more important than product in influencing human behavior; the four years of widely-shared work in developing this code are counted on to be more influential in changing ethical practices of psychologists than will be the publication of this product of their work. Finally, psychologists recognize that the process of studying ethical standards must be a continuing one; occasional publications such as this statement mark no point of conclusion in the ongoing process of defining ethical standards—they are a means of sharing the more essential discipline of examining professional experience, forming hypotheses about professional conduct, and testing these hypotheses by reference to the welfare of the people affected by them (3, p. v).

In addition to the study by Smit mentioned in a previous section (58), several other studies on the use of the critical incident procedures as a basis for evaluating teaching effectiveness have been reported. One of these was a study conducted under the joint sponsorship of the Educational Research Corporation and the Harvard University Graduate School of Education with funds provided by the New England School Development Council and the George F. Milton Fund. This was an exploratory study of teacher competence reported by Domas (6). Approximately 1,000 critical incidents were collected from teachers, principals, and other supervisors. Although this was an exploratory study, it was felt that it made an important contribution to the general problem of relating salary to teacher competence.

The second of these studies was conducted as part of the teacher characteristics study sponsored by the American Council on Education and subsidized by the Grant Foundation. This study is reported by Jensen (32). Teachers, administrators, and teachers in training in the Los Angeles area contributed more than 1,500 critical incidents of teacher behavior. The incidents were classified under personal, professional, and social qualities. The category formulation indicated that there were about 20 distinct critical requirements. These were recommended as a basis for teacher evaluation and as an aid to the in-service growth of teachers.

Another study was that of Smith and Staudohar (59), which determined the critical requirements for basic training of tactical instructors in the United States Air Force. From 130 training supervisors, 555 tactical instructors, and 3,082 basic trainees, a total of 6,615 usable incidents were obtained. The authors comment that:

> The training supervisors report a predominance of ineffective incidents in the major areas of: Sets a good example and maintains effective personal relations. The tactical instructors report more ineffective incidents in the area of Makes his expectations clear. Basic trainees show a predominance of ineffective incidents in three areas: Sets a good example, Considers trainee's needs, and Maintains effective personal relations (59, p. 5).

Another study on the evaluation of instructor effectiveness was carried out by Konigsburg (33). This study involved the development of an instructor check list for college instructors based on the critical incident technique and a comparison of techniques for recording observations. Its principal findings were the very low correlation coefficients between the total scores from the Purdue Rating Scale for Instruction and the instructor check list. When these two instruments were each given to half the class on the same day, the average correlation coefficient was found to be .29. The other principal finding is that the planned performances of a total of 46 predetermined behaviors were better reflected by the results obtained on the instructor check list than by the results on the Purdue Rating Scale.

A somewhat related study has been reported by Barnhart (4). This study collected a large number of critical incidents for the purpose of establishing the critical requirement for school board membership. The author applied his findings to the problem of evaluating the effectiveness of school board members.

Another type of application of the critical incident technique to the development of bases for evaluating behavior is the previously mentioned study of Eilbert (7). His list of 51 types of immature reaction based on a collection of several hundred critical incidents describing manifestations of emotional immaturity is believed to provide a useful guide to further investigation and appraisal of persons with behavior problems. It is believed that the results of this study provide substantial encouragement to the application of the critical incident technique to similar problems in the field of clinical diagnosis and evaluation.

MEASURES OF PROFICIENCY (STANDARDS SAMPLES)

A closely related use of critical incidents is to provide a basis for evaluating the performance of persons by use of standard samples of behavior involving important aspects of the activity. Such evaluations are called proficiency measures and are differentiated from the evaluation of typical performance on the job primarily on the basis that a test situation rather than a real job situation is used. Measures of this sort are especially useful at the end of training courses as checks on the maintenance of proficiency, and when the tasks assigned to participants vary a great deal in difficulty or are not directly observed by the supervisors.

One of the first applications of critical incidents to the development of proficiency measures was Gordon's study on the development of a standard flight check for the airline transport rating (28, 29). This study was done by the American Institute for Research under the sponsorship of the National Research Council Committee on Aviation Psychology with funds provided by the Civil Aeronautics Administration. In this study data from analyses of airline accidents were combined with critical incidents reported by airline pilots to provide the basis for developing an objective measure of pilot proficiency. The flight check consisted of the presentation of situations providing uniformly standardized opportunities to perform the critical aspects of the airline pilot's job as indicated from the study of the accidents and critical incidents reported. The new check was found to yield 88 percent agreement on the decision to pass or fail a particular pilot when examined on flights on successive days by different check pilots. The previous flight check when used on the same flights gave only 63 percent agreement, which was little better than chance under the conditions of the study.

Similar studies on the development of flight checks at the American Institute for Research have been carried out by Marley (36, 37), G. S. Miller (39), and Ericksen (9). These studies, sponsored by the United States Air Force and the Civil Aeronautics Administration, were concerned respectively with objective flight checks for B-29 bombing crew members, B-36 bombing crew members, and private pilots flying light civilian aircraft. Ericksen also developed a light plane proficiency check to predict military flying success (10) on a similar project sponsored by the U.S. Air Force Human Resources Research Center.

A similar set of proficiency measures was developed by Krumm for Air Force pilot instructors (34, 35), also under the sponsorship of the Human Resources Research Center. These measures were based on more than 4,000 critical incidents collected from student pilots, flight instructors, and supervisors.

The critical incidents were classified under three main headings: (a) proficiency as a pilot; (b) proficiency as a teacher; and (c) proficiency in maintaining effective personnel relations. The proficiency measures developed in connection with this study included paper-and-pencil tests presenting critical situations and requiring the instructor to select one of several proposed solutions.

Another development of this type carried on at the American Institute for Research was the construction of tests for evaluating research proficiency in physics and chemistry for the Office of Naval Research by M. H. Weislogel (71). This study was based on the critical incidents for research personnel (20) discussed in a previous section. The items for these proficiency measures were based on detailed rationales. The items described a practical research situation in considerable detail and outlined five specific choices concerning such matters as the best thing to do next, suggestions for improving the procedure as reported, etc. The critical behaviors tested in the items were taken directly from the critical incidents. The method of developing tests through the use of comprehensive rationales has been discussed generally in another paper (16).

Three studies have been reported by the American Institute for Research in which critical incidents were used as a basis for developing situational performance tests for measuring certain aspects of the proficiency of military personnel. These included the study of Sivy and Lange on the development of an objective form of the Leaders Reaction Test for the Personnel Research Branch, Department of the Army (57). This test included 20 situational problems based on the critical requirements of the noncommissioned combat infantry leader as determined on the basis of critical incidents collected in military maneuvers and during combat operations at the front in Korea. A second proficiency measure of a somewhat similar sort was developed for other types of personnel by R. L. Weislogel (73). The third study of this type was carried out by Suttell (61) for the Human Resources Research Center. This study was based on critical incidents collected in previous studies of the American Institute for Research and reported the development and preliminary evaluation of the Officer Situations Test. This test was designed to measure nonintellectual aspects of officer performance through the use of 16 situational problems requiring about six hours of testing time.

Because of the great difficulty in obtaining valid and reliable measures of typical performance, accurate measures of proficiency are essential for many types of activities. It is apparent that a comprehensive set of critical incidents can be of great value in constructing such measures.

TRAINING Many of the applications of the critical incident technique to training problems have been carried out for the military in special situations so that the reports are classified security information. In addition to work by Preston, Glaser, and R. L. Weislogel, R. B. Miller and Folley have utilized critical incidents in establishing training requirements for specific types of maintenance mechanics (47) in a study for the Human Resources Research Center.

Similarly, Ronan has used critical incidents as a basis for developing a program of training for emergency procedures in multi-engine aircraft (54) in a study for the United States Air Force Human Factors Operations Research Laboratory. On the basis of several thousand incidents reported by aircrew personnel regarding emergencies, three evaluation devices were prepared. These involved a conventional type multiple-choice test; a special multiple-choice test designed to measure the individual's information concerning the important cues in the emergency situation, the appropriate actions to be taken, and the basic troubles or causes of the emergency; and a "flight check" to be used in evaluating the performance of aircrew members in electronic flight simulators.

The obvious relevance of the behaviors involved in critical incidents and the specific details included make such incidents an ideal basis for developing training programs and training materials.

A recent study by Collins (5) uses critical incidents as a basis for evaluating the effectiveness of a training program. The types of incidents reported by mothers after a two-week training course were significantly different from those reported at the beginning of the program in a number of aspects relevant to the objectives of the program. The critical incidents appeared to provide a much more sensitive basis for revealing changes than other procedures used.

SELECTION AND CLASSIFICATION

Until recently, the customary approach of the research psychologist to the development of tests for selection and classification purposes has been as follows: A very brief period was given to study of the job. Following this, a wide variety of selection procedures was administered to a group of applicants or employees, and follow-up data were gathered. Since the research psychologist had little confidence in the accuracy of his analysis of the psychological elements required by the job, there was a tendency to try everything that was available and seemed even remotely related to the tasks involved. This has been called the "shotgun approach." It was hoped that with a wide scatter at least a few of the tests would pay off. The critical incident technique has lent substantial support to the more thorough study of the job prior to initiating testing procedures. There is increasing feeling at the present time that a much larger percentage of the investigator's time should be spent on determining the critical requirements of the job, so that the psychologist will have sufficient confidence in his tentative conclusions as to the nature of the important selection procedures to permit their use on a tentative basis prior to the collection of empirical follow-up data. This especially important in those situations where the follow-up requires a very long period of time or where the number of cases that can be followed up is so small that definitive findings cannot be anticipated.

One of the most important requirements for developing a system of job analysis that will facilitate a relatively accurate identification of the important job elements for a specific task is to establish a clear and specific set of definitions for these job elements in behavioral terms. The American Institute for Research has carried out a series of projects on this problem. The first of these was a study undertaken by Wagner under the sponsorship of the United States Air Force School of Aviation Medicine to define the requirements of aircrew jobs in terms of specific job elements (67, 68). Several thousand critical incidents were gathered from aircrew members, and these were classified into 24 job elements. These job elements were inductively formulated from the critical incidents and were grouped under the four area headings: (a) learning and thinking; (b) observation and visualization; (c) sensory-motor coordination; and (d) motives, temperament, and leadership.

The development of more than 100 proficiency tests to measure each of the various critical behaviors included in the 24 tentatively proposed job elements was reported by Hahn (30) for the School of Aviation Medicine. These tests were administered to a group of approximately 500 high school senior boys, and the intercorrelations were used to reformulate the tentative job elements. In a study just completed by Taylor (62) for the Human Resources Research Center, the results of applying an analytical procedure developed by Horst to study the interrelationships involved are reported. This analysis led to the formulation of a new set of 20 job elements for each of which a slection test has been developed. These tests have been administered to several hundred aviation cadets and follow-up data on their success in aircrew training should be available soon.

A similar project based on critical incidents collected from various civilian jobs has been reported by the present author (2, 18, 19). The Flanagan Aptitude Classification Test Series, published in 1953, provides aptitude measures for 14 critical job elements. The Applicant Inventory, also published in 1953, measures attitudes predictive of job adjustment for hourly wage employees.

An effort to adapt the critical incident technique to the problem of developing civil service examinations is reported by Wager and Sharon (64). In an exploratory study they collected about 100 incidents regarding on-the-job behaviors of maintenance technicians. These incidents were used a basis for determining job requirements in terms of behavior, and test items were developed for use in selecting applicants who could be expected to meet these requirements.

Another study that used critical incidents as a basis for developing tests to predict performance was carried out by O'Donnell (51). His test, designed to predict success in dentistry, was based on critical incidents collected by Wagner. The test includes items designed to predict, in part, the following three general areas: (a) demonstrating technical proficiency; (b) handling patient relationships; and (c) accepting professional responsibility. A follow-up study indicated moderate validity for these materials.

One of the few studies known to the author in which the critical incident technique was used in a project carried on outside the United States is Emons' doctor's dissertation (8). This study, carried out at the University of Liége, investigated the aptitudes of effective sales personnel in a large department store. A group of 40 supervisors provided 228 critical incidents. Nine categories were formulated from this group of incidents and recommendations made for an aptitude test to improve current selection procedures.

JOB DESIGN AND PURIFICATION

Inadequate attention has been given to the scientific design of jobs to promote over-all efficiency. Where a team has several different types of tasks to perform, it is frequently possible to design each of the team member's jobs so that only a few of the several tasks are involved. If the jobs have been studied by use of the critical incident technique, it may be possible to select and train each team member for only two or three of the critical job elements. This tends to maximize the effectiveness of performance with respect to each of the various types of tasks. Although such procedures have nearly always been informally used in planning the work of teams, the critical incident technique facilitates the collection of the data essential to this type of job purification.

Some preliminary work on this problem has been carried out at the American Institute for Research. Recommendations resulting from these studies for reducing the number of job elements required in certain common maintenance jobs are expected to lead to a saving of millions of dollars in training costs as well as to improving the effectiveness of job performance.

OPERATING PROCEDURES

Another application of critical incidents which has not been adequately exploited is the study of operating procedures. Detailed factual data on successes and failures that can be systematically analyzed are of great importance in improving the effectiveness and efficiency of operations. Such information can be efficiently collected by means of the critical incident technique.

Examples of such studies are provided by a series of three projects carried out by the American Institute for Research under the sponsorship of the United States Air Force School of Aviation Medicine. The first of these involves the collection of critical incidents relating to near accidents in flying reported by Vasilas, Fitzpatrick, DuBois, and Youtz (63). More than 1,700 critical incidents were collected from pilots and other aircrew members by procedures developed for this study. These incidents pointed to possible improvements in training job design and equipment design as well as in operating procedures.

The second of these studies was specifically concerned with the effect of the age of pilots and other crew members on aircrew operations. This study was reported by Shriver (56), and included tentative suggestions regarding various modifications in operating procedures.

The third study in this series, reported by Goodenough and Suttell (26), involved the collection of critical incidents regarding the impairment of human efficiency in emergency operations. These incidents provide a detailed statement of both the types of stresses that impair performance and the types of performance that are impaired under specific conditions. More than 2,000 critical incidents were collected in which impairment in performance on operational assignments was observed. These incidents were collected in Alaska and the Far East as well as in operational commands in the United States. This report contains suggestions for improving operations in emergency situations.

EQUIPMENT DESIGN An application closely related to that just discussed involves the collection of critical incidents to improve the design of equipment. Reports of specific incidents from the field have always been a basis for equipment modifications. The critical incident technique facilitates the collection and processing of this type of information. Too often in the past action was taken on the basis of informal reports from operating personnel. The collection of large numbers of critical incidents representative of operating experience provides a sound basis for modifying existing equipment and designing new models.

In the study by Fitts and Jones (12), mentioned above, which was carried out at the Aero-Medical Laboratory, 270 critical incidents relating to errors in reading and interpreting aircraft instruments were collected and analyzed. These led to a number of specific suggestions regarding modifications in instrument displays.

Other recent studies conducted at the American Institute for Research have used data from the critical incident technique along with other sources to develop procedures for designing jobs. The reports on these projects are classified for military security reasons.

Other projects at the American Institute for Research have used the critical incident technique as a supplemental procedure for task analysis of equipment in the design stage of development (9, 10, 34, 35, 39). These procedures have been found very effective when used by psychologists working closely with engineers on the preparation of design specifications for new equipment.

MOTIVATION AND The study of attitudes has been somewhat limited and difficult to interpret be-
LEADERSHIP cause of the almost exclusive reliance on verbal statements of opinions and preferences. The critical incident technique has been applied in a few instances to gather factual data regarding specific actions involving decisions and choices. These studies suggest that critical incidents of this type may be a very valuable supplementary tool for the study of attitudes.

A recent study carried out by Preston of the American Institute for Research for the Air Force's Human Resources Research Center (53) used critical incidents as a basis for studying decisions of airmen to re-enlist in the Air Force. It is believed that these specific incidents provide valuable information not contained in studies utilizing only data on opinions.

A series of reports by Ruch (55) contains critical incidents on combat leadership collected from senior officers in the Far East Air Forces. These incidents provide a factual basis for the study of motivation and leadership of Air Force personnel engaged in combat operations.

COUNSELING AND PSYCHOTHERAPY Another field in which current techniques emphasize over-all impressions, opinions, and reports of single cases is counseling and psychotherapy. There appears to be a trend, however, in this field toward emphasizing the collection of factual incidents. This suggests that the critical incident technique may be useful in this area also.

Exploratory work has recently been done at the University of Pittsburgh with the critical incident technique to establish areas of change accompanying psychotherapy. A series of three master's theses were carried out by Speth, Goldfarb, and Mellett (25, 38, 60). They collected 243 critical incidents from 11 psychotherapists. These incidents were collected about patients who had shown improvement and were replies to the question, "What did the patient do that was indicative of improvement?" Although these studies were primarily exploratory in nature, the tentative finding that different therapists stress different criteria of improvement and nonimprovement suggests that the critical incident approach may be of use not only in developing objective measures of improvement but also in experimental studies of the types of improvement resulting from the therapists' use of specific procedures.

A somewhat related type of study initiated by Diederich and reported by Allen (1) describes the use of the technique to obtain critical incidents from students reporting things that caused them to like a fellow high school student either more or less than before. This study is being continued to provide the basis for tests of specific value areas. An incidental finding of the study was that when an example of the kind of incident desired was shown on the form, 53 percent of the positive and 23 percent of the negative behaviors reported were in the same category as the example given.

SUMMARY AND CONCLUSIONS

This review has described the development of a method of studying activity requirements called the critical incident technique. The technique grew out of studies carried out in the Aviation Psychology Program of the Army Air Forces in World War II. The success of the method in analyzing such activities as combat leadership and disorientation in pilots resulted in its extension and further development after the war. This developmental work has been carried out primarily at the American Institute for Research and the University of Pittsburgh. The reports of this work are reviewed briefly.

The five steps included in the critical incident procedure as most commonly used at the present time are discussed. These are as follows:

a. Determination of the general aim of the activity. This general aim should be a brief statement obtained from the authorities in the field which expresses in simple terms those objectives to which most people would agree.

b. Development of plans and specifications for collecting factual incidents regarding the activity. The instructions to the persons who are to report their observations need to be as specific as possible with respect to the standards to be used in evaluating and classifying the behavior observed.

c. Collection of the data. The incident may be reported in an interview or written up by the observer himself. In either case it is essential that the reporting be objective and include all relevant details.

d. Analysis of the data. The purpose of this analysis is to summarize and describe the data in an efficient manner so that it can be effectively used for various practical purposes. It is not usually possible to obtain as much objectivity in this step as in the preceding one.

e. Interpretation and reporting of the statement of the requirements of the activity. The possible biases and implications of decisions and procedures made in each of the four previous steps should be clearly reported. The research worker is responsible for pointing out not only the limitations but also the degree of credibility and the value of the final results obtained.

It should be noted that the critical incident technique is very flexible and the principles underlying it have many types of applications. Its two basic principles may be summarized as follows: (a) reporting of facts regarding behavior is preferable to the collection of interpretations, ratings, and opinions based on general impressions; (b) reporting should be limited to those behaviors which, according to competent observers, make a significant contribution to the activity.

It should be emphasized that critical incidents represent only raw data and do not automatically provide solutions to problems. However, a procedure which assists in collecting representative samples of data that are directly relevant to important problems such as establishing standards, determining requirements, or evaluating results should have wide applicability.

The applications of the critical incident technique which have been made to date are discussed under the following nine headings: (a) measures of typical performance (criteria); (b) measures of proficiency (standard samples); (c) training; (d) selection and classification; (e) job design and purification; (f) operating procedures; (g) equipment design; (h) motivation and leadership (attitudes); (i) counseling and psychotherapy.

In summary, the critical incident technique, rather than collecting opinions, hunches, and estimates, obtains a record of specific behaviors from those in the best position to make the necessary observations and evaluations. The collection and tabulation of these observations make it possible to formulate the critical requirements of an activity. A list of critical behaviors provides a sound basis for making inferences as to requirements in terms of aptitudes, training, and other characteristics. It is believed that progress has been made in the development of procedures for determining activity requirements with objectivity and precision in terms of well-defined and general psychological categories. Much remains to be done. It is hoped that the critical incident technique and related developments will provide a stable foundation for procedures in many areas of psychology.

NOTES

1. Allen, C. D. Critical requirements in interpersonal behavior. Unpublished senior thesis, Princeton Univer., 1950.

2. American Institute for Research. *The applicant inventory.* Pittsburgh: American Institute for Research, 1954.

3. American Psychological Association, Committee on Ethical Standards for Psychology. *Ethical standards of psychologists.* Washington, D.C.: Amer. Psychol. Assn., 1953.

4. Barnhart, R. E. The critical requirements for school board membership based upon an analysis of critical incidents. Unpublished doctor's dissertation, Indiana Univer., 1952.

5. Collins, Marjorie G. Selected methods applied to the evaluation of a parent training course in child management. Unpublished doctor's dissertation, Univer. of Pittsburgh, 1954.

6. Domas, S. J. *Report of an exploratory study of teacher competence.* Cambridge: New England School Development Council, 1950.

7. Eilbert, L. R. A study of emotional immaturity utilizing the critical incident technique. *Univer. Pittsburgh Bull.,* 1953, **49**, 199-204.

8. Emons, V. L'analyse de la fonction de vendeuse de grand magasin par la méthode des exigencies critiques. Unpublished doctor's dissertation, Univ. of Liége, Belgium, 1952.

9. Ericksen, S. C. Development of an objective proficiency check for private pilot certification. Washington: Civil Aeronautics Administration, 1951. (*Div. of Res., Rep.* No. 95.)

10. Ericksen, S. C. Development of a light plane proficiency check to predict military flying success. *USAF, Hum. Resour. Res. Cent., Tech. Rep.*, 1952, No. 52-6.

11. Finkle, R. B. A study of the critical requirements of foremanship. *Univer. Pittsburgh Bull.*, 1950, **46**, 291-297. (Abstract)

12. Fitts, P. M., & Jones, R. E. Psychological aspects of instrument display. 1. Analysis of 270 "pilot error" experiences in reading and interpreting aircraft instruments. Dayton, O.: U.S. Air Force, Air Materiel Command, Wright-Patterson Air Force Base, 1947. (*Mem. Rep.* TSEAA-694-12A.)

13. Flanagan, J. C. The aviation psychology program in the Army Air Forces. Washington: U.S. Government Printing Office, 1947. (*AAF Aviat. Psychol. Program Res. Rep.* No. 1.)

14. Flanagan, J. C. A new approach to evaluating personnel. *Personnel,* 1949, **26**, 35-42.

15. Flanagan, J. C. Critical requirements: a new approach to employee evaluation. *Personnel Psychol.*, 1949, **2**, 419-425.

16. Flanagan, J. C. Use of comprehensive rationales. *Educ. Psychol. Measmt.*, 1951, **11**, 151-155.

17. Flanagan, J. C. Principles and procedures in evaluating performance. *Personnel,* 1952, **28**, 373-386.

18. Flanagan, J. C. *Flanagan aptitude classification tests.* Chicago: Science Research Associates, 1953.

19. Flanagan, J. C. Improving personnel selection. *Publ. Personnel Rev.*, 1953, **14**, 107-112.

20. Flanagan, J. C., *et al. Critical requirements for research personnel.* Pittsburgh: American Institute for Research, 1949.

21. Flanagan, J. C., *et al. The performance record for hourly employees.* Chicago: Science Research Associates, 1953.

22. Flanagan, J. C., *et al. The performance record for non-supervisory salaried employees.* Chicago: Science Research Associates, 1953.

23. Flanagan, J. C., *et al. The performance record for foremen and supervisors.* Chicago: Science Research Associates, 1953.

24. Folley, J. D., Jr. Development of a list of critical requirements for retail sales personnel from the standpoint of customer satisfaction. Unpublished master's thesis, Univer. of Pittsburgh, 1953.

25. Goldfarb, A. Use of the critical incident technique to establish areas of change accompanying psychotherapy: II. Relationship to diagnostic group. Unpublished master's thesis, Univer. of Pittsburgh, 1952.

26. Goodenough, D. R., & Suttell, Barbara J. *The nature and extent of impairment of human efficiency in emergency operations: the field study.* Pittsburgh: American Institute for Research, 1952.

27. Gordon, T. The airline pilot: a survey of the critical requirements of his job and of pilot evaluation and selection procedures. Washington: Civil Aeronantics Administration, 1947. (*Div. of Res., Rep.* No. 73.)

28. Gordon, T. The development of a standard flight-check for the airline transport rating based on the critical requirements of the airline pilot's job. Washington: Civil Aeronautics Administration, 1949. (*Div. of Res., Rep.* No. 85.)

29. Gordon, T. The development of a method of evaluating flying skill. *Personnel Psychol.*, 1950, **3,** 71-84.

30. Hahn, C. P. Measurement of individual differences with respect to critical job requirements. *USAF Sch. Aviat. Med.,* 1954, Proj. No. 21-29-014, No. 2.

31. Hobbs, N. The development of a code of ethical standards for psychology. *Amer. Psychologist,* 1948, **3,** 80-84.

32. Jensen, A. C. Determining critical requirements for teachers. *J. Exp. Educ.,* 1951, **20,** 79-86.

33. Konigsburg, D. The development and preliminary evaluation of an instructor check list based on the critical incident technique. Unpublished doctor's dissertation, Univer. of Pittsburgh, 1954.

34. Krumm, R. L. Critical requirements of pilot instructors. *USAF, Hum. Resour. Res. Cent., Tech. Rep.,* 1952, No. 52-1.

35. Krumm, R. L. *Development of a measure of pilot instructor proficiency based on the critical requirements of the instructor's job.* Pittsburgh: American Institute for Research, 1953.

36. Marley, F. W. Individual differences in critical aircrew elements: I. The determination of critical proficiency requirements for B-29 combat crews. *USAF Sch. Aviat. Med.,* 1952, Proj. No. 21-29-014, No. 1.

37. Marley, F. W. The development of performance flight checks for B-29 combat crews. *USAF, Hum. Resour. Res. Lab.,* 1952, Rep. No. 19.

38. Mellett, T. P. Use of the critical incident technique to establish areas of change accompanying psychotherapy: III. Differences among therapists. Unpublished master's thesis, Univer. of Pittsburgh, 1952.

39. Miller, G. S. *Development of B-36 bombardment objective flight checks and proficiency measures for use with reconnaissance crews.* Pittsburgh: American Institute for Research, 1953.

40. Miller, N. E. Psychological research on pilot training. Washington: U.S. Government Printing Office, 1947. (*AAF Aviat. Psychol. Program Res. Rep. No.* 8.)

41. Miller, R. B. Anticipating tomorrow's maintenence job. *USAF, Hum, Resour. Res. Cent., Res. Rev.,* 1953, No. 53-1

42. Miller, R. B. A method for determining human engineering design requirements for training equipment. Dayton, O.: U.S. Air Force, Air Development Center, Wright-Patterson Air Force Base, 1953. (*Tech. Rep.* 53-135.)

43. Miller, R. B. Handbook on training and training equipment design. Dayton, O.: U.S. Air Force, Air Development Center, Wright-Patterson Air Force Base, 1953. (*Tech. Rep.* 53-136.)

44. Miller, R. B. A method for man-machine task analysis. Dayton, O.: U.S. Air Force, Air Development Center, Wright-Patterson Air Force Base, 1953. (*Tech. Rep.* 53-137.)

45. Miller, R. B. Human engineering design schedule for training equipment. Dayton, O.: U.S. Air Force, Air Development Center, Wright-Patterson Air Force Base, 1953. (*Tech. Rep.* 53-138.)

46. Miller, R. B., & Flanagan, J. C. The performance record: an objective merit-rating procedure for industry. *Amer. Psychologist,* 1950, **5,** 331-332. (Abstract)

47. Miller, R. B., & Folley, J. D., Jr. *The validity of maintenance job analysis from the prototype of an electronic equipment.* Pittsburgh: American Institute for Research, 1952.

48. Nagay, J. A. The development of a procedure for evaluating the proficiency of air route traffic controllers. Washington: Civil Aeronautics Administration, 1949. (*Div. of Res., Rep.* No. 83.)

49. Nagay, J. A. The airline tryout of the standard flight-check for the airline transport rating. Washington: Civil Aeronautics Administration, 1949. (*Div. of Res., Rep.* No. 88.)

50. Nevins, Charlotte I. An analysis of reasons for the success or failure of bookkeepers in sales companies. Unpublished master's thesis, Univer. of Pittsburgh, 1949.

51. O'Donnell, R. J. The development and evaluation of a test for predicting dental student performance. *Univer. Pittsburgh Bull.*, 1953, **49,** 240-245. (Abstract)

52. Preston, H. O. *The development of a procedure for evaluating officers in the United States Air Force.* Pittsburgh: American Institute for Research, 1948.

53. Preston, H. O. *Events affecting reenlistment decisions.* Pittsburgh: American Institute for Research, 1953.

54. Ronan, W. W. *Training for emergency procedures in multi-engine aircraft.* Pittsburgh: American Institute for Research, 1953.

55. Ruch, F. L. Incidents of leadership in combat. *USAF, Hum. Resour. Res. Inst., Res. Memo,* 1953, No. 3.

56. Shriver, Beatrice M. Age and behavior: a study of the effects of aging on aircrew performance. *USAF Sch. Aviat. Med.,* 1953, Proj. No. 21-0202-0005, No. 3.

57. Sivy, J., & Lange, C. J. Development of an objective form of the Leaders Reaction Test. *AGO, Personnel Res. Branch, PRS Rep.,* 1952, No. 930.

58. Smit, JoAnne. A study of the critical requirements for instructors of general psychology courses. *Univer. Pittsburgh Bull.,* 1952, **48,** 279-284. (Abstract)

59. Smith, R. G., Jr., & Staudohar, F. T. Technical requirements of basic training tactical instructors. *USAF, Hum. Resour. Res. Cent., Tech. Rep.,* 1954, No. 54-7.

60. Speth, E. W. The use of the critical incident technique to establish areas of change accompanying psychotherapy: I. Function of age and education. Unpublished master's thesis, Univer. of Pittsburgh, 1952.

61. Suttell, Barbara J. *Development of a situation test to measure non-intellectual officer qualities.* Pittsburgh: American Institute for Research, 1953.

62. Taylor, M. V., Jr. *The development of aircrew job element aptitude tests.* Pittsburgh: American Institute for Research, 1953.

63. Vasilas, J. N., Fitzpatrick, R., DuBois, P. H., & Youtz, R. P. Human factors in near accidents. *USAF Sch. Aviat. Med.,* 1953, Proj. No. 21-1207-0001, No. 1.

64. Wager, C. E., & Sharon, M. I. Defining job requirements in terms of behavior. *Personnel Admin.,* 1951, **14,** 18-25.

65. Wagner, R. F. A group situation compared with individual interviews for securing personnel information. *Personnel Psychol.,* 1948, **1,** 93-107.

66. Wagner, R. F. A study of the critical requirement for dentists. *Univer. Pittsburgh Bull.,* 1950, **46,** 331-339. (Abstract)

67. Wagner, R. F. Development of standardized procedures for defining the requirements of aircrew jobs in terms of testable traits. *USAF Sch. Aviat. Med.,* 1951, Proj. No. 21-29-010, No. 1.

68. Wagner, R. F. Using critical incidents to determine selection test weights. *Personnel Psychol.,* 1951, **4,** 373-381.

69. Weislogel, Mary H. *Development of a test for selecting research personnel.* Pittsburgh: American Institute for Research, 1950.

70. Weislogel, Mary H. *Procedures for evaluating research personnel with a performance record of critical incidents.* Pittsburgh: American Institute for Research, 1950.

71. Weislogel, Mary H. *The development of tests for evaluating research proficiency in physics and chemistry.* Pittsburgh: American Institute for Research, 1951.

72. Weislogel, R. L. Critical requirements for life insurance agency heads. *Univer. Pittsburgh Bull.,* 1952, **48,** 300–305. (Abstract)

73. Weislogel, R. L., & Schwarz, P. A. Some practical and theoretical problems in situation testing. Unpublished manuscript. Pittsburgh: American Institute for Research, 1953.

74. Wickert, F. Psychological research on problems of redistribution. Washington: U.S. Government Printing Office, 1947. (*AAF Aviat. Psychol. Program Res. Rep. No. 14.*)

APPENDIX C EMERGENCY KIT STATISTICS

NOT NEARLY EVERYTHING YOU NEED TO KNOW ABOUT STATISTICS

We almost called this appendix "Almost Everything You'll Ever Need to Know About Statistics," but even in our most flippant of moods we couldn't bring ourselves to that. We've both logged many, many hours in statistics classes—and passed. But we wouldn't *think* of doing a major study without a *real* statistician on the team. Somehow that pontifical nod and muted "yes, that should be adequate" from a person who can look a curvilinear regression or an ANOVA in the raw without trembling is too reinforcing to be done without. Most of the social science researchers we know have statistician consultants they use for backup on their work. So never feel foolish or inadequate because you need help on the statistical parts of a survey, critical incident or other FTO project. We certainly don't.

Now, what's in this emergency kit? First, some refresher on the most basic statistics, the descriptive statistics, and then just a tad on the correlational statistics, but not much. As far as we've been able to determine, you don't really need a Ph.D. in behavioral science statistics to analyze and interpret the results of most survey studies. If you use the survey guidelines we laid down in chapter 13, about all you'll ever need are descriptive statistics—those simple, number-summarizing methods you learned in Business Math 14 or Introduction to Psychology 108.

All statistics do, says educational psychologist and measurement specialist Carol Taylor Fitz-Gibbon, is "help you crunch large amounts of information into usable numbers." That you can do with a hand calculator and a little common sense. About the only correlational method we think you might regularly need is a statistic called Chi-square, which can help you decide if the numbers in your "cross-tabs" are distributed evenly or by some underlying design. Chi-square is one of those indexes that allows you to make such impressive statements as, "Higher seniority employees perform at the same level as do low seniority employees but at a significantly higher level than trainees and others with less than one-year experience."

SIMPLE DESCRIPTIVE
STATISTICS

If you have any trouble with this little refresher, you probably need a basic statistics course. There are a number of good ones in programmed instruction format. Two we recommend are:

► *How to Calculate Statistics* by Carol Taylor Fitz-Gibbon and Lynn Lyons Morris, Sage Publications, Beverly Hills/London. Actually, this is one of eight books from *Program Evaluation Kit* developed by the staff of the Center for the Study of Evaluation, University of Los Angeles, under an HEW grant.

► *Introduction to Statistics* by Lloyd Homme and Donald Tosti, Individual Learning Systems, Inc., San Rafael, CA 94902. More than one graduate student has used this set of nicely programmed texts to survive the mandatory educational psychology statistics sequence.

These are the basic terms of descriptive statistics, the minimum for analyzing survey results.

A. *Mean*—The arithmetic average. All the scores added up and divided by the number of scores.
Example:

$$\text{Mean} = \frac{\Sigma x}{n} = \frac{\text{Sum of all scores}}{\text{Number of scores}} = \frac{4 + 5 + 6 + 7 + 8}{5} = \frac{30}{5} = 6$$

B. *Median*—The middle score. Count the number of responses and circle the middle one; the one right in the middle of the pack.
Example:

$$4 - 5 - 6] - 6 - [7 - 8 - 8$$
$$\uparrow$$
$$\text{Median}$$

C. *Mode*—The most common score. If supervisors report four absences per employee *most* frequently, then four is the mode.
Example:

$$4 - 4 - 4 - 5 - 6 - 7 - 8 - 8$$

Mode

When these three *measures of central tendency* are almost equal, you have a normal or bell-shaped distribution of scores or answers. When mean, median and mode are quite different, the scores or answers are referred to as *skewed.* When these three measures are different, it is a good idea to graph the data. Graphing gives you a visual understanding of how the numbers lay out, which in turn tells a lot about the population you are studying.

D. *Kinds of Skew*

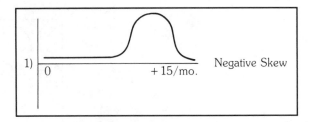

When scores are negatively skewed, that means they are bunched near the *high* end of the scale. If this was a graph of absences, you might conclude that there is a tendency among *all* departments to have high absences. As a problem indicator, this curve says "big trouble."

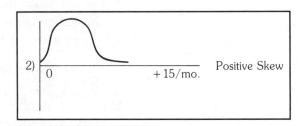

In a positive skew, scores clump near the low end of the scale. You might conclude from this distribution that departments tend to have low absences. As a "problem indicator," this curves says "no problem."

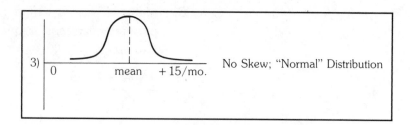

In a normal distribution, scores are evenly distributed around some central score. This is a great curve for selection test scores but a bad one for absences. As a problem indicator it doesn't tell a lot. If the *mean* that goes with the normal curve is *high,* then you have a general problem worth dealing with. If the *mean* is *low,* then the problem of higher absences on the righthand side of the curve may not be amenable to a cost effective *general* solution.

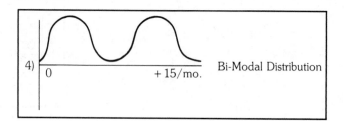

In a bi-modal distribution of scores, there are two "lumps" of data. This tells you that you may be dealing with two completely different groups of departments; high absence and low absence departments. You would look first to see what other characteristics separate the departments that produced these two different readings. One lump may be department's professionals and the other, work groups with lots of day labor, for example.

E. *Standard Deviation*—Standard deviation, sometimes represented by the Greek letter sigma (σ), is a measure that tells you whether the majority of scores are close to the value of the mean, or scattered all about. When the standard deviation of a set of scores is large, then the "mean" or "average" score doesn't tell you much about the "average" or "typical" department, student, branch, etc. When the standard deviation is small, most scores or answers are close to the value of the mean and the mean is a good representation of the typical response.

Calculating the Standard Deviation

The formula for figuring standard deviation is more foreboding looking than it actually is. It's all that Greek and statistical shorthand.

$$S.D. = \sqrt{\frac{\Sigma x^2}{n}}$$

Where

Σx^2 = sum of the squares of the differences between the mean and each score.

n = the number of scores

$\sqrt{}$ = square root

An example will clear up the Greek and the doubletalk. Here are 10 scores. Let's say they represent absences per year for 10 departments.

Absences Per Dept.		Difference (x) Score − Mean	Difference Squared (x^2)
48		+8	64
47		+7	49
43		+3	9
41	> Mode	+1	1
41		+1	1
---	Median		
40		0	0
38		−2	4
36		−4	16
34		−6	36
32		−8	64
400	Total	0	$\Sigma x^2 = 244$

Scores (N) = 10

Mean = $\dfrac{400}{10}$ = 40

Median = 40.5 (half-way point)

Mode = 41

$$S.D. = \sqrt{\frac{\Sigma x^2}{n}} = \sqrt{\frac{244}{10}} = \sqrt{24.4} = 4.9$$

What this example says is that most departments had 40 absences plus or minus about 5. It also means that 40 absences are a pretty good representation of departmental absences.

CORRELATIONAL STATISTICS

Chi-Square (χ^2)

This is a statistical test that tells us whether the scores in a table—like a cross-tabs table—are uniformly distributed or whether something is influencing the way the numbers fall. Calculating a Chi-square requires arithmetic, some patience, and a table of Chi-square significance. You can find a Chi-square table and an explanation of its use in any statistics book, but one sample table accompanies the following example.

Using Chi-Square

1. Suppose you were looking at production numbers and found out:
   - 9 departments produced above standard for the 1st quarter
   - 11 departments produced at standard for the 1st quarter
   - 10 departments produced below standard for the 1st quarter

2. You also find out that 17 departments are supervised by supervisors who graduated from supervisory training and 13 departments are supervised by untrained people.

3. You make a table of *production records* and *training status*:

	Hi Prod.	Average Prod.	Low Prod.	
Trained	7	8	2	17
Untrained	2	3	8	13
	9	11	10	30

Question: Is there a relationship between *supervisory training* and *departmental productivity*? To answer, calculate a Chi-square.

4. Start the calculation by constructing a table of *expected* outcomes. That is, make a table that assumes training makes no difference.

You do that by apportioning the production records backward to the cells of the table in proportion to the number of

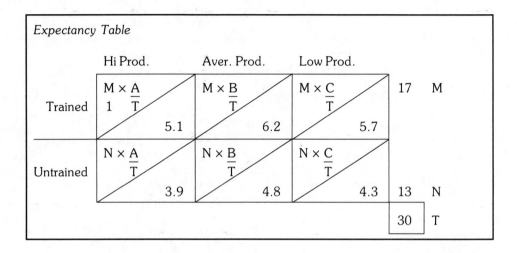

Expectancy Table

	Hi Prod.	Aver. Prod.	Low Prod.		
Trained	$M \times \dfrac{A}{T}$ 1 5.1	$M \times \dfrac{B}{T}$ 6.2	$M \times \dfrac{C}{T}$ 5.7	17	M
Untrained	$N \times \dfrac{A}{T}$ 3.9	$N \times \dfrac{B}{T}$ 4.8	$N \times \dfrac{C}{T}$ 4.3	13	N
				30	T

A = 9 departments with above standard production
B = 11 departments at standard production
C = 10 departments below standard production
M = Number of departments with trained supervisors (17)
N = Number of departments with untrained supervisors (13)
T = Total number of supervisors (30)

5. Calculate χ^2 using this formula for comparing each cell in the two tables:

$$\frac{(O - E)^2}{E}$$

O = actual production records that fit the description for each cell
E = expected production from the expectancy table

$$\chi^2 = (O - E)^2 = \left[\frac{(7 - 5.1)^2}{5.1} + \frac{(8 - 6.2)^2}{6.2} + \frac{(2 - 5.7)^2}{5.7} \right.$$

$$\left. + \frac{(2 - 3.9)^2}{3.9} + \frac{(3 - 4.8)^2}{4.8} + \frac{(8 - 4.3)^2}{4.3} \right]$$

$$= [.708 + .522 + 2.40 + .926 + .675 + 3.184]$$
$$= 8.415$$

6. 8.415 is the Chi-square score for the cross-tabs table comparing production levels of *trained* and *untrained* department supervisors. So what? The so what is that *if* 8.415 is a number that can occur by accident, then training makes no difference. If the odds of the number 8.415 being an accident are very *low,* then the original table is telling us that the difference between trained and untrained on the original cross-tabs is no accident.

	Hi Prod.	Avg. Prod.	Low Prod.
Trained	7	8	2
Untrained	2	3	8

The obvious interpretation, then, would be that trained supervisors have higher producing departments than untrained. Step 7 shows how to make that determination.

7. First you need to figure out a number which you need in order to use the Chi-square table: the df number—degrees of freedom. To find the df number, imagine a row and a column from the contingency table are blotted out and count the number of remaining cells. The number is the df number.

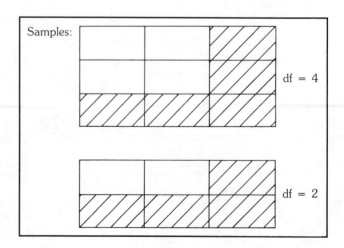

8. Now locate the tabled Chi-square by going down the left column to the appropriate df number, then selecting the Chi-square value from one of the columns.

df	Test at 10% error level	More stringent test (5% level)
1	2.71	3.84
2	4.60	5.99
3	6.25	7.81
4	7.79	9.49
5	9.24	11.07
6	10.64	12.59
7	12.02	14.07
8	13.36	15.51
9	14.68	16.92
10	15.99	18.31
11	17.27	19.67
12	18.55	21.03
13	19.81	22.36
14	21.06	23.68
15	22.31	25.00
16	23.54	26.30
17	24.77	27.59
18	25.99	28.87
19	27.20	30.14
20	28.41	31.41
21	29.61	32.67
22	30.81	33.92
23	32.01	35.17
24	33.20	36.41
25	34.38	37.65

The number 8.415 is greater than 4.6 and 5.99 so we know that the table is 95% a reflection of a *real* difference. In fact, on a full Chi-square from a standard statistics text, we would see that 8.415 is significant at the 2% level. So the table of production is good at a 98% confidence level. We can say that the chances are 95% pure that training makes a difference in production level—at least for the first quarter.

Spearman's Rank Order

Once in a while you want to compare rankings. For instance, in a recent survey study we had sales reps select and rank from 1 to 5 their toughest performance problems. We also had their supervisors select and rank the five things they believed were most effecting sales performance. We needed to know whether sales reps and sales managers agreed on the performance problems affecting sales. If they didn't agree, we were in a heck of a mess for guessing, and would have to throw both opinions out and do further research. If they reasonably agreed, then we could just spot check with observations and the like. Overall we ended up with ten high-ranked items.

Task Listed	Sales rep ranking of need for improvement	Mgmt. ranking of need for improvement
Overcoming objections	1	3
Motivating myself	2	7
Planning/organizing my work	3	10
Uncovering needs	4	2
Beginning the sales interview	5	5
Listening to my clients	6	8
Reading my customers	7	4
Finding decision makers	8	1
Fact finding	9	6
Making trial closes	10	9

The only way to rationally sort this hodgepodge is statistically. There is no "eye ball" test that can reliably tell us how close to agreement these two sets of rankings really are. The test is called Spearman's Rank Order Correlation Coefficient. The formula is:

$$\gamma_s = 1 - \frac{6 \text{ sum } (d^2)}{n \ (n^2 - 1)}$$

where

> d = the difference between the rank on one measure (x) and the rank on the other (y)
> n = number of cases

Here's how it works. Make a chart like the following; either rank can be x or y, and calculate the d and d^2 columns

x (rep's ranking)	y (manager's ranking)	(x − y) = d	d²
1	3	−2	4
2	7	−5	25
3	10	−7	49
4	2	+2	4
5	5	0	0
6	8	−2	4
7	4	+3	9
8	1	+7	49
9	6	+3	9
10	9	+1	1
n = 10			Σd² = 154

$$r_s = \frac{6 \text{ sum } d^2}{n\,(n^2 - 1)} = \frac{(6)\,(154)}{(10)\,(10^2 - 1)} = \frac{924}{990} = .933$$

Values of r_s greater than ± 0.80 indicate a very *strong* relationship. Values less than ± 0.40 represent a weak relationship. A relationship between two sets of ranks can range from $+1.00$ to -1.00. Positive numbers indicate that when one ranking is high the other is high. Negative numbers indicate that when one rank is high the other is low; this is referred to as an inverse relationship. Since the correlation between sales rep's rankings of performance improvement needs and manager's rankings of performance improvement needs is 0.933, we concluded that the agreement was very high. Therefore, only a small amount of qualitative research was needed to fully validate and explain the findings.

The Nomographic Test of Percentages*

Sometimes all we have for results of a survey is a group of percentages. For instance:

> of 65 women who responded, 47% said they felt they were fairly paid.

> of 188 men who responded, 59% said they felt they were fairly paid.

Question: Is the difference in satisfaction with pay between men and women (59% vs. 47%) a *significant* difference?

An easy way to answer the question is by something called a "Nomographic Test of Statistical Significance." It is a simple visual test using two graphs.

---

*Adapted from A. N. Oppenheim *Questionnaire Design and Attitude Measurement* (New York: Basic Books, 1966).

It works like this:

1. Look for the same sizes on chart 1 and look between them with a straight edge for a correlation coefficient. In the example:

$N_1 = 65$
$N_2 = 188$

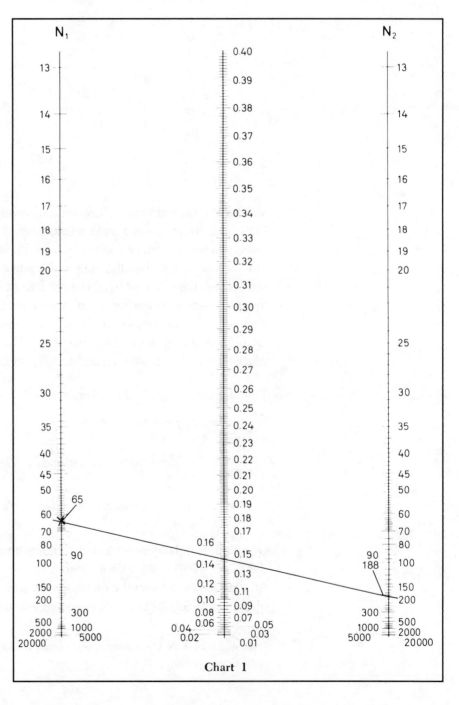

Chart 1

2. The correlation coefficient = 0.144, or at least someplace between 0.14 and 0.15.

3. Find the correlational values for the 5% and 10% level by running a line between the percentages of the two groups.

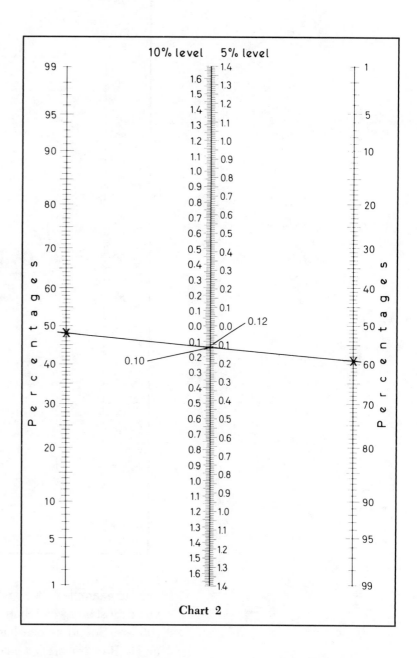

Chart 2

Is 0.144 larger than 0.12? You bet! So, the groups are *for sure* different at the 5% and 10% levels.

4. Find the correlation value for the 1.0% and 0.1% levels of significance, by running a line between the two percentages.

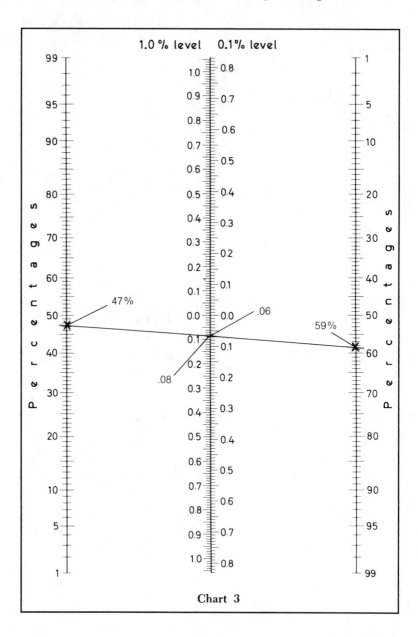

Chart 3

For our example to be significant at the 1% level, our significance value must be *greater* than .06. In fact, .144 is larger than .06 . . . Sound simple? It is! Here are "clean" copies of Charts 1, 2 and 3. Remember, *first* determine the significance number for the two groups; *then,* compare the actual percentages at the 10%, 5%, 1% and 0.1% levels of significance.

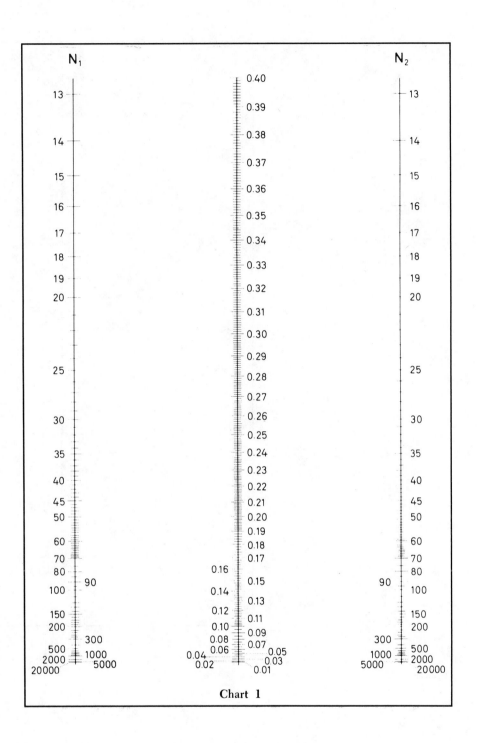

Chart 1

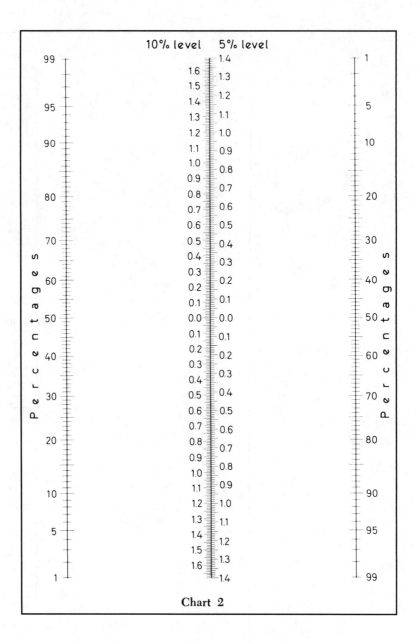

Chart 2

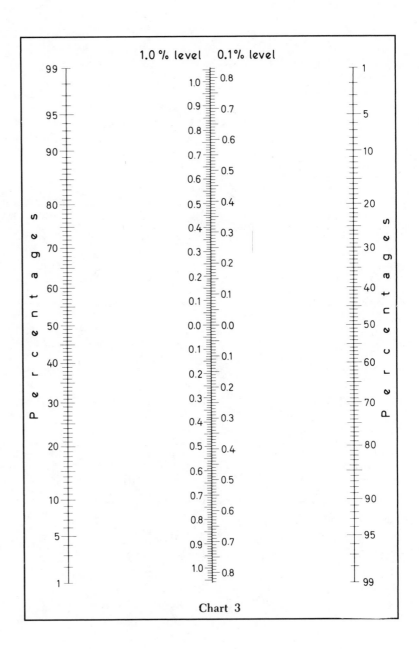

Chart 3

BIBLIOGRAPHY

Anastasi, Anne. *Psychological Testing.* New York: Macmillan, 1961.

Armine, H. T.; Ritchey, J.; and Hulley, O. S. *Manufacturing Organization and Management.* Englewood Cliffs, N.J.: Prentice-Hall, 1975.

Bandura, A. *Principles of Modification.* New York: Holt, Rinehart and Winston, 1969.

Bandura, A., and Walters, R. H. *Social Learning and Personality Development.* New York: Holt, Rinehart and Winston, 1963.

Borman, W. C.; Dunnette, M. D.; and Hough, L. M. *Development of Behaviorally Based Rating Scales for Evaluating the Performance of U.S. Navy Recruiters.* NPRDC TR-76-31. Minneapolis: Personnel Decisions, Inc., 1976.

Brightman, Harvey J. *Problem Solving: A Logical and Creative Approach.* Atlanta: Business Publishing Division, College of Business, Georgia State University, 1980.

Companion, Michael A., and Teichner, Warren H. *Application of Task Theory to Task Analysis: Evaluation of Validity and Reliability Using Simple Tasks.* Washington, D.C.: Air Force Office of Scientific Research (NL), Bolling AFB, 1977.

Connellan, Thomas. *How to Grow People Into Self-Starters.* Ann Arbor, Mich.: The Achievement Institute, Inc., 1980.

Davis, R. V., and Luthans, Fred. "Managers In Action: A New Look at Their Behavior and Operating Modes." *Organizational Dynamics* (Summer 1980): 64-80.

Deden-Parker, A. "Needs Assessment In Depth: Professional Training at Wells Fargo Bank." *Journal of Instructional Development,* vol. 1, no. 1 (Fall 1980): 3-9.

Deterline, William A. *Instructional Technology Workshop.* Palo Alto, Calif.: Programmed Teaching, 1968.

Fine, S. A. "Functional Job Analysis: An Approach to a Technology for Manpower Planning." *Personnel Journal* (November 1974): 813-818.

Flanagan, J. C. "Defining the Requirements of the Executive's Job." *Personnel,* vol. 28, no. 1 (July 1951): 28-35.

Flanagan, J. C. "The Critical Incident Technique." *Psychological Bulletin,* vol. 51, no. 4 (July 1954): 327-358.

Flanagan, J. C.; Marchese, A. C.; Tuska, S. A.; and Fivers, G. "The Clinical Experience Record for Nursing Students." Pittsburgh, Penn.: Psychometric Techniques Associates, 1960.

Foreman's Time Study Training Course Manual. St. Paul, Minn.: Gould Batteries, 1965.

Gagne, Robert. "Military Training and Principles of Learning." *American Psychologist,* vol. 17 (1962).

Gilbert, T. "Mathematics: The Technology of Education." *The Journal of Mathematics,* vol. I, no. 1 (1962).

Gilbert, T. *Human Competence: Engineering Worthy Performance.* New York: McGraw-Hill, 1978.

Granum, O. Alfred. *The Science and Art of Building a Life Insurance Clientele.* Cincinnati, Ohio: National Life Underwriters, 1975.

Handbook for Designers of Instructional Systems, vol. II. AFP 50-58. Washington, D.C.: Headquarters, USAF, 1973.

Harless, J. H. *An Ounce of Analysis.* Falls Church, Va.: Harless Educational Technologists, Inc., 1970.

Hays, William L. *Statistics for the Social Sciences.* 2nd ed. New York: Holt, Rinehart and Winston, 1973.

Landa, Lev. *Algorithmization In Learning and Instruction.* Englewood Cliffs, N.J.: Educational Publications, 1974.

Landa, Lev. *Instructional Regulation and Control: Cybernetics, Algorithmization and Heuristics In Education.* Englewood Cliffs, N.J.: Educational Technology Publications, 1976.

Mager, R. F., and Pipe, Peter. *Analyzing Performance Problems.* Belmont, Calif.: Fearon, 1970.

McCormick, Ernest J. *Job Analysis: Methods and Applications.* New York: Amacom, 1979.

Merrill, Paul F. "Task Analysis: An Information Processing Approach." *NSPI Journal,* vol. XV, no. 2. (1976): 7-11.

Metzler, Ken. *Creative Interviewing: The Writer's Guide to Gathering Information.* Englewood Cliffs, N.J.: 1977.

Michalak, Donald F., and Yager, Edwin G. *Making the Training Process Work.* New York: Harper & Row, 1979.

Miller, R. B. *A Method for Man-Machine Task Analysis.* TR 53-137. Ohio: USAF, WADC, Wright-Patterson AFB, 1953.

Mintzberg, H. "Power In and Around Organizations." *TRAINING Magazine,* vol. 14, no. 10 (1977): 35.

Olsen, Herb. *Guide to Gathering Information In Face-to-Face Interviews.* Ramsey, N.J.: Ramsey-Wallace Corp., 1967.

Oppenheim, A. N. *Questionnaire Design and Attitude Measurement.* New York: Basic Books, Inc., 1966.

Rundquist, Edward A. *Job Training Course Design and Improvement,* 2nd ed. Naval Personnel and Training Research Laboratory, San Diego, California, September 1970.

Schoner, Bertram, and Uhl, Kenneth P. *Marketing Research.* New York: John Wiley & Sons, Inc., 1976, Chapter 8.

Shriver, Edgar L. *Cue Response Analysis of A Maintenance Task.* Paper read at the American Psychological Association, 1958.

Snyder, M. B. "Methods of Recording and Reporting Task Analysis Information." *Uses of Task Analysis in Designing Training and Training Equipment Requirements.* TR 60-593. Ohio: USAF, WADD, Wright-Patterson AFB, 1960, pp. 11-31.

Steele, F., and Jenks, S. *The Feel of the Workplace: Understanding and Improving Organization Climate.* Reading, Mass.: Addison-Wesley Publishing, 1977.

Theologus, G. C.: Romashko, T.; and Fleishman, E. A. *Development of a Taxonomy of Human Performance.* Technical Report No. 5. Washington, D.C.: American Institute for Research, 1970.

Tregoe, B. B., and Zimmerman, J. W. *Top Management Strategy.* New York: Simon and Schuster, 1980.

Van Gundy, Arthur B., Jr. *Techniques of Structured Problem Solving.* New York: Van Nostrand Reinhold, 1981.

Von Bertolanffy, L. *1956 General Systems Theory.* Yearbook of the Society for the Advancement of General Systems Theory, no. 1, 1956, pp. 1-10.

Watson, Charles E. *Management Development Through Training.* Reading, Mass.: Addison-Wesley Publishing, 1979.

Zemke, R. "Sales Managers Specify Their Training Needs." *TRAINING Magazine,* vol. 16, no. 3 (March 1979).

Zemke, R., and Larson, D. *How Senior Managers Reward and Punish Middle Managers.* Unpublished Research Monograph, 1980.

INDEX

Absence analysis, 174
Absence control, 111
Absence rate study, 73
Absences, 178
Accurate discrimination, 206
Algorithm, 47-67, 120, 230, 237, 238, 240
  characteristics of, 50
  definition of, 47, 55
  developing, 51
  example, 49, 50, 55, 63, 65
  exercise, 65
  format, 62
  medical example, 52
  notational, 65
  for reader, 51
  symbols, 65
  task analysis
    examples of, 55
    guidelines, 61
  tips and tricks, 62
Algorithmization in Learning and Instruction, 47, 48
Alignment meeting, 164
Analyzing performance problems, 3, 18
  and gate, 194
Anderson, Al, 86
Anderson, John F., 159, 170, 246, 250
Arbitration, 149
Artifact study, 230
Attempts to sell, 78
Attention, focusing, 106
Average performer, 184

Bad news syndrome, 250, 252
Bandura, Albert, 21
Bank study, 75
  hypotheses, 75
  questions, 76
Behavior, 42, 80, 130, 133
  charting, 70
  counting, 70, 73
  frequency, 80
  frequency count, 234, 241
  guidelines, 79-82
  modification-based model, 21
  observable, 79
  observations, 76, 256
  pilot testing, 71
  pinpointing, 70
  rate of occurrence, 69
  rating instruments, 131
  study, 70
  subtle, 79
Behavioral algorithms, 47-67
Behavioral chain example, 204
Behavioral counting, 72
Behavioral differences, 78
Behavioral examples, 132
Behavioral frequency, 69, 70, 75
  counts, 69-81
  studies, 226
Behavioral modification, 70
Behavioral/reflexive task, 206
Behavioral repertories, 69
Behaviorally anchored rating scales, 127, 130-134
Berdie, Douglas R., 159, 170
Boolean algebra, 196

Bottom-line results, 183
Bottoms-up principle, 203
Bramson, Robert, 147
Brightman, Harvey J., 151
Brown, A. M., 117
Buy-in, 220

Campbell, David, 143
Chaining, 204, 211-212
Chi square, 132-134, 319, 324
Classification scheme, 79
Client image, 245
Cognitive component, 208
Columbo principle, 81
Commonality questions, 105
Communication of results, 245, 247
Competency questions, 105
Component task achievement, 271
Computer programming, 50
Concept forming, 207
Concept learning, 211
Concordance, 219
    procedure, 112-113
Connellan, Thomas, 72
Consensus
    grid, 143, 145, 146
    groups, 141-154
    leadership, 152
    ranking, 145
    survey, 151, 154
    techniques, 235, 242
    validation, 141
Consistency, 82
Constructive criticism, 107
Consultants, 183
Consultants Digest, 164
Correlation statistics, 324
Correlation coefficient, 328
Counter-exemplar method, 186
Creative Interviewing: The Writer's
    Guide to Gathering Information,
    109
Critical incident technique, 129-139,
    228, 232, 277-313
    background, 278-280
    current, 286-301
        aims, 287-289
        data analysis, 298-301
        data collection, 292-298

    interpreting/reporting, 301
    plans/specs, 289-292
    description, 133
    instruction sheet, 137
    rating scale, 135
    raw stories, 137
    scale for evaluating, 139
    studies, 280-286
    using, 134, 302-311
Critical job requirements, 129
Critical path values, 196
Cross-tabs, 162, 176-177, 319
Culture, 23
Customer contact behaviors, 79, 85
Customer studies, 222
Cut-off numbers, 188

Daniels, C. Aubrey, 70
Data collection, 82
Data gathering, 259
Decision variables, 213
Deden-Parker, Ann, 9
Definitional rigidity, 79
Delphi groups, 151
Delphi technique, 149, 150, 154, 233,
    236, 242
Delphi theory, 150
Demographics, 173, 231
    data, 172, 189
    example, 192
Descrimination making, 206
Descriptive statistics, 162, 249
Deterline approach, 39-46, 62
Deterline, William, 39
Df number, 327
Difference of opinions, 232
Discrimination, 43, 206-207, 211-212
Doktar, Robert, 10
Drucker, Peter, 13
Dunhman, Randall B., 170
Dunnette, Marvin, 130

Effective incidents, 130, 135
Ego, 82
Eighty/twenty rule, 12, 138
Employee absences, 111
Employee performance, 231
Evaluation, 134, 253, 255
Exemplary performance, 185

Expectations, 23
  table, 325
Experimental approach, 192
Experts, 168, 196

Face to face interviews, 84, 99–115,
    126, 240
Failure events, 194
Fault tree analysis, 193–200
  critical path values, 196
  definition of, 193
  diagram, 195–196
  example, 199
  logic concept, 194
  qualitative analysis, 196
  symbolic notations, 195
Field research, 255–260
Figuring Things Out (FTO), 99, 217,
    219, 224, 234, 243, 250, 253
  change, 260
  consensus, 260
  conducting, 7–15
  example, 256
  model, 22
  objectives, 232
  observational approaches, 27
  project, 319
  research, 218
  strategy of, 7–15
  study, 23, 25, 96, 255–256, 260
  tactics for, 7–15
  technique, 11, 236
First-line supervisors, 151, 173, 191
First-order causes, 219
Flanagan, John C., 129
Flextime, 151
Flow chart approach, 237–242
Focus group
  audiotaping, 96
  client meeting, 87–89
  data, 85
    internalizing, 91–92
  double-checking, 94
  goals, 85
  interview guide, 87–88
  moderator of, 86
  organizing and writing, 92–94
  phases of, 86–94
    analyzing results, 91–94

conducting, 89–91
    planning, 87–89
  pros and cons, 96–97
  reporting, 94
  results, 97
  tips and tricks, 94–96
  transcribing proceedings, 91
  videotaping, 96
Frequency, 69
  definition of, 69
Frequency-count approach, 70, 72,
    230, 241
  observations, 71
Friesen, Paul, 14
FTA. *See* Fault tree analysis
FTO. *See* Figuring Things Out

Gagne, Robert, 201, 263
  hierarchy, 202
"Garbage in, garbage out," 87, 198
Gilbert, Thomas, 21, 184,
    190
Granum, O. Alfred, 73
Griffin, Darrell R., 94
Group meetings, 151

Handle, Darwin, 249
Harless, Joe, 3
Hierarchical model, 202
Hierarchy, 212
High performers, 89, 188, 190, 202,
    259
High-performing group, 187, 189
Hisenberg principle, 80
Horabin, Ivan, 47
Hostile respondent, 120
Hubbard, James J., 118
Human competence, 184, 190, 191
*Human Competence: Engineering
    Worthy Personnel,* 21
Human performance
  causes of problems, 24
  model, 8, 17–25
    flow chart, 18–19
  problem model, 21
  theory, 17
Human resources development, 125
Hypotheses, 76
Hypothesis projecting, 209

Ideas, generating, 154
Inaccurate reports, 124
Incentives, 184
Individual actions, 205
Individual analysis, 9
Ineffective incident, 130
Information-gathering, 12, 99, 261
  by telephone, 117, 126
Instructional Regulation and Control:
    Cybernetics, Algorithmization,
    and Heuristics in Education, 48
Intent question, 105
Intercept survey, 241
Internal assessment of organizational
    health, 170
Intervention, 187, 259, 261
  locus, 190
  value of, 186
Interview, 40, 223-225, 232
  analyzing results, 111
  answers in perspective, 107
  attention, 106
  characteristics, 100
  conversational, 100
  concluding, 110
  conducting, 106
  criticism, 107
  disagreement, 108
  drawbacks, 115
  face-to-face, 104
  informal, 100
  introductory meeting, 101
  jargon, 101
  limits, 114
  managing time, 108
  note-taking, 108, 110
  one-on-one, 99-115
  open statement, 106
  open-ended questions, 102
  preparing for, 101
  questions, 102
  report summary, 111
  scheduling, 102, 104
  shorthand, 109
  starting, 104
  structured, 100
  verbal behavior, 100
Interviewees, 106, 114, 117
  assessment, 107
Interviewer training, 99

Job analysis, 34
Job content level, 226
Job description techniques,
    238
Job performance, 82
Job/task breakdown, 36

Kelly, Edward F., 251
KISS principle, 14, 159

Landa, Lev, 47
Lateness, 111
Latham, Gary, 99
Law of disproportionate distribution,
    138
Learning hierarchies, 201-213
Learning terminology, 205
Levels of learning, 210
Levinson, Harry, 155
Line managers, 13, 14, 223, 227
Logic gates, 195
Logical system, 212
Low performers, 187-189, 190, 202,
    225, 232
Luthans, Fred, 21, 215

Mager and Pipe model, 18, 21
Maier, Norman R. F., 152
Mail survey, 156
Management, 184, 224, 245, 255
Market research, 83, 85
Market Research: A Short Course for
    Professionals, 120
Mayer, Steve, 158, 250
McColland, David, 12
McLagan, Patricia, 233
Memory training, 110
Method analysis, 29
Metzler, Ken, 109
Military training and principles of
    learning, 263-276
  learning, 266-267
  tasks, 264-267
  training design, 267-274
Miller, Brenda K., 118
Miller, Larry, 70
Mintzberg, Henry, 10
Model of human performance,
    18
Models, 17-25

Moderator, 88
Motor performance, 43

Needs analysis, 184, 223, 224, 233
Needs study, 225
Nominal group, 147
Nomographs, 162, 330-335
  test, 329
Non-observational methods,
    231-233
Non-verbal reinforcement, 110
Norm, Thom, 124
Notational system, 61
Note-taking, 108

Objective logic, 145
Observable behavior, 41, 129
    principles, 82
Observations, 39, 82, 328
    selecting techniques, 229
    studies, 75, 80
    summary, 76
Observe-and-record procedure, 76
Observed transactions, 78
On-job trainer, 42
One-to-one interviews, 225
Open-ended questions, 190
Operation-chart analysis, 30
Operational analysis, 9
Operations studies symbols, 30
Operator/performer, 40
Opinion surveys, 234
Oppenheim, A. N., 170
OR gate, 194
Oracle, 150
Oral presentations, 250
Organization
    analysis, 9
    change process, 261
    culture, 23
    incentive system, 24
    mission and goals, 23, 227
Organizational analysis work, 9, 215,
    225
Organizational climate, 23
Organizational criteria, 217-226
Organizational goals, 197
Organizational obstacles, 226
Organizational surveys, 170
Organizational systems, 198

Overtime analysis, 174

Paredo, Alfredo, 138
Pareto principle, 12
Peers, 86
Perception-changing experiences,
    208
Performance
    algorithm, 62
    common denominators, 189
    criteria, 188
    data, 184, 192, 258
    difference, 77
    economic value of, 187
    effective, 73
    environment, 11
    evaluating, 132
    feedback, 23
    improving, 185
    ineffective, 73
    information, 183-192
    levels, 75, 189
    model, 112
    non-observable, 230
    obstacles, 228
    problems, 23, 164, 183, 217-225,
      328
      analysis, 183
      causes of, 218
      hypotheses, 189
    rating instrument, 131
    records, 187-192, 222
    review instruments, 127, 130, 184
    standard, 185
Personal interviews, 84, 99, 114-115
Personnel record, 226
Picking the pinpoint, 79
Pilot testing, 63, 250
Pinpoint-count-chart, 73
PIP. *See* Potential for improving
        performance
Polls, 156
Potential for improving performance,
    184, 185
    example, 191
    methods, 188
    ratio, 187
    technique, 192
Precise personal management, 70
Precision teaching, 70

Premature pinpointing, 79
Presentation, 250
    purpose of, 246
    of results, 246, 248
Prioritizing
    system, 145
    tasks, 234
    tool, selecting, 235
Priority grid, 151, 235, 242
Priority matrix, 142-144, 146, 154
Problem solving, 202, 209, 211
    activities, 210
    dimension, 213
Procedure, definition of, 204
Process/decision flowcharts, 53
Production records, 189
Productivity, 164, 183
Propriety questions, 105
Protocol development, 51
Pyramid of tasks, 202

Qualitative information, 231
Qualitative research, 329
Quality control circles, 219
    training, 200
Quantitative analysis, 197
Quantitative information, 231
Questionnaires, 108, 114, 127, 148,
        155-179, 224-225, 231-234,
        241
    crucial words, 167
    design
        and attitude measurement, 170
        guidelines, 165-169
        and use, 70, 159
    example, 161, 171
    guidelines, 159-162
    incentives, 167
    instructions, 167
    interpretations, 160
    sample, 160, 162
    scaled items, 160
    statistics for social sciences, 160
    yes/no items, 160

Random selections, 186
Rank ordering, 112
Reinforcement, 23, 69
Relationship tension, 104-105

Reporting results, 245-253
Requesters, 164
Research accuracy, 249-258
Response, 40, 42, 203
    generating, 203
    learning, 210
    sets, 169
Results
    audience, 246
    presentation, quality of, 245
    purpose, 246
    reaction, 259
Revealing artifacts, 240
Rule applying, 207, 208, 211
Rule of nine, 141
Rummler, Geary, 21
Rundquist, Edward A., 34

Sales opportunities, 77-78
Sales training, 83
Salesmanship skills, 132
Schiff, David M., 164
Schoner, Bertram, 120, 123
Selection technique, 220
Self-talk, 81
Sequence questioning, 107, 123
Sequencing, 271
Serial ordering, 272
Seven-step syndrome, 252
Shriver, Edgar L., 5
Simon, Herbert, 142
Simple consensus, 146
Simple observations, 29
Skewed data, 162
Skill clusters, 131, 143
SMEs, 51, 53, 63, 141, 147, 149, 152,
        154, 212-213, 219, 237, 241,
        259
Smith, Frank J., 170
Social learning, 21
Solutions, 255-261
Spearman Rank Order, 328
Spitzer, Dean, 169, 193
Spotlight treatment, 14
S-R. See Stimulus-response
Standard deviation, 322, 323
Statistics, 319-355
    calculating, 320
    introduction, 320

mean/median, 320
skew, 321
Stimulus, 40, 42, 203, 206, 233
  learning, 211
  recognition, 202-203
  response, 203
    discriminations, 43
    elements, classification of, 43
    learning, 45
    outline, 40
    pair, 203
    tables, 39-46, 213, 215, 228, 237, 240
Structured interview, 118
  anatomy of, 101-114
Structured questions, 115
Subject matter experts, 37, 48, 131, 141, 212
Supervision, 133, 219
Supervisors, 40, 41, 175-178, 328
Surveys, 120, 122, 127, 155-179, 258
  analysis, 175, 176, 178
  case study, 163
  cost, 156
  demographic data, 172
  definition of, 179
  do's, 165
  don'ts, 168
  drawbacks, 157
  format, 120
  garbage, 173
  group, 235, 242
  human insight, 155
  imagination, 178
  leg work, 158
  misinformation, 178
  multiple-choice, 155
  observation, 178
  pilot test, 163
  pitfalls, 163
  results, 170, 234
  standard conditions, 157
  study, 164
System failure, 193

Tactic, 13
Talking to people, 85-87
Tape recording, 108, 123

Task analysis, 5, 39-48, 50, 61, 193, 201, 204, 205, 208, 213, 255, 263, 271
  definitions of, 33, 39
  strategies, 211
  techniques, 29, 51
Task cost, 220
Task, elapsed time, 221
Task existence, 231
Task job description technique, 239
Task listing, 29, 33-38, 229, 237
Task matching technique, 228
Task needs, 215
Task observational technique, 229
Task selecting method, 217-226
Task, technical criteria, 227-236
Task techniques, 217, 227
  for agreement, 241
  selection criteria, 221, 238
Task tension, 104-105
Tasks, hierarchy of, 37
Tasks, observable, 229
Teaching application, 211
Teaching strategies, 210
Telephone consumer survey, 121
Telephone interviews, 84, 117-126, 223, 240
  accuracy, 124
  benefits, 117
  cost, 118
  minuses, 119
  mistakes, 124
  pluses, 119
  questionnaire, 119
  satisfaction, 126
  suggestions, 126
  time length, 118
  yes or no answers, 122
Telephone surveys, 120, 123, 126, 224
Tension, 105
Terminology, using, 205-206
Three-phase needs analysis model, 9
Time management, 13
Time studies, 29, 30
Time study chart, 30, 32
Top management strategy, 7
Trainees, 134, 205, 206, 210
  repertoire, 204

Trainer, 142
Trainer/researcher, 223
Training, 125
   development, 218
   need, 176, 190, 217
   program, 134, 257
Tregoe, Ben, 7
Trend lines, 74
Trends, 74
Troubleshooting, 209
Turnover analysis, 175
Typical performance,
   185

Uhl, Kenneth, 120, 123
Undercommunication, 80
Undesirable event, 194
Upper-management intuition,
   112

Valid criteria, 187
Variable values stimulus, 206
Verbal association, 205
Verbal background, 43
Verbal closing statement, 72
Verbal mediators, 46
Verbal performance, 43
Verbal transactions, 70-71
Videotaping, 32

Watson, Charles E., 130
Wilson, Larry, 104
Words, 4
Working hypothesis, 165

Yerkes-Dodson law, 105

Zemke-Kramlinger model, 22
Zimmerman, John, 7